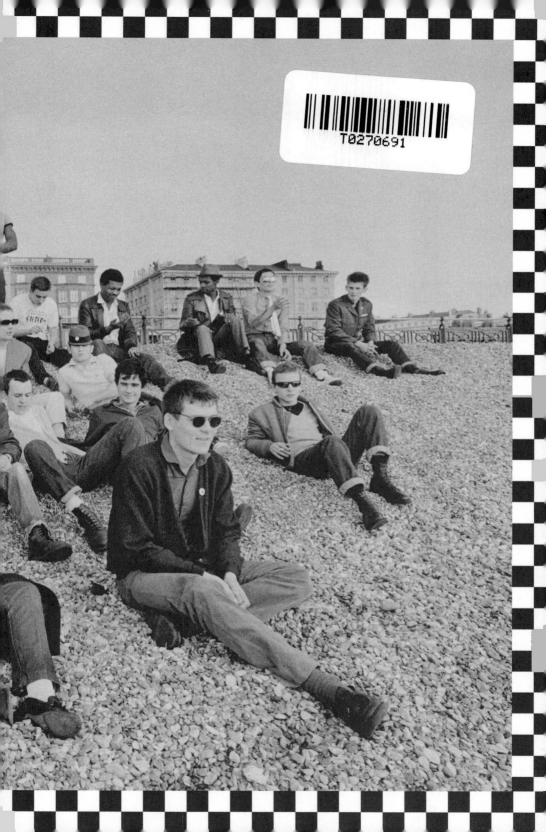

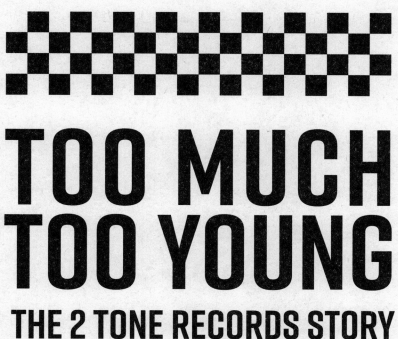

TOO MUCH TOO YOUNG

THE 2 TONE RECORDS STORY

RUDE BOYS, RACISM, AND THE SOUNDTRACK OF A GENERATION

DANIEL RACHEL

BROOKLYN, NEW YORK

Published by Akashic Books
©2024 Daniel Rachel
The moral right of Daniel Rachel to be identified as the author of this work has been asserted in accordance with the Copyright, Designs and Patents Act of 1988 (UK).

ISBN: 978-1-63614-189-3
Library of Congress Control Number: 2023949637
First Akashic Books printing

Originally published in the UK in 2023 by White Rabbit.

Akashic Books
Instagram, X, Facebook: AkashicBooks
info@akashicbooks.com
www.akashicbooks.com

For Matthew Rowland . . .
and all those Saturday adventures hunting down these records

"A new dance caught the feet of the nation's youth. Within months 2 Tone replaced the dying disco rump as the mass dance music of the nation's youth. It was unselfconsciously pop, it was teenage, it was for boys and girls, it had fashions and identity and it had a strong morality, a message even. It all happened quickly and without hype or pretension. Sold-out venues, multiple encores, a sense of unity, purpose, even of a crusade, all that and more conspired to give the whole thing legendary status, not least in the eyes of the participants."

—Garry Bushell, *Sounds*, March 1, 1980

CONTENTS

PRINCIPAL CHARACTERS

(listed in alphabetical order)

David "Compton" Amanor guitar, the Selecter
Charley Anderson bass, the Selecter
Stella Barker guitar, the Bodysnatchers
Mike Barson keyboards, Madness
Terry Bateman singer/saxophone, the Friday Club
Jane Bayley singer, the Swinging Cats
Jeff Baynes video director
Mark "Bedders" Bedford bass, Madness
Charles "Aitch" Bembridge drummer, the Selecter
Pauline Black singer, the Selecter
John "Brad" Bradbury drummer, the Specials/Special AKA/J.B.'s Allstars
Andy Brooks singer/guitar/songwriter, the Friday Club
Desmond Brown keyboards, the Selecter
Francis Brown guitar, the Apollinaires
Tom Brown guitar, the Apollinaires
Roddy "Radiation" Byers guitar/songwriter, the Specials
Sean Carasov merchandise seller
Simon Charterton drummer, the Higsons
Tony "Curly" Cheetham manager, the Apollinaires
Elvis Costello record producer, singer, Elvis Costello & the Attractions
Dick Cuthell flugelhorn/cornet, the Specials
Doug D'Arcy managing director, Chrysalis Records
Rhoda Dakar singer, the Bodysnatchers/Special AKA
Jerry Dammers founder of the Specials and 2 Tone Records
Chalkie Davies photographer
Neol Davies guitar/main songwriter, the Selecter

Joe Dunton visual concept and photographer, *Dance Craze*
Terry Edwards saxophone/guitar, the Higsons
Roy Eldridge head of A&R, Chrysalis Records
Eddie Eve keyboards, the Friday Club
Felicity Fairhurst editor *Dance Craze* magazine, married to Joe Massot
Chris Foreman guitar, Madness
Lynval Golding guitar, the Specials/Fun Boy Three
Pete Hadfield tour manager, 2 Tone Records
Terry Hall singer, the Specials/Fun Boy Three
John Hasler manager, Madness
Arthur "Gaps" Hendrickson singer, the Selecter
Paul Heskett saxophone/flute, the Swinging Cats/the Specials
Charlie Higson singer, the Higsons
Michael Hodges percussionist/songwriter, the Friday Club
James Hunt bass, the Apollinaires
Miranda Joyce saxophone, the Bodysnatchers
John Kehoe manager, the Apollinaires
Clive Langer record producer
Stephen Leonard-Williams flute, the Apollinaires
Penny Leyton keyboards, the Bodysnatchers
Roger Lomas record producer
Chris Long dancer/singer, the Swinging Cats
Gavrik Losey film producer
Julia Marcus press department, Chrysalis Records
Lionel "Saxa" Augustus Martin saxophone, the Beat
Jason Massot son of film director Joe Massot
Joe Massot film director, *Dance Craze*
Stuart McGeachin guitar, the Higsons
Graham "Suggs" McPherson singer, Madness
Peter Millen saxophone, the Apollinaires
Everett Morton drummer, the Beat
John Mostyn agent/manager, the Beat
Frank Murray tour manager, manager of the Bodysnatchers
Danny Nissim video producer, Chrysalis Records
Sarah-Jane Owen guitar, the Bodysnatchers

Horace Panter bass, the Specials/Special AKA
Judy Parsons drummer, the Bodysnatchers
Jeff Perks film director
Chris Poole head of press, Chrysalis Records
Ranking Roger singer, the Beat
Joe Reynolds saxophone
Rico Rodriguez trombone, the Specials
Rick Rogers manager, the Specials/Trigger Publicity
Errol Ross record producer
Bob Sargeant record producer
Richard Scott Rough Trade
Dee Sharp singer, J.B.'s Allstars
John Shipley guitar, the Swinging Cats/Special AKA
John Sims art director, Chrysalis Records
Cathal Smyth aka Chas Smash singer, Madness
Lizzie Soden video director
Neville Staple singer, the Specials/Fun Boy Three
David Steele bass, the Beat
Tim Strickland bookkeeper/singer, Coventry Automatics
Jayne Summers drummer, the Bodysnatchers
Nicky Summers bass player, the Bodysnatchers
Lee Thompson saxophone, Madness
Kraig Thornber drummer, the Apollinaires
Paul Tickle singer, the Apollinaires
Geoff Travis Rough Trade
Holly Beth Vincent singer, Holly & the Italians
Dave Wakeling singer, the Beat
Valerie Webb singer, the Swinging Cats
Graham Whitby bass, the Friday Club
Juliet de Valero Wills (de Vie) manager, the Selecter/Trigger Publicity
Alan Winstanley record producer
Adele Winter singer, the Friday Club
Laurence Wood saxophone, the Apollinaires
Daniel "Woody" Woodgate drummer, Madness
Steve Wynne bass, the Swinging Cats

A Dr. Marten boot pounds down on a sprung dance floor, stomping to the rhythm of an infectious African diasporic beat. An audience rises and falls to the music. The singer urges everybody to clap their hands as the bass drum beats a tribal rhythm. The music begins to accelerate. Sweat drips down off the walls. Mist sweeps across the stage. Smiles spread across faces. In this moment, nothing exists in the outside world beyond this mass orgy of jumping, screaming and dancing. The noise reaches a cacophonous high and then collapses into a deafening roar. This is the biggest band in the country. They are Jamaican. And British. Black and white. Women and men. They are Coventry. And London. And Birmingham. They talk of youth and identity. Of harmony and solidarity. They dress like you and me and tell us that this is our time. Our generation. The chance to confront the ills of society and to look to a brighter future. They are on television and in the papers. On the radio and at the top of the charts. Together, as one, it is a movement. A way of life. A Street Feeling.

And then there is a scream. A body goes down. A punch is thrown. Spit and sharpened coins fill the air. There is confusion. Fighting. Racism. Misogyny. The gratuitous spectacle stoked by tabloid hostility. This is no longer a mini drama revolving on a turntable. It is a country in decay. Jobs being lost. Lives at risk.

Somebody stabbed. A band arguing. Loyalty challenged. Walkouts. Conflict. Then, abruptly, the beat changes. An eerie siren whistles across the airways. Music and politics intertwine. The mood wrapped up in a three-minute song. People line up. To oppose the state, the police, Thatcherism, apartheid, and give themselves to song. To come together in celebration, to dance and sing. To feel the power of mass communion. A place of unity. A house of belonging. They call it madness—it is. They say nobody is special—they are not. They tell us to enjoy ourselves—we do.

This are 2 Tone.

FOREWORD

BY PAULINE BLACK, THE SELECTER

On a cold Monday night in late 1978, I saw a band at a small Coventry night club called Mr George's. I had no idea what to expect, but I had been told that they'd supported the Clash on a recent UK tour. At the time, I was trying to start a reggae band with a friend of mine, so I was more interested in the support act that evening, Hard Top 22—a tight, roots-infused collective of local musicians, who were each paid that night with a free pint. Monday night was reggae night. As all musicians know, it's the worst night of the week for getting a paying audience through a venue's doors, vividly illustrating the level of commitment to reggae-influenced music in this provincial city at the time.

Both bands that night left an impression, but I had no idea how much of an imprint they would make on a generation of youngsters, both Black and white, who were rapidly outgrowing punk and new wave and hungrily looking for something to replace it. In truth, I was one of those youths, too. After I heard both these bands, I felt reinvigorated to try that little bit harder, because I could see they were on to something new. The name of the headline band was the Special AKA.

By 1979, many of those performers would coalesce into the Specials and the Selecter; the latter being the brainchild of guitarist/songwriter Neol Davies, whose instrumental, also called "The Selecter," ended up on the flip side of the Specials's new single "Gangsters." This first 2 Tone label release rapidly climbed the charts, spurring Neol on to form a band, of which I became lead singer. These founders of the 2

Tone movement in Coventry enabled like-minded bands—Madness and the Bodysnatchers from London, and the Beat from Birmingham—to develop a new inclusive sound, blending the rhythms of Jamaican ska and rocksteady with a punk rock sensibility. A killer black-and-white visual style cemented the look. The architect of this new sound and image was Jerry Dammers.

Three years earlier, the infamous right-wing politician Enoch Powell had let loose his incendiary "Rivers of Blood" speech, calling for a stop to immigration and for enforced repatriation. A famous rock musician had also given vent to a drunken rant, along similar lines, during his set at the Birmingham Odeon, proving that an intolerant, jingoistic, postwar Britain was still alive and well, and was having none of this mixing and blurring of the Black and white lines of society. Like all good ideas, 2 Tone came to the fore when the progressive youth among us, spearheaded at the time by the Rock Against Racism movement, decided to put their foot down and invited us to take that one step beyond.

Over forty years ago, us 2 Tone musicians, just like our audiences, were all young, fit and full of vigor and creativity, not a care in the world, other than to make a mark on this unruly and inequitable place we had been born into. We were all children of the fifties and sixties, and the main thing we had in common was that we lived in Britain—a country that had hugely benefited from immigration, but curiously had an innate antipathy to the ideas of multiculturalism and diversity that we still struggle to embrace today.

The author, Daniel Rachel, has managed to capture the essence of that contradiction in those Margaret Thatcher–governed years, with this comprehensive, cautionary, but nonetheless celebratory saga of the 2 Tone label.

History is made up of the stories and recollections of often frail and complicated individuals, who are just trying to get through life as best they can, but still have a story to tell that's bigger than themselves.

The story of 2 Tone is framed here as that of Jerry Dammers.

His voice is loud and clear throughout. He had a vision, born from his unique perspective on life, which probably had much to do with the progressive ideas he was introduced to when he was a child. Through his singular composing skills and the ability to wrangle some of the unruliest, but nonetheless talented, musical individuals who were around at the time, he started a movement, by generously giving an opportunity to other like-minded bands to record on his new record label—which arguably did more than any other label to challenge racism and class prejudice in Britain. Indeed, the Selecter were so invested in 2 Tone that we recorded four singles and an album, *Too Much Pressure*, that all charted between 1979–80. We believed Jerry Dammers when he said: "It was quite a new idea, so it's kind of like a sublabel. But it was all about maintaining artistic control over the output and also having the opportunity to give other bands a chance."

Jerry helped change the mindset of a deeply divided country, whose division continues to this day. Divided it still may be, but among us are those who heard Jerry's best work, "Too Much Too Young," "Ghost Town" and "(Free) Nelson Mandela," in the early eighties. The historical impact of these songs is still as strong today as it was back then. They encapsulate a time when all things seemed possible if you could just marry excellent dance music with progressive social and political messages.

In March 2023, the remastered movie *Dance Craze*, and accompanying soundtrack, was released to droves of ecstatic 2 Tone fans. To have read this book and seen the movie again after all these years, I was struck by how the purity of purpose demonstrated by the bands has been captured in both mediums.

2 Tone championed all that was good about humanity, despite sometimes being infiltrated by the negativity of a small number of vocal naysayers.

To celebrate these releases, it would have been nice to organize one big event where all the bands that were involved in the 2 Tone movement over forty years ago could have reunited, but sadly, that did not happen. However, many of the individual bands that made up that movement are still performing, and since the Selecter is one of them, we will be enjoying ourselves as much as possible for the foreseeable future. I joined a band not to preach to the converted, but to start a long-overdue conversation. The music and ideas of 2 Tone live on, still influencing social attitudes and debates. Not a bad legacy for a movement that started in a grim Midlands nightclub on the worst night of the week, but is now embraced as the jewel in the crown of Coventry's City of Culture 2021 bid.

INTRODUCTION
PEOPLE ARE REALLY RATHER AFRAID

This is a story fraught with contradiction. A tale of ideals versus reality, of a working-class fan base led by middle-class musicians, of women challenging male privilege, of cultural identity fought out on dance floors across the country. But above all, 2 Tone is the story of a record label. One that inspired a movement and promoted a sound rooted in ska but delivered through a prism of rock, punk and soul. It was antiracist and antisexist but struggled to uphold these founding values. It was a radical alternative to the music industry but marketed and bankrolled by the establishment. Its imagery and iconography were black and white but it played out in a wash of hue and color. It is also the story of some of the greatest records ever made.

2 Tone was born in seventies Britain, into a beige landscape of Formica tableware, smoky barrooms and casual racism. Bigotry permeated every level of society where prejudice was an everyman currency lodged in the heart of popular culture, unchecked and policed by forces happy to maintain a discriminatory status quo. Put simply: racism was the very oxygen of British society.

What hope for the next generation? Unemployment was on the rise. Industrial strikes crippled the economy. Manufacturing commerce was on the verge of collapse. Trade union power was running rampant. In 1978, more working days were lost to labor disputes than since the General Strike of 1926. National pride was polarized. Tensions ran high. There was violence on the streets. Neo-Nazis freely marched through immigrant-populated towns and cities, protected by the police. Social division was extreme. Optimism was low. Disaffected youth rallied behind punk demanding a year zero in music, art and fashion to a conflicting cry of nihilism.

A year before her election as prime minster in May 1979, Margaret Thatcher appeared on the ITV current affairs program *World in Action*. Using immigration as a campaigning weapon, she cunningly spoke the language of the far right. "People are really rather afraid," she said, in a tone barely shy of condescension, "that this country might be rather swamped by people with a different culture." The skillfully judged phrase unsurprisingly provoked outrage: the leader of a political party addressing the nation in flagrant discriminatory overtones to woo National Front support toward the Conservative Party. Considering the UK population of ethnic minorities was 1,771,000 (3.3 percent), Britain was hardly a country "swamped." The "no future" punk rock outlook had never looked as bleak and as gray. Since the Sex Pistols's premature implosion in early 1978, and the Clash's subsequent search for broader musical expression, the country had witnessed a cultural wedge dividing clean-shaven pop commercialism from an alternative street-level embrace of art. British youth were in search of a new home. A place of belonging. In the void, vast swaths of unconscionable teenagers increasingly looked vulnerable to the persuasive camp of nationalism, booted marches and Union Jack flag-waving. In the cultural no-man's-land, race was pitted against patriotism, Black against white, skinhead against punk.

Salvation was to come from Coventry. A city rebuilt out of the ashes of the Second World War. Its resurrection a symbol of solidarity and hope. Here was a community who defended themselves against National Socialism and then forgave their enemy. Past foes were welcomed into a new world order where bombers had once darkened their skyline. In the immediate years following the war, Coventry blossomed, strengthened by dramatic buoyancy in the car industry. Then, just as rapidly, the fifties and sixties boom years deliquesced as the short-lived prosperity succumbed to a future of economic recession and government neglect.

And yet, for a second time in its postwar history, Coventry rose from depression and bestowed upon the city a sense of renewal and belief. Coming to the fore at exactly the same moment as the newly elected Conservative government, 2 Tone presented as a socialist co-operative in a period of monetarist ambition. It promoted collectivism and compassion for your fellow human being as an antidote to the prevailing doctrine of individualism and "the self." At its center was a Marxist thinker, humanitarian and staunch antiracist. Jerry Dammers was a visionary with a myopic sense of justice. His music addressed class and race division. It reflected a Black history and carried a social message. For a brief period, the effect was transformative and inspired a generation of followers.

I first heard the infectious rhythms of 2 Tone as a schoolboy. I was ten years old and, although perhaps not consciously, my heart pulled to the pumping bass; the dual chopping guitars and the deadpan vocals wrapped up in the mind-altering two-minute blast of the Specials's first number one, "Too Much Too Young." From the pages of *Look-in* and the small screen, I devoured the dapper outfits of bands like the Specials and Madness: the three-button jackets, ankle-cut Sta-Prest trousers, porkpie hats and black brogues. But most of all it was the songs; the warnings of teenage pregnancy and violence on the streets; of *ghost dances* and *red radios*; calls for Black and white to unite; clothes, music and social politics wrapped up in a British youth movement that landed on *Top of the Pops* and swept through the school playground.

2 Tone offered a way to look at the world and a soundtrack to dance to. In Birmingham, you made your choices: Blues or Villa, *Swap Shop* or *Tiswas*, Rude Boy or Mod. It was the thrill of decorating your Harrington with badges of the Beat and Walt Jabsco. Of hunting down cheap Fred Perrys in the Bull Ring market and scratched-up copies of Prince Buster singles. 2 Tone inspired you to look back and discover the cultural riches of sixties Jamaica. But it also documented the battleground of a new British landscape where the terror of neo-Nazis selling fascist literature outside your school

gate or on football terraces was usurped by 2 Tone's message of anti-racism and promises of seductive Beat Girls.

I carved the 2 Tone man—printed on the sleeve of each single release—on the school walls, imagined myself at the "Nite Klub" and blushed at the thought of *piss stains on my shoes*. I learned about the imprisoned Nelson Mandela, the horror of rape, and Israeli bombs dropping on Beirut. 2 Tone carved a deep groove in my soul and, thanks to the oxygen of airplay on Radio 1, the mind-blowing visuals of *Dance Craze* and the glossy pages of *Smash Hits*, my black-and-white world ignited with a life-affirming boom of colorful brilliance.

But the story of 2 Tone, and more particularly Jerry Dammers, is one of tragedy. Having formed the band the Specials and kickstarted a youth movement, Dammers increasingly struggled to communicate his vision. 2 Tone buckled under the weight of success. Its downfall is a fable of human frailty. Of betrayal. Of people trying to be the best version of themselves but discovering that ideals are prey to the irresistible lure of money and fame.

Still: it should always be remembered that at its heart, 2 Tone was high-energy dance music. Faster and more furious than its influencing predecessor Jamaican ska, and closer to the English rhythms of punk and guitar rock. It sold records in the millions and achieved incredible commercial success. Fans flocked to wear its iconoclastic fashions and espouse its political rhetoric. For a brief, bright, burning moment, 2 Tone shaped British culture. In its glowing embers, the country changed. We now live in a society where many of the values of 2 Tone are a standard way of life, where racism is unacceptable, sexism part of the national dialogue, and where institutionalized bigotry is increasingly exposed.

2 Tone was a catalyst: a story to be told.

PART I
EVOLUTION

CHAPTER I

MOONLIGHT SONATA

COVENTRY CATHEDRAL. MOTOR CITY.
BLACK AND WHITE MIX

Coventry Cathedral in the wake of an air raid, 1940.

On a cloudless, moonlit night on November 14, 1940, 300 German planes dropped 500 tons of explosives and 33,000 incendiary bombs over Coventry, a small Midlands metropolis 110 miles north of London, setting the city ablaze. During the eleven-hour assault, the Luftwaffe systematically destroyed the metropolitan industrial base and military infrastructure, ending a three-month campaign of heavy bombing raids. Operation Moonlight Sonata claimed the lives of 568 civilians, leaving a further 420 seriously injured and a city center of a quarter of a million square feet destroyed. Daimler Motor Company became an inferno; the Triumph car plant razed to the ground; a third of key industrial factories and more than half of the homes flattened; the hospital destroyed; and as many as forty churches and fourteen schools decimated. In the morning light, all that remained of St. Michael's Cathedral, which had stood at the heart of the city for almost six centuries, was its stone façade and spire. It was the most concentrated attack on British soil during the Second World War.

The obliteration of Coventry was a wanton act of destruction orchestrated by Adolf Hitler to wipe out the city's medieval architecture as revenge for the Allied bombing of Munich a week earlier. Many historians believe the British high command had advance knowledge of the attack and sacrificed Coventry to preserve intelligence information decoded at the top-secret Allied base at Bletchley Park. A fortnight earlier, on November 2, Ernest Bevin, the minister of labor, implored the prime minister, Winston Churchill, to strengthen the Midlands's antiaircraft fortifications. The complaint *was* acted upon. Indeed, per capita, Coventry had five times as many antiaircraft guns as London. Still, the city perished. And in Berlin, Joseph Goebbels, the Reich propaganda minister, boasted of plans to "*Coventriert*" (to decimate) other Allied cities.

On November 16, King George VI made an unannounced visit to the ruins of Coventry Cathedral, flanked by the home secretary, Herbert Morrison. Reportedly reduced to tears by the king's presence, locals gathered and welcomed the royal gesture of solidarity and its galvanizing effect on the city. Of 10,000 evacuation places offered to its citizens, only 300 people left Coventry. And yet there was more devastation to come. Bombing campaigns in April 1941 and August 1942 claimed more than 400 lives, with several thousand more injured.

In October 1945—little over five months since Victory in Europe—the local council published plans to construct a vibrant modernist city. And so began the long process of healing and reconciliation. "Future Coventry" promised a pedestrian precinct, the first of its kind in the country, and the creation of estates and prefabricated homes on the outer edge of the city to cater to a desperate housing shortage. In the same year, the Ministry of Information sponsored a twenty-two-minute film directed by John Eldridge and scripted by the poet Dylan Thomas. *A City Reborn* rejoiced in a historic metropolis famed for its trade of wool, cloth and silks, its mystery plays and pageants, and its industry and engineering. Told through the eyes of a young couple planning their future, viewers were informed that the "days of cramped houses and crippling streets" and of "slums still living on in a lingering death from the last century" were over.

In 1962, after delays due to bomb damage, work started on a two-mile elevated inner ring road circling the city center. This physical reshaping of Coventry would have a controversial and lasting effect on its indigenous communities. By 1970, less than half of properties in the Hillfields area had hot water or an indoor toilet or bath. Those fortunate to find work elsewhere deserted and, in time, the neighborhood became a haven for low-paid immigrants working in public services and insecure factory jobs, the homeless, sex workers and drug users. Thereafter, an unlikely community emerged mixing white with Afro-Caribbean and people of Bangladeshi, Pakistani and Indian heritage. It would become the hothouse for 2 Tone.

Affectionately known as the "British Detroit" because of its production line, the Daimler Motor Company built the first British car in Coventry in 1897. By 1950, twelve automobile manufacturers operated in and around the city, including Jaguar, Chrysler, Rover and Humber. Coventry, as Jerry Dammers would later describe it, was a *boomtown*. Boasting an average wage 25 percent higher than the rest of the country, the rapidly expanding "motor city" benefited from an influx of workers from the Caribbean. The movement of cheap labor was spearheaded by the then minister of health, Enoch Powell—after the British Nationality Act 1948 confirmed the right of Commonwealth citizens to settle in Britain—and endorsed by Harold Macmillan in a celebrated prime ministerial pledge, in which he said, "The doors of this country will always be open to the Commonwealth."

In 1947, SS *Ormonde* and SS *Almanzora*, two ships coming from Jamaica, entered Liverpool and Southampton docks, bringing small numbers of overseas British citizens to UK shores. A year later, 420 Jamaican passengers—many of whom had served in the Allied forces—arrived at Tilbury Docks on the HMT *Empire Windrush*, attracted by the promise of a prosperous life in the mother country. By 1962, over 300,000 people had arrived from the Caribbean, of whom half were Jamaican.

Compared to bigger cities like Birmingham, immigration to Coventry was relatively small, but the assimilation of the newcomers by the indigenous workforce reflected a spirit of postwar community. Following the German port of Kiel in 1947 and the Jamaican capital Kingston in 1962, Coventry adopted Dresden as its twin. Reduced to rubble by the Allies during the war, in 1965 peacetime Coventry was visited by a delegation of German youth from Dresden to help rebuild the vestry of the old cathedral. It was an incredible act of reconciliation, but in truth, Coventry was on the brink of industrial collapse. As swiftly as mass production had offered prosperity, the car industry fell into rapid decline, a victim of increased production in Europe and America. In 1975, Jaguar collapsed. Soon after, the Triumph plant closed down. By the turn of the eighties, more than half the workforce had lost their jobs.

Significantly, while adults negotiated the shifting world of employment and low-paid work, their children mixed in schools and at youth clubs, sharing their musical passions: white kids were introduced to the exotic and intoxicating sounds of ska and calypso; Black kids discovered the exhilarating pop explosion of the Beatles, the Who and the Kinks. "There was a crossfertilization happening," says Pauline Black, lead singer of the Selecter. "Lots of second-generation Black kids who'd come here with their parents listening to white pop music began to see a way of developing that conversation between white and Black music." Here was the first generation of teenagers not conscripted into National Service since its termination in 1963, entering into mixed friendship groups, open-minded and unburdened by traditional prejudices, freely sharing ideas, styles and records, and looking back into British and Jamaican culture with equal enthusiasm to looking forward. "If you found an old bluebeat record it was like gold," says Neol (pronounced Neil) Davies, guitar player with the Selecter. Recalling hordes of would-be musicians rummaging through charity shops on Gosford Street, hoping to find records to learn and perform, Davies says he remembers Jerry Dammers playing a Horace Andy record on his Dansette in his flat. "It was magical," he says. "You'd hear it once but then Jerry wouldn't play it again, in case you ripped it off."

Although few parents of 2 Tone musicians lived or worked in Coventry—rather they found employment in towns and cities such as Luton, Gloucester and Rugby—their children's subsequent move to the Midlands spearheaded the city's second dramatic revival in the postwar period. Where a flourishing motor industry had reversed Coventry's economy after the destruction inflicted upon it during the Second World War, now music gave renewed hope to the city after its collapse into rececession in the 1970s.

The population of Coventry was small, approximately 350,000 people. Accordingly, the pool of musicians to form bands was finite. Yet, as Pauline Black observes, it had one key advantage: "If a music scene developed it was easier to get into it." But whereas the Selecter formed simply because of who was around, the Specials came together in a more calculated way. "Some of my Black friends couldn't understand what I was doing," says guitar player Lynval Golding. "'What's wrong with you, man? You play in a punk group. You should be playing strictly roots.' They never understood what [the Specials] music was saying and how we were going to pull people together."

Looking back at the national pop charts, the mixing of Black and white musicians was not unusual—Hot Chocolate, the Equals, Heatwave, Thin Lizzy, Cockney Rebel, Darts, Showaddywaddy and Ian Dury & the Blockheads—but it certainly was not common. By contrast, the Specials would present themselves as Black and white musicians working as equals. It was a statement and a hallmark of their identity. In 1979, this hybrid of musical identity would give birth to a new British sound. They called it 2 Tone.

CHAPTER 2

SON OF A PREACHER MAN

JERRY DAMMERS

A middle-class son of a church dean, Jeremy David Hounsell Dammers was born on May 22, 1954, in Ootacamund, Tamil Nadu, a former province of the British Raj in southern India. His father, Horace, was a master of arts from Cambridge University and a staunch Labour voter. In September 1947, he married Brenda Muriel Stead. Jerry was their second son and the youngest of four children. In 1957, the family returned to the UK, first to Sheffield and then to Coventry, where Dammers senior took up the position of canon residentiary and director of studies at Coventry Cathedral. In 1972, he founded the Life Style Movement with the philosophy to "Live Simply" so that others may "Simply Live." Built around the ethos of finite resources, the movement attracted followers who believed "there is enough for everyone's need, but not enough for anyone's greed."

In 1965, Jerry passed his 11+ and accepted a place at King Henry VIII Grammar. Today, the school's website informs parents of its "proud history dating back to 1545 when King Henry VIII instructed his hanaper, Sir John Hales, to found a school in the city of Coventry," adding that it has "evolved through many different guises since that day, but the legacy of our founding monarch has remained." The school time line includes royal visits by Elizabeth I and James I. It marks the poet Philip Larkin's position in the junior department and the admission of girls in 1975. But for all the school's historical pomp and prestige, Jerry Dammers was a troubled pupil. At age fifteen, the rebellious youth absconded for two weeks to the island of Dorinish off the west coast of Ireland, purchased in 1967 by John Lennon and subsequently offered rent-free to the "King of the Hippies" and founder of the Digger Action Movement, Sid Rawle. "It was awful," recalled Jerry. "I went over there with this mate of mine and they put us to work ploughing the fields. Every night we'd be given a bowl of flour and water. The fields were laid out in the letters of the word *L-O-V-E*. That's when I stopped being a hippie and became a skinhead."[1]

Missing front upper teeth are the first thing you notice in Jerry's company. They smashed when he went over the handlebars of his bike as a child. "It was dead funny," he says. "I crawled into this house all covered in blood and I rang my mum. She sounded shocked and horrified, but her voice sounded a bit odd . . . then I realized I'd dialed the wrong number." In a separate incident at a Coventry nightclub, Jerry lost a second set of teeth during a physical altercation. By seventeen, life revolved around wanton acts of vandalism and excessive alcohol consumption. "I used to get pissed and put my foot through windows and things like that," he says. On a trip to Torquay, Jerry climbed on top of a holidaymaker's car and in a fit of stomping exuberance caused the roof to collapse. Summoned to court, he received a £250 fine.

Leaving school with one O level in art, Jerry took a foundation course at Nottingham Art School. Then, securing an interview at Leeds Art College, he attended the meeting without a portfolio, informing the admissions panel that he wanted to create a work of "Pop Art" like a "modern version of the Who." Playing a tape of himself singing a self-penned composition, "Little Bitch" (later recorded on the debut Specials album), Jerry said, "The professor just laughed and shook his head in disbelief and showed me the door."[2] History turns on such rejections. Had he been accepted, says Jerry, "The Specials and 2 Tone as we know it might not have happened."[3]

Realizing his folly, Jerry gratefully accepted a place at his second choice, Lanchester Polytechnic in Coventry, and quickly set about using the facilities to make animated films. An early four-minute short replayed the 1955 world heavyweight boxing bout between Rocky Marciano and British champion Don Cockell to show the stupidity of fighting. A second feature—*Far Gosford Street*—involved a dramatic mixture of live film referencing the IRA mainland bombing campaign and themed animation of a homeless alcoholic walking the streets of Coventry city center. However, it was a third short about a Birmingham nightclub which had the most bearing on Jerry's future career. Lasting only two minutes, *Doing the Bump at Barbarella's* exposed a line of chorus girls dancing to a "funky reggae-ish" instrumental soundtrack created by Jerry and a student from the year below, Horace Panter. The music would later morph into the Specials's live favorite "Nite Klub."

Completing art college, Jerry refused to attend the graduation ceremony and accept his degree certificate in protest against privilege and success. Formal education had served its purpose. Jerry's part-time embrace of music would now take center stage and essentially dictate the direction of his adult life. Having abandoned piano lessons as a young child, Jerry became a "mini mod" inspired by the Who's performance of "My Generation" on *Top of the Pops* in 1965. The BBC archive is long since lost, but an appearance by the four-piece on *Ready Steady Go!*, filmed earlier in the year, is an explosive assault of distorted guitars, aggressive drum rolls and vocal stutters. Watching the Who, fashioned in tailored two-tone longsleeve shirts and target motifs, an eleven-year-old Jerry Dammers was entranced by the group's pulsating electric rhythm, and determined that one day he would be in a band of his own.

Equally attracted to the early R&B rhythm of the Rolling Stones and the Small Faces, Jerry's taste in music sharply developed. "A friend of my brother's came round—my brother was in a soul band at the time—and he had this record with him, 'Al Capone' by Prince Buster. He put it on, and I thought, *What the hell is that?* I'd never heard anything like it."[4] Rejecting the developing rock sound of the late sixties in search of music with more subtlety, Jerry drifted to the on-beat soul of Tamla Motown and, in *Prince Buster's Greatest Hits*, the offbeat of Jamaican ska.

Optimistic and ever resourceful, one of Jerry's first attempts at connecting to the pop mainstream was to send a demo tape to John Lennon. In May 1968, the Beatles launched Apple Records and placed an ad in the music press requesting tapes from aspiring musicians. Beneath the heading "This man has talent . . ." a guitar player sang into a microphone, surrounded by instruments and with a bass drum strapped to his back. "One day he sang his songs to a tape recorder (borrowed from the man next door)," the copy continued. "This man now owns a Bentley!" Hooked, Jerry posted his music with great expectation. "My brother was saying, 'You're an idiot.' I was going, 'No, no, no, it's going to happen!'" It didn't. Apple never contacted the budding musician.

Next, and claiming to be a drummer, Jerry joined the Southside Greeks. Described as "a school rock 'n' roll, R&B–style band," the Southside Greeks's repertoire included cover versions of Desmond Dekker's "007" and Harry J Allstars's "Liquidator," facetiously renamed "The Masturbator" to persuade various reluctant members within the group to play reggae. Further stints followed in Ricky Nugent and the Loiterers, a Teddy Boy rock 'n' roll band, and a country and western outfit from Leamington Spa called the Lane Travis Country Trio.

By 1975, and now twenty-one, Dammers joined the semiprofessional outfit Nite Train, a soul covers band led by local singer Ray King. An influential figure on the Midlands live circuit, King would be a pivotal figure in the emergence of 2 Tone, as Lynval Golding explains: "All of us played at one time or another with Ray. He was this sort of Geno Washington–type figure. People would serve their apprenticeship with him. That was our foundation. If it wasn't for Ray, there would never have been a 2 Tone." Born Vibret Cornwall, the self-titled Ray King came to the UK from Saint Lucia in 1961 and recorded the acclaimed *Live at the Playboy Club* as the Ray King Soul Band. Next, King formed Nite Train. "We did lots of gigs over eighteen months doing cover songs like 'Love Train' and 'No Woman No

Cry,'" says Neol Davies. "Then we went to Djerba, a little island off the coast of Tunisia, and everything went wrong." From playing on a stage on the beach behind a row of scantily clad English dancers, the chastened musicians returned to the UK penniless. "The final insult," says Davies, "was when the exhaust fell off the van thirty miles from Coventry." Disillusioned and hoping to persuade King to be "less cabaret and more funky," Jerry says, "it was hopeless . . . and Ray walked out."

Broadening his horizons, Jerry began traveling to the Golden Eagle in Birmingham where DJ Mike Horseman hosted a roots reggae club night called Shoop for a mixture of "dreads" and, later, "punks." Reggae was available over the counter in Virgin Records or certain specialist shops, but as Jerry discovered, if you wanted to dig deeper, it was harder to find. "There was this funny little old white lady that used to sell roots records. You'd go into her living room and she would have these U-Roy records. It was very strange."

Exasperated by the limited musical opportunities in Coventry, Jerry joined Birmingham outfit the Cissy Stone Band, spending weekends playing funk-soul covers in workingmen's socials and nightclubs around the country. "I was learning the tricks of the trade," says Jerry, who at the time was still studying at art college but was becoming increasingly frustrated without an outlet to play his own material. Determined, Jerry borrowed a Revox tape recorder from Neol Davies and began to explore ideas, incorporating reggae with classic sixties pop songwriting. "That's where it all really started," says Jerry. "The time had finally come for me to get my own band together to do my songs." Edification came courtesy of "Not If It Pleases Me," a country-rock-tinged song recorded by Graham Parker & the Rumour. With its arrogant chorus refrain of, "You can't stop me not if it pleases me," the song's uncompromising stance provided a fillip to Jerry's burgeoning confidence. "That was the first song that made me think I could do something of my own. The record also had 'Don't Ask Me Questions' with a credible reggae backing." Then punk hit, and with it a sense that it was suddenly acceptable to do your own material. "That was the big change," insists Jerry.

CHAPTER 3

BLUEBEAT ATTACK

PUNK AND REGGAE. ROCK AGAINST RACISM.
COVENTRY AUTOMATICS

As a genre, punk had little if any trace of Black musical influence. Where punk was unrestrained, often rejecting melody and musical proficiency in favor of attitude and spirit, reggae relaxed the heart rate, pumping deep drum and bass grooves to stir the soul and shake down aggression. Punk and reggae appeared to be diametrically opposed to one another. Then, in 1977, everything changed. First the Clash. Then the Ruts, the Members, the Police and a host of white musicians began to incorporate reggae rhythms into straight-laced English grooves. The Clash introduced a cover version of Junior Murvin's "Police and Thieves" into their set, recorded with the legendary Jamaican producer Lee Perry, and as the "(White Man) In Hammersmith Palais" declared *a bluebeat attack,* a generation of white youth discovered a hypnotic reggae groove. It was a welcome balm to the high-octane energy of punk rock and, significantly, brought to the stage what many were experiencing at blues parties and enlightened clubs. "It was bound to happen one way or the other," suggests Jerry Dammers, "because that was the music we grew up with, that inspired us. Punk and reggae are very separate kinds of music; and although it embraced reggae, punk was a separatist movement and very much white. For me, reggae made punk gigs bearable. The lyrics may have been good, but the music was more or less unlistenable. To actually sit down and listen to a Sex Pistols LP . . . I mean, who'd do that? It gave me a headache. I wanted to create a more mixed atmosphere."

And yet, smoldering beneath the surface of the unlikely alliance between Black and white youth was an increasing undercurrent of hatred and resentment. As a country respected for its racial tolerance, England looked challenged. Ideologically opposed to racial integration, the National Front and other similar right-wing groups had increasingly gained electoral support throughout the 1970s. Advocating voluntary repatriation of all nonwhite, English-born citizens, the National Front rallied to slogans like "Keep Britain White" and "The Red, White and Blue Swastika," and spoke of Adolf Hitler showing "a proper, fair and final solution to the Jewish question." Its leaders shared photographs of themselves attired in Nazi regalia. By 1979, the National Front was finishing third at the ballot box and pledged to field candidates in all 635 constituencies at the next general election, guaranteeing the right to a party political broadcast on national television.

Matching their political aspiration, the National Front organized marches through immigrant-populated towns and cities, inciting fear and violence. This increase in racial tension became coupled with established rock stars, such as Rod Stewart, Eric Clapton and David Bowie, and punk rock leaders like Johnny Rotten and Siouxsie Sioux, flirting with Nazi rhetoric and imagery. Whether the engagement was ideological or merely fashion at play, it was sufficient to trigger the formation of Rock Against Racism, and thereafter the Anti-Nazi League.

In August 1976, Eric Clapton made a series of obscene racist comments at a concert in Birmingham, spouting ugly denunciations of "foreigners" who should "go back home," that England was "a white country in danger of becoming a colony within ten years," and that "we should all vote for Enoch Powell," whose infamous "Rivers of Blood" speech incited white nationalism. Witness to Clapton's diatribe from the front-row stalls, Dave Wakeling, lead singer of the Beat, says, "Then there was a lot of saying 'wogs' and 'get 'em out.' It was typical to hear people saying 'wog' but not from somebody on the stage and certainly not from someone playing a Bob Marley song ['I

Shot the Sherriff']. All you could hear was, 'What a bleeding nerve!' I wrote a letter to the *NME*. But it turned out there were loads of letters that said more or less the same thing. I was pissed off because most of them hadn't been there."

Red Saunders, a left-wing activist who called for "a rank-and-file movement against the racist poison in rock music" and the formation of Rock Against Racism (RAR), wrote one such letter of disgust. The response was instant. Correspondence poured in from all corners of the country. Acting quickly, RAR organized gigs billing white (punk) groups with Black (reggae) acts. Then, at the end of the evening, musicians came together to "jam" as a political statement and a visual symbol of racial unity. Inspired by Rock Against Racism, Jerry Dammers envisioned forming a multiracial punk reggae band with both Black *and* white musicians. "It was a subtle but important difference," he says.

In July 1977, Jerry recruited bass player Horace Panter, a middle-class art student from the sleepy market town of Kettering, Northamptonshire. Panter had arrived in Coventry to a stark warning: "The chap in charge of the halls said, 'Be careful when you go out at night because people get murdered.'" Finding relative safety in a college group and then a local soul and funk combo, Panter recalls meeting Jerry for the first time. "He was this strange mod character with sideburns and tartan trousers, who whistled skinhead reggae and pounded out Fats Domino and boogie-woogie on the pub piano."

Continuing his quest, Jerry enlisted, or more accurately pilfered, a clutch of local musicians to complete the inaugural lineup of the Specials. "We started rehearsals at the Heath Hotel," says Neol Davies. "I went for a few weeks, but it soon became apparent that Jerry and I being in the same band wasn't going to work." One day, Neol arrived at rehearsal only to discover Lynval Golding playing guitar in an authentic trebly reggae style: "Oh, I understand," Neol spat out. "See ya."

Born on July 24, 1951, in Mendez, a district of St. Catherine in rural Jamaica, Lynval Golding grew up in humble surroundings, with middle-class heritage. The Goldings are one of the five families descended from British-born Daniel Golding, who settled on the island in 1685. At age ten, Lynval left Jamaica to join his father and stepmother in Gloucester. "When I arrived I locked myself in the outdoor toilet and cried." If the shock of arriving in the west of England was traumatic, the disturbing reality of racism was an unforgiving introduction to life in the motherland. "I had a kid spit in my face and call me a Black bastard. I had no idea what he was talking about. When I realized he was insulting me, I got mad and smashed his face in. I was one of about ten Black kids and hated school. I just wanted to get out." As a young adult, Lynval ventured to Coventry where he formed his first band, the Meritones (a name taken from Jamaica's first sound system) with organ player Desmond Brown. By the time Lynval graduated to playing with Ray King—in his soul band and for a short spell in Pharaohs Kingdom—he became aware of Jerry Dammers sitting in on their weekly Sunday residency at the Pilot Pub. "Jerry was crafty," says Lynval. "He knew who he wanted in his band." Invited to listen to a "couple of ideas," Lynval was impressed. "Jerry had this great big old church organ in his house. He had no money to offer but I thought, *I like this. This is really interesting.*"

As a four-piece, Jerry, Horace, Lynval and newly recruited Barbadian drummer Silverton Hutchison, another contemporary of Ray King, set about rehearsing a mix of funk and reggae songs. "Lynval was the first Black person I met in my life," says Horace. "I was twenty-two and quite naive." Impressed by his well-spoken English, Lynval christened his bandmate Sir Horace Gentleman and taught him the rudiments of reggae bass. "Lynval and Desmond [Brown] would come round my flat with various records, and say, 'Listen, man! This is how it goes.'" Over time, Horace came to regard reggae in a similar vein as African drumming, where each individual instrument combines to make a whole sound. "Everything is the rhythm section," he explains. "The keyboard plays conga rhythms, the bass drum and the hi-hat play a steady thing and the snare improvises and the whole thing is held together by the bass, which plays the melody. Everything is arse about-face in terms of rock 'n' roll. I realized that

I had quite an important role to play in this group." Then, abruptly and unexpectedly, Lynval announced he was quitting and moving to London. He was unimpressed by the early rehearsals; Jerry says, "I had to beg him to come back."

The last addition to the lineup was vocalist Tim Strickland, described by Jerry as "a kind of Lou Reed wannabe who couldn't sing but had a good sort of punk attitude." Making their debut in October 1977 at the Heath Hotel, the newly dubbed Coventry Automatics squeezed onto the small stage. When it became apparent that Jerry's organ would not fit, he set up in the audience and faced the band. Adding to the comedy, Strickland thought it would be "funny and punk" to read Jerry's lyrics off sheets of paper and then sit down during instrumental passages. "On one occasion," he says, "I went to the bar and bought a pint during the gig." After eight months, Strickland was out. Brushing aside notions of being the "Pete Best of the Specials," he says, "I was quite a naive and not very confident individual. And I was in it just for a laugh. In the year of punk," he adds with disarming sincerity, "I was kicked out for not being able to sing."

The Coventry Automatics: (L–R) Roddy Byers, Silverton Hutchinson, Terry Hall, Lynval Golding, Horace Panter, Jerry Dammers, Neville Staple. Queens Road, Coventry, 1978.

* * *

A set list from an early Coventry Automatics gig includes a cover version of the Wailers's "Mr. Brown" and an original number called "It Ain't Easy" (rewritten in 1980 as "Pearl's Café"). "It was like two separate bands," says Horace Panter, searching for a suitable analogy to describe the group's sound. "We played a reggae song and then a punk song." Insistent that they share bills with straight punk bands, Jerry also stipulated that the support group would headline. "We would go on first," says Strickland, "even though it was an Automatics night."

At the Heath Hotel, the bill included Roddy Radiation & the Wild Boys and a local punk outfit calling themselves Squad. "It was just like *1-2-3-4*, make a noise for two minutes and then stop and say *1-2-3-4* again," says front man Terry Hall.[5] Jerry had previously seen Squad at a gig in Birmingham and explains that despite their crude attempts at making music they were "a lot more popular than the Automatics at the time. But I think Terry could see that there was no real future in that, so I persuaded him to join us."[6]

Born in 1959, Terry Hall lived in Hillfields, on the edge of Coventry city center. His mother was a sometime cleaner and a trimmer at the Talbot car plant, his father, of German Jewish descent, a technician at Rolls-Royce. At age twelve, Terry was sexually abused by a teacher on a school trip to France. The traumatic experience would define his teenage and adult life and feed a dependency on prescribed drugs to balance a later diagnosed bipolar disorder. Morose and sarcastic, Terry left school without qualifications, passing through a stream of unsuccessful employment opportunities including bricklaying, an apprenticeship as a hairdresser, and office work as a clerk at a stamp and coin dealer. Replacing Strickland in December 1977, Hall had a rather different approach to stage presentation. "Terry wore makeup and a black beret that slid halfway down the side of his face," noted budding journalist and early supporter of the Automatics, Simon Frith. "If Tim [Strickland] had looked like an extra from Lou Reed's *Berlin*, Terry looked like a character out of Christopher Isherwood—nervy, intense and absent-mindedly disturbing. He sang in the punk style of detached anger."[7] Watching the new front man at a gig at Tiffany's, Strickland says, for reasons that now escape him, he walked to the front of the stage and "threw half a pint over Terry."

Unconvinced by Terry's wannabe posturing, Jerry told him that punk was "a moment not a career" and was in danger of becoming a home to copycat followers, and that he (Jerry) was the "real deal" because he had worn Dr. Martens, tartan trousers and a mohair jumper since 1974. "I told Terry that the Clash and the Sex Pistols were about my age and that pogoing and wearing a leather jacket didn't make him a real punk. To do something truly original, like they had," he continued, "would be real punk spirit." Singling out a group of fans jumping up and down, Jerry told Terry that they were not "true punks" because they just aped what everybody else did. To make his point, Jerry suddenly invented a dance on the spot, allowing his limbs to spasm out of control. "I was hopping around like a frog, saying, 'That's a true punk, Terry! It's not about copying.' I tried to explain that punk had developed from a small creative group of people around Malcolm McLaren and Vivienne Westwood in London trying to do something original. I think I got through to him that it was about creating fashion not following fashion."

Adopting a strong English visual identity, the Automatics plied their wares in local pubs, regularly attracting audiences of between one and two hundred people. Before long, the Automatics became "kings of the heap" and started playing farther afield. Offered a support slot with reggae band Steel Pulse at the Top Rank in the center of Birmingham, the Automatics struggled to win over a largely Black audience. "We rocked up and all of Handsworth turned up to see the Handsworth revolutionaries," says Horace Panter. "And here's this support band with these four white and two Black guys trying to play reggae. It was dreadful but we toughed it out."

In the audience, one plucky music fan saw great potential in the Automatics and wanted in. DJ Pete Waterman—later of eighties production team Stock, Aitken and Waterman—had been playing Jamaican records at various clubs across Coventry since the early seventies and owned a record shop in the city precinct. Offering to manage the Automatics, Waterman stumped up £600 and booked a session at Berwick Street Studios in central London. It was a great opportunity. Urgently in need of a second guitar player, Jerry singled out Roddy Byers.

The son of a trumpet player who by day worked at the Jaguar factory on leather finishing, Roderick James Byers was raised in the small mining village of Keresley. Learning guitar as a thirteen-year-old, Roddy joined a succession of groups playing anything from jazz to Indian rock. Given the nickname "Radiation" by his brother because he would go red in the face when he drank alcohol, the nom de plume was perfect for the exploding punk scene. After forming Roddy Radiation & the Wild Boys, the group landed a prestigious support slot with Manchester's Buzzcocks.

Foreseeing how punk guitar could complement Terry Hall's vocal style, Jerry approached Byers to come to London the following day and record with the Automatics. Unwinding from a day job as a painter and decorator for the local corporation and happily inebriated in Domino's, a former gay club and now a popular punk hangout, Byers agreed to play on the session. "I staggered off home and next morning I was awoken by someone banging and kicking my front door. It all came back to me . . . recording—London—Dammers. I was lying in bed thinking, *Fuck me, they meant it!* At the front door were Jerry and Pete Waterman. They helped me load my Vox AC 30 and Gibson Les Paul into a taxi and we caught the train to the big smoke."[8]

Channeling the guitar playing of the Stooges and Johnny Thunders, Roddy played a raw punk style that was the perfect foil for the Automatics's reggae backbeat. Although crude and underdeveloped, the four songs committed to tape in London—"Dawning of a New Era," "Jaywalker," "Too Much Too Young" and "Little Bitch"—suggested a group operating outside of the norm but with exciting commercial potential. "Great little tunes with acid lyrics," pitched Peter Waterman.[9] Lynval, who was impressed by the unusual but distinctive front man, says Terry recorded his vocals in one take. "He had only been with us a couple of months. Pete came in and said, 'Fucking hell! Where did you get him from? He's fucking brilliant!'"[10]

To complete the transformation, Waterman advised Terry to start wearing a black polo-neck sweater and a chain to draw attention to himself, before adding, "All we need then is to stick a rocket up your arse!" Maintaining that Terry "couldn't sing" but had "a unique voice," Waterman qualifies, "The public like people with unusual voices, something distinctive." Yet the de facto manager's optimism was met with wholesale rejection when touting the tape to record companies. But Waterman did manage to persuade Seymour Stein at Sire to see the Automatics live. Giddy with excitement, Waterman attempted to teach Terry to dance. "Some hip-swinging cross between the Watusi and the Shag," laughs Jerry, noting in his diary: "Manager fails to pay studio bill, tries to teach Terry to dance, and is dismissed."

Chris Gilby, the next appointment, was the manager of the UK-based Australian punk band the Saints. Gilby organized a second recording session in a studio based in a housing estate in Tower Hamlets, and the Automatics cut four new tracks: "Nite Klub," "Concrete Jungle," "Racquel" and "Rock 'n' Roll Nightmare." Unimpressed by the results, Gilby attempted to oust Terry from the band and as an alternative suggested to Jerry that he should approach Johnny Rotten, who had recently walked out on the Sex Pistols.

Examples of groups who struggle to rise above local mediocrity litter the pages of small-town histories. As the Automatics attempted to hone their craft, few would have predicted their dramatic reversal of fortune. Rehearsing at the Binley Oak, Roddy recalls sharing half a lager with Lynval and "going twos-up on a cigarette" while Horace was "bringing wood in to burn on the fire in the back room" to alleviate the cold. Still, there would be opening slots supporting Generation X, Ultravox and XTC at Tiffany's dance hall in the city precinct. And starting on January 2, 1978, a three-month Monday nightclub residency billed as the "Dawning of a New Year At The Mr George, With AUTOMATICS."

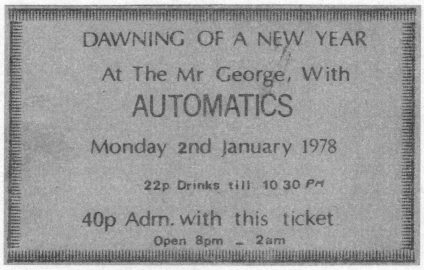

Handbill for the Coventry Automatics, January 1978.

Then, on January 24, the Automatics stood in for the Clash when they pulled out of a booking at Barbarella's nightclub in Birmingham. Ever the opportunist, Jerry asked his friend Roadent (Steve Connolly), who worked as a roadie for the Clash, to introduce him to the manager Bernie Rhodes. Connolly obliged. While meeting in London, Jerry told Rhodes about the Black and white mix of people in the Automatics and their punk/reggae credentials. Rhodes was intrigued and offered some opening dates with the Clash. "I couldn't believe I managed to blag our way onto the tour," says Jerry. "Bernie hadn't even seen us play!"

As luck would have it, the American electronic proto-punk duo Suicide, booked as the main support act, could not make the initial dates. Rising to the occasion, the Automatics opened the show, watched by the Clash's lead singer. "They were rough, but I enjoyed their energy," observed Joe Strummer. "You could tell they had something going, even if they weren't sure what it was. A lot of bands were doing the punky reggae thing at the time, us included, but they were taking it all very seriously, very rootsy. The Automatics, though, had a different approach, which was down to many things, but mainly,

I think, Terry's voice. He didn't have a reggae voice, and he didn't even try. He sounded so English and that was the difference."[11] Musicality aside, the Automatics offered the Clash further enticement, as Horace explains: "Neville [Automatics roadie] started supplying Mick Jones [Clash guitar player] weed and we were allowed to stay."[12]

On July 8, after receving a letter from a lawyer representing the recently signed London Automatics, and just four hours before showtime at Friar's, Aylesbury, the Coventry Automatics changed their name. Having previously toyed with a clutch of variations—the Automatics, the Jaywalkers, the Hybrids, Coventry Specials—they became the Specials. "We were mostly technically fairly basic musicians and singers," says Jerry, by way of explanation, "not that 'special' individually." Further believing that the band as a whole could be collectively much greater than the sum of its parts, he adds that "Specials" sounded "reggae-ish" in Jamaican slang—a "special" was a gun—and also came from an in-joke. In typically sardonic fashion, Terry proposed the name "the Six Petals," which to Jerry amusingly sounded like "Sex Pistols/Specials when you tried to say it pissed."*

---

* In the back of his mind, Jerry says, Michael Dyke's 1975 reggae song "Saturday Night Special"—"Leave your Saturday night special at home"—may have also informed his choice.

Jerry's notebooks list a comprehensive selection of potential names forwarded by each member of the band, a handful already in use. They include: Copasetic, Double Agents, Thrown, Stupid Marriage, the Riots, the Rubbers, Scratch, Blood Pressure, Paragons, Comets, Kickers, Viceroys, the Sheiks, the Tongues, Beatitude, Crystalized, the Natives, Thrillers, Attackers, Pleasurers, the Daylighters, the Keys, the Turnkeys, the Barons, the Sharks, the Treetops, the Invaders, the Enforcers, the Rulers, the Competition, the Lyrics, the All-stars and the Sure Shots.

A second list includes: Sent to Coventry, the People, Rough Diamonds, Bad Blood, Agitation, Springhill Jack, Cut the Tribe, Sounder, Battery, the Mashers, the Originals, the Cards, the Cloth, Pickpockets, Foot Pads, Javelins, Stiletto, Cresta, Rain, the Directors, Boss, Big Shot, Sultans, Hooker, Growler, Monkey-engine, Midnight Oil, Albany and Belvedere, the Sorrows, Moodies, the Affectives, the Daggers, the Quitters, Venom, Studio Cave, the Loose Leaves, the Trojans, Mailings, Rudelox, the Beaconaires, 4+2 = Harmony, the Empires, the Dub Buddies, the Jah Gents, Strictly Six, Stroots, the Charms, the Thundering Vibrations, Doctor Dick, Harrow, the Heath, Combo, the Hunters, Small Steam, Top Flight, the M6, the Night Out, the Wrong and the Plumb-bobs.

Reviewing the gig for *Sounds*, Garry Bushell noted the group's multiracial punk reggae dynamic, further observing that "the two cultures don't so much clash as entertainingly intermingle. Whereas the Clash play punk songs and reggae songs, the Specials's ditties combine elements of the two." Singling out Terry's voice ("sounded like Pete Shelley") and Horace's dancing ("a bit naff"), Bushell concluded, "But what the hell? They're competent, and enjoyable. Check 'em out."[13]

In the afterglow of their first national review, impending pop stardom met with the harsh realities of life on the road. The Specials were earning £25 a night (later doubled at Joe Strummer's insistence), and constant hunger and cold nights saw the band pitching by the roadside and sleeping in the van on top of the equipment. "I used the drum carpet as a blanket," recalls Lynval. "The next morning I'd dust myself off from the dirt." Money was in short supply, and with most of the group in their twenties, their mettle was tested on a daily basis, typified by Jerry spending a night in a freezing-cold police cell in Liverpool for the theft of a beer glass. "The tour was exhausting but brilliant fun," says Roddy. "Sometimes the crowd gave us a chance and we would retire from the stage happy, even though we were covered in gob." Moreover, Horace says that the three weeks spent on tour with the Clash set the benchmark for a Specials performance, to which they owe a tremendous debt of gratitude. "The Clash would give 150 percent every night. They were just full-on. We started that tour as civilians and ended it as a combat unit. It was our rock 'n' roll boot camp."

Performing to volatile audiences, Jerry witnessed a growing antagonism between tribal youth groups. Evidence of the bloodshed and violence—as much initiated by bouncers as rival fans—is evident in the documentary film of the tour, *Rude Boy*, directed by Jack Hazan and David Mingay as they traveled the length and breadth of the

---

Neville added the New Rave Regia, System One, Dem and Wee, Slax, Driver, ITZ, Loose End and the Blues.

Terry also proposed the Nobbers and the Klan.

country shooting the Clash for a cinematic release. Matters came to a head at the Glasgow Apollo where Mick Jones is seen shouting at the audience to stop fighting, and at Crawley Sports Centre where a contingent of National Front supporters disrupted the show. "The Sham Army [a loose term for Sham 69 fans, which included some violent skinheads] turned up, got onstage and attacked the lead singer of Suicide," says Jerry. Horrified by the ugly display of violence, Horace recalls "loads of pretty nasty-looking skinheads with NF badges and tattoos. You could palpably sense this kind of malevolence. Alan Vega [Suicide] came backstage and hurled a chair: 'I'm on the next fucking plane home.' It was just really heavy. That was a wake-up call to us. It was very much brought home to me that we're not going to be *just* a pop group."

Dismayed by the gratuitous violence, Jerry says, "That was the night the Specials concept was born. I wanted us to become part of the scene and change it, so it didn't become affiliated with the far right."

CHAPTER 4

THREATENED BY GANGSTERS

REGGAE. SKINHEADS. PARIS

The popularity of reggae in the late sixties and early seventies and the emergence of skinhead subculture are as linked as the Beatles and Merseybeat explosion of the early sixties, or the detonating fizz-bang of punk rock and the Sex Pistols in 1976. Reggae grew out of ska and rocksteady and is characterized by a slower rhythm, an organ shuffle, delay on the rhythm guitar and strong melodies to complement a shift in the bass and drum pattern. Between 1969 and 1972, reggae exploded onto the British musical landscape. "The Israelites" by Desmond Dekker & the Aces sold over one million copies and toppled Marvin Gaye's "I Heard It Through the Grapevine" from the number one spot. "It Mek" breached the top ten, followed by "Liquidator" (Harry J Allstars), "Red, Red Wine" (Tony Tribe) and the Upsetters's instrumental classic "Return of Django." There were hits for the Pioneers ("Long Shot Kick de Bucket"), Jimmy Cliff ("Wonderful World, Beautiful People"), the Maytals ("Monkey Man"), Bob & Marcia ("Young, Gifted & Black"), Nicky Thomas ("Love of the Common People"), and, in May 1971, "Double Barrel" by Dave and Ansel Collins was the best-selling record in the country for two consecutive weeks.

In April 1970, a Caribbean Music Festival attracted 10,000 fans and a host of reggae stars to the Empire Pool Arena, Wembley, including the Ethiopians, Bob & Marcia, the Pioneers, Millie Small, the Maytals and Desmond Dekker. A twenty-minute film of the festival simply titled *Reggae*, directed by Horace Ové, showed Black and white youth arriving at the concert dressed in sharp suits and button-down shirts. Asked what reggae meant to them, one boy replied, "It's the beat; it's fantastic," while an elderly Jamaican gentleman opined, "Reggae is a sound only the Black man understands." White working-class skinheads disagreed. Claiming to identify with the rebel stance of reggae, vast swaths of youth began dressing in high-waisted trousers, button-down Ben Sherman shirts, Levi's Sta-Prest, braces, Crombie overcoats and a healthy splash of Brut aftershave. The brutal look was glorified in an underground literary sensation when, in 1970, Richard Allen—a writing pseudonym of forty-eight-year-old James Moffat—published his debut novel, *Skinhead*. It told the story of sixteen-year-old Joe Hawkins and a life enthralled by football, music and violence.

On the page, Hawkins vented his aggression at hippies, but in the real world, skinheads displayed no shortage of racist hatred, often determined not by the color of one's skin but by degrees of cultural differences; where Black people were often tolerated, Pakistanis were singled out. Speaking in 1985, Terry Hall disclosed, "I knew what Paki-bashing was 'cos I used to do it. I knew what it was about. I knew the reasons and the reasons were that there were no reasons. Like football violence—there are no reasons."[14]

Rejecting any romanticized image of skinheads as a united working-class movement, Jerry Dammers says, "If there was bashing of Asians or hippies there was just as much bashing of other skinheads, either at football or just another gang three streets away." Jerry remembers being a teenager and seeing a local rock band at Baginton Youth Club on the outskirts of Coventry. A disco followed the live music and suddenly the previously placid audience came alive to the infectious rhythm of "Liquidator." Jerry recalled thinking, *If only the skins didn't act according to the stereotype: kicking the shit out of hippies or immigrants; if only all that energy and anger was directed into something positive and against the system, which brutalized them in the first place.*[15]

The contradiction of reggae on the dance floor and racial violence on the street spoke of confused young adults in search of an identity and a need to belong. This cultural ambiguity would become a key factor in the 2 Tone story, both uniting and dividing its ambition. Having previously supported Sham 69 in both Birmingham and Coventry, the Specials were all too aware of the problematic skinhead following they were attracting.* At the London School of Economics in February 1978, the so-called "Sham Army" chanted "Sieg heil" at Sham and daubed the walls with Nazi paraphernalia, causing £7,500 worth of damage. "It was obvious the skinhead revival was coming," said Jerry. "The idea was to tap into it and reflect it, to make sure it didn't go the way of the National Front. I idealistically thought, *We have to get through to these people*. That's when we got the image together and started using ska rather than reggae. It seemed to be a bit more healthy to have an integrated kind of British music, rather than white people playing rock and Black people playing their music: ska was an integration of the two."[16]

While on the verge of a fundamental reappraisal, a serendipitous event during the Clash tour would dramatically shape the Specials's future and result in the group expanding from six to seven members. Yet, over time, how Neville Staple came to join the Specials has left a mythological trail. Some say Staple was interjecting lyrics from the mixing desk during a set at the Music Machine in Camden and Bernie Rhodes persuaded him to jump up and join the Specials. "All I knew is I needed to get on that stage," Neville wrote in his 2009 memoir, *Original Rude Boy*. "Without a second thought, I took one bound and found myself next to Terry. Straightaway I was on the mic and I belted out my toasting." In an earlier account, Staple said the Specials were soundchecking in Leeds: "The atmosphere was bloody electric and I remember hearing the lads running through 'Guns of Navarone,' so I just plugged in the mic and off I went."[17] A third, and

---

* A year later, on April 8, the Specials opened for the Damned and UK Subs at the Lyceum in London, where a skinhead contingent first saw the band and would subsequently follow them around the country.

perhaps less glamorous version of events, given by Lynval Golding in an interview with the *New Musical Express* in September 1980, has Jerry playing keyboards in the dressing room before the gig and Neville singing along to "Monkey Man." "And then it [and Neville] was in the set from then on," says Lynval.

The Staple family moved to England from Jamaica when Neville was twelve and settled in Rugby in search of work and a better life. An only child, Neville found it difficult to adjust. "I was a bit rugged at the time and wouldn't take no for an answer. What I wanted, I would go out and get. Nobody got in my way." At fourteen, Neville found himself in a young offenders' institution after being involved in a post office robbery. Leaving school a year later, his teenage years revolved around remand centers for crimes ranging from house burglary and drug dealing to extortion.

One day, Neville was at the Holyhead Youth Centre in Coventry and heard an unusual mix of punk and reggae coming from the sound system in an adjacent basement room. "We used to keep parties where I had the Jah Baddis Sound System," explains Neville, at this point unaware of the Specials's [né Coventry Automatics] existence. "I was intrigued and popped my head round to listen." Impressed by what he heard, Neville asked if he could help and tidy up wires. Taken on as a roadie, Neville traveled in the back of the group transit van sitting on top of the speakers. "My original idea for him was to mix," says Jerry. "I built a little mixer with switches, and I wanted the whole band to go through it and Neville to switch instruments in and out while we played to get live dub effects. Instead, he became the official first roadie superstar!"

Fresh from the success of the Clash tour, the Specials promptly disappeared from public view. The group, having agreed to work with Bernie Rhodes, were instructed to cancel all further live dates, move to London, and practice five days a week. They were housed in a converted British Rail warehouse in Chalk Farm, the accommodation a damp upstairs room among mounting detritus, foul odors and the company of rats scampering across the bare floorboards. Sleeping on broken chairs and old settees, the band survived on occasional handouts for fish and chips and the offer of £35 weekly wages if they signed a management deal. "It was more than we were getting on the dole," says Roddy. "Me and Lynval said, 'Oh! That sounds good.' But thank God Jerry said no."

With the band uprooted and rehearsing in miserable conditions, Rhodes harangued them with outmoded punk rhetoric. "You gotta be good enough so some kid'll buy your records as opposed to a new pair of shoes,"[18] he told the Specials, convinced they were not ready to make it. "What Bernie didn't realize," counters Jerry, "was that there was seven people going halfway round the bend. We were literally cracking up." After an aborted attempt to convince Terry to join the Black Arabs—later to feature in *The Great Rock and Roll Swindle* playing disco versions of Sex Pistols songs—Rhodes decided to toughen the group up. And so, in November 1978, he sent the Specials to Paris for a five-night residency at the Gibus Club, on Rue du Faubourg du Temple. For all its excitement and sense of adventure, the trip was a disaster.

Dumping them in Dover, Rhodes ordered the band to unpack the van, carry the equipment onto the ferry where, on arrival in France, another vehicle would meet them. Setting the scene for what would be five days of mayhem, Roddy recounts the eventful journey. "We pushed the gear to the ferry on a handcart and Jerry's case burst open and his Y-fronts and stuff blew across the ferry station, much to our amusement. At the other side, Jerry dropped on his knees and claimed France for England by putting a handful of sand in his mouth. Silverton was sent home at customs—no visa—and Jerry tried pleading with the gendarme, but forgot he had all his money in his hands—bribery! The van sent to meet us was tiny, and because we were told the French didn't pick up Black hitchhikers, me, Terry, Horace and Jerry put out our thumbs."

Arriving in Paris, the group were met by a woman, described by Roddy as "an English hooker/heroin addict—sent to look after them." Escorted to their hotel, the group were outraged to discover they were liable for damages incurred by the Damned a fortnight earlier. When they protested, the manager confiscated Lynval's and Roddy's guitars. The situation rapidly escalated and in the resulting disagreement, a glass door was shattered. During the standoff, Roddy and Terry ventured down to the club where they fell into conversation with an "Italian-looking guy" who offered them a mint. As he opened his jacket, "We saw a gun," says Roddy. Troubled to learn of their accommodation predicament, the club owner accompanied Roddy and Terry back to the hotel. "This gangster, this really heavy character, came along," says Jerry picking up the story, "and, put it this way, he managed to get our gear back!" If the Clash tour was "our Battle of Britain," muses Horace, "Paris was our Dunkirk."

Less enthralled by the escapade, Terry firmly points blame at their new manager. "Bernie said it was character-building, which I guess it was, but it's no fun turning up in the middle of Paris at three a.m. and not have anywhere to stay or no money. Character-building I can do without. I'd rather have no character."[19] Once the band were safely back in Camden, they wrote a new song inspired by the Paris debacle. Making oblique reference to the ill-fated trip, *confiscated guitars,* and shady characters, "Gangsters" was written on the back of Joe Strummer's guitar. "I never understood the lyrics, although I wrote them," says Jerry. "But I knew it was about the sharks and wide boys that try and make money by pretending to run the music business."[20]

CHAPTER 5

SKA IS DEAD, LONG LIVE SKA

SKA

During the Clash tour, Jerry Dammers became aware that mixing modern heavy reggae with punk rock was not working. Where reggae was slow and laconic, punk was fast and furious: opposing rhythms with the beat too far apart. "We just couldn't get any continuity going," says Jerry. "Then I heard a song called 'Smoking My Ganja' by Capital Letters, which had a ska offbeat." Realizing that the combination of punk and ska would be more effective because they were both uptempo music, Jerry says, "That was the eureka moment."

To young Jamaicans, ska was what their parents listened to. It was music from another era, a time long since passed, with little modern vogue. Moreover, its popularity in the UK had passed its sell-by date. But that was all about to change.

To appreciate ska and its relationship to 2 Tone we must go back to August 6, 1962. After almost 300 years of British rule, and in the presence of HRH Princess Margaret, Jamaica regained its independence. The soundtrack to the momentous historical change was ska. An indigenous rhythmic expression elevated to celebrate Jamaica's break from its colonial past. The origins of ska are a matter of debate. What we know is, after the Second World War there was an influx of imported rhythm and blues records from American GIs stationed in Jamaica. Simultaneously, those fortunate enough to own a radio could pick up music transmitting from cities in the US Southern states such as Miami, Memphis and New Orleans. Over time, Jamaican artists began to record their own versions of these records. But rather than replicating them, there was a subtle accent shift from the on-beat to the offbeat. Thus, instead of emphasis being placed on the first and third beat of the bar, it moved to the second and fourth. The result was a musical revolution.

Taking its name from the onomatopoeic description of the guitar offbeat, ska was music born of the common man. Initially it featured brass and reed instruments and tended toward instrumentals. But as a wave of violence swept across Jamaica, exacerbated by an influx of cocaine, armed gangs and police corruption, ska increasingly spoke of hardship and drew attention to social and cultural divisions between uptown and downtown Kingston. Adopted by the disenfranchised, ska became the music of the outlaw.

In 1964, ska exploded into the British conscience with "My Boy Lollipop." Eighteen-year-old Millie Small sounded like no other singer. Upbeat, quirky and unforgivingly optimistic, she delivered the song with a dazzling breath of infectious pop innocence. With the tune lasting barely two minutes, white audiences discovered the jerky rhythms of a hitherto unknown Jamaican sound. Small had revolutionized British tastes. Four million records sold worldwide and, in an instant, England became the gateway for an abundance of Caribbean artists. Jamaicans settling in the UK received a live injection of homegrown music while white music fans, and particularly the burgeoning mod scene, found a rhythm to dance to and a style to be fashioned by.

Affectionately known as bluebeat—named after the Blue Beat record label established in 1960 as a subsidiary of Melodisc—over 700 releases of this new genre flooded the market between 1960 and 1967. Suddenly Prince Buster was on British television performing "Al Capone." The BBC aired a thirty-five-minute documentary, *This Is Ska*—presented by future prime minister of Jamaica Edward Seaga—featuring artists such as Jimmy Cliff, the Maytals and Byron Lee & the Dragonaires, familiar to audiences as the house band in

Dr. No. As a stream of live performances gave way to lessons in how to dance to the new authentic craze, a voice-over informed viewers of a "hypnotic sound of surging excitement and power" propelling people into a "frenzy" and moving to a "pulsating, almost religious beat."

Brimming with style and swagger, ska, and its evolution into reggae, became an integral part of British youth culture. The Beatles dropped their first attempt into the middle eight of "I Call Your Name" and four years later dedicated the rhythm of "Ob-La-Di, Ob-La-Da" to their newfound love of Jamaican music. As an adolescent, Jerry Dammers was a fan of "Yeh, Yeh" by Georgie Fame & the Blue Flames, which, although not strictly ska, had a Caribbean feel. Acquiring a copy of *Reggae Chartbusters*, Jerry was soon playing in the style of his new infatuation. His first attempt to play reggae on the piano was "Reggae in Your Jeggae" by Dandy Livingstone. Listening to records by the likes of the Beatles, the Rolling Stones and the Small Faces, Jerry traced the influence of American R&B on British beat groups and asked himself a fascinating question: what if an English group created a new beat from the influence of Jamaican music?

The ska offbeat and the classic English rock rhythm were in perfect synergy: the former exactly double the speed of the latter. "We've got two cultures in this country now," Jerry told *NME*'s Adrian Thrills in May 1979, "so the obvious thing is to go back to the roots of reggae and the roots of rock and try to form a new dance music. Original ska is much closer to rock music because it's just like a basic rock drumbeat with offbeat guitar thrown in." Neither wishing to revive an antiquated style wholesale, nor indeed reject punk outright, Jerry envisioned a British version of ska: putting their own lives into the music, their own lyrics, and stretching its parameters with other musical elements. "We're just trying to show some other direction," said Jerry. "You've got to go back to go forward."[21] Lynval was horrified: "Ska's old-man music!" He hollered in patois, "Music must forward!" Like Lynval, Silverton Hutchison watched on aghast. Already struggling to meet his mortgage repayments, the drummer began to miss rehearsals. But playing ska was too much. In a fit of anger, he called Jerry "a wanker" and walked out on the band.

Despite the encumbrance, Jerry set about adding "musical quotations" to preexisting songs: to "Gangsters" the riff from "Al Capone," and in "Too Much Too Young" elements of "Birth Control" by Lloydie & the Lowbites. Roddy looked on at a loss. Unfamiliar with ska, he realized his carefully constructed guitar parts no longer fit the new musical direction. Forced to reevaluate his approach, Roddy was thrilled to discover that all his favored Chuck Berry, Duane Eddy and Johnny Thunders licks suited the ska-based approach.

The set took on a new identity, and the rhythm through the songs solidified the sound. "Ska unified our songs," says Horace Panter. "Our punk songs slowed down and our reggae songs sped up. Everything was a lot more danceable. We fused the energy of punk and the sinew of reggae and produced a music that combined both influences." Jerry remembers that as soon as they started playing ska everybody in the band started jumping up and down. "It was that African roots rhythm," he says. "It survived all those years of slavery and ended up in Coventry."

Three centuries ago, Alexander Pope suggested, "A little knowledge is a dangerous thing." Suddenly, the Specials were a dance band. And ska was in the air. The Leyton Buzzards recorded "Saturday Night Beneath the Plastic Palm Trees" and sang about *dancing to the rhythm of the Guns of Navarone*; while Arthur Kay capitalized on the recent George Lucas film of intergalactic battles in a galaxy far, far away and issued "Ska Wars." On Planet Earth, British reggae band Matumbi succumbed to a fit of nostalgia and asked the question: [Where is] "Bluebeat & Ska?"

Certainly, the Specials had limited knowledge of Jamaica's indigenous sound. Lynval and Jerry played the offbeat on their respective instruments but essentially the Specials remained a rock band. "The ska we played was very different," says Jerry. "It's actually a strange fusion: bits of skinhead style, bit of mod style, and a bit of Jamaican rude boy style." Even the cover versions—"Monkey Man," "Too Hot" and "Long Shot Kick de Bucket"—were not exact copies. They were fresh, updated interpretations infused with a unique English take. "If you listen to the original versions and then you listen to the way we do them, there's a fairly big difference," Roddy told *Smash Hits* in 1979. "We do them more rock style. There's disco basslines, heavy metal passages, rock riffs and all sorts coming out over the ska."[22]

Now, without a drummer, unsigned, and with no discernible or coherent image, the Specials were unlikely candidates to convert an uninitiated public to rhythms long forgotten or at best regarded as passé. Yet, 1979 was to be the year of 2 Tone, and the Specials its musical sensation. With Dammers's audacious idea to self-finance a debut single and kickstart a homegrown independent record label, the fate of the band, and indeed the course of British youth culture, was about to change. "I was like the naughty boy in the chemical laboratory," says Jerry contemplating the imminent experiment. "If you mix ska and rock together there'll be an explosion." Unable to resist, he combined them and, as he says, laughing, "There was an explosion. It was completely mad. I don't want the credit for it. I want the *blame* for it!"

CHAPTER 6

DON'T CALL ME SKA FACE

GANGSTERS. KINGSTON AFFAIR

1979 was the biggest year for record sales in British music history. Disco, new wave and country dominated the charts. On BBC One on a Thursday night on *Top of the Pops* you were as likely to see Chic, Sister Sledge and the all-singing Nolan sisters, as you were the Dooleys, Tubeway Army or the fresh-faced eighteen-year-old Janet Kay singing "Silly Games." Reggae was a big part of the "anything goes" musical landscape, and its offbeat rhythms stretched from Dennis Brown singing "Money in My Pocket," to "Walking on the Moon," "Roxanne" and "Message in a Bottle," the crossover hits pumped out by the Police.

Looking on with envy, the Specials languished in the backwaters of Coventry, let down by managerial ineffectiveness and record industry indifference. They decided to take matters under their own control. "We'd been through so many guys who claimed they could manage us," says Lynval Golding. "They claimed they could do this and do that, and in the end they do fuck all. We tried to do everything the normal way but were told by record labels to get out of it. Send them back to Coventry. Nobody wanted to know. That's when we said we'd do our own single and just fuck them all."[23] Disillusioned with a London-centric music industry and hell-bent on dictating the terms of their musical and financial future, Jerry set out a plan: the Specials would record an independent single, establish a label, and become pop stars.

And so, as unlikely as it sounds, or perhaps entirely plausible depending on your life experience, somebody knew a friend who knew somebody who could help. In this instance: Fraser, a friend of Neville's, who knew a local businessman named James O'Boyle (aka Jimbo). Asked about the connection, Roddy gives a look of concern. There is a long pause. "Some of Neville's mates used to do a bit of minding for Jimbo," he says hesitantly. "You daren't repeat the stories you've heard because people might be still alive." After some reflection, Roddy continues, "I heard that Jimbo had taken some business partner out into the country and made him dig his own grave. He pretended to shoot him, pushed him in, and drove off. Let's say: Jimbo had a certain reputation."

Beyond part-owning a plastic factory and investing in skateboard rinks across the country, there is little online knowledge of Jimbo. Neol Davies remembers him as quite short and stocky. "He was mixed race, an ex-boxer from Belfast. I beat him at pool one day, to my horror. I thought, *Shit!* He was an exciting character to be around. You knew he was involved in all kinds of no good. You could label him as a gangster. That was the irony of him funding the record."

Explaining the unlikely connection between Jimbo and the Specials, Terry Hall recalled "this bloke" arriving on the scene "with £2,000, wanting to get involved with us," he said to *Sounds* in April 1979. "He told us to make a record and that's what we did. He's a good bloke." While the band agreed to 15 percent interest on the loan, some members were not overly keen on borrowing the money. Concerned about the consequences if they could not make the repayments, Roddy's anxieties were confirmed when they went to pick up the advance. "We sat in his car, Jimbo reached into the glove compartment and there was a gun." Desperate for the deal to go through, Jerry says, "I would have done anything to get my music out there. Porkpie hat? I probably would have worn a porkpie on my head if it meant the music would have got heard. Records were something that was made in London by aliens. The idea that you'd get anywhere near a recording studio was just another planet. Then, suddenly, the idea that you could make and produce your own record was incredible. So we just got on it."[24]

Emboldened by the independent success of the Buzzcocks's *Spiral Scratch* EP—released two years earlier with money borrowed from family and friends—the Specials booked time at Horizon Studios. A fortnight before the session, John Bradbury was recruited as the new drummer. Known to most as the man behind the counter at Virgin Records in the city center, Bradbury had enrolled in an art foundation course in 1971 at Lanchester Polytechnic before studying fine art at Hull College of Art. Of Irish working-class parentage, Bradbury supplemented his student days earning money in numerous cover bands and regularly gigging in workingmen's clubs. Thrown in at the deep end, Horace says, "We rehearsed 'Gangsters,' recorded it and then taught Brad the set."

Owned by local businessman Barry Thomas, Horizon Studios was a two-story Victorian warehouse located next to Coventry station and part of the old railway goods yard. It was located on the first floor of the long narrow building, and the Specials made use of the sixteen-track facilities; with the aid of engineer Kim Holmes, they recorded three songs—"Gangsters," "Nite Klub" and "Too Much Too Young." "'Gangsters,'" says Terry, "was the best of the three songs."

Opening with a screech of car tires—lifted from Prince Buster's "Al Capone" and regarded as one of the first examples of sampling on a British pop record—a deafening wail pierces the speaker tweeter as Neville announces, *Bernie Rhodes knows, don't argue!* Suddenly a pounding rhythm bursts through, creating a tense atmosphere over a falling riff. *Why must you record my phone calls?* asks a high-pitched male voice. Double-tracked, to give a disturbing feeling, Terry recorded a "bored" and an "angry" vocal. "I'd heard it done by Jim Morrison on 'Riders on the Storm,'" explains Horace. "Two vocals with the same phrasing, but a different timbre . . . it sounded incredible."[25] Adding to the discombobulating vocal, a guitar line reminiscent of the Fry's Turkish Delight ad promised the enticing flavor of a "rare

Eastern essence." "Gangsters" was a compelling slice of dark pop, broody and sinister, inviting the listener into an eerie world of unsettling overtones, simultaneously pointing accusingly while offering protection to those who dared to step inside. But having completed its recording, the Specials unexpectedly faced a problem. "We didn't have a B-side," says Terry, "so I suggested we put on this song Neol Davies had done." Lynval presented the idea to him. "It didn't take me long to say yes," says Neol, grateful that a song he had recorded almost a year earlier was going to see the light of day.

In December 1977, as the influence of punk spread nationwide, Neol Davies was at home watching a television play when a soundtrack featuring a 1930s-style dance band caught his attention. "I had no idea what it was," says Neol, "but I was dabbling around on the guitar and came up with the idea of a riff, almost Cole Porter's 'Begin the Beguine.'" Eager to record the strange-sounding instrumental idea, Neol tracked down local producer Roger Lomas, who owned a small four-track studio in the garden of his house on Broad Street, Foleshill. "Neol knocked on my door, and said, 'I've come up with this great idea for a new song but I've got no way of recording it.' When I heard it, I thought, *Blimey! He's got something here.* I didn't know what it was. It wasn't like anything I'd heard before."

Over the next two months, Neol began layering instruments: first guitar, then bass. Needing a drummer, he asked John Bradbury—who had been badgering Neol to cut an independent record for several months—to lay down a rhythm. Limited to two microphones, Lomas placed one above the kit and the second in front of the bass drum. "It was all I had," he says. "There were no cymbals or tom-toms."

When Neol suggested the track needed a trombone solo, Bradbury proposed his brother-in-law, Barry Jones, who owned a local newsagent. Duly summoned, Jones was horrified when Lomas added a flanged delay effect to his brass part. Unconcerned, and now on a roll, Lomas's final touch was to layer a percussion track combining a tambourine and two pieces of sandpaper rubbed together. "I put a delay on them too, and it made a rhythm all of its own."

Giving it the title "Kingston Affair," Neol had an acetate of the recording cut at Midland Sound Recorders in Balsall Common on the outskirts of Coventry. Then, mocking up a record cover on black card, Neol attributed the track to "The Selecters," written in white ink in the bottom center of the sleeve. Often presumed as a reference to "selectors" who picked records at sound system clashes, the differently spelled name was taken from the auto-changer used to stack records on Neol's hi-fi unit. "I liked the look of the three 'e's," he says casually.

The black label on the plain inner sleeve read, "Kingston Affair—The Selecters—©1978—BRADBURY—DAVIES." "I only credited Brad because he instigated the whole process," says Neol. "If he hadn't said, 'Let's make a record,' I wouldn't have. He didn't have anything to do with writing it. It was my drum pattern, my bassline. I played guitar and I composed the trombone line."

Success beckoned when Roger Lomas secured a publishing deal for the writers with Desert Songs/ATV. "They said they had interest from a Japanese advert," says Neol dolefully. "It never happened." Nevertheless, instant enthusiasm greeted Neol and Brad when they played the record at Mr George's nightclub during the Coventry Automatics's weekly residency. "I was absolutely amazed," says Jerry Dammers, unable to believe that "mere humans" could cut a single. The record industry was shrouded in mystery, so much so, says Jerry, that when pop stars visited Coventry, "it was like they'd come from Mars or something." Similarly impressed, Horace Panter recalls Neol and Brad "standing at the back of the room grinning."

To marry "Kingston Affair" with the ska-influenced "Gangsters," Jerry suggested overdubbing an offbeat rhythm guitar on the recording. He then proposed that Neol retitle the track "The Selecter" and credit it to a fictitious group of the same name.

After the double-sided record was pressed, the musicians gathered around to listen to the acetate. To their horror, the needle scratched and slid across the glistening vinyl. "The heavy bass blew the needle out of the record's grooves," says Horace, barely suppressing his pleasure. To compensate, Jerry overdubbed "a treble-heavy piano," allowing the record to be recut. Next, Brad pilfered 2,000 white cardboard sleeves from Virgin Records, and Horace purchased a set of rubber stamps from Clarke Marking and Stationery Co. on Warwick Row, at a total cost of £8.75. In Horace's front room, members of the band began the laborious task of hand-printing the plain covers. Inspired by the design for a poster advertising a sound clash between "Jah Shaka VS Alpha Sound," the sleeves were franked in bold capital letters: *THE SPECIAL A.K.A. GANGSTERS VS. THE SELECTER.**

In the weeks leading up to the do-it-yourself activity, Jerry worked on a portfolio of hand-painted prototype paper labels and sleeves. The artwork included a monochrome image of his girlfriend in a "Bonnie and Clyde–type pose" stamped across the palm of a black handprint, and a die-cut window sleeve revealing the title "The Selecter" when the vinyl disc was removed. Across all the images ran black-and-white checkers. "It was a sixties Pop Art thing," explains Jerry. "When I was twelve and a 'mini-mod' I used to decorate my bike with black-and-white tape. It was an image of that time because we were doing the sixties revival with the ska. Later, people saw the black-and-white checks as a statement of racial unity. It wasn't consciously supposed to reflect that but when people read that into it, I had no problem with it." Citing the two-colored checkers on Chess Records sleeves, Jerry adds that there was nothing particularly "novel" about the design.

When it came to giving the record label a name, Jerry toyed with the idea of "Tonic" or "Tonik," which, as he explains, was "another name for the iridescent [two-tone] material from which suits were made in the late sixties." Again, often misunderstood or otherwise interpreted, Jerry qualifies that "two-tone" meant "a type of material—two colors at once—not black-and-white check." Horace continues: "The name '2 Tone' was cool. It came with its mod sixties thing. I remember going round to Jerry's house with notepads. 'Okay, what are we going to call our record label?' We came up with all these ideas and logos." Tracing an outline on rough paper, Jerry drew the digit "2"

---

* Although "Gangsters" was credited to the Special AKA, hereafter the band is referred to as the Specials to avoid confusion.

in front of the word "Tone." Horace then recalls shifting the "2" above the "Tone." It sealed the label's iconic graphic.

There remained one final design component: Walt Jabsco. The cartoon image that would soon become synonymous with every 2 Tone release owes its creation to the cover of the *Wailing Wailers* album featuring Bob Marley & the Wailers posed as the American soul band the Impressions. Tracing Peter Tosh's (the Wailers) upright outline, posed defiantly attired in a suit and wraparound shades, Jerry says, "I just thought he epitomized that look . . . so it was an impression of an impression of the Impressions." Replacing winkle-pickers with a pair of loafers and positioning hands in pockets, Jerry christened the animated figure "Walt Jabsco." The name came from a vintage American four-buttoned bowling shirt bought when Jerry played in Tunisia with his former band Nite Train. The front of the shirt had "Walt" written on it and on the reverse "Jabsco." "I had this idea of a 'fish'-style cartoon character," Jerry elaborates. "I had a friend who worked in Newcastle with the people who founded *Viz*. I've always thought that the cartoon character Billy the Fish was influenced by the original Walt Jabsco."

CHAPTER 7

RUDE BOYS IN THE JUNGLE

ROUGH TRADE. SIGNING TO CHRYSALIS

Meeting at Coventry station and clutching a freshly cut recording of "Gangsters" and "The Selecter," Jerry and Neol boarded a train to London and made their way to Rough Trade at 202 Kensington Road. Neol recalls arriving unannounced, walking straight up to the counter and declaring, "'We've got this record! We've been selling it locally.' They played it and we got a great reception." Located in a house off Portobello Road in west London, Rough Trade was a record shop–cum-distributor with ground-floor space and a rented office on the first floor used by the publicity department. Opened in February 1976, Rough Trade soon established itself as a hub for burgeoning punk do-it-yourself culture. It was cofounded by a former student of Churchill College, Cambridge, Geoff Travis, who would go on to discover an unexpected connection to Jerry Dammers. As an undergraduate in the early seventies, Travis had shared student accommodation with Jerry's brother, Chris. "He was quite a strange individual," Travis recalls, "almost an opposite character to Jerry." Recollecting his first encounter with the Specials, Travis says the whole group arrived and sat on the floor against the wall behind the shop where distribution happened. "We made them tea and they played a tape of 'Gangsters.' It was amazing so we organized to have it mastered. That was an unforgettable experience. Jerry rejected it about four or five times. This was a totally new experience to us. Normally we'd master a Fall single and it would take about twenty-five minutes. Jerry was an incredible perfectionist: beyond the realms of normality."

Joining Rough Trade in 1977 with a view to expanding the reggae section, Richard Scott says it was common for bands to turn up with a cassette hoping to broker a deal. Contradicting Travis's memory, Scott recalls meeting the Specials upstairs. "The room was fairly full. Bernie Rhodes was there. He was saying that they shouldn't sign to a label because Terry couldn't sing. I always liked that!" Settled with a gentlemen's handshake, Rough Trade agreed to press and manufacture "Gangsters" and pay the dealer price less 20 percent distribution costs. "We paid up front," explains Travis, "which was quite radical. That gave people cash flow. Normally you'd wait six months to get paid and then you'd have to haggle. We were the opposite. We paid on the spot. The whole point about the independent distribution network was to compete: to enable people to have hits and keep their bands without having to go and sign to a major."

When "Gangsters" was put on sale the response was immediate. "It went crazy," says Travis. "We sold two thousand really quickly." Short of precise figures, Travis recalls a second pressing of 5,000, which also sold out, and third and fourth pressings of maybe 10,000 and 20,000. Laughing at the ad hoc arithmetic, Richard Scott concedes that "records flew out of the door," adding that although sales were healthy, they were not big enough for "Gangsters" to be sold in Woolworths or WHSmith. However, Rough Trade's involvement with the Specials would be short-lived. "The next thing we knew they'd done a deal with Chrysalis, said thanks for your help and went off into the sunset," recalls Travis, with evident regret. "In a way you could say it was our lack of business acumen. If we had been thinking more coherently and had a bit more money and wish, we might have said, 'We could be your partner.' It was too early in our evolution. We weren't ready for it."

Advance copies of "Gangsters" were sent out, and media interest swiftly followed. *Melody Maker* applauded the "original punk-reggae" band's "wonderfully eccentric self-production," while quick off the mark, *Sounds* reporter Dave McCullough praised the release as "an instant, potentially classic, killer, with one of the great, understated hooks of all time." A month later, on May 7, 1979, influential DJ John Peel introduced the record on his late-night radio show. "Where do they all come from, these bands?" he asked listeners with typical understated reverence. "I mean, you've not heard of them before. Obviously, people who know the Specials have heard of them and have gone to see their gigs and so on, but I mean this is their first record and I think it's an absolute gem. I really do. In fact, I shall play the other side of it, 'cos the other side's very good and I seem to have got a little time on me hands."

Flipping over the seven-inch disc, Peel played "The Selecter" but mistakenly credited the track to the Specials. Neol Davies was incredulous. "You're in your sitting room at home and all of a sudden you're on the radio: 'He's playing the record!' Then he said, 'That's "The Selecter" by the Specials.'" Without a second thought, Neol picked up the phone and asked the operator to put him through to the BBC. To his surprise, the call connected directly to the Radio 1 studio. "They put me through between records and I told Peel the whole 2 Tone story. He went back on air and said, 'I've just been speaking to Neol Davies . . .' And then he played both sides again!"

With further reviews running in the music press, critical opinion of "Gangsters" fluctuated between praising "Coventry's pride and joy" (*NME*) and criticizing the Specials's "tweety and bouncy" sound and a vocal that was "irritatingly shrill." More forgiving, Jon Savage pronounced in *Melody Maker*: "'The Selecter' has the sinuousness; 'The Gangster' has the muscle . . . both sides swing."

The sudden interest in the Specials was largely due to the involvement of the recently established Trigger Publicity fronted by Rick Rogers. Rogers had spent his teenage years humping gear for the Edgar Broughton Band before working as a press officer for Stiff Records. During the punk rock explosion, he traveled with the Damned, the Sex Pistols and the Clash on the infamous Anarchy tour.

Trigger operated out of a small run-down office at 5 Kentish Town Road, directly above A. H. Holt (soon to be the prime supplier of Dr. Martens footwear to Madness) and adjacent to the Rock On record shop and the offices of Chiswick Records.

"That was when Jerry walked into my office," explains Rogers. "Somebody at Rough Trade said, 'You need some PR. I know just the person for you. Go and see Rick.'" Coincidentally, Alan Harrison, a part-time tutor at Lanchester, shared a house with Rogers in Crouch End and advised Jerry to seek him out. Emboldened by two independent endorsements, Jerry arrived at Trigger with a cassette copy of "Gangsters." "I thought it was amazing," says Rogers; he played the track and immediately expressed an interest in working with the group. "But I want to see you live," he added.

(L–R) Steve, Rick Rogers and Juliet de Vie in the 2 Tone office, Camden, London, circa 1979.

Listening from the upstairs bathroom, Trigger partner and Trinidadian-born Juliet de Valero Wills was mesmerized by the "incredible and familiar ska beat filling the stairwell. I came out of the loo and I was so excited I launched myself down the last couple of steps, cracked my head on the top of the doorframe and landed in the office. That was my introduction to Jerry Dammers!"

Schooled in Scotland and ejected from home, de Valero Wills landed in London at age fifteen with the intention of studying at Kingsway Princeton College. Sidetracked by the engulfing wave of punk bands flooding the capital, she found work as an assistant to the press officer at Miles Copeland's fledgling label, Faulty Products. Shortening her paternal Spanish surname to the simpler "de Vie," Juliet worked on campaigns for the Police, Squeeze, Wayne County— as he became a she and transformed into Jayne County—and the neophyte punk-ette Toyah Wilcox. As punk evolved into new wave, de Vie climbed the rickety stairs at Trigger and joined forces with Rick Rogers.

In March, Rogers traveled to Warwick University to see the Specials and was stunned. "They were far and away the best band I'd ever seen live," he says, "just amazing. They had all the attitude and energy of punk but playing a music that just moved you both physically and mentally. They had an incredible stage aura. You couldn't take your eyes off them. It was a whirlwind, like you were having a party that was being led by these characters and the barrier between performer and artist wasn't there. It was absolutely extraordinary."

The university date had been organized by local booking agent John Mostyn. "The Specials had just gone through this rotten time with Bernie Rhodes and Jerry came to see me on this wet February day, quite unannounced. The doorbell rang and there was this odd-looking chap standing there. I had no idea who he was. He said, 'Are you John Mostyn?' I said, 'Yes.' He said, 'I've made a record and I'm really worried about selling it. Can you get us some gigs?' He put 'Gangsters' on the turntable and after thirty seconds, I turned to him and said, 'You're going to be alright.'"

Securing live engagements across the country—including John Bradbury's debut at Birmingham University, marking the Specials's first UK date in almost six months—the twenty-eight-year-old promoter was sent into raptures about the group's live prowess. "They were the best band I'd ever seen," says Mostyn with evident pride. "It was love at first sight. They had everything: accomplished playing and a desire to entertain. The whole room would be dancing by the end of the first number. You don't see the likes of that very often." Mindful of the goal of building a fan base across the country, Mostyn accepts that the intense touring schedule throughout early 1979 "must have been bloody hard work for them. But it laid the foundation. They played virtually every day of the week for two months."

Assuming responsibility for gigs in the capital, Rogers booked a fortnight of showcases to introduce the Specials to industry movers and shakers. The strategy was simple: three dates in the first week, two in the second. "I knew that if I had the maximum number of journalists in the first week, in the second week the reviews would be in the music papers. It meant they went from playing to a handful of people to selling out the Nashville in Kensington."

On March 18, the Specials returned to the live circuit and played to thirty people at the Moonlight Club in west London. Reviewing the gig for *Sounds*, Dave McCullough noted that despite receiving "a deservedly stunned reception" there was no doubt that the group "are preparing for an attack upon your musical sensibilities. The Specials can knock shit out of the many great pretenders around."[26]

A month later, McCullough interviewed the group for their first feature in the national press. Under the banner heading "Rude Boys in the Jungle," McCullough reminded readers of the depressed hometown environment the Specials belonged to: "Coventry is all concrete. Huge monoliths of planning diarrhoea stretch mercilessly to the blue sky above like they own the very souls of the few beings that totter out from their concrete cocoons, faceless and drained. The 'area' is dissected with subways that seem to throb with an invisible tension and deserted 'play spaces,' swings and trickling streams that poke fun at the surrounding slabs of gloom."

Turning his lyrical observation to recent London shows at the Hope & Anchor and a second outing at the Moonlight Club, Mc-Cullough pitched the Specials "cutting it again impressively in front of the guest-listed throngs of hobnobs and very important twats. The two gigs were in fact simply staggering." Proclaiming that the "wiry bunch of street-corner rude boys" were "gonna-be-big," McCullough wagered they had the "most instantly appealing and stimulating sound since those early days of grit and sandstone punk. It's dance music with a vengeance." He advocated that the Specials "flex their dance-beat muscles through the richness and sheer integrity of Dammers's pithy, uncompromising, terribly effective lyrics, covering the compassionate, the embittered and dramatically frightening. They are as musically and extra-musically fierce as they come."

The plan to create a groundswell of support was paying dividends. "The first gig at the Moonlight was not completely full," recalls Juliet de Vie, "then there was another one not that long afterward, and in that short gap it was completely rammed. There was a queue outside. Inside, everybody was into it from the beginning and dancing like crazy. There was a sense that something was happening and you were not sure who was controlling it."

Traveling from Coventry with the band and a coachload of fans, one supporter, Jamie Moore, recalled sweat dropping off the ceiling in the west London club. "My clothes were covered in these droplets of sticky brown gunk. It was so hot. Everyone was clambering on each other's shoulders, arms around each other, feeling a part of something, when life outside gave you nothing. Punk was over, a joke; it had promised us a future but didn't deliver. The Specials spoke about what was happening right then. We felt part of something important."[27]

Looking on at the wild scenes inside the Moonlight Club was a thirty-year-old former music journalist who had made a name for himself writing for *Melody Maker* and *Sounds*. Latterly employed by Chrysalis as a press officer and then an A&R man, Roy Eldridge expected little more of the Specials than "another band caught up in the mod revival" and to be out of the club within fifteen minutes and on to the next gig. Instead, what Eldridge saw stopped him in his tracks. "They were incredible," he says, still marveling some four decades after the event. "They had real presence onstage. It was all these contradictions: you had the deadpan Terry quite static in the middle, Lynval and Neville dancing backwards and forwards, Jerry grinning inanely on the keyboards and then this rock-solid rhythm section." Today, managing Liam Gallagher among a rostrum of high-profile artists, Eldridge regards the Specials as the best unsigned live group he'd seen, and unlike anything he has ever known. "They had energy, passion and a sense of the political. They made you dance. They made you think. I was mesmerized."

Eldridge talked his way backstage and says the group were shattered and quite intimidating. "Thankfully I knew Rick from when I had tried to employ him at Chrysalis. I said, 'We've got to do something. Come in the office and meet everybody. Let's take this to the next step.'" Recalling the introduction, Rick Rogers says Eldridge was "bursting with enthusiasm and raved about what he had seen. He didn't start throwing money like the rest of them; he was simply engrossed in the band and the music. That counted more than anything."

Bounding into Chrysalis the next day, Eldridge boomed, "THERE'S THIS BRILLIANT GROUP. WE'VE GOT TO DO THE DEAL."

Desperate to sign the Specials, Island, Virgin, EMI, CBS, Warner Bros. and Arista entered into a bidding war. "There was enormous pressure in a very short period of time," says Rogers, whose responsibility was not only to secure a deal for the Specials but to negotiate an agreement to establish 2 Tone as an independent label. "Jerry wanted to put out singles by other bands that would be A&R'd by 2 Tone and not be held to any contract. If a band wanted to stay, they could, or if not then they were free to go. It was completely unheard of, and to most people mad."

Such was the industry frenzy that when the Specials played at the Fulham Greyhound in May, a scrum of record companies huddled anxiously around the bar in a venue packed to the rafters with mods and skinheads. "Rick came backstage," says Horace Panter, "rubbing his hands together going, 'Great!'" Roddy walked in, saw Mick Jagger holding court and walked straight back out again. "I couldn't handle

it," he says. But signing to Rolling Stones Records did not interest Rick Rogers in the slightest. "We wanted to sign to a company
that had an identity and, frankly, the Rolling Stones didn't fit that at
all. We looked at Mick Jagger as this old man." Perhaps unaware of
their misgivings, Jagger told the press, "I think the Specials are great.
They're into a music with deep roots and that's something I like. I
really get off on the Specials."

Unimpressed by the charade of courting and flattery on show,
Roddy commented, "We found a lot of record companies were telling
us what records to release and what songs they thought would make
good B-sides before we'd even signed anything. I think the people in
bands usually know better than the record companies, anyway. The
labels don't really know what the kids are thinking or what's going
on."[28] As far as Rick Rogers was concerned, the only person who understood "the concept and the sociology and politics of it all" from
the beginning was Roy Eldridge. "He wasn't put off by these crazy,
unworkable, mad ideas."

Established in 1968 by Chris Wright and Terry Ellis, Chrysalis (a
portmanteau of "Chris" and "Ellis") had experienced almost immediate commercial success. Following a slew of top ten singles and albums from artists including Ten Years After, Rory Gallagher, Steeleye
Span and Jethro Tull, in the midseventies Leo Sayer had a dazzling
run of hits including the number one single "When I Need You." In
the same year, 1977, Chrysalis signed Blondie, a New York–based
quintet. Fronted by Debbie Harry, Blondie's success over the next five
years would eclipse most acts on the British charts. Yet, having signed
only one overt punk act, Generation X, Chrysalis desperately needed
a notable postpunk act to usher in the new decade.

Pointing to punk bands who signed to major labels—Sex Pistols
(EMI and A&M), the Clash (CBS) and the Slits (Island)—the managing director of Chrysalis at that time, Doug D'Arcy, says, "There
was not the culture of independent labels at the time that 2 Tone
appeared. The label was such a good idea. It would have been wrong

of us to miss the opportunity to work with the Specials. Our only problem was Ellis and Wright. Terry [Ellis] particularly hated the idea of a subsidiary label under our wing."

To ratify the agreement, it would require Chrysalis to suppress their identity within 2 Tone. It was an incredible proposition: an unsigned band negotiating a record deal while simultaneously demanding their own label to release singles by groups they had not yet heard, let alone found—all obligation-free. "We didn't have a clue who that was going to be," says Eldridge. "But it was, 'Okay, if that's what they want let's just go with it.' I didn't care what it took. If we didn't do that, we wouldn't have got the Specials."

Jerry was convinced that a collectivist approach would carry greater long-term benefit, and recalls, "The whole point of 2 Tone was everybody working together. That instead of competing, we should work with like-minded bands. Like the Specials: the whole was greater than the sum of the parts. It was strength in numbers. We took that idea to different record companies but Chrysalis was the only one that could see that idea of a sublabel."

For Jerry, understanding the philosophical root of his magnanimous approach elicits fascinating self-analysis. "General ideas of justice and fairness and not wasting resources must have been influenced by my upbringing to some extent," he says, "but most of it was just common sense and hopefully some sort of intelligence of my own." Questioning the right to be defined as a Marxist—"because I never read Karl Marx"—Jerry settles on socialism. "Politically, most of my influence would have come through the sixties: through Black music and rock music, which had a lot of political counterculture messages, and *IT* and *Oz.*"

With Chrysalis closing in on the deal, the fine detail of establishing 2 Tone Records as a subsidiary independent label presented challenges. "We had conversations with Rick and Jerry and a quite difficult lawyer," says Eldridge. Negotiating the number of singles 2 Tone could release per year, Rick Rogers says, was a struggle. "We ended up with a deal that allowed us to record up to ten singles a year by other artists, of which Chrysalis were committed to releasing six. And that none of those additional artists would be obliged to the label." The key clause meant new acts would sign one-off single deals with 2 Tone, not Chrysalis; and Chrysalis would pay £1,000 for recording costs. Accordingly, on a typical release the artist would receive 10 percent of the retail price, the songwriter 3 percent per side, and 2 Tone 2 percent for running costs and publicity expenses. The remaining 85 percent covered pressing, printing of sleeves and the promotion of the material. Furthermore, Chrysalis had no contractual obligation to enforce the 2 Tone identity outside of the UK.

Essentially, the deal with Chrysalis gave 2 Tone unmitigated freedom. It could operate independently and without accountability. Bands would benefit from the weight of major record company backing but remained free to come and go at will. "What you must remember," emphasizes Rogers, "is that the Specials didn't want to turn 2 Tone into a record company." Signed acts would have total control over recording and marketing; "the rest," he says, "was up to Chrysalis."

The historic deal gave the Specials unprecedented autonomy. But at what cost? In 1976, the Sex Pistols signed to EMI for £40,000 returnable against future royalties and the Clash made a five-album deal with CBS for £100,000. By contrast, the Specials signed a five-album deal and received a £20,000 advance, paid in full on completion of their first long player. On the face of it, Chrysalis were bankrolling 2 Tone by offering the Specials a reduced fee. Nevertheless, Jerry insisted each member of the band receive a weekly wage of £40, including Rick Rogers. "I was made an equal partner in the band in the role of 'organizer,'" says Rogers. "I was treated like the eighth member. There was no management percentage. If they got paid £50 one week, I got paid £50. When record royalties came through, they were divided equally. It was generous to a fault."

Then, as the contract was prepared for the Specials to sign, Rogers received a phone call from a relatively new independent label. "I know exactly what you're getting paid," its founder told Rogers. "I'll double it. Come and sign to us." Holding his ground, Rogers told him it was not "about the money." The executive tried a different tack: "If you get them to sign a contract with us we can talk about this label, I guess." Fobbed off again, his final tactic was to offer "a very large personal bribe," at which point, says Rogers, "it was just, 'Fuck off!'"

Signatures secured, the first priority for Chrysalis was to rerelease "Gangsters." After taking over distribution and marketing from Rough Trade, "Gangsters" was repressed and issued in a die-cut black-and-white paper sleeve. Given a sheet of paper with a label-sized image of Walt Jabsco, sketched by Jerry in pen and ink, John Sims in the Chrysalis art department says his immediate thought was shock. "This is the label design! It's too small." Redrawing a larger master, Sims sent the artwork to production. He then received a phone call from Jerry. "That's not what I wanted. It's too clean. It's got to be rougher. It's got to replicate the grainier authentic look of a Prince Buster record." Acting quickly, Sims requested a suspension of production, only to be informed, "Sorry, we've just printed 250,000 sleeves. We've got to get the single out now."[29]

"Gangsters" sleeve bag, March 1979. Courtesy of Chrysalis Records/Jerry Dammers.

The rushed release brought instantaneous rewards: not only continuous play on John Peel's late-night Radio 1 show, but a prestigious slot on the BBC's influential weekly review program, *Roundtable*. Judged by a panel of experts, special guest Elvis Costello declared "Gangsters" "one of the best records of the last ten years." The following week, the *Sun* determined, "If it's rude, it must be Special." Tipping the group for the top, the daily tabloid informed readers that the Specials "have been adopted as the musical representatives of the rude boys, that special brand of aggressive youngsters, who are a cross between mods and skinheads."

Although available since April, "Gangsters" registered dramatically on the national charts, prompting a television debut on *Top of the Pops*. In the company of the Boomtown Rats, Abba and the week's best-selling single, "We Don't Talk Anymore" (Cliff Richard), the Specials presented as an oddity. Radiating indifference, Terry eyed the camera and stayed rooted at the microphone stand while Neville danced relentlessly across the stage, turned out in a monochrome jacket, porkpie hat and dark sunglasses. Behind his keyboards, Jerry grinned a toothless grin as the rest of the band oozed pop-star cool in shady suits and impenetrable glares. Within four weeks, "Gangsters" had climbed into the top ten and rooted itself at number six. Selling in excess of 250,000 copies, it was by any standard an immense feat and a vindication of the two years of hard slog. "There was something happening before the media blew it up," says Jerry, keen to emphasize that chart success was not a result of hype. Recalling a gig in June in Lincoln at A. J.'s Club when the Specials played to a largely uninitiated audience, Jerry says, "We won them over and they demanded five encores."

Excited by their immediate triumph, Terry likewise linked the breakthrough of "Gangsters" to the group's staunch work ethic. "We were working for eighteen months before that, hoping to reach that point. It almost felt like, well, we deserved it because when you know that you're doing something good it breeds a lot of confidence. I think we all felt like we were ready for it and it was time for it to happen."[30]

Happen, it would. By the year's end, "Gangsters" would be declared the largest-selling independently pressed and distributed single of the year. And 2 Tone Records would become one of the greatest independent success stories in recent memory, prompting favorable comparison to the supreme self-managed record label, Motown.

Ad for "Gangsters," June 1979. Courtesy of Chrysalis Records/Jerry Dammers.

CHAPTER 8

AN EARTHQUAKE IS ERUPTING

MADNESS. THE PRINCE

On May 4, 1979, Margaret Thatcher stood on the steps of 10 Downing Street as the newly elected prime minister. Quoting from Saint Francis of Assisi, she addressed the nation, "Where there is discord, may we bring harmony. Where there is error, may we bring truth. Where there is doubt, may we bring faith. And where there is despair, may we bring hope." Surrounded by jubilant crowds waving Union Jacks and celebrating the first Conservative government elected to office in five years, Thatcher added, "And to all the British people—howsoever they voted—may I say this. Now that the election is over, may we get together and strive to serve and strengthen the country of which we're so proud to be a part."

Life in the United Kingdom would never be the same again. Thatcher would govern the country for an unprecedented eleven years while the Conservative Party would stay in office for a further seven. By which time—1997—a social and political revolution would have transformed the country in almost every conceivable manner. For those like Jerry Dammers, who read the script and foresaw the consequences of Thatcherism, these were troubling times. 2 Tone would offer an uncompromising alternative to the mainstream agenda: a balm to alleviate the pain and counter the flow of right-wing rhetoric. Where there was bigotry, it would offer hope, and where there was adversity, it would provide sanguineness.

Yet, ironically, when the Specials came to prominence during the last months of Jim Callaghan's Labour government, they were railing as much against the inadequacies of socialism as the oncoming dark clouds of Thatcherism. On the last day of polling, the Specials played the Moonlight Club in West Hampstead. Taking to the stage, Terry Hall stood at the microphone motionless. "I haven't got much to say," he starts, announcing the first song with characteristic sardonicism, ". . . it's the eve of the election, and 'It's Up to You.'" Behind him, the band crash into the introduction: Neville leaps into the air as Jerry pumps at the keyboards and the room fills with the sound of instruments rising and falling. Abruptly the music stops and Lynval's clean electric guitar oscillates between a major and minor chord. "What you gonna do . . . ?" asks Terry to an oncoming heavy reggae groove. In unison, the audience sing along, assuming the song's polemical stance: *We can't force you to enjoy this music*—the political—*Looks like a case of the blind leading the deaf*—and in the last verse, the inescapable, *They want the whole world painted gray.*

The following day, as the electorate awaited news of a predictable result, the Specials drove across to north London for an engagement at Dingwalls. Booked to support, John Cooper Clarke, the fast-talking Mancunian poet, watched the headline act and then, putting his head around the dressing room door, imparted a single comment, "Belting!" Far from their hometown constituencies, none of the Specials had voted. Margaret Thatcher's victory confirmed, the group readied themselves for a clutch of gigs in the capital. However, unbeknown to the Coventry septet, they had, albeit unintentionally, invaded the territory of a rival gang.

Over the passing years, how Madness first encountered the Specials is a contested myth. Now, Suggs remembers reading a double-page spread in *Melody Maker* and being shocked how similar the Specials looked to Madness. "They were not only wearing suits and the same sort of porkpie hats that we did, they seemed to be doing exactly the same music as we were doing." A regular at the Hope & Anchor in Islington, Suggs says he first heard "Gangsters" at the pub's critical meeting point: the jukebox. Given free license "to put on whatever we wanted," Suggs recalls someone dropping the B-side "The Selecter" and being astonished: "What the hell is that!" he exclaimed. "It was the sound of it," he says. "The bassline and then that out-of-tune trombone. I really loved that. We loved an instrumental. And then someone flipped it over!" Familiar with "Al Capone" by his beloved Prince Buster, Suggs says hearing "Gangsters" was "an amazing moment. The sound was as it should be. At that time, you had cod reggae: 10cc doing *I don't like reggae, I love it* in a Jamaican accent or *underneath the plastic palm trees* by the Leyton Buzzards. It was all a bit novelty: white people doing reggae. But the bass and everything on the Specials's record was deep. 'Gangsters' had authenticity. It was really inspiring."

Impeccably timed, a poster appeared at the Hope & Anchor advertising the imminent arrival of the Specials. "The next thing they bowl in looking exactly like us," recalls Suggs, "a strange looking gang of fellas bursting in through the doors: all smart suits and Frank Sinatra porkpie hats. I didn't know whether to feel jealous or vindicated that we were on to something after all. It was a revelation that someone else out there was like us." Accompanied by bandmates Lee Thompson and Cathal Smyth (known to his friends as Carl or Chas Smash), Suggs ventured downstairs to watch. Billed as a local Rock Against Racism night, the gig ranks among Suggs's most memorable. "They [the Specials] went off like a packet of crackers. I remember Neville Staple blowing holes in the ceiling with a starter pistol and then they stormed into 'Gangsters.' Within seconds of the first chords, they were jumping up and down like lunatics. They were fucking brilliant. It was probably one of the best gigs I ever saw, certainly one of the most important for me and the rest of the band, and completely informed us, in terms of performance, pretty much from then onward."[31]

The origins of Madness stretch back to 1976 and a loose association of friends playing cover versions of rock 'n' roll songs, Motown and reggae. "We had all kinds of musical influences," says founding member Chris Foreman. "The drummer, John Hasler, wrote our first song, which was called 'Mistakes.' It was like, 'Ah! You can write your own songs.' It was a real moment." Built around the nucleus of Foreman, Thompson and keyboard player Mike Barson, Madness would undergo many lineup changes until they settled as a seven-piece. The complexity of those tyro days forms the text on the inner sleeve of their second album, *Absolutely*, and provides a wonderfully idiosyncratic history of the group's formation:

First meeting 'round Mike's '77 done none. We meet again, 'round Mike's John takes up drums and Chas Smash learns bass! We practice 'round Mike's and dig up Suggs from the bar. Off goes Carl. Along comes Gavin. Off goes Kix [Lee Thompson]. Along comes Lucinda for one gig! Gavin can't handle chaos off he goes. Off goes Lucinda and back comes Kix. Practice place found in Finchley Road. Off goes Kix again. Off goes Suggs with the arrival of the football season. Along comes Bedders [Mark Bedford] who beats a bass. Hasler drops drums and tries his hand at vocals. Garry introduced by rockin' John Hasler, takes over drums. Neither can handle the noise—off they go! His other team let him down so we decide to give his job back to "The Suggs," our almighty leader. Without anyone noticing, Woody [Daniel Woodgate] gets behind the drums. Kix thinks, "Mmm . . . interesting" back he comes and off we go!

Established in north London, the Invaders became Morris & the Minors, became the North London Invaders, and, finally, after Chris Foreman randomly picked out a Prince Buster title from their set list as a joke, Madness. Playing a mixture of ska, soul and rock 'n' roll, Madness proved to be a difficult group to categorize. "We were Madness," says Chas Smash definitively. "We were different to everyone else around. We started spraying and painting DMs [Dr. Martens] before anyone else did. We had a different image. Then one day Lee wrote on the back of one of his Levi jackets in bleach, 'That Nutty Sound!' And it was!"

Filled with notions of bumper cars and fairground rides, Lee Thompson envisaged the sound of something discordant and weird, a nutty mesh of bluebeat and rock 'n' roll. "He had this circus idea, something a bit nutty, and we knew what he meant," says Mike Barson, whose distinctive piano playing centered the sound of Madness and gave it a music hall edge.

Traditionally looked down upon by the British musical intelligentsia, "reggae," says Suggs, was "music that yobbos in Mecca ballrooms danced and fought to on a Saturday night. As far as they were concerned, it had very little musical merit." Dismissed as simplistic and repetitive compared with the complex and indulged world of rock, Suggs says, "the music's vigor and subtle infinities of rhythm passed them by. But not us."[32] Heard in roller discos, youth clubs or at house parties, reggae was all about the way it made you feel. "Exactly!" cries Suggs. "It's what it felt like. You'd hear the bass and the drums and you'd want to dance. Lee Thompson used to do this dance and would say, 'The bass is my feet, the hi-hat is my hips, the snare drum is my arms, and my head is the top.' In '75, '76, we were hanging around with kids who were into progressive rock, blankets over the lights and all sitting around on the floor smoking dope. Then you'd see the Black kids going, 'We're going to get charged. We're going to go out and dance.' That was the thing. You had to get through that subtle paranoia of what grass does to you, to actually get on your feet. There was no ego. It was like a machine: everyone playing their part, and no one stood out necessarily. You made this machine of dance."

Confronted by a pervasive belief that "white people can't play reggae," or "you have to be Black," Madness often played to audiences indifferent to offbeat rhythms. "At one point," Suggs told *Smash Hits*, "we just dropped all the bluebeat numbers because they never got any reaction." Contradicting his latter recollection, Suggs adds, "Then I started hearing about the Specials through friends of mine. So we went down to the Hope & Anchor [March 18 or possibly May 5] when they were playing there but we missed them."[33]

After the Specials's show, Suggs introduced himself to Jerry Dammers. Bonding over the selection of ska on the pub jukebox, Jerry shared his plans to start a record label. "He said it was going to be an English Motown," Suggs recalls. "Then he told us he didn't have anywhere to stay so he came back to my mum's flat." It was located above Maples, a furniture shop on Tottenham Court Road. Conversation about Jerry's vision for 2 Tone lasted long into the night. "He was talking about it being self-sufficient, all-encompassing and racially integrated," says Suggs. "I didn't think it would ever happen."

Earlier in the year, Jerry had been left baffled by some prominent graffiti—"North London Invaders," "Chalkie," "Toks," "Bird's Egg"—around Euston Station when he had come to London to meet Rough Trade. "Sometime later I realized this was the work of Madness and their road crew," chuckles Jerry. Inspired by a television documentary about artists in New York, various members of Madness had invented graffiti tags: *KIX681* (Lee Thompson), *Chrissy Boy* (Chris Foreman), and *Mr. B.* (Mike Barson). It gave them a sense of importance, if not notoriety, in the surrounding boroughs of north London. Suggs, however, turned to his mother's encyclopedia of jazz musicians. Randomly opening a page, his finger pointed at the name of a Kentucky drummer named "Peter Suggs." Skipping over the forename, a nickname was born.

News of the Specials caused much surprise in Madness's camp. "There was us in London and the Specials in Coventry," says drummer Woody, "two completely different parts of the country, and both ironically influenced and playing music from a part of history. We had the same dress sense and were all listening to exactly the same stuff—it was just incredible." Running off a cassette tape and two sheets of photocopied publicity, Madness mailed their cack-handed promotional material to Jerry's home address in Coventry.* Alongside Polaroid photographs of each of the six members of the group (Chas was not yet an official member) and

* The recently discovered artifact, stored away by Jerry for over forty years, was displayed at the 2 Tone Lives & Legacies exhibition hosted at the Herbert Museum in 2021.

helpful biographical details—name, age and instrument—a typed history gave information about the band and their forthcoming bookings: "Madness—a new group from North London—have been practicing in secret for one & a half years and have finally mastered 'The Nutty Sound,' which will be played in addition to Blue Beat and ska influenced songs at the following venues: Hope & Anchor: May 3rd, Nashville: May 4th, Windsor Castle: May 7th, Windsor Castle: May 11th."

Dismissive of a "lightweight, comedy/novelty" Nutty Sound logo, Jerry tore off the second page of the promotional pitch and "threw it away." Regarding Jamaican music as "Deadly Serious," Jerry nonetheless heard potential in the "very rough-and-ready" enclosed music. "They were just like a school band," he laughs. "They did a bit of Prince Buster and rock 'n' roll covers and some of their own songs. I seriously don't think anyone would have signed them at that stage—but there was 'My Girl.' I could see they could write a real song, so I offered them a chance to put something out on 2 Tone."

Concurrent with Jerry's judgment of the music, Elvis Costello recalled seeing the Specials and Madness share a bill at Eric's in Liverpool. "The Specials went on first so Madness had all evening to get drunk, and they came on like this gang of football hooligans— completely pissed. They opened with 'Madness' and were absolutely fantastic for one or two numbers, but then it disintegrated into a total shambles. They were like a gang who could play . . . a bit. It didn't seem like they could even remember their own songs. That was the first time I saw them and I really thought they were just a novelty act. I thought it could be something that would only work live, but they were really good fun."[34]

On June 8, the Specials signed to Chrysalis. When they arrived at Stratford Place, situated in a small cul-de-sac opposite the Bond Street tube station, Lynval Golding says, "being chauffer-driven, from my background—that's film stars! It was amazing." Popping the cork on bottles of ice-cold champagne, the band then made the short journey across to North End Road, Kensington, for a double-headline gig with Madness. The Nashville Rooms was a small venue with a capacity of 600. But with the growing reputation of both groups, demand for tickets was at a premium. "There was a queue around the block with kids all dressed like us," says Suggs. "Jerry told me that John Lydon jumped out of a car, came up to this kid in the queue and goes, 'Are you for real?' The kid goes, 'Yeah! We fucking are. Fuck off, you old cunt.' I walked into the club and everyone was dancing. It was like, 'Oh my God.' This was not just us in some funny little pub in Camden Town. This was starting to become something much bigger.[35] We'd been quite happy in our own little bubble, but suddenly something was happening and we just happened to be right in the middle of it."

On the back wall of the Nashville, a handwritten banner crudely scrawled in black marker hung across the stage. It read, "Return of the Rude Boys." "It was amazing!" says Madness drummer Woody. "We walked in and everyone was all in the suits and the whole gear. It was like, 'What is this?' A massive great room full of Mikes and Suggs and Lees and what have you."[36] There had not been such a music industry buzz about a group since the Sex Pistols. "The Specials were incredible," says Mike Barson. "They all had suits on and were jumping around when they were playing, so there was a great energy. I remember thinking, *Wow! It really sounds like those old reggae records that we're* trying *to do*. It was so weird."

"They were like us but turbocharged," exalts Suggs. "We were still diesel at that point. They'd gone that bit further, while we were still doing a bit of R&B. The Specials gave us this revelation that the uptempo stuff was really fucking exciting. No one else seemed to have realized what a fertile vein that music was, how potent it was live. But suddenly we were aware we were not alone. We learned a lot about how to turn a basically easygoing rhythm into something quite high-octane and speedy. Things started to change after we saw them."[37]

Meanwhile, while the nutty boys came offstage at the Nashville in west London, a group of fans was growing impatient at the Dublin Castle due north. Madness had double-booked. Hastily packing their equipment into two ex-GPO vans, the group hurtled through Shepherd's Bush and Notting Hill Gate, swinging right onto the Westway and taking a left at Regent's Park to complete the three-mile journey to Camden Town. Arriving to tumultuous applause, a roomful of skinheads, mods, rude boys and a splattering of aging hippies celebrated a group on the crest of mainstream success. In a matter of months, the six members of Madness—and the dancing Chas Smash—would be on *Tops of the Pops* as 2 Tone took the country by storm. "This is the purest form of dance music that I've heard for many a long gigging session," raved *Sounds*.

Interviewing the group for their first national feature, under the heading "Madness Are Not Rude Boys," Robbi Millar provided a recipe of influences. "Take a sound of the Specials, fairground style, and add some cockney Kilburn (High Roads) type vocals, throw in a saxophone for good measure to pick out a spine-tingling melody along the way, and you've got it. Madness!"

On the verge of breaking into the pop world, Madness needed to release a record. And quick.

Owned by Mike Finesilver, Pathway Studios was located on a ground floor on Grosvenor Avenue, Newington Green, and was decked in fifties-style aerated boards on the wall. Madness arrived on June 16 with enough money to record three songs. "It was a tiny studio," says guitarist Chris Foreman. "It was only eight tracks but it had a good mixing desk and microphones." Tuned up and ready to record, the band awaited the arrival of their drummer. Reconstructed for Madness's 1981 biopic *Take It or Leave It*, Woody is seen driving around the back streets of Islington on a motorbike searching in vain for the studio. "They lost £200, which was quite a lot of money," says producer Clive Langer of the aborted session. To remedy the situation, Langer paid a visit to Rob Dickens at Warner Bros. and negotiated payment for a second weekend at Pathway in return for the group's publishing rights on any original tracks recorded.

Two weeks later, Madness reconvened at Pathway and, so says Chris Foreman, "We'd got a lot better in the time in between." More rehearsed but apprehensive, Suggs says, "We were very nervous." As a member of the band Deaf School, Langer says, "I wasn't really a producer. But I knew that I knew more than they did about making a record." Screened off in individual cubicles, the group worked quickly until Bedders hit a low note on the bass and smashed the glass on the VU meter. Levels restored, Madness recorded the first of three tracks, "The Prince." Composed as a tribute to Prince Buster, Lee Thompson says, "It wasn't difficult to write at all," as he had explained in the group's oral memoir, *Before We Was We*: "I had the melody in my head, but I wasn't able to get it out. So, I hummed it to Mike, and the band as a whole. Mark [Bedford] picked it up, he got the rhythm going, and then Woody came in on the drums. It was done in the time it took a kettle to boil."[38]

Essentially a twelve-bar blues in structure, "The Prince" was unusual for its unapologetic extended instrumental passages. "A lot of the records we did at that time weren't in a format," upholds Suggs. "When you think about 'The Prince,' there wasn't a chorus. It was the same with 'Embarrassment' and 'Night Boat to Cairo'; the chorus was in the saxophone. Lee's playing was so potent we'd often just go, 'We don't need a chorus. Just let Lee play the sax.'"

Carefree, unpredictable and a self-confessed kleptomaniac, Lee Thompson's misspent youth had earned him a fourteen-month spell in an approved school. Inspired to play the saxophone by listening to Andy Mackay (Roxy Music) and Davey Payne (Ian Dury & the Blockheads), Lee meticulously practiced along to records by Fats Domino and the Coasters. Though he was dedicated and diligent, it soon became apparent that the young saxophonist was nonetheless ignorant to the finer tuning of his chosen instrument. "He played a semitone out because he didn't have his mouthpiece on properly," says Clive Langer. Describing Lee as "a bit whacky," Langer continues:

"He'd turn up a day after you'd expect him, and he was quite often out of tune." To mask the ad hoc pitching, the saxophone was filtered through an Eventide Harmonizer. It became Lee's sound. "We were just trying to get him in tune," quips long-serving Madness engineer Alan Winstanley with a wry smile.

Songwriting, it turned out, was another domain rife for thievery when it transpired that elements of "The Prince" owed a debt of gratitude to the godfather of ska. Pilfering references to earthquakes, ghost dances and *uptown Jamaica*, Lee liberally duplicated "bits and pieces" from Prince Buster's collection of hits, *Fabulous*. Stuck for a saxophone solo, Lee also fesses up to playing "bits of" "Texas Hold-Up." Ten years old when reggae took off in the UK, Suggs says that "those records were always in the firmament. Obviously, we had other influences, like Ian Dury and the Kinks, but I think the common thread was a kind of comic malevolence. There was an attitude that people like Prince Buster had. It was funny but it was serious at the same time. We became real aficionados."

Originally recorded by Prince Buster, "Madness" would not only become the homonymous signature tune of the north London septet, but in time would be adopted as a staple set closer of most artists signed to 2 Tone. Jaunty, with subtle political overtones, the ska classic was played by Madness with the swashbuckle of a rock'n'roll song. "It's a very odd rhythm compared to the original," explains Suggs. "Often what's great about English groups, especially when they're young, is you take a form of music and you get it slightly wrong. We put it all on the four and took a lot of the swing out of it and did a bit more bashing and banging."[39]

Having recorded two songs blending modernity with authenticity, the group turned their attention to the song that had first impressed Jerry Dammers, "My Girl," written by Mike Barson in the back of his Fyffe work van. Based on an argument with his girlfriend, "My Girl" is unusual in the 2 Tone canon for its overt balladry and tackling of the perennial struggles of teenage romance. Centered around a "moody" major–to–minor chord progression, Barson fused a rock rhythm with a reggae offbeat inspired by Elvis Costello's break-through hit "Watching the Detectives." "That was a big inspiration," confirms Mike. "I started with those chords and then I just carried on from there." Barson had sung "My Girl" live, but in the clinical surroundings of a recording studio, his limited vocal ability was exposed. "It didn't sound like a hit single," says Alan Winstanley bluntly. Nonetheless, as Clive Langer suggests, "My Girl" stood out as "an amazing pop song" whoever sang it. "It was mature but quite naive."

Hawking the tapes around industry contacts, Langer was surprised to meet a series of rebuffs. "Most record companies weren't interested. Even Stiff [later to sign Madness] turned it down." Then, unexpectedly, Jerry Dammers contacted Suggs and told him that his dream of starting a record label was now a reality: 2 Tone was official; did Madness want to put out a single? At a meeting with Jerry over lunch at the Spread Eagle in Camden, Rick Rogers says, "We talked about doing a single with them. In fact," he qualifies, "putting out the single that they'd already recorded as a demo." Rogers then told the group that the recording needed tweaking. "When Jerry heard 'The Prince,'" says Clive Langer, picking up the story, "he wanted the offbeat turned up on the guitar, so we went back and did a remix." In July, Mike marked the occasion with typically dry appreciation in his diary: "Remixed 'The Prince' and 'Madness' to get rid of hum on sax solo. Mix of 'Madness' shit."

Despite Mike's misgivings about the recording, Madness signed to 2 Tone in a Greek Cypriot café on Camden High Street. While there is some debate as to whether an official contract existed, Chas Smash was not party to the agreement. Since jumping onstage at the Camden Music Machine, Chas had earned a position as Madness's dancer. "Next thing you're thinking, *He's pretty good*, and people like him," says Chris Foreman. "He was definitely a visual icon." Not signed to 2 Tone nor a contributor on the recordings—at this point, he was not yet accepted by Madness as a full-time member—Chas nonetheless found a way to make his mark, inscribing the inner groove of the vinyl master: "CHAS SMASH SAYS 'THAT NUTTY SOUND.'"

Ad for "The Prince," August 1979. Courtesy of Chrysalis Records/Jerry Dammers.

* * *

Earmarked for a summer release, "The Prince"—backed with "Madness"—was advertised with the "catch line": "Nutty new single from Madness." "It had to be done very quickly," says John Sims, who prepared the artwork while the group were on tour. "The night before, I saw them at the Electric Ballroom and they had these white lights and there was a great big shadow of Chas Smash on the back wall doing his nutty dancing. So I redrew Walt Jabsco as a dancing figure. It went to press and the following day I got a phone call from Neol Davies, saying, 'What the fucking hell are you doing with our Walt Jabsco logo?' But people loved it and thought it was great. Although, I don't think Jerry was particularly enamored with it either."

While Madness diligently prepared for a performance at the Lyceum supporting the Pretenders, John Hasler arrived at their rehearsals in Archway with copies of the new single. "It was like a football team winning the FA Cup!" squawks Suggs. "And like all great British people, we put traffic cones on our heads and ran around the roundabout with shopping trolleys. It was that fantastic thing of fresh vinyl with our name on it and the black-and-white 2 Tone label."

When the record was released on August 10, 1979, *Melody Maker* proclaimed, "No jukebox should be without a copy!" Excited, Suggs and Chas ventured to their local branch of Woolworths in search of their new single. "We were white herberts so 'The Prince' was in the novelty section," says Suggs. "Carl went up to the counter and went, 'That's gotta go in the reggae section, mate!'" Raising their spirits, John Peel played both sides of the single on consecutive nights. "Hearing 'The Prince' was amazing," says Woody, who played a straight rock beat on the track. "But it sounded like no other record on the radio, and it was like, 'Oh God! Is this good enough?' It didn't have that kind of high-fidelity sound: it was all a bit echoey. And yet it was really good."[40] Impressed by what he heard, Peel offered the group a coveted Radio 1 session* as Madness set off on a short tour of the UK. A fortnight later, "The Prince" dented the low regions of the UK chart. It prompted a provisional invitation to perform on *Top of the Pops*. Called to the 2 Tone office at the break of day, the group nervously awaited news from the BBC. When the phone rang, there was a tangible air of excitement. "Sorry," came the word, "but Secret Affair [mod revival band] are higher than you." Dejected, the group trundled home.

Then, dramatically, "The Prince" started to climb the chart, and five weeks later reached the top twenty. Summoned by the BBC, Madness arrived at the *Top of the Pops* studios at nine o'clock in the morning to make their television debut. They were not required on set until the afternoon, and mayhem ensued. "They wouldn't let us go in the bar," Chris Foreman frowns, "so we found out how to get in by climbing out the window and going round the fire escape." Hopelessly intoxicated, the group made their way to the studio floor. As the cameras rolled, Lee popped up on-screen with a silver plastic

---

* Madness recorded "The Prince," "Bed and Breakfast Man," "Land of Hope and Glory" and "Stepping into Line." The session was produced by Bob Sargeant and broadcasted on August 27.

saxophone. "I knew we were miming so I took a toy one along and half the keys snapped off it. Woody thought it was hilarious. He was taking the piss . . . just superb!"[41] Similarly disposed to giving Auntie the runaround, Suggs sauntered into shot while Cliff Richard was performing his number one record. "We had a love/hate relationship with *Top of the Pops*," laughs Suggs. "We got banned four times for messing about and not miming properly. I remember the poor plugger, Sonny—God rest her soul—going to me, 'Will you stop it? There's a lot of people who would give their right arms to be on *Top of the Pops*.' They couldn't bear it but we kept having more hits and so we kept being asked back."

Introduced by Peter Powell—"With a sound they call 'the nutty sound'"—Madness commanded the stage as if they had performed on television all their lives. Dressed in a £50 Johnson & Johnson mauve suit, Suggs jerked and skanked to the swirls of Mike Barson's Farfisa organ. By his side, suited, booted and with a porkpie hat tilted across his forehead, Chas Smash projected the dancing rhythm of British ska into an estimated nineteen million households. "They were pretty dark times at the end of the seventies," says Suggs. "But all of a sudden this mushroom of hope, 2 Tone, sprouted out of the darkness. There was a lot of energy and an idea that music had got a bit pretentious and self-indulgent and it was time for something for really young people that wasn't manufactured."[42]

In the Specials and Madness, 2 Tone could now boast two certified pop acts; watching closely, Neol Davies knew it was time to act. Though Davies had spent many years in Coventry, mainstream success still eluded the twenty-seven-year-old guitarist and songwriter. Yet, in name only, the Selecter had a top ten hit. The trouble was, no such band existed. Desperate for a slice of pop stardom, Davies called a meeting of selected local musicians and proposed the formation of a new band. "We're guaranteed success," he told the assembled throng. "2 Tone is ours for the taking."

CHAPTER 9

GOING TO A GO-GO

THE SELECTER. ON MY RADIO. TOO MUCH PRESSURE

T hroughout 1978, the Transposed Men—a name taken from Dwight V. Swain's series of science fiction novels—shared a rehearsal space with the Specials opposite the art college in the center of Coventry. Decked in tiled black-and-white checkers, the floor design of the Binley Oak foreshadowed a future elusively waiting in the wings. "You had to burn wood in the fireplace to keep warm," says Neol Davies, who had formed Transposed Men with John Bradbury after listening to "Watching the Detectives" and agreeing that Elvis Costello's record provided a blueprint for merging reggae and pop. Abetted by a nineteen-year-old bass player, Steve Wynne, who by day worked in the precinct market, guitarist Kevin Harrison and keyboard wunderkind Desmond Brown, the four-piece produced a sound which Neol says propitiously was "very similar to the Specials after Brad joined them."

A surviving rehearsal tape, recorded on a mono portable cassette player, offers a revealing insight into the group's ambition and introduces many songs that would later form the basis of the Selecter's debut album, *Too Much Pressure*. Alongside "Out on the Streets" and "Street Feeling" is a rudimentary version of "On My Radio," a song that would in time define Neol Davies and introduce the Selecter to the public at large. Built around a pumping Motown-styled backbeat and galloping snare rolls, "On My Radio" promised greatness. But an unconvincing lead vocal meant it fell short of delivery. When Virgin Records traveled to Coventry to see Transposed Men play live, the melodic weakness screamed out. "They were very impressed, but the general consensus was that I wasn't a strong enough front person and my voice wasn't cutting it," admits Neol. Left in a state of flux, the fate of the group was determined as the first drifts of snow welcomed in a rare white Christmas. Popping into the Binley Oak one winter night, Jerry Dammers casually asked if John Bradbury was available to help the Specials. "I can't find Silverton and we're in the studio next week." Apprehensive, Neol replied, "Ask him. I can't stop him." Pulled into record "Gangsters," Bradbury never returned.

As a twenty-two-year-old white fan of the blues, Neol Davies accepted an invitation to a jam session at the Holyhead Youth Centre. Established in 1974 by Bob Rhodes, the center provided a space for young musicians and artists who were experiencing drug or alcohol abuse, unemployment or homelessness, to promote culture in the city. Charley Anderson was a voluntary youth worker and recalls receiving a £300 grant from the Cadbury's Trust to renovate the premises: "I went to a city meeting with Courtenay Griffiths [now a KC] and pleaded our case with the community relations committee. They granted us access to the basement and gave us £25 to help paint the place. Then we started Jah Baddis Sound System with Neville Staple and ET Rockers."[43]

The center became a convivial meeting point for outcasts and outsiders. When Neol Davies arrived with an electric guitar in hand, he developed an immediate affinity with bass player Charley Anderson and two other budding musicians: Desmond Brown and Arthur "Gaps" Hendrickson.* "Neol came along and played some lead guitar," Anderson told *Sounds* in 1980. "I thought it was great, like Hendrix coming in over the top of reggae." Honed on blues guitar players

---

* "Gaps" or "Gappa" was a nickname given to Hendrickson by friends to deflect police harassment. "We would be coming home from a blues and they would pick us up and take us to the police station. We gave each other a nickname like 'Mule' and 'Sugar,' and mine was 'Gappa.'"

like Peter Green of Fleetwood Mac, Howlin' Wolf and "Smokestack Lightning," Neol remembers plugging in his Gibson and playing blues licks over reggae rhythms. "We'd jam all night," he says. "'Yeah, man! The white guy's cool.' I didn't know how to play reggae at that point. But from Desmond cajoling me about my rhythm, it enabled me to become an authentic player and eventually I passed the Desmond test."

Calling themselves Chapter 5 and procuring the services of singer Joy Evering, the group played a mixture of reggae covers and Booker T & the MGs–type soul. Invited on occasion to play lead guitar, without knowing it, Neol Davies had discovered the nucleus of the Selecter. The cross-fertilization of Black and white musicians comingling across a variety of half-formed and short-lived groups informed what would become the defining sound of Coventry. Players joined and left bands searching for the right outlet for their creativity. Alongside Chapter 5, Pharaohs Kingdom, Earthbound and Nite Train, a miasma of ad hoc groups entertained future members of the 2 Tone society. However, one group, more than any, represented the cultural melting pot that would become synonymous with 2 Tone.

Hard Top 22 was a tough dub reggae band, six of whose members would eventually form the Selecter. Further still, Jerry Dammers attributes a brief stint with the group as his breakthrough to understanding how to play reggae. Untutored, Jerry played the offbeat with one hand on the keyboard and the bassline with the other. Introduced to the reggae "bubble" by Charles "Aitch" Bembridge, Jerry received an unforgiving lesson in discipline. "Jerry would press the keys down and when he lifted up to come off the beat I'd hit the back of his hand," says Bembridge. "I did it until his hand was red."

Alongside the Coventry Automatics, Hard Top 22 secured a residency at Mr George. "We probably only got a pint of beer each for playing," says singer and guitar player Gaps Hendrickson. "It was a small community of musicians and we all knew each other." Looking in one night was a twenty-five-year-old folk singer named Pauline Vickers. "That's when I first saw both bands, just as 'Gangsters' came out," she says, before adding with characteristic dryness: "I preferred Hard Top 22." Born to a Nigerian father and a white, half-English, Jewish mother, Vickers would later complete the lineup of the Selecter and change her name to Pauline Black. Adopted by a middle-aged white couple in Romford, Essex, Black never knew her birth parents. The only Black child at her school, Pauline says she was never a particularly friendly adolescent. "Everyone I ever related to was white," she told *Melody Maker* in 1980. "Then, when I was fifteen, people stopped patting me on the head and saying, 'What a nice little Black girl with pink ribbons in her hair,' and started seeing me as a Black mini-woman. Then all the prejudice comes flooding in." Growing up with a white uncle who revered Enoch Powell, Pauline says of her contradictory upbringing, "I went through eighteen years of conditioning to think a certain way, which gave me all kinds of hang-ups."[44]

In 1972, Black accepted a place at Lanchester Polytechnic to study combined science after reading a novella by John Wyndham—*Consider Her Ways*—centered on a female biochemist. Then, in her second term, her boyfriend committed suicide, hanging himself outside the student union building. Pauline was devastated and soon after dropped out, unable to bear the daily reminder. Transferring to Coventry School of Radiography, Black defined herself politically. "I wanted the overthrow of capitalism and for socialism to link up internationally with other countries in that fight." Connecting her Marxist outlook with songwriting, Black began performing in the back rooms of pubs and folk clubs, offering protest songs to largely indifferent audiences. "Singing wasn't a thing I set out to do," she says. "My role models would have been people like Diana Ross, Joan Armatrading and Poly Styrene. These were singers talking about identity. If you were of mixed heritage, you looked for other people who had had a similar experience growing up."

Pauline first heard reggae in the fifth-form common room where white kids would put records on and dance in formation to the Pioneers and Prince Buster. "I remember thinking, *Wow! That's really cool*." She then saw the Rolling Stones and was mesmerized by Mick

Jagger's ease connecting with a live audience. During this time, Black met Lawton Brown, a political science student at Warwick University who encouraged her to read books about Black consciousness. They began to write songs together. "Pauline was a classical guitar player and Lawton was giving her lessons," remembers Aitch Bembridge, who at the time shared a house with Brown. "My first introduction to Aitch was when I caught him coming out of the loo naked carrying a mop and bucket," laughs Pauline. "I was waiting in the kitchen for Lawton and suddenly Aitch appeared buff naked. He looked mortified and scuttled off." Forming the nucleus of a band, the three musicians teamed up with Desmond Brown and Silverton Hutchinson and began rehearsing at the Wheatsheaf pub on the Foleshill Road.

Since John Bradbury's departure, Neol Davies's ambitions for Transposed Men had crumbled to nothing. Working as a cost clerk at Lucas Aerospace supplying parts to the military, Davies would spend his lunch hour watching the Specials rehearse. "It was a frustrating period," he says. "I saw them getting better and better while I knew I had some really good songs sitting there." When "Gangsters" took off—backed by "The Selecter"—Neol was desperate to catch the slipstream of the Specials's sudden success. "They were playing a lot of gigs up and down the country, building up an audience. It was all beginning to shape up. People were dressing like them. It was set up to go. I could see that if I formed a band it was going to be successful."

As fate would have it, Hard Top 22 were falling apart. "There was a lot of argument and disagreement," recalls Gaps. "We were about to call it a day. I was at home one evening and Charley Anderson knocked at the door and said, 'The Specials want to have a meeting.' I told him to fuck off. I said, 'I'm not interested. I'm fed up with it.' But Charley said, 'No, this is serious. The Specials are on the verge of breaking through. John Peel's playing both sides of the record.' So I went to this meeting [to discuss the formation of a new group called 'The Selecter'] and they had it all sussed out and were saying, 'You guys are coming along with us.' I thought, *This is big! But can we really pull it off?"*

Arriving at Charley Anderson's terrace house at 33 Adderley Street, Pauline Black thought she was just going along "for a bit of a chat." Lynval Golding had recently dropped by at a rehearsal and proposed to Black that she should come and meet these people. "When I walked in the room, I met Neol Davies and his wife sat on the sofa. Everyone was a little high. Neol played 'The Selecter' on a red Dansette and it was like, 'Woah! That's amazing!' It was just so eerie, so weird and strange and other-worldly." Addressing the room, Neol pitched the idea of "The Selecter." "He had it all sussed out," says Pauline. "He said he needed a band to build on the success of the single. Then breaking into a broad smile, he started singing, *Do you wanna be in my gang, my gang, my gang?* We all shouted back in unison, 'Oh yeah!'"[45]

A rehearsal was hastily organized to see how the seven musicians gelled. Presenting a couple of songs, Pauline suggested jamming around "They Make Me Mad," which she had cowritten with Lawton Brown. "A girl singer was the last thing that any of us wanted," admits Neol. "But Pauline wasn't like the other girl singers that we'd had. She was completely different. Her voice was just so loud and powerful. We just looked at each other and said, 'This is going to work! You're in!'" Guitar player Compton Amanor was not convinced. "I thought it was a sellout," he says. "We were on a mission with Hard Top 22, very much mired in the 'Back to Africa' movement. We had our own repertoire. I was dragged into it kicking and screaming."

On July 2, 1979, the newly formed group performed their debut gig in Worcester. Although they'd been originally booked as Hard Top 22, Aitch recalls arriving at the venue and announcing, "Tonight we are the Selecter."* As the band opened the set with a cover version of the Upsetters's instrumental track "Soulful I," Pauline took to the stage sporting pink spandex pants and a tight white T-shirt scattered with pink sequins. Lyrics strewn across the front of the stage, Pauline

---

* Jerry Dammers suggested and designed the name "The Selecter" instead of "The Selecters," as it had appeared on the acetate of "Kingston Affair."

and Gaps ran from side to side creating a dynamic visual image. "It was not an auspicious event," confesses Pauline. "We were all over the place: the sound system was appalling; and we all needed some serious restyling."

Eight days later, the Selecter played their second gig at the F-Club in Leeds supporting the Specials, watched by Elvis Costello, who earlier in the year had scored a number two hit with "Oliver's Army." Much to Jerry Dammers's surprise, the Selecter had refashioned themselves as a carbon copy of their hosts. While Pauline noted, "The Specials tore the place down," reviewing the gig in *Melody Maker*, Frank Worrell described the Selecter treading with "an exhilarating ease, forcing even the weariest limbs into action . . . [They] are going to be real contenders." If there was any doubt the group would need time to learn a completely new repertoire and bed in their adopted style, Jack Bowers's review in *Record Mirror* after seeing a show at the Limit Club in Sheffield heralded the Selecter's arrival. "They create a truly modern sound blending ska, dub and rock in a vital mix," he regaled. "The stage crackles with energy, providing a show I haven't seen equaled in many moons."

On July 21, the Selecter made their London debut, joining a triple bill hosted by 2 Tone with Madness and the Specials at the newly refurbished Electric Ballroom in Camden. Three coachloads of fans made the journey from Coventry and joined the hundreds of people on the street clambering to squeeze into the venue. "It was one big party," marvels Gaps. "The walls were sweating and the whole building was shaking." With steam visibly rising off the audience, the mass of energy was a remarkable sight. The night was "unbelievable," says John Mostyn, "dynamite, just ridiculously brilliant. It didn't come better than that." Reviewing in *Sounds*, Giovanni Dadomo wrote, "The Selecter conspire to make dancing the only way to walk." Drawing attention to the "two all-action vocalists," Dadomo continued, "one of these wears a bluebeat hat, mohair jacket and roll-up jeans and introduces the songs in a squeaky Oop North accent somewhat reminiscent of the late Clitheroe Kid," before concluding that the

Selecter handled the ska rhythm "with grand and dexterous zest." For the encore, all three bands came onstage for a riotous performance of "Longshot Kick de Bucket" before collapsing in a small backstage area, their clothes drenched and steaming with sweat and heat.

If 2 Tone's ceremonious introduction was in need of validation, the night at the Electric Ballroom was its communal confirmation. Barely registering on the UK charts, and with only two records to its name, 2 Tone was poised to take British youth culture by storm. Improbable as it sounds, by the year's end, 2 Tone would have commercially eclipsed punk.

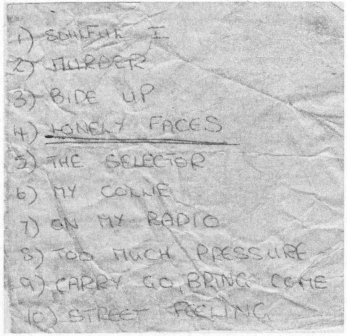

Set list for the Selecter at the Coventry City Centre Club, July 31, 1979.

* * *

Critically lauded as a live band, and barely six months after forming, the Selecter signed to 2 Tone and readied to record their debut single. "It was suggested we might be overshadowed by the Specials, and we considered that," commented Charley Anderson. But in truth, it was unthinkable the Selecter would sign for anybody but 2 Tone. Booked into Horizon Studios over three days—August 23, 24, 25—the Selecter had one pressing concern: what to record. "I saw them supporting the Ruts," recalls producer Roger Lomas. "'On My Radio' jumped out as the obvious choice. But when we booked into the studio, I didn't have a clue what it was called. They played all their songs, and I was thinking, *Am I going mad? They haven't played it.* Somebody said, 'Well, there's "On My Radio," but it's like a bloody Eurovision Contest song!' I said, 'That's the one!'"

Concerned that it was "too poppy," Neol Davies says there was a feeling that "On My Radio" "wasn't substantial enough." Inspired to write the melody after hearing a blackbird tweeting, Neol says "the angularity of the singing" prompted him to pick up the guitar. "*It's just the same old show on my radio* just came out. So I had the chorus before the verse." Repeating two chords, Neol conjured images of buying his *baby a red radio*, only for it to be playing *the same old show*. Convinced the song was a hit, Roger Lomas was dismayed that the group favored "Too Much Pressure." "There was complete disagreement, so as a compromise, I said, 'Right, we record both of them and let the record company decide.' I rang Chrysalis and said, 'Look, we've got a problem here,' and Roy Eldridge said, 'Okay, we'll pay you to record two A-sides and a B-side.'"

Tackling "On My Radio" first, and new to the studio environment, Pauline Black laid down a stunning lead vocal. "It was her very first take!" exclaims Lomas. "I'd always say to singers, 'Can we run through it once to get a level?' Pauline did a great take, and I said, 'Great, let's do it again!'" Much to Lomas's surprise, Pauline replicated the performance. "Both vocals were so good, I put one on the left-hand side, one on the right-hand side and a delay in the middle." Lomas then suggested that Pauline should sing the chorus in falsetto.

Written in an unusual time signature—7/4—the chorus of "On My Radio," according to Neol, had "seven beats: a bar of four, and a bar of three. It felt odd but good." The radical switch to the on-beat was dynamic, says Aitch, who at first resisted the change. "You were playing ska, then all of a sudden this time signature kicks in—*it's just the same old show*. It was militant." Pushing the arrangement further, Neol wanted a drum break leading into the chorus to last longer than a listener would expect, influenced by a similar device employed in "Get Off of My Cloud" by the Rolling Stones. "They all thought I was mad," says Neol. The daring move accorded "On My Radio" an unlikely but memorable hook. Yet, while the band were willing to overcome a musical challenge, the choice of producer was increasingly becoming a point of contention and festering resentment.

Trouble began when the regular use of the term "boy," meant as a greeting by Lomas, was misconstrued as a racist slur. "They referred to people as 'boy' in the days of slavery," says Gaps. "It offended me because it offended the others." Ever the polemicist, Pauline says, "It wasn't nearly as bad as being called 'nigger' but not that far off. It was annoying but certainly not meant in any kind of racial manner. However, there were more sensitive souls in the band than me and Neol." One of those, Aitch, now contends, "Roger wasn't saying it to make you feel like he's master and you're a slave. It was slang. He even got me saying it. 'Alright, boy!'" Far from having racist overtones, Lomas says, the phrase originated from Steve Wright's afternoon show on Radio 1. "He used to have loads of characters and one of them was Sid the Manager. He'd answer the phone and his only line was, 'ALRIGHT, BOY!' The band took that totally out of context. I don't think they understood my sense of humor."

A dark shadow hung over the session. Criticism begets criticism and, suddenly, the producer's credibility was an issue. "I thought, *What does this guy know about reggae music?*" concedes Aitch. "He was coming from a completely different background. But when I saw the direction it was heading, I thought, *Yeah, it's for the pop scene. He knows what he's doing*. We provided the reggae and he was mixing in a poppy commercial vibe to reach the people. I thought, *Let him continue*." Four decades on and Roger Lomas has little encouraging to draw from his time with the Selecter. "I have to be honest; they were never a good band to work with. They were an argumentative bunch of bloody people, to say the least. I have nothing positive to say about it. Everything was a bloody issue. I thought they were a great band but they were hard work. I could do a gig with them and it would go down a storm. The crowd would be going nuts for more. I'd walk backstage, and they'd all be bloody arguing. It was like, 'You did this,' and, 'You did that.' I'd be like, 'Hang on a minute. If you're leaping all over the place and the crowd is going nuts, who cares if somebody played a bum note?' It just made for a bad atmosphere."

The six members of the Selecter other than Neol were mixed race or Black. In the aftermath of the Second World War and the subsequent rebuilding of the country, the Selecter belonged to the first generation of the Black diaspora in the United Kingdom. Bass player Charley Anderson came from Montego Bay and grew up to the thunderous sounds of ska. Also born in Jamaica, keyboard virtuoso Desmond Brown had known Anderson since he was fifteen. Asked how the Selecter formed, Brown told *NME*, "Music, school days, friendship, fighting in the same gang and sharing the same sort of experience." In 1962, at age eight, drummer Charles "Aitch" Bembridge flew BOAC from Jamaica to start life in Gloucester. At age thirteen, vocalist Arthur "Gaps" Hendrickson left St. Kitts and boarded a boat bound for Southampton Docks. "I was so excited because I was going to join my parents, who I hadn't seen for almost ten years. We arrived in England and my eyes filled with tears because everybody disappeared, and my brother and I just sat there waiting. Eventually a policeman came and took us to the station. He gave us a shilling and I bought a Kit Kat. About seven o'clock in the evening a man came to the door and said, 'Yeah, they're my boys.' It was my father."

Like many Black kids in the seventies, guitarist David "Compton" Amanor started wearing red, gold and green tams. "You're not sure what you're doing, it's being pushed on you," he says. Raised in Ghana by a Black mother and a white father, Compton came to England when he was nine. "Rasta encircled itself with the myth of roots, which in the end takes your identity away and gives you more hang-ups. You'd talk to kids and say, 'Where are you from?' and they'd say, 'Africa'—but they were born here."

Understandably, the mix of differing cultural backgrounds influenced the Selecter's reading of unfamiliar social situations. As they found their feet in the confines of the recording studio, tension mounted between band and producer. The next song scheduled was the appropriately named "Too Much Pressure." It was written as a snapshot of daily life, and Neol says, "I'd gone home for lunch and my wife and I had a terrible row. We were struggling for money and I was really angry and frustrated." Fuming, Neol returned to work. While seated at his desk, a young woman asked what was wrong. "It's just . . . just . . . just too much fucking pressure," he blurted out. "Hang on . . . that's a good phrase." Hastily gathering a piece of company notepaper, Neol scribbled down the four-word phrase, "It's too much pressure," and on a stave, a six-note melody. Developing the idea, Neol compiled a list, alternating frustrations and hang-ups between the catchphrase "too much pressure." Within fifteen minutes, he had a completed song. "As far back as I can remember I've always been angry," says Neol, whose mother died when he was nine. "I've always been aware of the injustices of the world and wanted to say something about it. I'm from that generation that saw the execution of the Viet Cong prisoner who was shot in the head live in front of a television camera, and South African police using wire whips on Black people."

Interpreted by the Selecter, "Too Much Pressure" railed against the ills of modern society and spoke of police harassment and youth unemployment. Yet, when Neol initially presented the song to the group, it met with resistance. "We looked at various songs to go forward with," explains Aitch. "One of mine was called 'Under Pressure.' It went, *This man under pressure, pressure got to stop, pressure got to stop, pressure got to stop till you can't even drop.* We used to play it in Hard Top 22. We played them all and voted." Losing out, Compton claims he was totally against it. "But we said, 'We can't have two songs called 'Pressure,'" and went for Neol's." The song needed an introduction, and Compton distinctly remembers saying, "How about this?" and mimicking a heavy metal guitar riff over the chords A G A D. To his amazement, Neol shrieked, "That's it!" Reminded of the incident, Aitch rejects Compton's claim. "I took the intro from 'Beat Down Babylon' by Junior Byles. I said, 'Let's take that and rock it up.'"

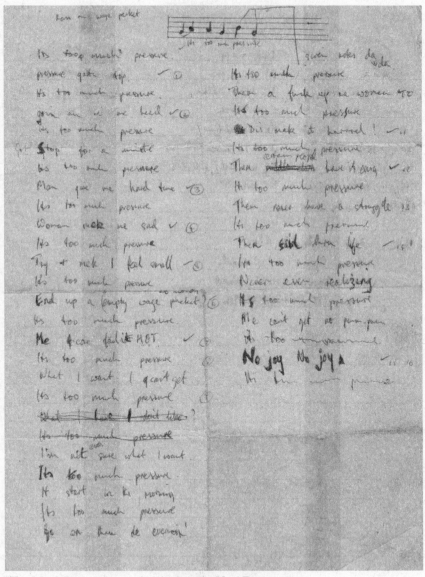

"Too Much Pressure" lyrics, handwritten by Neol Davies.

Having recorded the backing track of "Too Much Pressure," there were further arguments when Gaps refused to sing what he regarded as profane lyrics. "The original line was *Dem a fuck up my woman*, but Gaps wouldn't sing the word 'fuck,'" says Neol with righteous indignation. "He substituted it with 'fumble.' It completely changed the line."

The Selecter's debut 45 showed two sides of a great band. After it was released on September 28, HMV Oxford Street reported an unprecedented demand for it. Overwhelmed and understocked, the store's staff resorted to raiding the nearby Chrysalis headquarters for additional copies. Reviewed on BBC Radio 1 *Roundtable*, "On My Radio" received a rapturous endorsement from a twenty-one-year-old Kate Bush as the record began a slow climb up the charts. Six weeks later, it breached the top ten. "The record was a Trojan horse in a way," says a bemused Juliet de Vie. "Radio 1 heard the title but not the payoff line: *It's just the same old show*. It wasn't a celebration of radio. But it was very jaunty and up." Reaching a similar verdict, Jon Savage described "On My Radio" as "catchy, infectious, timely ska," informing *Melody Maker* readers that the song was "tricksier" than either the Specials or Madness. "If they now do a good *Top of the Pops* performance," he predicted, "the next dance craze, if not the world, is theirs."

Duly booked by the BBC's long-standing weekly chart program, the Selecter filled the screen in a hue of blue, brown, Black and white, and conquered the studio audience with three minutes of perpetual movement and irresistible rhythm. When they were whisked off to Holland for another television appearance, Gaps was thrilled to hear they were flying from Luton. As a young teenager raised in the Bedfordshire town, he used to make regular trips to Coventry to enjoy its superior nightlife. After seeing Desmond Brown and Lynval Golding perform in a band called Cool Interrogators, Gaps went back to Luton and considered his future. "I had a serious talk with myself: *Is this what you want to do for the rest of your life: go to bed, get up, go to work?* So I said to my friends, 'I'm moving to Coventry. I'll see you guys around.' They said, 'We'll see you in about six weeks when your money runs out.' I said, 'The next time you see me I'll be on television.' One of them said, 'Yeah, on *Police 5*.' We went down on a Sunday evening and I went to the pub where I knew my friends would be. I walked in and the whole pub went quiet because they'd seen me on *Top of the Pops*."

Ad for "On My Radio," September 1979. Courtesy of Chrysalis Records/Jerry Dammers.

On October 10, with a hit single under their belt, the Selecter made the decision to continue their relationship with 2 Tone. This was by no means a given; A&R man Tarquin Gotch had attempted to woo the Selecter to Arista. Arriving unannounced outside Charley Anderson's two-up-two-down in Hillfields, Gotch parked his Rolls-Royce and flashed a wad of banknotes. "Us, in our infinite wisdom, said, 'No, no, no. We're staying with 2 Tone,'" chuckles Pauline. They signed directly to Chrysalis for £20,000, and Compton believes they could have got £100,000. "We traded that for the right to bring in other bands," he says ruefully. "I cried the day we signed to Chrysalis. I thought we were selling out."

CHAPTER 10
RUDE BOYS

FASHION. THE SPECIALS ALBUM

2 Tone conjures images of a culturally unified and cohesive look—clothing, visuals, iconography—wrapped up in an identifiable sound. It has come to represent a movement opposed to racial and gender discrimination; a force rallying against a government seemingly waging war against the working class and the disenfranchised. Songs addressed issues that affected young people directly and on a day-to-day basis: street violence, sexual violence, teenage pregnancy, unemployment, the threat of nuclear war. 2 Tone was a modern form of protest music, echoing sixties pioneers such as Bob Dylan and Joan Baez, and delivered to audiences a belief in collaborative social and political unity.

Nevertheless, such clarity of purpose is disingenuous and overlooks the formative, undefined infant years of 2 Tone. In the early days, Rick Rogers says, Jerry Dammers was not always "as coherent about what drove him" as he became later. "My interpretation of Jerry's vision was building a movement around the label that would be guided by the ideology of equality and fairness." Jerry envisioned a British equivalent to Motown and saw 2 Tone having an identifiable sound that would change and develop gradually over time. It would act as a launching pad for groups to forge independent careers and, at its core, be an antiracist movement for a generation to unite around.

"It's all very idealistic at the moment," Jerry told *Sounds* in April 1979. "If we could start a cult of our own, I dunno, call 'em rude boys, if you like." The casual suggestion betrayed years of deep thought and fancy. The idea was explosive. This was a message calling out to disparate tribes, sending a smoke signal to the lost souls of punk, the lingering clan of Teddy Boys and the burgeoning revival of mods. The new alternative was 2 Tone. 1979: the year of the rude boy.

The lineage of the rude boy dates back to midsixties Jamaica and the musical transition from ska to rocksteady. Following the country's independence in 1962, a short-lived wave of euphoria gave way to rising unemployment and growing turbulence, in particular on the streets of the capital. The majority of Kingstonians were not violent or antiauthority, but in the lead-up to the 1968 election, a slew of artists released records addressing a rise in social unrest and in turn gave rude boys a disproportionately high profile. Typically male, young, urban and unemployed, rude boys engaged in criminal activity armed with blades and firearms. They became the focus of many protest songs; Prince Buster cast himself as "Judge Dread" and sentenced rude boys *Adolphus James, Emmanuel Zechariah Zechipaul and George Grab-and-flee* to 400 years' imprisonment. In response, Desmond Dekker's "007" accepted that *dem a loot, dem a shoot, dem a wail* but urged that *them must get bail*. From a cell, Honey Boy Martin presented a meeting of the *rougher than rough* rude boys and cautioned: *Don't be a fool, play it cool.*

The conflict between violence and lawfulness was at the heart of rude boy lyricism. But such was the success of the genre that it was debatable whether the catalog of songs acted as a deterrent against criminal activity or celebrated the rude boy as a revolutionary hero. In August 1979, Neville Staple addressed the question in an interview with *NME*, where he regarded himself as a "rude boy" because he was "rude," "cool" and "hard." Drawing attention to his sense of dress style ("slick") and his music taste ("ska, bluebeat and some up-to-date reggae"), Neville said that he did not class a rowdy skinhead as a rude boy. "If he goes around kicking people at gigs, then he's no rudie. A rude boy is a rebel that don't go around causing unnecessary trouble. He enjoys himself and dresses nice." Interviewed by the BBC a few months later, Neville refined his definition of rude boy to "a rugged ruffian . . . it's like a young boy over here, now, in England, getting into trouble, breaking into houses, vandalizing places, setting places on fire. They get to about sixteen and they're doing things heavier than that." Interceding, Lynval Golding added that the group's message to rude boys was to keep out of trouble. "It's not worth it. Listen to Prince Buster sentencing the hooligans to 400 years in prison. It's not about glorifying being a rude boy. It's about why you shouldn't be a rude boy."

Visual identity had long concerned Jerry Dammers. The Specials, and by default 2 Tone, needed a strong image to attract the audience they desired. Heeding the advice of Bernie Rhodes "to get a scene together," Jerry says that the best pop music reflects the audience. Where youth culture divided into cults and tribes—mods following the Jam, skinheads Sham 69, and punks the paucity of likeminded groups—Jerry says, "It just felt like every band had to have a tribe of followers." Adding, "Bernie [Rhodes] once said to me, 'Don't ever think that the fans dress like you. You have to dress like the fans.'"

Casting aside flares and loud checkers, leather jackets and pointed haircuts, the Specials unified their image, merging a triumvirate of sixties mod, skinhead and rude boy clothing. In came mohair and tonic suits, white button-down shirts and slim pencil ties. Pants cut short above the ankle, white socks and loafers, brogues and Dr. Martens, a trilby or porkpie hat and wraparound shades. Suddenly, a disparate group of old-wave musicians looked cool. "It was really important that we were identified with punk and the new wave," says Jerry, "but I had to persuade some of them to dress differently." Chief among them, Lynval Golding. Expressing horror at the notion of buying old suits from charity shops, he cried out in alarm, "Me not wear dead man's clothes!" "I'd worn those suits before and moved on," explains Lynval, who slowly accepted the need to conform. "We took a step backwards to what I was wearing when I was seventeen, eighteen."

Similarly reluctant to give up his leather jacket, zip trousers and Teddy Boy shoes, Roddy Byers reluctantly slipped into a secondhand tonic suit, matched with black Dr. Martens, a black leather porkpie hat, and a studded belt and wristband. "On the Clash tour, Paul Simonon wore a tonic suit and Fred Perry and looked as cool as fuck. Next thing I know we're all wearing it. I said, 'If I've got to wear this gear I'm going to do it in my own way.'"

The Specials's change in style neatly fit a nascent mod revival spearheaded in no small part by the release of the Jam's third long player, *All Mod Cons*. The outer sleeve showed Paul Weller in black monkey boots and light-blue Sta-Prest riding high above the ankle. On the inner sleeve, a photograph of sixties-influenced ephemera included a vinyl copy of *Sounds Like Ska*, a high-fidelity compilation of rocksteady and reggae favorites. Six months later, the mod revival exploded when a film of the Who's rock opera received a theatrical release. Set in 1964, *Quadrophenia* was awash with scooters, parkas and amphetamines. Such was its impact, swaths of British youth refreshed their wardrobes and embraced an antiquated mod sensibility. "We were more following fashion than creating it," Jerry told *Record Mirror*. "It was dead obvious that after punk that mods and skinheads were coming back."

But significantly, where the Specials may have represented a continuation of the mod and skinhead tradition, they would be separate from the burgeoning scene. "We're not specifically a mod band or a skinhead band," explained Terry. "It's more a mixture of both. If we played the same music and looked like hippies, we wouldn't even get noticed. Bernie Rhodes was right, sometimes you have to hit a nail on the head really hard with a hammer to drive a message across for people to be made fully aware of what you're trying to say. You've got to cover every aspect: how you look, what you say, your haircut. Then people tend to buy into it a bit easier."[46]

On September 6, the Specials appeared on the front cover of *Smash*

Hits looking moody and sullen, attired in dark suits with fixed glares. In the Chrysalis publicity department, Chris Poole was delighted. "Getting a mixed-race group on the cover was almost unprecedented. It was before the album had been released and the media were in frenzy about them." There were further interviews in the *Guardian* and the *Times*. "We even did the *Sun*," says Poole. "Jerry was dragged kicking and screaming into that one. There was fantastic coverage. It happened intuitively and organically, as much driven by the band and the management as the label." Working alongside Poole, Julia Marcus says, "Chris was really cool and had an innate understanding of the right things for the band to be doing. I think Chrysalis was really patient and respectful of what the Specials wanted to do. Rick had a really good relationship with the label. But in terms of the heart and soul of 2 Tone, Chrysalis didn't meddle or mess with it. The press loved 2 Tone. It allowed the bands to choose who they wanted to engage with. Jerry was a revered character and there was a lot of good feeling toward the label. People wanted to write about it."

Elvis Costello had spent much of the summer traveling up and down the country to see the Specials perform, sustained by half a bottle of gin and a pocketful of little blue pills. Impressed by such faith and commitment, the Specials invited Costello to produce their debut album. "We chose him," says Jerry, "because he said that he'd like a go at producing us. He was the only man for the job." For his part, Costello says, "I thought it was my job to learn everything I could about the band before some more technically capable producer fucked it all up and took the fun and danger out of it."[47]

Session time was duly booked at Ramport in Battersea, a studio owned by the Who and used by the Clash during the early stages of *London Calling*. According to John Bradbury, the Specials intended to record "Too Much Too Young" "before we realized that 'Gangsters' was doing so well, so we put back the new single."

Consumed by a cavernous live room, Ramport proved to be ill-suited to the Specials's gritty sound. In search of a less sterile environment, the group moved to TW Studios. Located on Fulham Palace

Road, the twenty-four-track facility shared an air vent with an up-stairs Laundromat. As wafting odors of washing powder and antiseptic conditioner engulfed the claustrophobic basement, the Specials recorded the aptly titled "Too Hot."

"The first few days felt a little overwhelming," said Terry Hall. "Major label . . . album . . . London. I was very young and it became a real eye-opener . . . As things settled down, it proved to be a great experience." At one point, Costello leaned back on his swivel chair only for it to promptly give way and leave the producer in a heap on the floor. "Definitely an icebreaker!" Terry tweeted in 2020 during Tim Burgess's online listening party to celebrate the album's recording.

Elvis Costello (center) and Neville Staple recording the first Specials album, TW Studios, London, September 1979.

Convinced he knew how the Specials should sound, Costello wrote in his memoir, *Unfaithful Music*, that "Jerry's dogged pursuit of his ideals and the improbable chemistry of the lineup did the rest." John Bradbury looked on admiringly. "There's no two ways about it," he commented midsession, "the guy *can* produce; no matter what doubts anyone else may have about his lack of experience in the field, he lets us all have a hand in the production. Jerry, in particular, has worked a lot with him on the backing tracks. There are a lot of new arrangements, and there will definitely be stuff not used in the set at present, and one, maybe two completely new numbers. One thing is for sure, though: this album is going to prove that no way are we just a live band."[48]

Regarding him as "just a normal, easy-to-get-along-with sort of bloke," Roddy was somewhat taken aback to discover that Costello wanted him sacked. "He couldn't really hear my rock 'n' roll punk guitar fitting in," recounts Roddy. "He took Jerry aside and said, 'Lose the punk . . . he's trouble.'" Unbeknown to Roddy, Costello's concerns extended deeper, forewarning Jerry that Roddy's limited guitar ability and attitude would eventually "wreck the band." Speaking in 1980, Roddy suggested that Costello had not understood the Specials's ambition. "I think he still thought that it was like one section of reggae, then the next section's a heavy section, then another section comes along. But I'm not knocking him at all. He got a great drum sound, and he was a lot better than having some hotshot producer who wouldn't even let us into the mixing sessions."[49]

Less generous in his appraisal of the producer, Horace Panter describes Costello's input as minimal. "He was just basically around in the studio saying, 'Okay, we'll do this one now,' making sure everybody was in the right place at the right time to play the right song. The production was as much to do with Dave Jordan." An experienced engineer respected for his live work with the Rolling Stones, Horace continues, "Dave did the legwork while Elvis would be getting Terry to record a vocal in a toilet or somewhere, or breaking bottles for the background noises in 'Concrete Jungle.'"[50] Venting his frustration because Roddy wanted to sing "Concrete Jungle," Terry says snidely, "He was always insistent on 'My song, my voice,' as in, 'My football, my game.'" Matters came to a head when Chrysalis heard the recording and suggested it as a new single. But, alleges Roddy, "because he hadn't sung on it, Terry vetoed it."

Housed by Chrysalis in a rented apartment two miles from the studio, the Specials enjoyed partying into the night and waking late. They were a self-confessed drinking band, and Roddy recalls a couple of over-the-top parties where the toilet was blocked and a group of skinheads arrived. "Elvis barricaded himself in one of the bedrooms," he says laughing. Walking down the King's Road, Julia Marcus (before working at Chrysalis) remembers "these boys shouting out of a top-floor window for us to go upstairs to their flat. We went up and it was tiny. They were rolling spliffs and being really sweet and chatty. They had these thick Coventry accents and I remember thinking they were a little bit parochial. They said they were in a band and they'd been signed by a label and they were staying in this fancy flat. I was like, 'Whatever.' The penny dropped two months later when I started working at Chrysalis and saw them in Brighton on the 2 Tone Tour. I thought, *I remember them!*"

Terry described it as a "typical sort of late-night drinking album." Booze was encouraged by the producer and lent the sessions a distinct party atmosphere. "Everyone was pissed," recalled Jerry. "We spent most of the time in the pub over the road and then we used to work during closing time, which was between four and six in the afternoon."[51] To record "Nite Klub," Costello ordered a crate of beer and crammed the band, their friends and a girl "wearing a skin-tight red rubber S&M suit" into a small cubicle between two doors, switched off the lights and recorded the resulting sounds. "It was raucous and heavily staged," tweeted Terry, "until someone dropped their trousers. It captured what the band was all about." On hand to add backing vocals to the unruly melee was Pretenders lead singer Chrissie Hynde. When she doubled up on *girls are slags* and provided heavy breathing on "Stupid Marriage," Costello said, the band were "cheering like kids," adding, "We'd been at the vodka gimlets."[52] Much to Roddy's amusement, he says, "Chrissie tried to get off with Terry. She gave me her phone number as well, but I never called."

Forging ahead, Costello made use of the studio's concrete floor and placed a sheet of metal on the step of the door leading to the control room. He then proceeded to whack it with a broom handle to augment the snare drum. In another fit of sonic quirkiness, Costello fed the drum kit through a little Fender amp in the bathroom, cranking up the distortion and then kicking it hard with a Dr. Martens boot to create an explosion. When Neville occupied the facilities, a live microphone captured him remonstrating, "You can't come in," only to later discover the phrase had been recorded for posterity and tagged on to the introduction of "You're Wondering Now." Then Neville bought a .45 pistol at a replica gun shop on Fulham Palace Road, loaded it with blanks and opened fire in the studio. "The noise was deafening," cackled Costello. "Our ears were ringing all day."

The spirit of the record was punk and shambolic, says Horace, who in his excitement played a wrong note on "It's Up to You." "I played a C as opposed to an A when the chorus comes back in after the quiet bit," he admits. The recording would earn John Bradbury the nickname Prince Rimshot. "Brad does a reggae rim shot [a drum stroke in which the stick strikes the rim and the head of the drum simultaneously] but he's also doing a rocker's beat," marveled Lynval Golding. "The way he combined it together in one song was incredible." Another revelation was Terry's cool, detached vocal delivery on tracks like "Doesn't Make It Alright" and the dub section of "Too Much Too Young." "Terry was able to sing quietly for the first time," says Jerry. "It brought out a sad and plaintive side to the songs. It was always meant to be there but hadn't really revealed itself in the live shows up until then."

The sparse production of the album may have surprised many who had experienced the visceral attack of the live Specials sound, but, says Jerry, "Elvis caught our feelings just right. I always wanted the Specials to be a classic British band. I couldn't see the point in doing it unless you try to do something really good that would give the Clash and the Jam a run for their money. If you go in the studio, you have to think, *Would David Bowie have been satisfied with this?* You've got to set your goals high otherwise there's no point. I remember saying that to Roddy. He thought I was crazy. He was going, 'We could never do anything like that!'"

Recorded in two and half weeks, the fourteen songs on the Specials's eponymously titled debut album reflected the landscape of contemporary Britain. They spoke of social concerns, youth culture and the everyday realities of street violence and social injustice. Many of the lyrics, written by Jerry as a teenager, recounted drunken episodes and female rejection. The personal attack of "Little Bitch" conjured the uncomfortable misogyny of many sixties songwriters. It was the "Stupid Girl," "Under My Thumb" and "Bitch" of the Rolling Stones, or John Lennon's sermonizing "Run for Your Life." However, as Elvis Costello noted, the Specials sang about things that were "obvious but which were direct," or in this case juvenile and naive.

One day, photographer Chalkie Davies received a phone call from Elvis Costello: "You should meet Jerry Dammers," he said. "Go to *Top of the Pops* on Wednesday." Acting on the tip-off, Davies says, he went to the BBC studios to observe the Specials "and saw seven very different and wonderful people; each one of them was like their own band. I really liked them." Traveling to Coventry a week later, Davies and his Canadian partner Carol Starr shot the cover for the Specials's debut album. "Jerry had all the locations figured out," recalls Davies. "He said, 'I've got two records to show you, but I've forgotten one of them.' He showed me *My Generation* by the Who and then later he told me, 'Oh, I remember the other one now, it was *Help!* [the Beatles].'" Standing on the first floor of an abandoned building at the Canal Basin near to the city ring road, Davies photographed the seven musicians in a triangular formation—"Just look at me," he said—as Starr simultaneously took a Polaroid from below—"And now from the side [for the back of the album]—please don't move." Describing his unusual collaboration with Starr, Davies says, "We had two cable releases to the same camera so we could both take pictures. It was like having two sets of eyes." Shooting just one black-and-white roll of film, Davies says one frame featured Jerry holding a suitcase. "I asked him why he'd brought it, and he told me, 'I want to get the fuck out of Coventry.'"

The Specials: (L–R) Horace Panter, Terry Hall, Neville Staple, Jerry Dammers, Roddy Byers, Lynval Golding, John Bradbury. Album shoot, Canal Basin, Coventry, 1979.

* * *

Monochrome, homemade and with a graphic street feel, the cover art for *The Specials* was as much a reaction against the slick album covers that defined much of the seventies as a tribute to Jamaican reggae artwork. Having spent many hours experimenting with photographs of the group—painting out the background in white and overlaying single images—Jerry asked Davies to cut out the front-cover image "badly." Obliging, Starr expurgated the individual members of the group using a pair of plastic paper scissors and created two groups of four and three on a white background "to look cheesy."

To create the band logo, Starr used Letraset and, as per Jerry's instruction, made the lettering "bold, heavy and nondescript." Measuring exactly two inches, the height of the lettering ensured the sleeve would be clearly visible in a record shop rack. After affixing a roll of black-and-white checkered tape to stretch alongside the band name, the final request was the inclusion of seven deliberate mistakes. They included "roughing up" the typography to include smudges and uneven lines, song titles running "downhill" and a nick clipped into the base letter "c" of "Specials." "That was for Chalkie and Carol," says Davies. "We had become Davies & Starr but Jerry thought that was impersonal, so I suggested taking a little bit out of the band lettering."

On the back cover, the only mention of Chrysalis ran in small print at the foot of the sleeve, with its traditional butterfly trademark substituted for the 2 Tone logo. Preempting disapproval, Davies delivered the artwork on a Friday, at the close of day. "I didn't want anybody to know what we were doing. Chris Wright phoned me and said, 'If you want this record to come out, you'll put that butterfly back on the sleeve.' I phoned Roy Eldridge and said, 'Who the fuck is Chris Wright? He's got some fucking nerve—this is a 2 Tone release.'"

When it was issued on October 19, 1979, Tony Stewart wrote in *New Musical Express*, "You just can't shake the tunes out of your head, can't stop beating your feet to the heat as the Specials's unique excitement surges through the speakers. One irresistible song follows another." Further describing it as "musically fathomless" and predicting it would "probably establish the Specials as true hopes for the '80s," Stewart concluded that the record was "essential for anybody who wants to know what's going on in rock 'n' roll today." Concise and to the point, Don Waller of the *New York Rocker* surmised, "This album will make your brain dance."

Less enamored, Dave McCullough attempted to offer a "piece of constructive reflection" for readers of *Sounds*. "The Specials seem to have lost the attacking, forward-looking, forward-moving, forward-thinking, almost militant momentum that was witnessed and promised from the beginning." Waxing lyrical under the heading "Rudies in a Rut," McCullough accused the Specials of appearing "content to cruise comfortably along the Costello-groomed, Chrysalis-waged axis as dahlings [sic] of the big-city rock elite, living up to their ideas of roots credibility and, on the commercial side, as pop stars." And on he moaned: "There is little edge, little scope and little raw nerve, little that takes you by surprise or thwarts the unspectacular and unending Costellofied rattle of conveyor-belt white reggae." Clearly impressed by his own quick-fire typewriter soundbites, McCullough fell prey to his own linguistic hubris at the "disgust at the way this album hints (just hints mind you) at the sort of jolly-niggers-in-the-hands-of-the-record-company-men attitude that I thought perished in the fifties and sixties."

The shocking vocabulary did McCullough no credit. Neither did the self-importance of journalist Vivien Goldman, who decided the "album's drawbacks are exposed all the more vividly in the light of its missed potential. After all," she informed *Melody Maker* readers, "the Specials have supposedly saved us from overdosing on Rasta clichés." Accusing Elvis Costello of being incapable of producing either a pop or reggae rhythm, Goldman argued, "The forward momentum of bass, guitar and drums (think of Sly & Robbie, think of Clinton, think of Chic) should have been the bottom line of this record." After being described as having a "reedy" and "whining" voice, Terry Hall responded onstage at Brighton Top Rank by dismissing Goldman as a "stupid cow."

Ignoring the bovine music press, fans clamored to buy the new record. Listeners were not disappointed: the album was a stunning portrait of a newly invented hybrid genre, Britsh ska. It was exciting, viscerally raw and packed with musical nuggets. Hard-edged social commentary crossed with a risible interplay. Original songs seamlessly mixed with radically updated interpretations of Jamaican classics, punk crossed with ska and reggae, rock with elements of funk and disco. Seemingly out of nowhere, a new music existed and there was no shortage of upward trajectory. In November, the Specials each received a silver disc for 60,000 sales, and a month later saw the figure double. Spending forty-five continuous weeks on the UK album chart, the record topped one million sales worldwide.

CHAPTER II

BATTLE OF THE GAP

2 TONE TOUR

I f punk had carried an air of despondency and a willfulness to reject a generation's future, 2 Tone encouraged audiences to be positive, engage with music as an active tool of change, and above all to enjoy themselves and have fun. Never was this more evident than on the inaugural 2 Tone Tour in October 1979. The ambition was simple: a Motown-style revue offering three chart bands; three hours of music and a spectacle of skanking and dancing in unseated dance halls over forty back-to-back dates, all for the mouth-watering cost of £2.50 at the door.

To promote the event, the participating groups—the Specials, the Selecter and Madness—agreed to rendezvous for a photo opportunity at the Blue Boar service station on the M1. Aligning schedules proved as difficult as planning a military invasion and, true to the analogy of war, when the twenty-one musicians assembled, all hell broke loose. "The famous Battle of the Gap," groans John Hasler, excusing what happened next with the caveat, "Everyone was just in a great mood: drinking and just high being on the road and being young and full of buzz." Mounting a plastic table, Lee Thompson started a food fight. It was instant mayhem. Sausage rolls and bacon butties filled the air as unsuspecting customers ran for cover and delivered a flurry of complaints to put-upon staff. "Suddenly all these police vans screech up and Neville and Lynval were slammed up against the windscreen," recalls Chris Foreman. Woody was shocked by the overt show of racism: "I mean, instantly like, 'Why are you picking on me? I've done nothing!' 'Come on here, Sambo.' A lot of the band members just weren't having it, so it kicked off."[53] Running in different directions, chased by the police, John Hasler remembers Neville having his collar felt. "Then they got Lee round the back by the kitchens and there was some old-fashioned police brutality. I was only twenty-one and trying to be the responsible manager. Probably because they were motorway police and didn't have cells to put us in, they ended up letting us go."

And so the tone was set. On October 16, the three bands met for rehearsals at the Camden Roundhouse, replete with its new cutting-edge sound system. Equipped on departure day with his touring luggage—a single carrier bag—bass player Mark Bedford asked singer Suggs, "Where's your gear?" "In there, mate," replied Suggs, pulling out a wad of £20 notes. "That's all you need to go on tour!"[54]

When the fifty-five-seat Trathens coach arrived, there was much coaxing required to persuade the musicians, who had happily wiled away the hours propping up the bar, to board the transport. "The atmosphere was buoyant, full of optimism," observed Allan Jones, covering the momentous occasion on behalf of *Melody Maker*. "Madness were quaffing light and bitters, being noisy, looking like a gang of roughneck schoolkids waiting to be taken for a day at the seaside." Weary from three days of alcohol consumption and wary of what was to come, Madness's thirty-three-year-old tour manager, John "Kellogs" Kalinowski, commented, "They make me feel so old. They just don't stop. Up till four in the morning boozing. They're on top of the fucking world."[55]

For most of the musicians, the 2 Tone Tour would be their first experience of life on the road: three bands doing it on their own terms and challenging how the music business worked. "We'd created a label in a little provincial city and gained national success," says Neol Davies, using "we" in the broadest sense. "We felt empowered." As the plan started coming together, Rick Rogers says, it was the beginning of the movement. "There was nothing more natural than all three bands touring together. It was continuing the idea of celebration and doing something that was worthwhile: here we are, off on the road, doing it, and going out on this amazing package tour."

2 Tone Tour poster, October 1979. Courtesy of Chrysalis Records/Jerry Dammers.

Transport organized. Hotels booked. Instruments rented. Flight cases secured. Juliet de Vie says organizing the tour was insane. "Trigger was transitioning from PR publicity into a management company. The instruments were a nightmare. These were bands with Hammond organs and Leslie speakers. It wasn't like a keyboard you could throw in the back of the van. These were fucking great heavy bits of kit. Desmond Brown! God help you if he couldn't have his own Hammond. It was the detail." On the eve of the first date, Juliet and her sister Sarah—roped in to help out—photocopied, assembled and stapled stacks of tour itineraries as arrangements changed by the hour into the morning light. "So as we were launching off up the motorway I was completely exhausted," sighs Juliet, "and then seeing everybody not giving a shit and tearing off the bottoms of the paper to make roaches, I was like, 'Great. Thanks. Cheers.'"

To mark their territory, a cardboard 2 Tone man was positioned behind the backseat facing out of the window. "It was literally one of those take-the-OAPs-to-the-seaside coaches, with a driver in a shirt and jacket," says Mark Bedford.[56] In place of the elderly, the youthful travelers made an altogether different atmosphere. "Like being on a school trip without the teachers," says Horace Panter. Seating was arranged according to drug of preference, with Suggs recalling drinkers at the front, amphetamine users in the middle and, through the clouds, Jamaican trombonist Rico Rodriguez smoking on the backseat. "The chatty, shouting, sticking-your-arse-out-of-the-window gang, i.e., Madness, were in every section. It was just a blur of arms and legs and hats flying in the air." Pauline Black, in her midtwenties at the time, says Madness were "just out of school. We would probably have been their teachers. With age, I've mellowed from what I thought about them then."

The only woman among forty testosterone-fueled men (Juliet would on occasion work at the London office), Pauline had never seen the male animal in such close proximity. "I was like, 'Woah! What are these people doing?' That was quite an adjustment." Outwardly confident, Pauline held her own. "It was generally accepted that you didn't get in an argument with me because you were likely not to come off best. I was good with words. Neville Staple used to say, 'Oh God, here comes Pauline, she's swallowed a dictionary again.' Pretty much people left me alone."

Flanked by his two friends, Trevor and Rex (the Specials's roadies), Neville says, "We were the Black boys off the street. I think we were a bit rough-cut for the rest of 'em: ganja-smoking boys. They weren't used to people like us: 'Bloodclaat . . .' We were too much in people's faces." Wise beyond her age at twenty-one, Juliet de Vie now says, "They'd all come from nowhere: shitty jobs, shitty bedsits, no money, trying to get things off the ground. There was an overwhelming sense of adventure. The whole 2 Tone ideal was about to be lived and borne out in these dance halls across the country. I had just a flash of that moment before I went back to being tired and worried."

As the coach neared the south coast, Chalkie Davies requested an impromptu photo shoot at the seaside town of Hove. "I said, 'Everybody off the bus. School photograph.'" With everyone scattered across the pebbled beach, Davies had time to snap one group shot before somebody spotted Rick Rogers in the distance holding the tour per diems. The next shot, Davies says, was of everybody chasing Rogers to get their daily allowance. Davies was thrilled to have at least captured one image of the entire entourage and a moment of 2 Tone history, but Jerry Dammers later teased the photographer when he noticed that both Commie and Gaps from the Selecter and Chas Smash from Madness had skillfully avoided the lens.

When the groups arrived in Brighton for the first date, an army of 2 Tone supporters welcomed them. Taking advantage of a work jolly organized by Chrysalis, Julia Marcus negotiated her way to the front of the Top Rank and says that the moment the lights went down the audience went insane. "It was a hotbed of sweating, writhing, jumping bodies just having an amazing time. You knew it was something really special."

Introducing a set of songs mostly unknown to the audience, the

Selecter opened proceedings by launching into an instrumental version of the Upsetters's "A Live Injection." Building up to "On My Radio" and "Too Much Pressure," the group showcased a heavy reggae version of the James Bond theme, dramatically intensified by Gaps acting out the agent licensed to kill dressed in a gabardine mac and armed with a fake air pistol. "There's never been a British band like them," raved Paul Rambali in the *New Musical Express*. "Not that they reject all that has gone before or anything, it's just that no one's ever arrived at their combination." Praising their "subtlety, vigor and strong identity," Rambali noted the Selecter's "remarkable feat of slipping between rock, reggae and funk rhythms on pop soul songs." Naturally delighted, Neol Davies says, "We were an unstoppable force onstage. We were explosive. Nobody had seen a Black band play like that before. It was completely different. If you ever saw us play live, you'd never forget it as long as you lived. It just built and built and built."

Night after night, a heaving mass of fans bounced up and down in the auditorium, firing up the bands onstage. Balconies buckled under the weight of devotees dancing and pounding their booted feet. "We had quite a few people jumping off the balconies," recalls Pauline Black. "In Bristol, I looked up and saw this guy sailing over the barrier twenty-five feet down into the crowd below."

"They were going fucking nuts," says Juliet de Vie, grinning with delight. "There was an incredible atmosphere. People just excited by what was happening, excited by the music, and excited to be a part of this thing. Being able to dance well was as important as being up there. You were contributing. The shows were like a steam train: the crowd would become this one mass of energy. You couldn't stop it."

Each morning, late risers found themselves chivied along and ushered onto the coach destined for the next town or city. Occasionally the driver would get lost, prompting rounds of the show tune "What's It All About, Alfie?" Whenever an opportunity arose to pull into a service station, Rick Rogers would frantically push coins into pay phones to book additional dates or upgrade to larger venues. "It was snowballing before our eyes," says Suggs. "It was becoming this phenomenon."

Second on the bill, Madness's show was all adrenaline and vigor and raising energy levels as they steamrolled from "Tarzan's Nuts" and "The Prince" to a rousing encore of "Shop Around." Tour manager Frank Murray had never seen the like. "I remember speaking to Dave Robinson at Stiff. I said, 'Tell me about Madness.' He said, 'Okay. There's six guys and a dancer.' I said, 'A what?' He said, 'A dancer.' I said, 'What do you mean a fucking dancer?' He says, 'You'll see . . . and there's two roadies that dance too, called Chalky and Toks.'"

Since jumping onstage at the Music Machine earlier in the year, Chas Smash had raised the spirits of Madness audiences through sheer exuberance and indefatigable onstage energy. Asked by Lee to introduce the band, Chas would take the microphone and reel off his signature oration. "Hey you, don't watch that, watch this. This is the heavy, heavy monster sound. The nuttiest sound around. So if you've come in off the street, and you're beginning to feel the heat, well listen Buster, you better start to move your feet to the rockinest rocksteady beat of Madness! 'One Step Beyond.'" Under a tide of uncontrollable enthusiasm, the next forty minutes would produce scenes of mania. Woody recalled fighting his way backstage at the Mayfair Suite, Newcastle: "It was just like the Beatles, wasn't it? Did you see them all crushed at the front of the stage—mostly girls screaming and climbing up the sides, grabbing anything they could get hold of as souvenirs?"[57]

Three weeks into the 2 Tone Tour and Suggs was having the time of his life. "Fuck me!" he hollers. "It was absolutely mental. We were all in it together. It was unbelievable. Literally, anything and everything could happen. Stage invasions. Stages collapsing. Every night was just chaos. There was just this raw sulfate-fueled energy flying around." One night, various members of Madness and the Specials dismantled Rick Rogers's hotel room, meticulously unscrewing all the fixtures and fittings. "Rick got back at the end of a long day," says John Hasler, shuddering at the memory, "and found everything stacked up in the corner. It was a great joke, but Rick wasn't a tough guy at all. He was a genuine, caring person and was literally in tears." Roddy Byers says Madness "took the piss a lot. They were more like kids having fun. They'd mess you about backstage: take your hat off you; take the mickey." When Neville loaded a starting pistol during "Gangsters," Chris Foreman says, "We had this rubber chicken and when he fired the gun, we threw it in the air. I had to hide. It was nuts!"

At the shows, Chas's younger brother Brendan sold a selection of ties, badges, posters and Madness's latest T-shirt creation: "Fuck Art, Let's Dance." Confronted by fans proudly displaying the offensive slogan, one hotel manager insisted it be covered over in gaffer tape. Underwritten by Chrysalis, the cost of the tour crept up to an estimated £53,000. "The T-shirts and ties kept us going," says Rick Rogers. "As soon as the doors opened there was a swarm of people who wanted to get this stuff. I had to jump across the table and start helping. It was insane." Regarding the low door price—rising from £2.50 to £3—Rogers says, "In 1979, you went on tour to sell records, rather than today where you put out a record to sell tickets. So ticket prices were just less than half of what it would cost you to buy an album, rather than five times more, which it's like now."

On November 2, as they prepared to play the University of Lancaster, the Specials learned that their album had entered the chart at number four. Receiving a congratulatory telegram from Elvis Costello, six of the band celebrated with champagne; the seventh, Jerry, "went into a sulk and threw his organ on the ground," says Horace without explanation. Taking to the stage, the Specials kicked into "Dawning of a New Era" and unleashed a whirlwind of energy. "[They] are one of the liveliest, most invigorating, and most innovative of new British bands around," gushed *NME* journalist Deanne Pearson, "molding, building, and finally producing a sound so fiercely addictive that the punters are drawn to it as if hypnotized. The Specials's music is the ultimate in dance music, when there is neither time nor opportunity to think of anything but movement. It is a drug without side effects."

Recalling the Specials's chaotic exuberance, Frank Murray says there was constant motion onstage offset by the solitary Terry Hall standing center stage. "He would walk out and just look so fucking tense. Then he did that first jump and all the tension came flying out." Watching the tour in Norwich, Charlie Higson (later of the Higsons) recalls a definite feeling that *the* band was the Specials. "They seemed to have the strongest songs, the strongest identity and were definitely the best known of the three acts." Before the tour, the Selecter's bass player Charley Anderson described the three-band billing as a "family of music, the Coventry Stax if you like. This is what 2 Tone is all about. We're not aiming for competition. We're not going out to say that the Selecter are trying to run off the Specials or that Madness aren't as good . . . it's a matter of trying to present each band at its best." Horace Panter is not convinced. "We all tried to blow one another off each night," he says. "We were on the top of our game. The audience were dancing from the word go. The feeling of joy and abandon. That was the apogee of 2 Tone. We had a mission. It was righteous. We were converting people to this amazing new music." Guitarist Compton Amanor agrees, saying the spirit of it was, "'Now top *that!*' Then at the end of the night, we'd all come together onstage and do 'Madness' by Prince Buster or 'You're Wondering Now' with the Specials."

If there is a single event which cemented the arrival of 2 Tone into the homes of the British public, it was the appearance of the Specials, the Selecter and Madness on the same edition of *Top of the Pops*. Thursday, November 8, 1979, the day 2 Tone became the sound of young Britain. Looking back at the running order of the BBC flagship music program, one can readily see why 2 Tone represented a radical shift in popular culture. Performing alongside the likes of Matchbox (English rockabilly), Dr. Hook (American rock) and Lena Martell (spiritual country), the three 2 Tone bands spoke of the *now*, while somehow agitating against an inglorious past. Over the previous twenty years, *The Black and White Minstrel Show* had been the pinnacle of BBC light entertainment, parading white actors made up to mimic and stereotype Black performers. Suddenly here were Neville Staple and Lynval Golding, Pauline Black and Gaps Hendrickson, confidently projecting "On My Radio" and "A Message to You Rudy" and expressing their talents in neatly constructed three-minute pop songs. Black, proud and performing as equals alongside their white bandmates, the swing from institutional cultural racism to the multi-ethnic face of 2 Tone was nothing short of revolutionary.

Performing "One Step Beyond" on a stage decorated with a cardboard cut-out of Walt Jabsco, Madness contravened decades of television tradition by walking offstage, circling the audience in a staggered "Nutty Train" conga and rejoining an onlooking Woody, grinning from behind his drum kit. Midsong, Suggs pulled out a toy instrument from his jacket pocket and made a half-hearted attempt to mime a saxophone solo. This was filmed on a Wednesday, with all three groups due to play in Bristol the same evening.* Chasing down the clock, Madness chartered a private plane. "We had to go from *Top of the Pops* to the airport, get on this scary little tiny aircraft, fly to Cardiff, then get to the venue," says Chris Foreman. "The Specials got a five o'clock train and arrived about ten minutes after us. I think Jerry insisted that they travel second class."

When the program was broadcast a day later, Madness were to be found in the East Midlands "hotfooting it around dank, dreary Derby," as described by Deanne Pearson, "desperately searching for a pub with a television to watch themselves, rifling frantically through pubs, launderettes and Chinese takeaways." Finding a promising location, Chas introduces the group to the bar staff and customers and "begs that he be allowed to switch channels: 'We're in a band and we're on *Top of the Pops* tonight,' he announces proudly, offering to buy them all a drink, doubles, if the barman will let him turn over for just five minutes. 'Come on,' Chas shouts in exasperation to his wilting entourage, 'let's find somewhere else. Thanks a lot, mate!'"

---

* The Selecter's performance of "On My Radio" was recycled from their appearance three weeks earlier, while during the Specials's mimed rendition of "A Message to You Rudy," Jerry pranced around onstage playing Lynval's cream-bodied Fender Telecaster.

At the next pub, Chas resorts to direct action, offering the barman a fiver if he will switch to BBC for "a mere five minutes": "Please mate," he pleads, "we're a band called Madness." After being denied again, a stranger befriends the group and, as Pearson describes, they are shepherded into a tiny, prefabricated taxi office where Chas "hastily turns on the set and selects *Top of the Pops*. 'It's alright, it's alright,' Chas pants feverishly, 'we were on fourth, we're on next.'" Grateful for the show of kindness, Madness distribute signed copies of "One Step Beyond" and free invitations to the gig at the King's Hall. Onstage at the gig, Chas continues with the platitudes: "I'd just like to say that if any of you lot out there want taxis home, get Eagle Cars. They're the best!"

Waking up the next day to discover their van had been broken into, Madness spent the morning detained at the local police station reporting stolen clothing and portable television sets. Such mishaps and shenanigans shadowed the tour. In Bristol—voted the second-best gig of the year, after Pink Floyd's *The Wall*—reports of a three-in-a-bed orgy circulated. "Ah, yes, the porno film," sniggers Lynval Golding. "That was mainly the naughty security man, Steve English, and Neville, who picked up a couple of girls, took them up to their room and filmed it all." In his memoir, *Original Rude Boy*, Neville remembers it as a night of blow jobs and charlie "being snorted off bare skin."[58] Allegedly circulated in record company offices, Pauline Black smirks and says, "But I never saw it, unfortunately." Addressing the issue of young women mixing with male musicians, Pauline explains, "Those that thought they were coming back for a cup of coffee got disabused of the idea fairly quickly and occasionally were to be found in the corridor having a little cry. If I saw some poor creature, I'd let them crash in my room. Of course, they'd be seen in the lobby the following morning and then everybody thinks you're a dyke."

Contemplating the virile culture associated with touring, Juliet de Vie says Neville was king of the rock 'n' roll life, intent on "shagging as many girls as he could get through. You saw and heard about all sorts of things going on," she says. "The young feminist in me could be quite appalled and be thinking, *You can't treat young women like this.* And then the other part of me would be, *But you're my friends. I work with you. I like you and you treat me well.* This was the late seventies and deeply sexist attitudes were the acceptable norm. Rock 'n' roll was, and is, a deeply macho culture and universally accepted as a lifestyle. There was no accountability because there was no accountability in wider society toward those attitudes. In the same way as there was casual and institutionalized racism everywhere, there was also casual and institutionalized sexism. I was a single girl in the midst of all of that, so you're going to get knocks on your hotel door at one o'clock in the morning that you knew definitely not to answer. Most of the time you were dealing with guys that treated you perfectly well. And then you saw this other side. I was conflicted." Contemplating the contradictions, de Vie adds, "You can espouse political and social ideals, but everybody struggles to actually live up to them completely. 2 Tone was about Black and white integration. Sexism was not on the agenda."

By dint of her gender, Pauline says she felt like an outsider surrounded by stereotypical rock star behavior. Added to which, she had never publicly defined herself as a Black woman. Taking stock of the dramatic change in her circumstances, Pauline decided it was time to identify who she really was. "I was working in the radiography department at Walsgrave Hospital and having days off, saying I was ill but really doing gigs. There was a music fan in the department who didn't know I was in the Selecter, but I thought he was going to see my adoptive name, Pauline Vickers, in the music papers. So I thought, *Fuck it! I need another name.*" When she ran the idea past her bandmates in the dressing room of the Lyceum, Charley Anderson started riffing aloud. "Pauline . . . Pauline," he kept repeating. "What is she? She's Black." Suddenly, Pauline screamed out, "'YES! I AM BLACK'—it was the one thing about me that was absolutely definitive." Excited by her new identity, Pauline borrowed a dove-gray fedora with a dark-gray ribbon band and, placing it on her head, declared it was just perfect. "That's the day Pauline Black came together," she says.

Resplendent in beige Sta-Prest, Ben Sherman shirt and a gray, double-breasted sharkskin jacket and penny loafers, Pauline single-handedly invented the persona of the rude girl. Commonly called out for her mod-like androgyny, Pauline says she would never adhere to wearing "a straitjacket of conventional dress for womanhood. The appropriation of a male way of dressing made me feel powerful. I was sticking up for any feminist beliefs by just existing, wearing what I wore, and having the attitude that I had. Wearing dresses onstage made me feel un-powerful. To go on a stage, I had to feel powerful—and I still had full slap on."

Like many bedazzled by Pauline's image, Chrysalis press officer Julia Marcus says the effect was groundbreaking. "You'd never seen anything like that before. It was such a great look and so easy for young fans to put together and emulate. That was massive. You didn't have to go to some big designer store and buy stuff. You could put the look together from secondhand shops and church jumble sales." Also an admirer, Juliet de Vie says, "Women didn't look like Pauline. They didn't act like Pauline. They didn't talk like Pauline. She said what she thought and didn't play the game. But the tough persona also contained a softer, caring and empathetic person that was carefully guarded for much of the time. Loneliness is notoriously a big thing on the road, and we were good company for each other and mutually supportive as two young women in this intensely male environment."

And so the tour rolled on.

At the Sheffield Top Rank on November 4, the police turned the power off at eleven o'clock, leading to impromptu vocal versions of "Guns of Navarone," "Gangsters" and "A Message to You Rudy," and several pointed chants from members of the Specials directed at the boys in blue. In Plymouth, Desmond Brown lost the plot, attacking a bouncer and taking a bite out of Chris Foreman's cheek. Turning twenty-six, Pauline Black was serenaded onstage with a round of "Happy Birthday" and presented with a huge card signed by all the bands. As Neol Davies walked into the backstage dressing room, a dart hit the board on the back of the opening door. "A couple of seconds later and it would have hit my face," he says in horror. "Chalky and Toks [Madness's roadies] thought it was hilarious. They were probably coked out of their head." Perhaps in a display of empathy, Lynval Golding showed Neol and Chris Foreman how to play the perfect ska upbeat. "It's not as easy as it looks," says Chris. "All the other bands had two guitarists. Madness only had me, doing the work of two men: Laurel and Hardy!"

In the media world, the tour was all the rage. Decorating their front page in black-and-white checkers, the *Sun*'s headline screamed: "IT'S 2 TONE MANIA!" In *Smash Hits*, David Hepworth announced, "2 Tone are taking Britain by the scruff of its neck and making it dance to their tune in a way that hasn't been seen since the early days of punk." Likening the package tour to a "ska machine," *NME* journalist Mark Ellen wrote of the ska spectrum stretching to both ends with the Specials dead center, "seesawing around a strict, brassy Blue Beat with the Selecter veering off to a reggae fringe and Madness keeping their wheels grinding against the curb of basic R&B. At some point in [Madness's] set it dawns on me that if this isn't heaven, it has to be the place next door." Catching the tour in Edinburgh, Garry Bushell reported the "greatest show on earth" was currently "merrily moon-stomping the charts and selling out the nation's polys, Top Ranks and Tiffany's," further informing readers that "Britain is in the grip of Madness."

On November 14, the north London septet bid farewell to prepare for a prearranged tour of the US. Bowing out at Ayr Pavilion, Madness exited doing a "nutty train" through the middle of the Specials's set, carrying suitcases and waving goodbye. It was the final act of a memorable extended fortnight, cataloged by Suggs a decade later in *Q* magazine. "Driving round Glasgow in a car with no doors, having eaten the wrong kind of mushrooms; dancing the Watusi on a PA stack; swinging perilously over audiences; and balconies bouncing within inches of collapse."

The following day, Dexys Midnight Runners joined the bill. Bunking the train from Birmingham to Carlisle, Dexys arrived carrying their instruments and asking to borrow backline amplifiers. "I think Jerry paid for some bed-and-breakfasts for them," says Frank Murray, who was more familiar with tour-managing the likes of Thin Lizzy and Elton John. "Dexys would come round in the morning and eat our breakfasts. It was a totally different situation from what I was used to working with, but it added to the greatness of the tour."

Earlier in the year, Dexys had in fact turned down the opportunity to record on 2 Tone after Jerry and Neol saw the group play first in a pub in Birmingham and then at the Romulus Club in August 1979, supported by Joy Division. "It was packed out and they were fantastic," recalls Jerry. "I considered the drummer [in Dexys] before Brad joined the Specials." Asked why Dexys had turned down the offer to sign with 2 Tone, singer Kevin Rowland told *NME* in January 1980, "We didn't want to be a part of anyone else's movement. We'd rather be our own movement." The group's guitarist, Al Archer, continued, "We were very conscious of the fact that we might become too closely associated with that very strong 2 Tone image. A lot of people have already come to expect a certain type of music, a particular beat and a most definite image, from every new band signed to the label, and automatically it's all down to whether or not you're as good as the Specials."

Sullen and grumpy, Dexys kept their distance and sat at the back of the tour bus. "After Madness they didn't seem part of the gang," says Rick Rogers. "They were a regimented unit in themselves and had their own philosophies and agenda." On one occasion, Kevin Rowland (singer and de facto leader) bullied a roadie who worked for the Selecter. "He tried to give him a hard time," says Lynval Golding, "and Hartford thumped him."

On November 29, the 2 Tone carnival arrived in Coventry. Fans queued for over four hours to welcome home the returning heroes and an estimated 2,000 forgeries were uncovered. Conducting their own nefarious activity, Chas Smash, Neville Staple and Specials trombonist Rico Rodriguez sold £5 bags of weed to kids coming in and out of the soundcheck. "Rico used to score grass. Then me and

Neville would sit with him, roll it up in a newspaper and sell it," says Chas. "It was a street thing." Described by Roddy as "this little Chinese-looking bloke with a woolly hat and a padded coat," Rico (born in Havana to a Cuban father and a Jamaican mother) would go unnoticed. "He'd just walk through reception leaving the smell of a big spliff behind him."

Inside Tiffany's dance hall, the atmosphere was incredible. "It was an amazing night," says Gaps Hendrickson. "It was like, 'We are Coventry!'" Second on the bill, the Selecter were welcomed onstage by a rousing round of "We are the mods" and unleashed a set of un-bridled energy. Expressing his thoughts on behalf of *NME*, Mark Ellen spoke of "steam locomotive bluebeat . . . jangling with angular chords, rattling with percussion and fronted by Gaps and the frenetic, wide-eyed Pauline who belt around like a couple of yo-yos wired to the mains." Likening the atmosphere to a football match, Lanchester student Lizzie Soden says, "Everybody was skanking."

Reduced to tears by the overwhelming reception, Horace Panter says the reaction during the Specials's set was unbelievable. "I felt as proud of the people in that club as they felt proud of us." Lead-ing the audience through riotous versions of "Skinhead Moonstomp" and "You're Wondering Now," the encore involved various members of Dexys and the Selecter. "People were going mental," says Soden. "Everybody got on the stage and Jerry was in the middle on top of his organ."

Completing a momentous five weeks on the road, the tour cul-minated with London weekend shows at Lewisham Odeon and the Lyceum Ballroom. "The kinetic chaos that spills from the stage as six people make like their shoes are on fire establishes the basic thrust," wrote Paul Rambali in *NME*, in awe of the Specials's relentless dy-namism. "Underestimated and at odds with the exuberance onstage around him, Terry Hall's immobile glare and deadpan voice is in fact the perfect foil. The one thing you're bound to focus on because ev-erything else is moving too fast—and the perfect persona to deliver sullen and disgruntled lyrics."[59] Miles ahead in vibrancy and vitality, according to Garry Bushell, the Specials dealt "a winning hand of twenty sparkling dance delights, tight, professional and above all enjoyable."

Reflecting back on a mammoth undertaking, Charley Anderson neatly summed up the scale of the achievement. "That tour could never be repeated. Whoever witnessed it will never forget. We shook some dust off the venues up and down the country. The audience got their money's worth; they got to sweat three, maybe four times over, with so much energy. Sometimes we could actually feel the whole building shaking. It was fantastic"[60]

CHAPTER 12

NICE BAND, SHAME ABOUT THE FANS

HATFIELD. FOOTBALL VIOLENCE

O f the seven new towns built in the postwar period, two of them, Hatfield and Crawley, would become synonymous with violence at 2 Tone concerts. As regional locations determining their self-identity—like Coventry's displacement of residents to its outer boundaries when the city landscape was reimagined in the fifties and sixties—male teenagers asserted their status through a base impulse to fight. On October 27, 1979, midway through the 2 Tone Tour, an unprecedented display of brutality erupted at Hatfield Polytechnic. During the Selecter's set, an estimated thirty to forty men burst through a plate-glass exit door. Wielding knives and razors, the unidentified faction lashed out indiscriminately at members of the audience, "whacking anyone within arm's reach," intent on inflicting maximum damage to the people watching the gig. "It was horrible," says Mark Bedford, who was standing at the front watching the Selecter.

The 2 Tone Tour had witnessed a unique gathering of cult factions, each with their own style of dress and a shared love of music. Youth culture had never seen the like. "This was more than just going to see your favorite band," suggests Rick Rogers. "It was kids all together onstage. That's what it made you want to do. It was completely inclusive. And therefore a political statement. Black kids and white kids made to feel the same. It was extraordinary. Never seen before and never seen again."

But for all the unity and harmony, a 2 Tone gig was increasingly becoming a meeting place for tribal violence. "The mods and skinheads were natural enemies," says Juliet de Vie. "Skins saw reggae as their music and felt they had some sort of proprietorial right over it, whereas the mods had come to ska from soul." As a child of the sixties, Jerry Dammers had reached the conclusion that youth cults divided people. "They thought they were rebels and fighting each other whilst the people keeping everyone down just stayed in power. Hopefully music can bring people together and put a message across. You want songs to inspire the way people think. If you can make the music emotionally echo the message you're trying to put across in a successful way, it will influence people."

To make his point, Jerry wrote the muscular "Do the Dog" with its tongue-twisting, quick-fire introduction: *All you punks and all you Teds, National Front and natty dreads, mods, rockers, hippies and skinheads, keep on fighting till you're dead.* "It was a call for unity," explains its author. "The music and the general left-wing socialist message and the visual side were all part and parcel of something people could relate to. White rock music was always limited in what it could achieve politically because it wasn't that inclusive and alienated as many people as it involved. Black music was more universal and on a global scale, more popular than rock music."

Popular maybe, but its attraction for many was surface deep. Infiltrated by the National Front and right-wing factions, 2 Tone gigs and their growing skinhead following increasingly became fertile territory to recruit impressionable teenagers. "I had big issues with skinheads," says Frank Murray. "I'd been around at the first incarnation when they were into queer-bashing and Paki-bashing. The term 'aggro' came out of that. If you were a hippie and they caught you they'd cut your hair. There was a real sense of violence." Discussing the questionable skinhead presence, Terry Hall told *Sounds* in April 1979 that the group did not want to have to tell people what to do, preferring that they just came to the gigs and danced. "If you treat people like morons, they tend to behave like morons. If we attract an

NF skinhead, that's even better. If we get him to like us, it's even better, irrelevant of whether there's Blacks or whites in the band." Naive to the consequences of such an open invitation, and perhaps regretful in later years, Jerry echoed Terry's provocation, stating that the band had an easygoing attitude to their audience. "If people want to be racists that's their problem. They've got to make up their own minds. As far as we're concerned, racism isn't an issue. Racism as far as we're concerned is like some kind of mental illness, like fear of spiders."

Rumored to have been carried out by members of the fledgling left-wing antifascist group Red Action, the display of violence at Hatfield was deeply shocking. "Kids about fourteen were getting cut up," said Chas Smash. "I couldn't go onstage that night. I had to sit it out." According to Lee Thompson, they had Stanley knives, batons, and, "I might have seen a machete at one point. They were attacking the merchandise stall, smashing everything up with these baseball bats." Looking on, aghast, Mike Barson says, "It was just a violent bunch of fucking idiots. They were some sort of political group who for some reason thought cutting people with a razor blade would do something or other."

Earlier in the day, the Selecter had arrived in Hatfield and gone into the town precinct looking for somewhere to eat. Talking to *NME*, Charley Anderson recalled meeting a group of "fascist drunken bastards saying they were coming to the gig later to cause some fun" because they had "nothing better to do." With rumors circulating, Neol Davies recalls, "There were lots of unpleasant-looking characters walking around. I remember being quite scared at one point. It felt like something was going to happen." Convinced the agitators belonged to a branch of the Clapton Anti-Nazi League, John Hasler says they were "looking for a fight. We were having breakfast in a café and they came in and tried to engage us in conversation. 'Are you against fascism?' 'Yeah, course we are. Now go away. Leave us alone.' They were just obnoxious arseholes who had decided that *they* were the people to fight fascism. They turned up at the gig, maybe a dozen of them, and pushed through the main glass doors, kicked over the merchandise stall and just started attacking fifteen-year-old kids with short hair. I remember getting the band backstage, then going back out and one guy had a girl by the hair and was trying to cut her face. The next thing, Chalky flew in from nowhere and BAM! Took him out."

Terrified, Frank Murray says, "When you see somebody getting kicked around, your stomach tends to tighten up. It's not a nice feeling. For some reason everybody seemed to conclude that Madness's fans might be responsible in some way or other, so they played a shorter-than-normal set so we could get the Specials on." Scheduled to perform at 10:45 p.m., most of the Specials missed the incident. "When we turned up, the dressing room was just full of kids with cuts and bruises over their faces and horrible stabbings and stuff," says Terry. "It was our responsibility 'cos we staged the gig. It felt like it was getting out of control. It's like when you go to football; it's only a handful of people kicking off, but it can feel like a lot of people doing it at the time."[61] Smuggled out at the end of the night, Pauline Black recalls standing in a car park "freezing cold and being very worried because it looked as though we were going to get a battering. The police were called and then of course it got in the papers."

Ten people treated in hospital, eleven arrests and an estimated £900 worth of damage was sufficient for the *Daily Mirror* to declare it a "riot," while *NME* reported "a gang of razor-wielding idiots" forcing their way into the gig and hospitalizing a number of people. Excited to be seeing the Specials for the first time, Rhoda Dakar (latterly of the Bodysnatchers) says, "It was stupid and unpleasant and violent and aggressive." Mindful that the violence was subsequently attributed to both fascist and antifascist groups, she adds, "Whether it was bully boys from the right or bully boys from the left, it didn't legitimize the action." Over time, the gig has become "the stuff of schoolyard myth," cautions Jerry Dammers. "It's like, 'Did you actually see what happened or did you just hear what happened?' All in all it was a very unpleasant and sobering night that took some of the euphoria out of the 2 Tone Tour."

Dismayed that the antiviolence message at the heart of songs such as "A Message to You Rudy," "Concrete Jungle" and "Doesn't Make It Alright" had done little to deter the perpetrators, the Specials issued a statement: "Everyone involved in the 2 Tone Tour wishes to make it clear that they detest violence under any circumstances and that anybody looking for a fight is completely unwelcome at any 2 Tone dance." Speaking retrospectively, Terry Hall said it was the gig where he started questioning "what was going on. I also had a bit of grievance with Madness because I didn't think they were taking responsibility. I think they should have made a stand. It was up to them to denounce it."

Unwittingly, Madness had increasingly attracted right-wing support. In Oldham, security guards uncovered a stash of weapons among fans including knives and a homemade mace. In Huddersfield, when a coachload of fans arrived from Middlesbrough and were denied entry to the gig, the group's van was smashed up. At Brighton Polytechnic, Woody recalls brushing past a group of British Movement supporters at the bar "talking very loudly about Adolf Hitler." Accusations of previous associations with neo-Nazi groups began to circulate. In an interview with the antiracist fanzine *Guttersnipe*, Suggs said, "When I was fourteen/fifteen I was in a gang that went Paki-bashing, at sixteen not so much and at seventeen I finished with all that when I saw a mate's dad strutting about in a Nazi uniform. Now my old mates come up to me and tell me they like the band but why do we play nigger music?" Making light of associations with racists in their youth, Frank Murray argues, "It would be like growing up in Belfast and saying you knew somebody in the IRA; of course you would. If I were racist, I wouldn't go on tour with Black people. That in itself disproves the idea. When the press were looking to point the finger, they went at Madness."

Singled out as the only all-white band on 2 Tone, Madness incurred the wrath of the press as racist incidents continued to blight their concerts. At the Electric Ballroom on November 18, a majority skinhead audience, fronted by a larger than usual National Front presence, harassed the support act, Red Beans & Rice, with a volley of insults and racial prejudice. Ashamed by their behavior, Suggs came onstage to berate the offenders and ended up kicking a microphone stand over and storming off. "They were spitting and Sieg heil-ing at the lead singer Laverne," says Chas Smash. "I had to come out and say, 'Stop fucking around. We wanted this band on the bill.'" Jumping into the crowd to "have a word," Chas was punched in the face and "kicked up the bollocks. It's the herd instinct," he ranted. "You've only got to stop a few leaders and then it's alright. Remove the cancer and the rest of the apples will fall back into the barrel."

Nevertheless, controversy plagued Madness. Featured in an *NME* interview—"Nice Band, Shame About the Fans"—Chas incensed his bandmates when he suggested, "We don't care if people are in the NF, as long as they're having a good time." It was a PR disaster. In the wake of the disorder at Hatfield, journalist Deanne Pearson pressed for an explanation. "It's got nothing to do with us," retorted Chas defensively. "Who cares what their political views are? We don't ask them, like we don't ask them if they're Conservative or Labour when they come through the door. There's no difference, they're all kids." Attempting to defuse the situation, Woody intervened to assure Pearson that Madness were not a political band. "We see our music purely as entertainment and our only concern is that everyone enjoys themselves." Undeterred, Pearson pushed on: "So do you sympathize with them or don't you?" "No," they replied as one. "We don't."

Changing tack, Pearson suggested that Madness owed it to their audience to make a stand against racist infiltrators. "It's best to just ignore them," responded Chas, rising to the bait. "Most of them don't know what they're talking about anyway. They stick a [Nazi] armband on and they don't know what it means. It's just like supporting a foot-ball team and wearing their scarf." Then revealing that some of the culprits were, in fact, friends of the group, Chas continued, "They're good kids. They know I don't agree with their views, and so what if they wear Union Jacks and Nazi swastikas? I don't care about that."

Desperate to set the record straight, Woody once again intervened. "Can I just say that the rest of us do not have friends in the NF and do not like having NF supporters at our gigs?" Ignoring the act of mediation, Pearson goaded her prey by suggesting that the group were encouraging them even by ignoring their political views. Incensed, Chas exploded, "You just don't understand, do you? They're just a group of kids who, like any kid, have to take out their anger and frustration on something. Some it's football, some it's music. NF don't really mean much to them. Why should I stop them coming to our gigs? That's all they've got. Well, I'll tell you something, you print a word of this and I'll deal with you personally." Flabbergasted, the rest of the band turned. "Shut up, Chas!"

Deflated, Woody snapped. "Don't take any notice of him. He's just the compère, he's not really in the band, these are just his views." Silent throughout the argument, beyond uttering asinine phrases such as "eggs and bacon and sausages, with tomato sauce, please" and "how do you like your eggs?" Lee Thompson suddenly asked, as if sensing an impending media furor, "If they say, 'Don't quote me,' you won't?" Pearson said she would not. However, when the article was published a fortnight later, she wrote, "But no one asks not to be quoted."

Mulling over the incident four decades later, Chris Foreman says Deanne Pearson had an agenda and, although it did the band no good and the remarks were ill judged, he insists Chas was not racist. Clearly still troubled by the lingering uproar, Chas revisits the interview. "I was trying to say that we didn't want to be in politics; that you have to communicate with idiots to change their minds. You have to let them in. I was trying to say, how can you have change through distance? You have to have proximity to cure it. It's a fucking disease. You can't cure a patient from a hundred yards away. You've got to be in the room with him. You have to recognize the disease, locate it, and lance it. Proximity, not fear. Not shouting at it. You can't help a person if they don't feel comfortable with you. Even if the guy's a fucking racist shit. You've got to be an agent of change, not punishment. I wasn't very eloquent and she [Deanne Pearson] misunderstood me. It was very hurtful. Chris thought I was a fucking idiot. His girlfriend was Black and they all thought I was racist. I felt absolutely fucking insulted."

Acknowledging the shortcomings of youth, Suggs now says, "We were just trying to work through ourselves, through people like Jerry, to understand a different perspective, how you behave and what you say, and how you say what you say. But there wasn't a racist bone in any of our bodies." In 1979, Suggs's defense struck a similar chord. Pointing out that Madness's first single was a tribute to Prince Buster "who is Black all over," he added, "If we were fascists, what would we be doing playing ska and bluebeat? If we wanted to talk about politics, we'd have formed a debating society, not a fucking band." 2 Tone made the difference, concludes Rick Rogers. "Once Madness saw and were part of it, they were 100 percent signed up to the agenda. There's no question about that."

In 1975, the introduction of camera surveillance at football grounds, to crack down on violence, was accompanied by longer jail sentences imposed by the judiciary. But while the police monitored activity on the terraces, gangs would often maraud through city centers after matches looking for "bother." "You have to factor in football violence," says Suggs. "It was a rite of passage. A load of boys running around chasing each other up the street. When I went up to Coventry, they had those fucking plastic seats you used to have at school just sort of nailed to the concrete. Coventry was particularly scary in them days. It was sort of the murder capital of the planet." Friendly with some of the staff who worked at the cinema, the Specials would run into the Odeon on a Saturday afternoon to avoid confrontation between rival fans. At Highfield Road (the home of Coventry City and where Jerry Dammers had worked as a turnstile operator), and at Stamford Bridge where Suggs cheered on Chelsea, crowds were entertained at halftime, or when the home team scored, with a blast of "Liquidator." For many it was their first introduction to reggae. Music and football were closely associated. "We used to play the Golden Eagle in Birmingham," says Roddy Byers, "and because we were from Coventry you would get football chants at the start. So during 'Liquidator' we would chant, 'CCFC OK.'"

As the clampdown on violence strengthened, football hooligans increasingly turned to rock concerts as a forum to release pent-up aggression. Mixing this with alcohol consumption, fighting was an inevitable consequence. "'It's Saturday night, let's get really pissed,'" mocks Horace Panter. "They'd all be there glowering at one another from separate corners of the room. It was the British working-class predilection for drinking too much and hitting one another." To mimic opposing fans taunting each other during a match, the Specials added the popular terrace chant, *You're gonna get your fucking head kicked in; you're going home in a fucking ambulance,* to the introduction of "Concrete Jungle." At early concerts, Lynval Golding would further inform audiences that in Coventry he witnessed a gang of white youths chasing a lone Black male, accompanied by the threatening chant.

Augmented by handclaps and a tribal drumbeat, the effect was transformational. As Terry sang about street violence and being chased by the National Front—or on occasion *being chased by a couple of cunts*—the band attacked one another with theatrical bottles made of sugar. Jerry ran across the stage and jumped on Neville's back. Upended and kicked to the ground, he limped back behind his keyboard. "It was having fun," says Neville, "playing out what we were singing. Kids used to sing that at football matches but also skinheads walking down the street."

On the dance floor, rival football gangs rubbed against cultural, sectarian and tribal factions: white against Black against Asian; Irish versus Scottish; Teddy Boys versus punks versus mods versus skinheads. "It was almost like fashion," submits Suggs, "just some weird adjunct of wanting to have a fight, wanting to be nasty and getting up the nose of other people. I knew kids I'd grown up with on the estate with the swastika tattoo but the wrong way round. There was that terrible dichotomy between real skinheads who were into reggae music and the whole NF thing. The real skinheads would go to Black clubs to dance and were into the aesthetic of what the Black kids were wearing—the porkpie hats and the suits. Then a lot of the football-hooligan types transferred their allegiances to bands. There was always that problem: you'd see a group of skinheads coming toward you and you'd never know until you got close up to see the badges. Then you'd realize they'd got a swastika on or an SS badge or NF or BM. It was tribal. I've got friends and for them it was a war."

By 1979, the National Front and the British Movement were using 2 Tone gigs to recruit fresh blood. "It comes back to young boys who want to feel part of a gang," Compton Amanor told *Hot Press*. "They don't really question what it is they're following or what armband they're wearing. All they know is that they're with their mates and having a good time. You see them doing Nazi salutes or chanting, but I've been at gigs where they've done this and five minutes later, they're back into the music, enjoying it and relating to it. All we're asking is to get them to question that contradiction because once they question it, they'll begin seeing things."

Concerned by reports of violence the farther south groups played, John Mostyn drew a thirty-mile radius around central London. "I wouldn't book anyone within that, other than the main London venues. 2 Tone represented everything they hated: Black and white having fun together, showing you can get on." Nevertheless, seemingly oblivious to the overt show of unity, right-wing extremists tagged 2 Tone groups according to their Black members. Thus *Selecter + 6* and *Specials + 2*. "It came from the uneducated types," rages Neol Davies, "mainly London racist skinheads who didn't like Black people but liked reggae music. It was a small minority but they had a large voice." Similarly outraged, Rick Rogers says, "They couldn't even add because at that time there was nine people onstage in the Specials, three of whom were Black."

To add insult to injury, areas of the media castigated 2 Tone as being instigators of violence and complicit with right-wing factions infiltrating gigs. Judged a threat to society by the *London Evening News*, a headline implored readers, "Don't Rock with the Sieg-heilers," above a picture of the Selecter—a seven-piece band with six Black members. "The media ran with the idea that in some way or another we were on the side of these racist skinheads," sighs Pauline Black. "That caused a lot of anger and consternation." If the adverse publicity was privately cause for concern at Chrysalis, today Doug D'Arcy is contemptuous of the sideshow. "As long as the bands kept on putting out good records, we knew it would go away. I didn't think it was important, put it that way." Equally dismissive, Roy Eldridge adds, "The National Front was irrelevant to the Specials. The group's message was a positive statement. I thought it would go away and it did."

In the short term, perhaps. But as 2 Tone continued to garner broader media attention, increased record sales and greater national support, so the weight of dissent grew. Conflict and accusation would increasingly blight 2 Tone concerts and, in time, challenge the very existence of the bands and the label.

CHAPTER 13

MAN FROM WAREIKA

COOPERATIVE. RICO. A MESSAGE TO YOU RUDY

"On the back of the 2 Tone Tour there was a sense of: what do we do now? How's it going to work?" says Juliet de Vie. Taken on in Brighton on the first day of the tour, Juliet was an obvious choice to manage the Selecter. Neol Davies says, "It was another expression of us as a cutting-edge band, going against the grain. We didn't have a standard record company, acceptably suited manager type. Quite the opposite. Juliet had been involved from the beginning and was clued up to what it was all about." She was twenty-one, peroxide-blond and fired up; Pauline Black says it was unusual to have a female manager. "She was respected in the band and within the industry. It was probably very hard for her going into boardrooms and meeting with accountants. But she held her own. It was good to have another female to bounce off."

Practical help to establish 2 Tone as a legitimate label was much in demand during its meteoric rise. The immediate answer was a legal document recognizing the fourteen members of the Specials and the Selecter as a cooperative. "It was a great idea," insists de Vie, "but it was going to take a small army of admin people to sustain it. 2 Tone wasn't making that kind of money. The bands weren't making that kind of money. They were selling records but only the Specials had made an album. The huge success was based around singles. None of it was cheap. They were expensive bands to run. Seven people. You can't travel in small vans; you needed a coach. The hotel bills. Everything was magnified. We attempted to have meetings but it was a nightmare."

Neol Davies remembers meeting the Specials in a café in London to agree on the financial split of the inaugural 2 Tone single, "Gangsters" and "The Selecter." "Brad [John Bradbury] was playing on both sides so something had to be worked out," he says, "because nobody wanted him to be paid twice. We decided to pool the money from both records." It was the nearest 2 Tone came to a formal agreement. Placing great emphasis on protecting each group's identity and artistic control, the majority view was not to be "hampered" by legal documents. "I know that sounds a bit idealistic," Brad told Deanne Pearson in October 1979, "but we'd rather just deal on a trust basis. It's more conducive to this familial thing because we're all in this together, and nobody's trying to outdo anybody else. We are beginning to talk about contracts now, as we expand. But what we'd really like to be able to do is offer groups contracts involving advances for wages—say, enough to record an album—and then sign them up for two or three years."

Having chosen to stay with 2 Tone after the runaway success of "On My Radio," the Selecter formed the cooperative with the Specials. Run on the principle of fairness and equality, Rick Rogers says, 2 Tone was a mini socialist republic. "There were no formalized or partnership contracts whatsoever. Everything was a handshake." Neither registered formally nor instated on public record, 2 Tone existed in name only. As Jerry was fond of saying, "It's more like a piss-take of a record company."

By winter 1979—and due to the demands of touring, recording and promotional activities—Juliet de Vie says, "You couldn't get fourteen people around the table. Straight after the 2 Tone Tour the Specials were in America and the Selecter in Europe. The pressures on them were huge. They didn't want to let go of this idea, but it became impossible: to get them together; to make decisions about artwork; who they were going to sign, and on what terms; or to make anything happen beyond their own careers, which were going nuts. There were a lot of phone calls, lots of notes: 'So-and-so said this.' There was no email. Communication was limited. You were relying on landlines. They're on a tour bus. They're in a hotel. They're doing a gig. Transatlantic calls weren't easy. Then you had the time difference to deal with. You were relying on the odd phone call trying to get a decision out of Jerry. All the bands came up against the hard realities of being in a commercial industry: 'We need to make records, sell records, otherwise we won't be able to do gigs because the audience won't come.' The pressure was to do all that and sustain the momentum."

Rejecting established music business practice, 2 Tone offered an alternative to groups who did not immediately want to sign to a major label. "We don't tell bands what to record," explained Terry Hall. "They send a tape and if we think it's good, it's okay with us to put out a single. There are piles of tapes at Jerry's house. We're very much involved in operating the label, but you can't get so involved that your own musical ability slips." In the absence of formalized meetings, the groups often made A&R decisions on a tour coach to shouts of "Sign them!" or "Rubbish!"

Increasingly, and perhaps inevitably, 2 Tone leaned on Chrysalis for support. "2 Tone never had a budget or paid for anything," says Neol Davies. "The label was a front." Responsible for marketing and distribution, Chrysalis offered a team of experts. Nevertheless, unlike the Specials and the Selecter, who had signed directly to Chrysalis, the one-off singles—Madness, and later the Beat and the Bodysnatchers—were deals made by 2 Tone, according to Roy Eldridge. "Jerry would play us a record and say, 'I want to go with this one.' Then we'd work out a release date and a strategy to promote it. He never came to us for approval. It was just, 'Here it is.'"

Meeting the Specials for the first time, John Sims of Chrysalis says, "We were more used to pop stars breezing into the art department on a cloud of cologne whereas Jerry would shuffle in anonymously with a carrier bag full of bits and pieces." Resistant to anything that appeared "unduly sophisticated or clever," Sims admired Jerry's eye for design detail. "We might do a beautifully crafted piece of typography and then he would tell us to 'knacker it up' by photocopying it a couple of times or by putting things out of focus. He was, in the nicest possible way, a complete nightmare to work with because he had such a clear idea of what he wanted. He would end up doing things over and over again in a very obsessive way until he was happy with it. Ninety-nine times out of a hundred he was right, and when it came back from the printers, it was spot on."[62]

"It was a constant battle to stop the art department smoothing things or turning things into gimmicky 'fun'-type cartoons," says Jerry about his relationship with Chrysalis. "I had to watch everything like a hawk and direct every detail of the artwork to try and keep it properly in the 2 Tone style." To everybody's consternation, Chrysalis refused to print black-and-white paper labels on singles above the first print run of 25,000. "They were too expensive," concedes Doug D'Arcy. The decision to use a cheaper plastic silver label and substitute 2 Tone imagery with plain text still angers Juliet de Vie. "It was a small thing but it mattered a lot," she says. "Plastic was a compromise. They didn't have the same emotive value. I hated it. It was going from cottage industry to mainstream label and working with a big pressing factory. It was the subject of a lot of discussion at the time. Nobody was happy about it. The way '2 Tone' was written as 'Two-Tone' was meaningless. It started to dilute it." Reflecting on the unique status of 2 Tone within the music industry, Terry Hall says it was "very odd because it was a record label that had success very quickly. But it wasn't really run as a record label. It was just an idea and a way that good bands could make records. In theory it was brilliant; practically it was not so great."[63]

More marketable than its predecessor, punk, Jerry says of 2 Tone, "There was always that tension between the commercial side and trying to keep the creativity and the politics all involved in it." Having expected the Specials to be little more than an underground band, suddenly, he says, they were pop stars. "There was an air of unreality about it because I had been looking forward to it for so long.

At the height of our success, John Hasler and I were in a tube station on a busy Saturday night and this train happened to stop loaded with gravel. I said, 'Come on, John,' and we both jumped on board. It was going through all these stations with crowded platforms and I was just waving to everybody like the queen as we went through. We ended up in this siding miles away [in East Finchley] and luckily came to a halt before we died of hypothermia. It was like *Top of the Pops* come to life in front of the passengers on a gravel train!"

(L–R) Chris Dawson (junior pasteup artist), John Sims, Neol Davies, and Juliet de Vie at Partridge Rushton Associates, Emerald Street, London, 1980.

* * *

On October 12, 1979, the Specials released their second single, "A Message to You Rudy," directed as a warning to the violent elements within their audience. "It's a message to them," cautioned guitarist Lynval Golding. "If you come out for trouble then the only place you're going to end up is in jail, 'cos that's where all the bad rude boys end up."[64] Written twelve years earlier, its composer Dandy Livingstone says it was a call to rude boys to "cool it" and "think about their future." After being picked out from a record collection owned by Lynval's father, the Specials's arrangement sustained its lilting rocksteady rhythm and introduced to the band lineup the legendary trombonist Rico Rodriguez.

Rico Rodriguez, London, May 19, 1979.

Born on October 17, 1934, in Mark Lane, Kingston, Emmanuel Rodriguez attended the celebrated Alpha Boys School, a Catholic institution renowned for its strict authority. Often compared to the Juilliard School of Music in New York, Alpha provided many boys with their only opportunity to receive a formal education. "There was a lot of discipline," recalled Rico. "Every day praying, working in the garden, and musical theory. But it was much better than cleaning shoes for tourists. And as soon our teacher was away, we just played our own things."[65] Schooled alongside many of the country's finest musicians—including trombonist Don Drummond, trumpeter John "Dizzy" Moore, and saxophonists Lester Sterling and Roland Alphonso—Rico was one of many who would later find acclaim as part of Jamaica's revered instrumental group the Skatalites. During the fifties, in between stints serving as an apprentice mechanic, Rico won first prize on Radio Jamaica's talent contest, *The Vere Johns Op-*

portunity Hour. It was hosted by a white journalist, and Rico says, "[Johns] was aware of the problems in our society and he used to have this show on Saturday nights. After I'd won, I couldn't enter again, so he used to have me on as a guest artist. The crowd was always behind me." During this time, Rico recorded with sound system producers Prince Buster, Count Boysie, Clement Dodd and Duke Reid; however, in December 1961, he made the decision to leave Jamaica in search of a better life in England. "I loved the excitement of music but I just wasn't making a living," Rico explained in 2003. "Jamaica is the land of my birth and I love it, but it just wasn't happening."[66]

Lauded on the London scene, Rico earned a living by working in a variety of menial jobs: at the gas works, on the production line at Ford's in Dagenham, and painting for the local authority. After Rico was signed to Island in 1977, the much-venerated *Man from Wareika* gave him a new lease on life—first supporting Bob Marley & the Wailers on their European tour, then finding session work and performing to white punk rockers at venues such as the 100 Club.

Hatching an audacious plan for the Specials's new single, Jerry tracked down the trombonist. "It was beyond our wildest dreams that Rico would actually come and play," he says. "I was so in awe of him, so I sent Lynval to ask him instead." Picking up the story, Rico told *Reggae Vibes* how Lynval found him in southeast London. "One day me daughter say, 'Some people look for you and them call every day and them would really like to get in touch with you.' One day them call and convinced me it would be good to join them. I realized they like what I was playing, so I join them and play."

Having contributed to the original version of "A Message to You Rudy," Jerry says, it was unbelievable that Rico recorded with the Specials. "He added real soul and feeling which took us to another level." Lynval says it was "like being with a legend. You can't find words to express the feeling. It's like amazing jazz players: they don't play the same way twice. That's what Rico was. He fit in the way we played the song. One take: BAM! You just had to let him play. Jerry would guide him and offer arrangements, but you can't arrange Rico. He arrange himself."

In recent years, Rico had formed a musical partnership with horn player Dick Cuthell, producer of *Man from Wareika*. Such was their impact, the duo were invited by Jerry to become the eighth and ninth members of the Specials. "Dick and Rico brought class to the music," says Frank Murray. "Being one of the elder statesmen of ska was like the icing on the cake. Rico's imprimatur was a seal of approval: 'I've worked with all the legends and now I'm working with these guys'— that was so important."

To promote the new single, the Specials recorded a promotional video directed by Martin Baker, the son of film actor Stanley Baker. Shot inside the Roundhouse, the newly expanded group bounced around against a white backdrop intercut with footage of a crowd of wayward rude boys causing mischief outside the Electric Ballroom. "There were a load of bread baskets," says John Sims, roped in to help on the shoot, "and one kid kicked it and it went flying." After attracting the attention of a passing police officer, a trumped-up charge of filming without a license led to the arrest of the cameraman. "It made a good story in *NME*," chuckles Sims. "'Ello, 'ello, 'ello. What's been going on here then?'"

CHAPTER 14

IF IT AIN'T STIFF, IT AIN'T WORTH A FUCK

MADNESS LEAVE 2 TONE

While the music press championed a ska revival and the Specials enjoyed a second top ten single, Madness took a step back. "The idea of 2 Tone was fantastic and we wanted to be part of it," reflected Mark Bedford. "But I don't know if we ever thought that we had to write songs in that style, as it were. We'd done one single and I suppose we felt it was time to move on."[67] A meeting was organized at the unofficial headquarters of 2 Tone, the Devonshire Arms on Kentish Town Road, where it was agreed that neither 2 Tone nor Rick Rogers would be able to offer Madness and the Specials equal attention. "It wasn't that we were ungrateful or anything," Suggs told *NME*, "we probably owe most of our success to the Specials—it was just that we couldn't stay under their wing forever." Acknowledging that Madness had to break out on their own and develop their own style, Suggs joshed, "I believe that every band has their ten minutes of glory, but I like to think we've left enough options open to give us *twenty* minutes."

The rise of Madness had been relatively quick, and with little hardship. Unexpectedly they were in the charts, swept up by the popularity of the Specials and 2 Tone. "It was like the lazy man's way to success," says Suggs. "We didn't have to do anything. A little bit of rehearsing and then all of a sudden, we were hitting it off where some people had been struggling for years. It's like suddenly this sort of wave came and we just had to slightly turn left, and we were on it and we were away."[68]

In north London, there had always been an air of notoriety attached to certain members of Madness from years of marking the territory with graffiti tags. "We were famous from round our way," says Suggs, "so we had no care for trying to become successful. But suddenly we were involved in this phenomenon that was way beyond anything we'd comprehended. We were young, naive kids. I was eighteen. And to meet people like Rico and Jerry, who was a very philosophical person, to open your mind to the fact that you're actually doing something worthwhile. It stopped us running around the streets doing things we shouldn't do. I don't think it really occurred to us that we were involved in something that was going to become important, but I'm so grateful that we were. Jerry had a vision that you could do something that would appeal to the underclass, stylistically and musically, and then change their minds. We were just in our own firmament. It was the attitude that we were into, not the concept. 2 Tone was very specific to do with geography, the Midlands: Coventry and Birmingham. We were from London. It wasn't the only thing we wanted to do. We wanted to be like Ian Dury and the Kinks and talk about our own geography."

With a hit record to their name, Madness had the music industry in a flurry. "We could have signed them," says Roy Eldridge. "There was talk about it, but our hands were full with the Specials and the Selecter." According to Doug D'Arcy, Chrysalis did not sign Madness because they were not willing to be number two on the label. "They felt that they wouldn't be the center of attention," he says. Madness saw it differently. "A deputation of them came to see me," recalls Chris Poole, "and said, 'Can't you persuade Chrysalis to sign us? We're desperate to stay here.' We didn't because Doug thought that the Selecter were the group that would be more successful. I thought they were great, but I didn't think that they had the commercial possibilities that Madness had."

Offering a rather different explanation, John Hasler says Madness did not sign to Chrysalis because one of the band insulted Leo Sayer at *Top of the Pops*. "That was it," he says. "They weren't interested after that. There was a lot of damage-limitation going on because they could be quite rude to journalists. They didn't mince their words. They weren't there to sell themselves and there was a healthy dose of arrogance involved. It got quite difficult at times. Chris and Mike seemed to think that they were running things. They'd turn up at record companies without an appointment: 'We've got a band. We're in the charts. We've arrived.' I was getting phone calls: 'Who the fuck are these people!' One day, Lee Thompson came into Trigger going, 'The lads have been talking. You're not doing enough.' He said, 'Off you go,' and sat in for me. When I came back, he said, 'Keep it. It's too busy.' The phone was going all the time: journalists, record companies. You had to keep it all spinning. It's like relationships. The person you fancy isn't always the person that fancies you. It's about getting the right one."

If Chrysalis had signed Madness, Chris Foreman says, "we would have done an album on 2 Tone. So Chrysalis lost out. Every record company was after us and offered us loads of money. But we thought, 'That's not what it's all about.' They couldn't see much further than 'ska' band." On one occasion, Mark Bedford recalls visiting one particular record company. "They said, 'Ah, right, you're . . . er . . . um . . . you're . . . er . . . Madness, aren't you?' We said, 'Yeah.' They said, 'Right, you've got a record in the charts.' We said, 'Yeah.' 'What is it?' It was like, 'Terry, go out and get a copy of the Madness record, would you?' We thought, 'It's not the company for us.'"[69]

On September 3, 1979, after much deliberation, Madness signed to Stiff after performing at the wedding reception of managing director Dave Robinson.* Earlier in the year, Robinson had signed the Equators, an all-Black, ska-influenced band from Birmingham whom he had seen supporting local group the Beat. Now, as far as Robinson was concerned, Madness were in competition with the Specials. He rushed the band into the studio to record their debut album, and

---

* Madness signed as a six-piece. Chas Smash was kept on a retainer.

Madness arrived just as the Specials left. "When we got there," says engineer Alan Winstanley, "there were some tapes lying around so we had a quick listen—just to check." "It actually sounded completely different," says producer Clive Langer. "We were always aware of competition and what was going on. Being in a band is competitive, like football: they're your mates but it's a creative competition, one ups the other."

Upping the ante, Dave Robinson insisted that John Hasler leave the 2 Tone office. "It was a big mistake," says Hasler. "The Specials were not our competition. They were our honeypot. We were in the hive together. If somebody goes out and buys a Specials LP with their pocket money this week, they're going to buy a Madness record next week and then the Selecter the week after. You might have a favorite band, but you'd still get the stuff that was part of the scene. Robinson really pumped the Specials as the enemy. It was ludicrous." Seeing it both ways, Mike Barson reasons, "We picked up a lot of ideas from the Specials. But when we first started, you're just two two-bob bands and you're thinking, *Oh, I like them*, and maybe copying them. So sometimes we'd be looking up to the Specials and thinking, 'We want to be like them,' and other times we'd be thinking, 'We don't want to be like the fucking Specials. We're better than them. We've got better songs.'" Less vitriolic, perhaps, Suggs pulls out a fitting metaphor. "The Specials were playing a tuba and we were playing a trumpet: theirs was more deeply resonating, but you could still hear ours from a distance!"

Visiting Madness at TW Studios, Dave Robinson heard "One Step Beyond" and exclaimed, "That's the first single!" It was barely a minute long, and Robinson overrode a flood of objections and instructed Alan Winstanley to remix it. "Double it up," he insisted. "Make it twice the length. Make it sound different on the second time around." Complaining that it would take all night, Winstanley quickly copied the song twice over and processed the second half of the track through a harmonizer as a demonstration. "Then before we knew it," he says, "Dave mastered the track, cut it and pressed it. So we never actually remixed it."

Originally recorded by Prince Buster in 1964—as the B-side to "Al Capone"—"One Step Beyond" was a different song fed through Madness's rhythm section. Playing a straight rock beat across a 6/8 feel, Woody's drumming nodded to ska but lent the track a modern, distinctive touch, punctuated with a little roll and a whack on the rim. Further distinguishing themselves on an album—also titled *One Step Beyond*—of sixteen tracks, Madness presented a veritable feast of pop as much in thrall to classic English songwriting traditions and American R&B as ska or reggae.

Within the same week, Madness landed in the top ten of both the single and album charts. "Entertaining but temporary," cautioned *Smash Hits*, "likable but short-lived. The sound of fashion. Good visuals, jolly 'allo myte' Chas 'n' Dave style vocals, busy instrumental touches, matey honky-tonk music with distinctly dubious lyrics about knicker knocking—more personality than real songwriting talent." Awarded an underwhelming 6/10, a *Sounds* review was at best noncommittal and, ironically, like the aforementioned review, criticized the enduring strength of the record: "capturing the essence of teenage working-class London: a bluebeat base from too many Saturday nights beneath plastic palm trees mixed with breezy love songs and Cockney character sketches, the whole lot embellished by their striving after the Nutty Sound . . ."

Packed with hits—"Night Boat to Cairo," "One Step Beyond," "My Girl," "Bed and Breakfast Man"—and rerecordings of their 2 Tone sides—"The Prince" and "Madness"—the group had little to worry about. *One Step Beyond* would spend over a year on the album chart and establish Madness as the foremost UK pop band of the eighties. Their relationship with 2 Tone was no longer contractual. But in the eye of the public—not least in the album's monochrome cover—they would remain every inch a part of the label's immediate and foreseeable future.

CHAPTER 15

A SHOW OF GLADNESS

THE BEAT. UB40. TEARS OF A CLOWN

One day in 1978, David Steele saw an ad in his local paper, the *Newport News*. It caught his eye. "Bass player needed to form a group with original songs—to shake some action." Recognizing the subtle nod to the Flamin' Groovies song "Shake Some Action," the seventeen-year-old Steele responded. He was the only one. Relieved, Dave Wakeling, who had written the ad with his friend Andy Cox, commented, "David must have been the only living bass player on the Isle of Wight. Most of the people there were very rich and over fifty. There were no Jamaicans. But there was one Indian fellow who worked on the buses. And he was a novelty."[70]

Steele had edited a punk fanzine and witnessed the Rock Against Racism Carnival at Victoria Park featuring the Clash and Steel Pulse. He had also written two songs: "Twist and Crawl" (cowritten with his friend Dick Bradsell) and "Mirror in the Bathroom." When he played them to Wakeling and Cox, he remembers them saying, "These are good. Maybe you should come to Birmingham and we'll get a band together." Emitting a hearty laugh, Steele says, "I don't think they ever expected me to turn up."

Working class but educated at King Edward VI Camp Hill Grammar School, Birmingham, Wakeling says he may have talked "different from the other lads in the street" but "enjoyed the ambiguity" of his mixed Birmingham accent. After befriending Andy Cox at college, the pair relocated to the Isle of Wight to build solar panels for Cox's brother-in-law. Living in a cliff-top cottage close to the Blackgang Chine theme park, Andy taught Dave how to play guitar. In September 1978, when they moved back to Birmingham, Steele followed. To earn money they found jobs—Wakeling on a building site, Cox in a factory, and Steele as a trainee psychiatric nurse—and set about expanding the group lineup. While Cox posted an ad for a Maureen Tucker–style drummer who could play reggae, Steele asked his work colleagues at All Saints Hospital. "There's this bloke who mends my car whose name is Everett," one nurse told him. "I'll send him round."

When he was fifteen, Everett Morton left St. Kitts to live in England. He harbored ambitions to be a drummer and would practice with a rolled-up newspaper. "Drums are very noisy," he explains, "so I'd settle the papers on my bed like a snare and tom-tom and just practice." By day, Everett worked in a kettle-spinning factory. He did so for twelve years. By night, he played in soul and reggae bands, and once sat in on a session with Joan Armatrading. "Her family and my mother were best friends. She was playing in Handsworth and I just did one thing with her." Meeting Cox, Steele and Wakeling, twenty-seven-year-old Everett listened as they played their songs on two acoustic guitars and a bass amplified through a little speaker. When they finished, he asked, "Are you sure it's a reggae drummer you want?" What he thought was: *They're terrible. It's all over the place. It's just three guys strumming and making a lot of noise.* Desperate to play drums, Everett agreed to come to a proper rehearsal the following week. It was little better. However, he had made an impression. "When I left they followed me to my Austin Maxi and said, 'Are you going to come back? Please come back.'" He did.

By late 1978, David Steele thought punk had become "boring" and "self-indulgent," while reggae was getting "soft" and "commercial." "We wanted a cross between the two—the excitement plus a bit of rhythm." Then, in December, Birmingham's popular city center nightclub Barbarella's closed down. It led to an increase in private parties. "People kept playing *Tighten Up Volume 2*," says Dave Wakeling, "so people got to looking in secondhand shops [for ska and reggae]. It was great—there was tons of these records at five pence each. And so we started playing them."[71] A fan of the exhilarating noise of punk and the hypnotic quality of reggae, Wakeling imagined combining the two into something both rhythmic and danceable. "Punk and reggae worked really well together. Rock'd get people up and dancing and reggae'd keep them moving." To this point, Wakeling, Cox, Steele and Morton had kept their strictly reggae numbers apart from their punk-influenced songs. Now the idea dawned on them to move them toward each other. In doing so, they discovered punky reggae. "The key was Everett," insists David Steele. "We'd already got our sound. We couldn't really change how we played so we had to find a way to stick it all together. It was an accident. Dave's not wrong but it wasn't so thought out."

Practicing weekly, the quartet attempted to blend a new wave sound with Everett's straight-four-on-the-bass-drum reggae beat. "We would have been doing 'Whine and Grine' and 'Jackpot,'" says Steele. "We moved to him and he moved to us." A month in, they decided to have a "big" sit-down talk. "Our rehearsals were half practice, half psychotherapy," explains Steele. "For the music to come together there had to be that social coming together as well." Frustrated by the practical lack of progress, Everett suggested doing a song that they all knew. They hit upon "The Tears of a Clown." Originally a transatlantic number one for Smokey Robinson & the Miracles in 1970, the burst of Motown pop cemented the sound of the flowering foursome.

Soon after, Andy Cox saw a gig advertising a local band called the Dum Dum Boys. Cox contacted the group and asked if his group could open for them. After Cox was told they would have to audition, what happened next would change the course of their lives. When they arrived at the Dum Dum Boys's rehearsal room above the Socialist Workers Bookshop next to Digbeth Civic Hall and plugged into their amps, Ranking Roger (then a drummer) recalls the four-piece playing "a loose version of 'Mirror in the Bathroom,' then 'Twist and Crawl,' 'Best Friend' and lastly 'Save It for Later.' I was like, 'Fuck me! We don't stand a chance!'"

Roger Charlery's parents had emigrated to England in the fifties with a plan to work and save enough money to go back to St. Lucia. "The system never paid enough," says Roger. "All the families I knew in our neighborhood were just hanging on." Schooled predominantly among white children, Roger says he recalls one teacher telling him, "'If it wasn't for us lot you'd be still walking around in grass skirts, and you wouldn't know how to use a knife and fork.' I was horrified!" When Roger was thirteen, he had a dream: "I could see a small circular room and people were standing up and clapping and I could see myself bowing. I woke up and I said to myself, *I'm going to be an entertainer. One day I will be famous, and I will be called Ranking Roger.*" He did and he was.

By sixteen, Roger stood over six feet tall and claimed to be the first Black punk in Birmingham. Dressed in a ripped Union Jack flag, bondage trousers and with orange spiked dreadlocks, he made a name for himself on the local scene MCing over records in pubs and at Rock Against Racism events. "Reggae was saying 'Chant Down Babylon' and punk 'Anarchy in the UK,'" he explains. "They shared the same attitudes." One night when the Damned were booked to play at Barbarella's, a group of skinheads started chanting "Sieg heil, Sieg heil" and "National Front" in front of the stage. In desperation, the DJ, Mike Horseman, turned to Roger and said, "You've got to say something to them." Picking up the microphone, Roger started toasting in time with the music, "Fuck off, fuck off, de National Front. Fuck off, fuck off, de National Front." The crowd picked up the chant. "Next thing, there was a riot: people fighting and throwing bottles, and antifascist punks attacking the National Front. Mike and I had to duck down behind the decks. After that I decided that I was going to do everything within my power to put a stop to racism."

On March 31, 1979, Roger watched Wakeling, Cox, Steele and Morton play their first gig at the Matador supporting his band, the Dum Dum Boys. The crowd went crazy. When they played a second gig at the New Inn in Balsall Heath, Roger saw them play again. Watching them whip through a version of Prince Buster's "Rough Rider,"

Roger had a sudden and urgent desire to toast with them. "You would see Roger performing in the audience," says Dave Wakeling. "Before I'd spoken to him, he jumped onstage, grabbed the microphone and started toasting."

The band still had no name, so Dave looked up "music" in a thesaurus. "The first thing I saw on the other side of the page in the antonyms was 'clash.' I thought, *This is fertile ground!* Then I saw the word 'flam'—I read it too quick and I thought it said 'sham.' *Woah! This is really fertile:* two *great band names* [Sham 69 and the Clash]." Looking in the antonyms under "harmony," Dave then read the word "beat." "We were named after the Clash," says Roger. "In the thesaurus, 'clash' is to *beat* two things together. It was very clever."

When the newly named Beat began a weekly residency at the Mercat Cross, behind the Digbeth bus station in the meat market, Roger, having left the Dum Dum Boys, became a regular. It was organized by John Mostyn, who had regularly attended the group's earliest gigs and was now helping to organize "stuff." The music agent says, "The first one we did we had about seventy people, the second one about a hundred. The third one I had to call the police! It was all word-of-mouth." In an attempt to attract wider support, Mostyn invited the social secretary from Aston University. When she was impressed by what she saw, Mostyn seized the moment. "Wouldn't they be great for your ball?" he asked her. "Yes," she replied, "but no one knows who they are." Then playing his trump card, Mostyn suggested, "'Why not have them and a Radio 1 DJ? Like John Peel?' When she said yes, I knew we were off!"

In May, exactly as Mostyn had hoped, the Beat supported John Peel at the university end-of-term ball. Watching the Beat perform, Peel was flabbergasted: "This has to be the greatest, the best band in the universe!" he exclaimed to anyone within earshot, before insisting that the group return to the stage and repeat their set over. Still not satisfied, Peel demanded the Beat swap their payment of £80 for his: a cool £360. "That was a special night," smiles Mostyn. "There were five hundred students who had no idea what they were about to see, and they went completely barking. They'd heard 'Gangsters' and sud-denly here was a band in front of them just as good as the Specials." Flushed with excitement, the Beat invited the Radio 1 DJ to sample a balti at their favorite curry house a short trip from the city center. Belly full, Peel left the restaurant only to discover the theft of his van. "It had a load of records in it," says Mostyn. "I remember just dying of embarrassment."

Bad luck followed. In rehearsal, the Beat read an article in *Melody Maker* about 2 Tone. Throwing the paper onto the floor in disgust, Andy Cox says, "I thought our chances were ruined. Two bands—Madness and the Specials—doing exactly the same thing but already getting recognition."[72] Acting decisively, John Mostyn sent a demo tape to 2 Tone and invited Jerry Dammers to see the Beat play at the Mercat Cross. When Jerry saw Ranking Roger onstage, his thoughts returned to an episode at Barbarella's a year earlier. He recalled Roger toasting over "I'm an Upstart" by the Angelic Upstarts, and the night continuing when a crowd of people had walked across town to Polly-anna's, a nightclub on Newhall Street that was notorious for its racist door policy; Roger was refused entry. Striking up a conversation out-side the venue, Roger had told Jerry about his band the Dum Dum Boys. "He said he would come to our next gig, supporting UB40 be-hind Digbeth Civic Hall. He came but we were terrible."*

In fact, Roger had only recently spurned an opportunity to join UB40, as he explains: "They were playing the New Inn in Moseley and I went up onstage with them and brought the house down. This was before Astro was in the band. They wanted me to come and do more with them, but I thought their music was too mellow. The Beat was more punk—more versatile and aggressive." With two bands of-ten sharing a bill, it was not until a meeting held in the summer that Roger chose the Beat over UB40. "They said to me, 'You've been quiet. Is there anything you want to say?' I said, 'Well, I've been hang-

---

* Unaware of the Specials until the release of "Gangsters," Roger once attempted to MC with the group at Cannon Hill Park. "There was a stage invasion and I jumped on the stage. I was just about to grab the microphone and do my little eight bars and they stopped because a wall collapsed."

ing around with you guys for a while. I want to know if I'm in or if I'm out?' They said, 'It's obvious! You're in or you wouldn't be here.' There was a big roar of laughter and that was it. I became the fifth member of the Beat."

Impressed by what he had seen, Jerry offered the Beat a three-week tour opening for the Selecter. Not so, says Neol Davies. When the Beat was booked to open for the Selecter at the Cascade Club in Shrewsbury, Neol says he watched them soundcheck, mouth agape. "I turned to Aitch and said, 'This band should be on 2 Tone.'" Inviting them to come on the road, Neol cautioned, "'We can only give you petrol money. But you can play whatever gigs you want with us.' I then went straight to Jerry and said, 'You've got to hear this band,' before being reminded that Jerry had kept an eye on the Beat since Ranking Roger joined the lineup several months earlier."

Over the summer, the Beat and the Selecter played together in Blackpool, Sheffield and the Midlands. On September 23, the mini-tour arrived at the Nashville Rooms in London. "It was a big thing," recalls David Steele. "Those gigs were so fast and so amazing: the whole buzz and excitement. We'd been playing in little pubs to about twenty people and then it was fifty, then a hundred, and now it was five hundred and another five hundred people outside. I think Madness came."

Terrified to see hundreds of skinheads shouting, "Sieg heil," and doing Nazi salutes in the crowd, Ranking Roger says the atmosphere was similar to a football match. "I was like, 'The first coin that's thrown at me I'm down in that audience.'" Full of nerves and trepidation, the Beat stumbled through the first song, "Whine and Grine." Watching from the side of the stage, Desmond Brown was fuming. When they came offstage, he cornered Andy Cox. "Don't you ever fucking do that again. If you get scared of an audience, you can just forget about being in a group or anything." Backstage, a contingent of skinheads came to talk to the band. "We were like, take a deep breath here then," says Dave Wakeling. "They said, 'We liked that: Black geezers and white geezers onstage together. It's alright.' We were like, 'Oh! Well, yes, if you like it, we did it on purpose!' In Birmingham," Wakeling continues, "it wasn't seen as anything special. Nobody mentioned that there were people of different color in the band." Looking on, wide-eyed, Roger says, "We were all going, 'London is fucking heavy.'"

Three weeks later, on October 13, the Beat supported the Selecter at the Electric Ballroom. At the end of the night, Jerry Dammers appeared backstage carrying a briefcase and a big smile on his face. "We want you to do the next 2 Tone single!" he hollered to huge whoops and cheers. "It was like a fairy story," says David Steele. "Put a single out on the best label in the world? 'YES, PLEASE! WE CAN DO THAT!' Then Jerry added an unexpected condition: 'We've got to do it quick. If you can do it in a week, we can get it out before Christmas.' We were like, 'WHAT!'"

When the Beat revealed in a television interview that they had come to fame after sending a cassette to 2 Tone headquarters, Jerry received hundreds of demos from bands desperate to sign to the country's hot property. "There were some hilarious cassettes. There was one and they were singing, *2 Tone is terrific, it really turns me on.* It was great. The chorus went, *Terry and Jerry.*" One serious contender was an eight-piece reggae band from Birmingham named after the unemployment benefit form for new claimants. British and multiracial, UB40 played their first gig in February 1979 and shared a mutual passion for ska, reggae and soul. Their highly original and politicized left-wing lyricism soon attracted attention from members of the Specials and the Selecter. Obtaining a copy of a three-track cassette, they auditioned UB40 on the 2 Tone tour bus. "When I heard, *I'm a British subject not proud of it / While I carry the burden of shame*, we got really confused," says Lynval Golding. "We didn't realize it was a white guy singing. It makes sense a Black British guy." Charley Anderson was also surprised. Taking Golding to see them play at a pub in Birmingham, he says, "We realized that they were white guys and Syrians and all different kinds of nationalities, Blacks and whites. I thought that this was a real 2 Tone band, playing soft, cool reggae. So I got UB40 to support us at the Lyceum, their first major gig in London."[73]

Now, Jerry admits it was a mistake not signing UB40. "I thought 2 Tone should build on its slightly twisted retro-ska identity. They were more like straightforward current reggae and I thought it might confuse the identity. I was also uneasy about the lyrics to 'King.' It was a beautiful tune but, *King, where are your people now? Chained and pacified, you tried to show them how and for that you died,* was hinting that Martin Luther King's policy of nonviolence might have been wrong, whereas it achieved a great deal." Whether 2 Tone turned down UB40 or the group simply had other plans is still a matter of conjecture. "I know Jerry thinks he turned us down," wrote Brian Travers on UB40's message board, indignant after years of unsolicited connection with 2 Tone, "but we wouldn't pass on a major label (EMI) to sign with a keyboard player (with no advance money) who was already under too much pressure. Truth is we were always going to develop our own label so needed the right deal to start with . . . and NO we would never have signed to 2 Tone. It was a complete shambles that made a few good records. We didn't want to be bagged with the 'ska' thing. We had our own ideas . . . loved the 2 Tone scene for entertainment but we took our work very serious and it was obvious it was going to burn out along with all the people associated."

Labeled in the press as one of a handful of new bands formed in the slipstream of 2 Tone, UB40 nevertheless benefited from a glut of exposure. "The whole business really pissed me off," drummer Jim Brown told *Record Mirror.* "Another ska band! Another Birmingham band! Every time we played anywhere, we were advertised as being straight off the 2 Tone Tour, just lumping us in with all the rest. We all like the Specials, the Beat and all the others, good luck to them. I don't begrudge them a thing—yet coming from the same place at the same time doesn't mean you have to be another clone band."

Decided by a vote, Rick Rogers says, 2 Tone was the obvious home for the Beat. "Where else would they have fitted?" he asks rhetorically. "They knew it, and as soon as we knew them, *we* knew it." Similarly convinced, Juliet de Vie says, "It was a no-brainer. UB40 were more of a traditional, laconic reggae band but with very clear politics. 2

Tone was still working out its politics. The Beat had Ranking Roger jumping around all over the place: this kid who looked amazing. He absolutely summed up that youthful energy of 2 Tone. He was Black, joyous and brought a huge smile and an open heart."

The toast of the town, the Beat accepted an invitation to record a coveted John Peel session. When they were called to the BBC studios in Maida Vale, producer Bob Sargeant recalls the group being "quite nervous." Born in Newcastle, Sargeant had enjoyed a stint as a musician playing with Mick Abrahams (of Blodwyn Pig and Jethro Tull), before finding employment with the BBC as a freelance producer. "It was an eight-track studio and we did five songs: 'Tears of a Clown,' 'Ranking Full Stop,' 'Big Shot,' 'Click Click' and 'Mirror in the Bathroom.' Talk about danceability; it was a hundredfold. The rhythm section rocked: they were really solid. You had your foot tapping all of the time." By six o'clock, and safe in the knowledge that all the tracks had been successfully recorded, the group decamped to the canteen. "John [Mostyn] bought me a cup of tea and a sticky bun," recalls Sargeant. "Then he said, 'We've got a single to do. The band seems happy with what you've done here today. Would you consider doing it?' I said, 'I'd be delighted!'"

After being told that they had "the 2 Tone sound," any sense of complacency was shattered when Jerry then requested the Beat record "Mirror in the Bathroom" as the first single. Convinced the song was not ready, David Steele says, "The arrangement was still growing," adding that neither guitarist, Dave nor Andy, "wanted to do a solo." Three days before the session, the Beat found their answer: Lionel Augustus Martin. In return for his initiation into live punk, Everett Morton took three of his bandmates to the Crompton Arms in Handsworth to savor the delights of a popular local Jamaican musician. "I said, 'Alright, now come to my den to see where my music is coming from.'" Looking on, the white trio were mesmerized by the sound coming from an aging saxophonist. Vowing that if they ever got good enough, Dave announced, "It would be amazing to have him in the band."

Saxa onstage with the Beat, Rock Garden, London, November 8, 1979.

Born in the parish of Clarendon, Jamaica, Lionel Augustus Martin (known to all as Saxa) was a graduate of the Alpha Boys School with Rico Rodriguez. Coming to England in the late 1950s, Saxa played in various pickup bands, touring with the likes of Desmond Dekker and Laurel Aitken and, as he frequently boasted, jamming with a budding Beatles in Liverpool at a late-night blues. With no time to waste, the group introduced themselves and asked Saxa to come and play with them at a party in Selly Oak. "I got in the van and there was this old guy sitting on the backseat wearing a floppy hat and earrings," recalls Ranking Roger. "He was at least thirty years older than me, and somebody said, 'This is Saxa. He's a friend of Everett's.'" At the soundcheck, asked if he wanted to know what key the song was in, Saxa responded, "Cha!" and kissed his lips. "You just play and me'll blow." Stunned by his rudeness, Roger muttered to himself, "'Who is this loudmouth?' He was friendly enough but he was loud and insistent: 'Get me another drink. What time are we going on?' He was a proper old Jamaican guy. Then he took out his saxophone and started warming up. I instantly felt my irritation melting; it was the way he blew the horn. It sounded like water drops. He had this warm, unique sound but all I could hear him saying was, 'Get me another brandy.'"

Onstage, Saxa was in his element. "You couldn't stop him," continues Roger. "It sounded amazing. He was playing jazz mixed in with calypso over punky reggae and improvised riffs. We came offstage and he said, 'You boys are the band for me. I've waited all my life for you boys. Me drop dead onstage with you. We's boys' musicians.'" Equally effusive, Dave Wakeling raved to *Smash Hits* about their newest member bringing a fresh feel to the sound. "Suddenly you could have a punky song and you'd get a slow mournful jazz solo played over it that really puts it in a different vein. The first time I heard 'Mirror in the Bathroom' with sax on it, I thought, *Oh yeah! That's what the song's about!* It clearly gave it a whole new meaning."[74]

Having found the missing link, the Beat readied themselves to record for 2 Tone. "We thought about doing one of our own songs but we had to be sure about the single," said Dave Wakeling. "It had to have impact so we were confident of doing well." Reasoning that "Tears of a Clown" better suited the 2 Tone ethos, John Mostyn adds, "We weren't going to give them our best song ['Mirror in the Bathroom'], nor Chrysalis the publishing rights for the next five years." Conscious of releasing a single late in the year and by a new band, David Steele says, "We knew we wouldn't have much time to get people to listen to the song, so we'd have to do one that they already knew, and 'Tears of a Clown' had already been going down well live. We'd always thought 'Mirror in the Bathroom' would be our single but it had quite depressing lyrics, hard lyrics, and it would have taken a few weeks for people to get into it, and right before Christmas it would probably have got lost."

Further reasoning that Madness played "Tears of a Clown" live, Andy Cox divulged to the *New Musical Express* that, if not the Beat, then another 2 Tone band would surely record the song. "I mean," he said, "the Merton Parkas have got a really terrible version and it could also be rereleased, so if we don't do it now, we may lose our chance."[75] More revealing, and contrary to popular memory, Ranking Roger claimed in an interview with *Record Mirror* in January 1980 that an-other song, "Ranking Full Stop," was to be the Beat's first single. "We tried to record it but it just didn't work out, so we had to put back the re-lease date. With Christmas only a few weeks away we decided to release 'Tears of a Clown' because we thought it would pick up more airplay."

Alluding to an aborted recording session at Horizon Studios, here, once again, memories are inconsistent. John Mostyn says the session was with Roger Lomas. For his part, Lomas says he cannot ever remember working with the Beat. Meanwhile, Bob Sargeant claims the session took place in the first week of November after John Mostyn said to him, "You don't mind coming up to Coventry to record this, do you?" Adding weight to his recollection, Sargeant tells a culinary anecdote with marked attention to detail. "So I made the trip to Coventry. I stayed in a well dodgy bed-and-breakfast called the Raja Guest House. It was cheap and cheerful. Then all through the night, I could hear people going up and down corridors and doors slamming. It went on until six in the morning. I thought, *What the fuck's going on here?* I went down for breakfast the next morning and a guy in a turban walked in and asked if I wanted tea or coffee. I said, 'Coffee, please.' He brought me a bowl that had Heinz baked beans in it, and a bowl of eggs that had been shelled and dropped into the beans, and a spoon. That was breakfast! When I went to Horizon, I hated the place. The drum kit was already set up and had a bass drum the size of a military band. It sounded terrible."

The recording of "Ranking Full Stop" was hampered by technical inefficiency when Roger reached the last line of the song, *I said stop*, and the track played on repeatedly. Defeated, Bob Sargeant turned to the band and said, "I think you should come down to London. I know a studio there back to front." "Yes!" John Mostyn cried from the back of the room. "Let's do it straightaway!" Relocated to Sound Suite in Islington, and with sixteen-track facilities at their disposal, the Beat worked fast. On the first day, the group recorded three takes of "Tears of a Clown" and overdubbed additional guitars and vocal parts. Mixed on day two, "Tears of a Clown"—the definite article now omitted from Smokey Robinson's title—featured a distinctly updated arrangement. Where on the original the introduction included a top line played by a piccolo and a harpsichord, complemented by oboe and bass bassoon, Andy Cox substituted the orchestration with a double-tracked guitar riff. "Keep it simple but melodic," enthused Sargeant, before replicating the guitar figure with an ornate xylophone descant. "The music has to make sense."

When the band turned their attention to "Ranking Full Stop," Dave Wakeling suggested that Roger should record his vocal in the bathroom for its natural echo. Still only sixteen years old at the time, Roger now says, "It was my chance to show my light." Freestyling at the microphone, Roger's youthful energy imbued the song with vigor and dazzling certitude. Dismissing the title as meaningless, Roger says he saw the song more as a dance: *I will really tell you and show you how to do the Ranking Full Stop: you move to your left and then move to your right*. Propelled into action with a dramatic drum roll, Everett Morton likens his trademark fill to "the sound of someone falling down the stairs. I'm left-handed," he says by way of explanation. "You're supposed to lead with your right hand but I lead with my left hand instead. That's what makes it so different."

Both songs complete, the Beat forwarded alternative mixes of "Tears of a Clown" and "Ranking Full Stop" for record company approval. Midway through the 2 Tone Tour, Jerry canvassed opinion by asking the traveling entourage to vote for their favored version. "I've always found that incredible," marvels Dave Wakeling. "Anybody can have their say in the running of the 2 Tone organization."[76] But one person not impressed was Laurel Aitken. Hearing "Ranking Full Stop," the Jamaican singer declared it a copy of his own song "Pussy Price" and threatened to take legal action. "I said, 'You tell me where your lyrics are on there?'" spits Ranking Roger. "It sounded nothing like our tune." Yet, another song, "Mr. Full Stop—written by Eddy Grant and recorded by the Original Africans in 1967—shared lyrical similarities. "I'd never heard 'Mr. Full Stop,'" remonstrates Roger. Then seemingly contradicting himself, he says that the Beat used to play "Mr. Full Stop" in their early days. "Dave said, 'Here you go, Roger. These are the lyrics.' I was like, 'What do you mean, these are the lyrics? You want me to toast another man's words. I can't do that. I've got my own style.'" Insistent that the likeness was coincidental, David Steele argues, "It's three chords, so it's a lot of songs. We did a few cover versions like that, the Jolly Brothers's 'Conscious Man' and 'Sweet and Dandy' by the Maytals, but they never quite worked out."

As 2 Tone pressed ahead with its release, the reaction was instant. Only a few months earlier, the Beat had played to small audiences, grateful to the few people who danced. Abruptly, all that changed. "Everyone went mad, right from the start," David Steele reflected after a gig at the Electric Ballroom. "Yet we were exactly the same group playing exactly the same stuff."[77] Dave Wakeling recalls the group going down badly on another occasion and the audience shouting. "So we announced that the next song was 'an old mod number' and they went crazy, dancing like fuck!"

Ad for the "Tears of a Clown" single, December 1979. Courtesy of Chrysalis Records/ Jerry Dammers.

* * *

On December 8, 1979, "Tears of a Clown"—coupled with "Ranking Full Stop"—entered the UK chart at number sixty-seven. Unconcerned by its lowly position, John Mostyn waited patiently, confident success would only be a matter of time. "We did our first *Top of the Pops* and two days later the record jumped to number thirty-one." The band were ecstatic. "It was bigger than getting the vinyl," says David Steele. "We grew up with *Top of the Pops*. It was surreal. It was like being on *Star Trek* and entering another world. We didn't have this long period of getting the band together, touring, finding members and writing new songs. Suddenly it just went BAM! It was like a silent film speeded up."

At the beginning of the year, Ranking Roger was a schoolboy. Nine months later, here he was on national television. "I remember the warm-up presenter saying to the audience, 'Twenty million people will be watching when this program is broadcast . . .' I was like, 'Woah! That's a third of the population!'" Introducing the band, DJ Mike Read reminded viewers of Smokey Robinson & the Miracles's number one success with "The Tears of a Clown," adding, "There's a new version out which is heading in that direction by a great new group . . . it's the Beat!" As the camera slowly zoomed in on the stage, the entire band began to dance, except one. "I didn't know what to do," says Roger. "Then I remembered being told by the floor manager, 'Make sure you smile.' All of a sudden I was grinning like a Cheshire cat!"

Soon after, the band received a telegram from Smokey Robinson. It read: "I have heard six different versions of 'Tears of a Clown' already this year. May I congratulate you on recording the best version." The record-buying public seemingly agreed. Week by week, the single climbed the charts, holding its own against the rush of Christmas releases, until in the second week of January it leapfrogged over David Bowie, the Three Degrees and the Police and landed at number six. After being playlisted on BBC Radio 1, the Beat received a second invitation to appear on *Top of the Pops*. "The problem was getting Everett to do it because he wouldn't quit his job at the kettle-spinning factory," says John Mostyn. "He said to me, 'I'll quit when we've got *Top of the Pops.*' When I said, 'We're recording Wednesday,' he handed in his notice the next day." Exuding confidence, Roger ditched his stage leathers and bondage trousers and stepped into the 2 Tone look. "I bought a shirt and a trilby and a secondhand green-and-purple-tinted tonic suit," he recalls. "At the BBC, a cameraman said to me, 'When you sing, *Tears of a clown I'm going down de town*, blow this party popper.'" Happy to comply, Roger danced freely onstage, prompting DJ Peter Powell to declare at the end of the performance, "They are something else!"

CHAPTER 16

CALLING RUDE GIRLS

THE BODYSNATCHERS. TOO MUCH PRESSURE

S tanding in the hot and sweaty basement of the Hope & Anchor in April 1979, Nicky Summers watched the Specials,
gobsmacked. Dancing solidly for an hour, there and then she
knew she had to form an all-girl ska band. But nine months earlier,
when the Coventry Automatics supported the Clash at the Music
Machine, Nicky had been unmoved. "They didn't set you alight. They
were interesting and a bit art school. They didn't sound like how they
became. When they became the Specials, they totally transformed.
They blew me away."

Born in Hackney, Nicky would often help on her father's green-
grocer's stall in Berwick Street Market, mixing with customers like
Lynne Franks and Paul McCartney. Leaving school with the intention to study modern languages at the Polytechnic of Central London, Nicky then declined their offer. "I remember being fifteen, sixteen,
seventeen, and being so tremendously bored. We were bored teenagers. *Top of the Pops* had gone stale. A whole generation was waiting for
something. There were no jobs. We had electricity blackouts, garbage
strikes. There were riots in Notting Hill. Something had to happen.
Something had to give."

That something was punk rock. Empowering a generation in music, art and fashion, it demanded destruction of the old order and the
creation of something new. "In those days girls rarely played electric

guitars," says Nicky. "Growing up there weren't girl bands. There was always this idea that men would take over or start directing you. I wanted an all-woman band to make a statement. It was very difficult to get together. Everybody said: 'How do you do it?' I didn't know." Inspired by the Slits—three women and (on record) one man—and the fusion of fashion and energy wrapped up in the Specials's live show, Nicky placed a series of ads in the music press.

RUDE GIRL types (guitar(s) with noisy vocals, drums) sought by similar bassist (rudimentary but improving) Ska, rock, reggae, early punk ideas for fast, emotive, danceable stuff. Sharp Brains Around 20 years. 01-886 9775 (Nicola).

FEMALE INSTRUMENTS/vocals needed for all girl group. Bluebeat, Reggae, early sixties danceable stuff. Must rehearse. No time wasters. Box No. 3798.

Ads placed by Nicky Summers in *NME*, May 26, 1979, and July 21, 1979.

"All I got was three months of dirty phone calls," says Nicky. "I thought a lot of girls would want to do it, but it didn't seem that way." After what felt like an interminable period of waiting, Jane Summers, a drummer and part-time lifeguard, responded. Having recently relocated from Dover, Jane arrived in London wearing a fake leopard-skin coat and bright-red lipstick, looking like, says Nicky, "a young Shirley MacLaine." Jane and Nicky hit it off and moved in together. "Jane assured me she had a drum kit, but I never saw it for six months," laughs Nicky. Next, they met Stella and Sarah-Jane.

Born in the naval town of Portsmouth, Sarah-Jane Owen says that both her parents could carry a tune and would "gather round the piano" on Sundays. As a child, Sarah-Jane had piano lessons and for her twelfth birthday requested an acoustic guitar. "That's an awfully strange thing to want for a girl of your age," her mother told her. First studying at Portsmouth Art College, Sarah-Jane then accepted a place at the Royal College of Art. After creating her own clothing collection while working for Jeff Banks, the *Sunday Times* tipped Sarah-Jane as a "bright young designer." Then, after a period of living in squats and teaching fashion one day a week at St. Martin's School of Art, she saw Nicky's ad in *NME*. "I was dating Pete Carney, who was the lead singer of Way of the West. He lent me his electric guitar and showed me how to pick and play barre chords and use an amp. He figured out the ska upstroke. It was all new to me. That's how I got the gig. I became the lead guitarist by default because I had an ear for playing little lines. I was quite proficient, but to play guitar on an offbeat was a new thing. I had to change my style of playing."

Stella Barker had taught herself to play acoustic guitar when she was fourteen. She studied French and Spanish at Edinburgh University and enrolled at Cambridge Tech to take a bilingual secretarial course. Having dabbled in local bands, Stella left England to work in San Francisco. Returning a year later, she landed a job as a secretary at EMI International in Seymour Mews but left disillusioned after twelve months. "Then I saw this ad in the *Melody Maker*," she says. "I spoke to Nicky and we met in a pub in Waterloo. We had a chat and at the end she said, 'You've got the job.' I thought, *I haven't played guitar!*"

In June 1979, Penny Leyton saw the Specials perform at Canterbury College of Art. "They were incredible," she says. "It was fresh music and had great rhythms. You could dance to it. After the gig, the group asked if anyone had anywhere to stay. I shared a big house so we said, 'We've only got the sitting room floor but you're welcome to it.'" Penny had played classical piano since the age of eight but never an electric instrument. "At school somebody played 'Monkey Spanner' and I remember thinking, *Wow! This is the music for me,* so

I started collecting ska and reggae." Having completed a bachelor's degree, Penny studied at St. Martin's, where she saw an ad for a keyboard player, pinned up by Sarah-Jane. Trembling with nerves, Penny picked up the phone and arranged an audition. "I went along and they had a piano in the rehearsal room, and I played Scott Joplin!"

Now a five-piece, the women extended their search for a brass player. To their surprise, Miranda Joyce suddenly appeared, pushed into the rehearsal room by a young man who practiced in the adjacent room, who announced, "This is my sister." Asked if she could play an instrument, Miranda replied, "No, not yet." Raised in the middle-class surroundings of Hampstead to parents who hosted "dinner parties" and "drank wine," Miranda was a sixth-former at Parliament Hill School and had been dating Mark Bedford from Madness—a pupil at the adjacent grammar school—since she was fourteen. "I was on my way to a summer job as a photographer's assistant and I bumped into a friend of a friend who said, 'Hey, there's a ska girl band starting.' My brother had a saxophone he'd got from the Salvation Army and I'd literally picked it up two weeks earlier. I was like, 'Oh my God, I want to do that!' So I learned how to play the theme from *Hawaii Five-0*, went to the audition and got in."

Six down. One to go. But where to find a singer? After work, Nicky would often go and watch bands in and around central London with her friend Shane MacGowan (later of the Pogues). One night, she saw him talking to a girl of mixed heritage. Intrigued by her striking image, she asked for an introduction. Born in 1959 in Belsize Park, Rhoda Evans De Dakar was registered after her Panama-born father's stage name, Andre Dakar. "I left school wanting to be an actress. My first job was at the Young Vic Theatre working in the order department. Then I was a civil servant on the personal-issue counter in the dole office. I heard the Mo-dettes were looking for a singer and thought, *Should I? Nah!* Then I saw them at Acklam Hall and wished I had." Working weekends in a shop on King's Road, Rhoda dropped in at the Fulham Greyhound one Saturday evening.

"I was chatting with Shane and he introduced me to Nicky. She said, 'Can you sing?' I went, 'Yeah! I sing in the bath.' 'D'you want to be in a band?' I went, 'Yeah, alright.' I thought if Shane knows her, she must be alright." Rhoda had in fact seen Nicky's ad in *Melody Maker* but, having answered many "dodgy ads" in the past, dismissed it. "I thought, *Oh yeah, another one. I won't bother*." Asked why a band rather than pursuing a career on the stage, Rhoda says, "Because singing was much easier than acting but not as demeaning as modeling. You were speaking your own words. It was about showing off."

Sharing her vision to be a female version of the Specials, Nicky laid it on the line from the get-go: "Okay. We're going to go places. Everybody's got to focus. We're not going to muck about. This isn't a hobby. You can't date people and not show up for rehearsal. We're going to be serious about this." Practicing three nights a week on Royal College Street in a basement shared with Adam & the Ants and the Vibrators, Nicky says, "We weren't very slick or professional musically, but that became our sound and reflected how we played." Abundantly aware that 2 Tone was a British take on Jamaican music, Nicky recalls, "You couldn't replicate Black music or a bluebeat record and do it justice. But you could do your contemporary take and put your input and life in it."

Plugging a Dansette record player into a light socket, the girls studiously listened to ska and R&B records—"Time Is Tight," "Monkey Spanner," "007"—to understand what made up the different elements of a song. "We had to figure out whose part was which," says Sarah-Jane. "We would work out what the bassline was doing, what chords and rhythm the guitars were playing. We taught each other structure and how songs formed with an intro, a verse, middle eight, and a bridge into the chorus. We learned a lot in a short amount of time." Enjoying the naivety of it, Miranda says, "It held together on a thread. Had it been all guys I would never have gone for the audition. It's terribly sexist I suppose, but I thought men would be better musicians or more judgmental. All the boys I grew up with who were getting into bands had been playing for years."

At age twenty, Penny was the only group member with knowledge of music theory. "A lot of girls seem to think that if they're in a band they've got to prove themselves instrumentally, or have got to put across some heavy point about sexism or feminism, so that in the end there's no fun in them at all and they end up downright boring."[78] Promoting a sense of fun, Sarah-Jane suggested calling the band Pussy Galore. Nicky was not amused. "It smacks of seventies sexism and dirty old men." Rolling her eyes, Rhoda says, "Now it would be funny; then it was fucking stupid. It was SJ's idea: 'Well, my mum thinks it's to do with James Bond.' I said, 'Yeah, I know. Where does your mum live? In a shed at the bottom of the garden? Fuck off. If you want to call this band Pussy Galore, do it without me.'" Rejecting Soft Cell and the Avengers, Stella suggested the Bodysnatchers, influenced by having recently seen the film *Invasion of the Bodysnatchers*. "It was the name that everyone hated the least," scoffs Rhoda.

After seven weeks of intense rehearsal, the newly named group accepted a slot at the Windsor Castle in west London supporting the Nips, organized by their manager, Howard Cohen, a friend of Nicky's. Advertised as the "Invasion of the Bodysnatchers—the first seven-piece, all-girl dance and beat band in this Galaxy," word quickly spread. In a *Guardian* interview, Terry Hall cheered on the "new seven-piece, all-girl ska band."

Marching across the sticky carpet at the Windsor Castle, the Bodysnatchers plugged in their instruments, assisted by Stella's and Sarah-Jane's respective boyfriends. Over the next thirty minutes, the packed room heard ten songs including "007," "Monkey Spanner," "Double Barrel" and two reggae-fied nursery rhymes: Eric Morris's "Humpty Dumpty" and Neville Hinds's "London Bridge." "My hands froze for the first song and we kind of fell apart toward the end," recalls Nicky. "We were ramshackle and chaotic but people loved it." Sarah-Jane agrees: "It was a little bit out of time but we sounded authentic: the rim shot on the drums sounded like a biscuit tin, and Nicky's Rickenbacker bass had a real low rumble. The sound was straight out of Jamaica." Gig over, the young women stood motionless. "We didn't even know to get off," laughs Sarah-Jane. "We looked at one another saying, 'What do we do now?'" The answer came from the uproarious audience and shouts for more. After the band insisted that they had played all the songs they knew, the crowd demanded the Bodysnatchers play them all again. "So we did that," says Stella. "It was amazing!" The night before, Stella's father, a York-shire farmer, had driven down to London in a VW to help transport the gear. "It became the band van," she says. "I could see him at the back of the pub with a pint in his hand surrounded by punks and a guy with a Mohican. After the gig, I said, 'What did you think, Dad?' He said, 'Not bad, but the beer's too warm.'" Likewise un-moved by the whole affair, Rhoda joshes, "I'd done Shakespeare at the Old Vic so some crappy gig on the Harrow Road didn't impress me much."

Ten days later, on Tuesday, December 4, the Bodysnatchers played a second show at the Windsor Castle, again supporting the Nips. "There were various timings going on so we practiced a lot between the first and second gig," says Nicky. "We played 'Time Is Tight' perfectly and I remember our friend Gaz Mayall saying he was disappointed because he preferred the ramshackle approach." Where the first gig had been regarded as a "tryout to test the water," the sec-ond had the added pressure of Neol Davies, Pauline Black and Jerry Dammers standing up front, and, says Nicky, "Richard Branson run-ning around shrieking: 'Has anyone signed them yet?'" "Straightaway it was Rhoda," says Juliet de Vie. "She jumped out. She looked fantastic and had such a great presence, such strength about her. She was doing a girlie sixties-look thing, but she had this empow-ered feel: very statuesque and composed. They were already a good band."

Sporting a beehive, Rhoda impressed Jerry by telling him, "I am the rudest of all the rude girls because I've got the tallest hair." Sarah-Jane remembers Jerry making his way through the crowd "spitting through his missing front teeth and saying, 'You girls are great!' He was smiling and just full of enthusiasm." Offered a tour slot with the

Selecter, Penny explains, "It was unheard of. But they also said, 'You have to go home and practice.' Basically, we had promise but we were a disaster musically and we had to get better."

News of the Bodysnatchers spread rapidly. At their fifth gig—at the 101 Club in Clapham—Seymour Stein (head of Sire Records) mixed among a horde of expectant journalists and record company scouts hustling for a view of the band. "The Bodysnatchers could be a lazy A&R man's identikit dream," wrote Peter Silverton in *Sounds* a month later. "Reggae. Girls."

On New Year's Eve, the Bodysnatchers saw out 1979 supporting the Selecter at Dingwalls, watched by Lemmy of Motörhead, Shane MacGowan and, barely a month into their gigging career, the first press naysayer. "Unfortunately, the Bodysnatchers, although heading in the right direction, have not yet found a route of their own," wrote an uncharitable Deanne Pearson in the *New Musical Express*. Reproaching the group for following too closely in the footsteps of the "Big Three" (the Specials, Madness, the Selecter) without introducing any new ideas, Pearson condemned the Bodysnatchers for allowing the 2 Tone stamp to hide their personal identity. "There is plenty of room for development but at the moment, with most of their concentration put into finding their way up and down fretboards and keeping in time, there is not much left for experimentation or diversification." Surprisingly, Pearson ended her review on an optimistic note: "The Bodysnatchers are definitely one of the bands to watch out for in 1980."

Made up of six Black members and one white, the Selecter were an experiment in cultural diversity: a unique amalgam of English, Jamaican, St. Kittsian and Ghanaian. "The music was an expression of our mixed-up identities," says guitarist Compton Amanor, "fighting and competing to be heard." Rejecting the notion that reggae was Black music played by Black musicians, and rock was white music played by white people, keyboard player Desmond Brown made a case for the

Selecter representing the underprivileged in society. "We're just like everybody else who is struggling to make something of life. In this situation we can say, 'Look, life is not all money, life is not all fun.' We have the same problems as them; we're operating from their level. That's why we play the music and lyrics we do. Like the line, *I was only having some fun and they come and take me away.* Anybody can relate to that."

Leading into the new decade and fresh from the success of the 2 Tone Tour, the Selecter block-booked Horizon Studios where, over a six-week period, they recorded their debut album, *Too Much Pressure.* Yet, before playing a single note, a disagreement over the choice of producer splintered the group's short-lived honeymoon period. Out went Roger Lomas and in came Errol Ross. "I got stitched up," says Lomas, forty years after producing the Selecter's debut single, "On My Radio." "It was their biggest hit. It sold over 240,000 copies. I should have done their album. It was as simple as that. It was down to Charley Anderson. He got his mate in who was totally unqualified to do the job."* According to Neol Davies, it was a decision made behind his back. "The six of them ganged up on me and told me at Maida Vale when we did our first John Peel session." The result was that six people did not want Roger. "It's not the same as six people wanting Ross," continues Neol. "It was horrible. I had to tell Roger. Both of us had assumed he would produce the album because he'd done such a great job on the single."

Jamaican-born Errol Ross had come to England in 1961 when he was eight years old. But by the midseventies, frustrated with the lack of opportunity in Coventry, he moved to London. Finding work as a studio engineer, he wrote and produced the self-titled album *Take It Easy on Yourself* for the Dutch label Ariola. Invited by bass player Charley Anderson to work with the Selecter, Ross found himself at the center of an unresolved dispute. "If I had produced a hit single and they brought somebody else in I wouldn't be too happy," he concedes. "But I was asked to come and do a job."

---

* Both Mikey Dread (the Clash) and Dennis Bovell (the Slits) were unavailable to produce the album.

Seeing the Selecter play for the first time in Bristol, Ross says, was an unbelievable experience. "The energy was amazing. I thought the balcony was going to collapse. The whole place was bouncing to the same beat, the same rhythm, the same force. I thought, *If we can capture this live energy in the studio, we'll be onto something good.*" Expecting him to put the band at ease and create a healthy working environment, Pauline Black took an immediate dislike to the producer. "I didn't like him after five minutes in his company," she says. "His unctuous demeanor coupled with his hustler mentality did not impress me." Never one to tergiversate, Pauline is unforgiving in her condemnation. "I loathed him. I thought he was full of shit. He single-handedly ruined the sound of our first album."

Forced to work with a producer he not only did not want but had no respect for, Neol claims Ross was out of his depth and lacked any sense of what the Selecter stood for. "He was musically and stylistically in the past. The way he dressed and talked. He was so false and pseudo-hip. He wore flares and a pimp coat [full-length leather]. As a nod to us he got a cheap 2 Tone hat from some market stall. It looked ridiculous."

Drummer Aitch says, "We were all thinking, *Who is this guy?* I realized the mistake when we started recording. He took something on he didn't know how to do." Today, vocalist Gaps maintains he had been in favor of sticking with Lomas, suggesting there was no reason to change producer for somebody with no previous experience. "There was bad feeling around Errol. That stained the atmosphere. Neol and me went into it reluctantly. But it wasn't like down tools or 'I'm going to leave the band.' Everybody was quietly excited with what was happening. That's what kept it together."

Festering resentment unsurprisingly expressed itself in irritation. Aitch complained that the monitor level in the control room was ear-splittingly loud. Compton protested that Ross was too hands-off. "Maybe he could have played more of the producer at times and said, 'You're too busy there,' or, 'You need to lay off there,' or, 'The guitar and drums are fighting each other.' Halfway through the session he brought in one of his own songs and said, 'Hey, try this!' I was stunned. It was like a seventies soul song. It wasn't in the spirit of what we were doing at all."

Speaking to Ross almost four decades after the event, he is reluctant to apportion blame. Rather, he points to a group with very little studio experience. "They had done enough gigs to have the confidence of knowing that their music was working. But then they were faced with four walls, mics and nobody to play to. It took some time for them to adjust." Further observing that "all the raw energy and anger within the Selecter gave the music an edge," Ross singles out Aitch's "very good, tight drumming," Pauline's "incredible voice," Compton's "steady skank rhythm" and Charley's "good bass playing." "But," he contends, "none of them were the greatest musicians. They were able to find the definitive line for the music and they had a fantastic energy together. But the trouble was, at moments everybody wanted to kill each other. We were trying to do some serious work and they were bitching, arguing and fighting. They were at each other's throats and I had to block that all out."

Compton agrees. "Discontent was always part of the band, right from the beginning. It's in the music." While Aitch says, "People took their emotions into the studio . . . a lot of it was captured in the performance but the vibes created a lot of animosity. People argued about the music; everything was taken the wrong way instead of trying to work together and compromise." Assuming a diplomatic position, Gaps argues, "We were getting used to each other, getting used to what it meant to be in a studio, getting used to what the music was actually really about, getting the rhythm and the sounds to sit right. It was a steep learning curve." Adopting a pragmatic approach, Ross suggested recording in shifts. "The band stuff was the band stuff. I had to keep cool and calm and adopt a strictly professional, nonpersonality role. So I said, 'Okay, guys. Today we record this. Get the tracks down. Get out of here. Then let the vocalists come into a fresh atmosphere. You come back to the studio at ten o'clock to hear what I've done.' If they had stayed it wouldn't have got finished."

As the session spilled into January, recording often took second place to outside demands. Yet, against the odds, an album began to take shape. Songs addressed adolescent frustration and male identity ("Street Feeling"—*Shut yer mouth, grit your teeth*), police harassment ("Danger," "Murder"), unemployment and the harsh realities of working life ("Time Hard"*—*Every day things are getting worse*). "The tunes made you think," says Neol, who wrote five of the eight original songs. "Everybody could identify with 'Too Much Pressure' and 'Out on the Streets.' That was the challenge: to write something deeply personal that didn't appear personal or to write a political statement without being sloganeering." As Pauline put it, the album was the musical autobiography of the Selecter: "It was confrontational." Reflecting on her own contributions—"They Make Me Mad" and "Black and Blue," written from commonplace experiences—Pauline explains, "It was saying: are you really going to buy this state bullshit? Are you going to live by those rules or are you gonna find your own philosophy? They were pretty explicit about my feelings toward the world."

The fusion of different cultures and genres spread the palette of influence across the Selecter's album, where ska mixed with disco on "Out on the Streets" and African highlife guitar led the spiritual "Carry Go Bring Come," featuring Rico Rodriguez and Dick Cuthell. By contrast, "My Collie" addressed the legalization of cannabis, humorlessly introduced by Pauline's ad-libbed mock government health warning: "Smoking can seriously damage your brain." Although essentially an updated version of Millie Small's breakthrough ska classic "My Boy Lollipop," the arrangement benefited from a layer of choral voices and, as the track fades, the shouted instruction to "Roll another one!" Writing in *NME*, Paul Du Noyer would later describe

---

* "Time Hard"—originally recorded by the Pioneers in 1972—was the first song the Coventry Automatics ever rehearsed and was later described by Compton Amanor in *Hot Press* as "a bluesy, sad song, which is pretty pessimistic, but if you watch us do it onstage, we're dancing around and bopping to it."

the song as "the group's finest recorded two minutes forty-five seconds so far."

But such platitudes did little to lift a flailing group spirit. Mixed and mastered, the completed album enraged its authors. "We were really unhappy with the production," lambasts Compton. "It didn't capture what we were live. I remember hearing the finished record and thinking, *Is that it? Where's the bass gone?* I resented Errol's production credit, and a lot of the band felt that he hadn't done a job that justified him getting an equal share of the royalties."

Reacting to subsequent decades of abuse and accusation, Ross says the Selecter had fantastic potential but scuppered their chances. "If you are an arsehole and have a shit attitude toward your band members, it don't last. I couldn't understand it. You're on the dole, you're struggling, and suddenly you have a golden ticket. All you have to do is keep a cool head and do your work as a professional. But all the personal stuff and constant fighting ruined a great thing. My memories are bittersweet." For years after, Pauline would oscillate between blaming the producer and deliberating whether in fact the group had recorded an album too early in their career. "I'd love to do those same songs over again," she says ruefully.

Committed to the record, the Selecter turned their attention to the cover artwork and an idea suggested by John Sims in the Chrysalis art department from an Oldham Gold Seal batteries ad. Taken from the 1956 textbook *The Typography of Press Advertisement*, the ad depicted a frustrated motorist leaning against a wall gripping a defunct starting handle, trilby fallen to the floor, and the caption, "The Day My Motor Died at Dawn." Sims's proposal was to update the image and, to avoid potential copyright infringement, cast a model to assume the same pose. "He couldn't get it," says Neol Davies about the photo shoot in Holborn Studios in London. "So a friend of ours, Steve 'Cardboard' Eaton, said, 'Let me have a go,' and that became the famous shot."

(Top left) Ad for Oldham Gold Seal batteries from *The Typography of Press Advertisement*, 1956; (top right) *Too Much Pressure* cover, hand-drawn by Charley Anderson; (bottom) *Too Much Pressure* album sleeve, Canadian issue, 1980. Courtesy of Chrysalis Records.

For the back sleeve, the group posed during soundcheck at Dingwalls on New Year's Eve. Nobody was happy. Complaining that the resulting picture was both too dark and a poor representation of the band, Gaps singles out Aitch's head—"It looked like it was stuck on"—and the image of himself singing in front of a microphone stand when the microphone was in his hand. "It was obviously blotted out." The artwork was in fact a composite of four separate photographs, including a press shot of Aitch dropped in behind the drum kit. Retouched at Chrysalis by artist Bernard Trower, microphone stands and drumsticks disappeared and the faces of the band were airbrushed to make them clearer. "As far as I'm concerned," snapped photographer Rick Mann, "it's a big fake. Why fuck about when they were perfectly good live shots already?"

The album was released in February 1980 to five-star reviews. Vivien Goldman praised the attractive "width and crispness of the sound" while admiring "the way that every single individual's part is distinct and separable, easily picked out and yet blended essentially into the whole. Something for everyone," she told *Melody Maker* readers, "a touch of Dread, some equally natty baldheads, a white boy, plus the most militant Black woman singer in the land." The Selecter may all have rejected the sound of the finished record, but it was a hit. A new entry at number five, *Too Much Pressure* spent thirteen weeks on the national chart, earning each member of the group a gold disc in recognition of 100,000 sales. Much to the chagrin of Chrysalis, the Selecter chose to omit "On My Radio" from the long player and a guaranteed bump in sales. "It was marketing craziness," says Compton. "But the band didn't want to put a single on the album because it would be a commercial thing to do."

Meanwhile, in an apartment in the Dakota building in New York, John Lennon was sitting at a black upright piano as Yoko Ono mumbled the lyrics to a new song. Motioning her to stop, Lennon was insistent the song required a "lively backbeat" to compensate for its lack of melodic variety. Then, as Frederic Seaman (butler/chauffeur) recounted in *The Last Days of John Lennon*, "John suggested trying a ska beat" and asked Seaman to bring him a tape of the Selecter, who they had been listening to on Long Island. "When I brought John the tape, he played it at loud volume, while fiddling with his drum machine, attempting to duplicate the frenetic beat of 'Too Much Pressure.'" Yoko was not interested and "demanded that John turn off the tape player and rhythm box. Gnashing his teeth in frustration, John complied."*

---

* In 1964, the Beatles recorded "I Call Your Name" with a distinct ska influence, and in a 1968, the album track of "Ob-La-Di, Ob-La-Da" with a reggae backbeat. A year later—in 1969—John Lennon and the Plastic Ono Band performed at the Lyceum, supported by a profusion of Black and reggae artists including the Young Rascals, Desmond Dekker & the Aces, Blue Mink, Black Velvet, Jimmy Cliff and Hot Chocolate Band, and Emperor Rosko as DJ between the performances.

CHAPTER 17

AN AUTUMN OF MISUNDERSTANDING

TOO MUCH TOO YOUNG. ELVIS COSTELLO

I980 was the year of middle-distance runners Sebastian Coe versus Steve Ovett at the Moscow Olympics. Sixteen million viewers gripped by the American television series *Dallas*, desperate to know "Who shot J.R.?" At home, Britain braced itself against the first effects of the "Thatcher Experiment" as Geoffrey Howe, chancellor of the exchequer, announced major cuts in public spending. The opposition leader Jim Callaghan called it the most socially divisive budget in fifty years. Inflation doubled to 21.8 percent and the country entered recession. Gas prices soared. Steel and shipbuilding industries collapsed. Unemployment rose to two million. Contemplating another winter of discontent, the prime minister told the Conservative Party conference, "I prefer to believe that certain lessons have been learned from experience, that we are coming, slowly, painfully, to an autumn of understanding. And I hope that it will be followed by a winter of common sense. If it is not, we shall not be diverted from our course."

In 1979, 2 Tone had chalked up five hit singles, launched four new acts and completed a sell-out package tour of the UK. The Specials and Madness topped readers' polls in *NME* while on the back pages 2 Tone-related merchandise flooded the market, offering deals on ties, three-button tonic suits, checkered sweatshirts and sew-on badges. 2 Tone would continue to flourish but challenges on the distant horizon loomed. Alongside the first signs of a new pop dandyism there was a concerning drop in music sales as record companies began to tighten their belts and drop acts, while Decca sacked 1,200 of its staff.

With the Specials very much riding the crest of the wave, 1980 could not have started better for them. In the early hours of January 29, Rick Rogers was woken to the news that "Too Much Too Young" had jumped an unprecedented fifteen places to the top spot in the UK chart. Overcome with joy, Rogers began to leap around his hotel room, much to the disquiet of his roommate, Jerry Dammers. "I woke him up and he was most annoyed," says Rogers, laughing. "He didn't give a toss and went straight back to sleep. It's the only time I've seen an artist genuinely not care about their success." The night before, the Specials had played in Norman, Oklahoma, on the third date of their first American tour. Nursing a hangover, Jerry urged Rogers to calm down. "I just couldn't face it," he says. Undeterred, Rogers popped the cork on a bottle of champagne and went in search of the rest of the band. "It was like, 'Whoa! Jesus Christ! We've got a number one record!,'" says Lynval Golding. "We never saw ourselves in the same league as the Stones or the Beatles or Rod Stewart. I was on top of the world." Clearly shocked, Horace Panter wrote in his tour diary, "I don't believe this. The feeling is tremendous and difficult to put into words. Indestructible is the nearest."[79]

Recorded two months earlier at the Lyceum in London, "Too Much Too Young" was the lead track on a five-song EP. Unlike the plaintive version recorded for their debut album, the live account was fast, furious and intense. It clocked in at a lightning one hundred and twenty-three seconds—only breaking the two-minute barrier courtesy of Terry Hall's three-second introduction, "Too much too young." Horace described it as "so fucking fast—it was like Motörhead!" No wonder. Approaching the end of the 2 Tone Tour, the Specials were at the zenith of their live power. A fortnight later, the group celebrated an incredible year with homecoming performances at Tiffany's in Coventry city center, which Horace says were the best shows he ever played: "The atmosphere was unbelievable." A medley of three songs—"Long Shot Kick de Bucket," "Liquidator" and

"Skinhead Moonstomp"—formed the flip side of the new single. It was billed as the "Skinhead Symphony," and there is no better illustration of the Specials's breathtaking musical dexterity. Driven by a tight rhythm section and swirling organ patterns, Neville urges all the *Skinheads, rude boys and rude girls to get up on your feet. Put your braces together and your boots on your feet. And give me some of that old moon-stomping.* Thousands of Dr. Martens boots pound the wooden dance floor, compelling the band to speed up until the music surrenders to a cacophony of noise and the ebullient stage announcement, "MAGIC! YEAH! THE SPECIALS!"

Once commonplace in the British charts, extended play records had long fallen out of vogue. "I didn't think radio would go for 'Too Much Too Young'" admits Rick Rogers, "but when Jerry said, 'We do a live EP,' it made absolute sense because the Specials were at their best live. That's where you experienced the three hundred and sixty degrees of the band."

It was scheduled for a January release, but an unforeseen disagreement blocking the release of all future Elvis Costello records threatened to derail the Specials's third single. In 1979, Radar Records, a subsidiary of WEA, financially collapsed. However, when Jake Riviera (Costello's manager) formed F-Beat—allegedly shortened from Fuck Beat and described by Costello as "the Stax to 2 Tone's Motown"—WEA served an injunction on the label's first release, "I Can't Stand Up for Falling Down." Livid, Riviera turned to Chrysalis. "I don't know exactly what happened," says Chris Poole. "Knowing Jake, he said, 'Right. Fuck you [to WEA]. If you don't release it, we'll put it out on 2 Tone.'" According to Jerry, Riviera then "cheekily printed up a few thousand Elvis Costello singles on the 2 Tone label, obviously thinking I would be delighted to have such a major star on the label, but I was having none of it, 2 Tone being strictly ska at the time. So Elvis was forced to give these singles away free at gigs."[80*]

---

* Thirteen thousand copies of "I Can't Stand Up for Falling Down" were given away on Costello's UK tour and, allegedly, a second pressing was sold outside the Palladium in New York at a Costello concert in January 1981.

When the legal dispute was resolved, Costello's cover of Sam & Dave's 1967 soul classic shot into the top five (on F-Beat) as "Too Much Too Young" slipped down from its two-week tenure at the head of the charts behind Kenny Rogers's country-crooned "Coward of the County." Capturing the unique relationship between the Specials and their dedicated following, "Too Much Too Young" was packaged in the first 2 Tone picture sleeve featuring a monochrome close-up of a jubilant audience, taken at a Selecter gig at the Hammersmith Palais. Jerry produced a "little black-and-white snap" of a skinhead fan and asked John Sims to cut out the image with a scalpel and "stick him in the bottom left corner of the photo."[81] It was sold at the recommended retail price "only £1.05," with an accompanying ad that positioned Walt Jabsco standing casually with a pint of beer in hand looking across the sleeve to a rude girl clutching a screaming baby. "They stole our logo [the Beat Girl]," laughs Ranking Roger. "It was like a sign of respect."

Ad for the "Too Much Too Young" single, January 1979. Courtesy of Chrysalis Records/Jerry Dammers.

The song's opinions on birth control and the instruction to copulating couples to *try wearing a cap* were sufficient for the BBC to ban the record, much to Chris Poole's delight. "The BBC was fairly reactionary about things like that," he says. "2 Tone was a continuation of punk in lots of ways and one of them was an antiestablishment, antiauthority attitude. Often it was better to be banned because you got lots of other coverage and your audience liked it."

Circumnavigating the problem, *Top of the Pops* aired a video of "Too Much Too Young" and simply cut the track short, omitting its last "contentious" verse. By today's standards, the controversial passage seems decidedly tame, but not the song's broader implication, as Nicky Summers argues. "I questioned the Specials lyrically. They were a bit misogynist in places. Slightly spiteful lyrics: you should be doing it with me not him." Rhoda Dakar is equally aggrieved. "It's all about *you* should take the pill. *You* should wear a cap. It's all *your* fault. I don't know at what age those lyrics were written but Jerry was old enough to know better." The charge leaves Jerry incensed. "Misogynist means hating all women. 'Too Much Too Young' was written about one woman and I didn't hate her. It was very rude, sarcastic and adolescent punky anger. The song was not about women in general. It was a very personal song: a lament, a cross between 'Young Hearts Run Free' and 'It Should Have Been Me.' I wasn't addressing the nation when I wrote it. It was written in the seventies when there was still pressure on people to settle down, get a steady job and a family by the age of twenty. Some people spent their whole lives in unhappy marriages. The point of the song was saying: at least put off having children; have a bit of fun first to help slow down the population explosion."

In a global context, "Too Much Too Young" pointed to China's extreme measure to limit population growth by restricting families to one child. The warning, *Do you really want a program of sterilization?* balanced with gentle persuasion: *take control of the population boom— it's in your living room.* "It was a really important song," maintains Juliet de Vie. "Having this very male band write a song with such a strong female sensibility spoke to girls." Ironically, two members of the Specials—Lynval and Roddy—were married and several of the band had children out of wedlock. Speaking to *NME* in February 1980, Terry Hall reasoned that birth control was about mutual consideration. "It's just as much on the boy's head as it is on the girl's. You've got to have two people to use contraception, and two people not to."

As the hullabaloo around the song settled, and seemingly in defiance of the BBC's moral stance, a cover version of "Too Much Too Young" appeared on Volume 78 of the compilation album series *Top of the Pops*. A year later, Jerry donated his silver disc, in recognition of 250,000 sales, to the Lanchester Polytechnic Student Financial Aid Fund's summer raffle. But it is perhaps a lesser-known piece of trivia that Jerry is most proud of. "Who is the only person to appear on two live number one songs recorded at the same venue?" he asks, grinning from ear to ear. "The answer is *me*! 'Too Much Too Young' in 1980 and Chuck Berry's 'My Ding-a-Ling' in 1972. I was in the crowd singing along. And they were both recorded at Tiffany's in Coventry."

CHAPTER 18

RUDIES COME BACK

BBC DOCUMENTARY. THE SPECIALS IN THE US

At thirty-nine years old, freelance film director Jeff Perks was perhaps an unlikely candidate to make a documentary about youth culture. Nevertheless, having made a spectacular film about Sham 69 and their right-wing following, Perks was certainly versed in the ugly realities of tribal warfare. Filmed in 1978, *Tell Us the Truth* profiled Jimmy Pursey's losing battle to unite opposing factions, culminating in the lead singer threatening to cut his own throat with a smashed bottle as he watched a Sham 69 gig descend into mindless violence. A year later, disturbances at 2 Tone concerts suggested the Specials were succumbing to a similar fate. "It was clear the Specials were already big and they were going to be even bigger," says Perks, who pitched the idea of a documentary about 2 Tone in a BBC bar. Having convinced commissioning editor Alan Yentob of a phenomenon people should be aware of, Perks likens the monolithic broadcasting institution to a castle with a moat around it. "From the battlements they'd see something going on in the distance and think, *That's interesting*, pull down the drawbridge, rush out, and film it." Given the green light, Perks picked up the phone to the 2 Tone office and organized a meeting with the Specials at a recording session in south London. The band liked the idea.

Shooting without a script, Perks says, "I like setting things up and then letting it happen. We knew we had a concert lined up but apart from that it was pretty spontaneous." Concerned about his age, Perks asked *NME*'s self-styled "cub reporter" Adrian Thrills to do the required on-camera narration and interviews. Arriving on an intercity train from London, Thrills made his way to 2 Tone headquarters in Coventry to "investigate the new musical sound taking the country by storm." Home to Jerry Dammers, 51 Albany Road was a semi-detached house adjacent to a barbershop and a poodle parlor. After being furtively given a makeover before the film crew arrived, friends rallied to give the first-floor front room a much-needed spring clean. "They did it up to look like a mod bedroom," says Roddy Byers. "It usually looked like somebody had broken in and strewn clothes everywhere. I shared a room with Jerry on tour. He was the kind of guy who'd forget to let the bathwater out or you'd go to clean your teeth and his socks would be in the sink." Asked to describe Jerry's home, Lynval Golding says with a hearty chuckle, "We as Jamaicans are brought up to believe that cleanliness is close to godliness. To imagine that a record label with all these hit records and you go in that house ... it was a tip." Suspicious and alerted by the possibility of nefarious activities carrying on behind closed doors, the police would regularly make visits to the property. "We'd be sitting there watching *Sgt. Bilko* and drinking cocoa," says John Shipley, a close friend of Jerry's, "and the police would come in and go, 'What's up?' It was an open house—the door was always open!"

Climbing the stairs of the rented abode, the filmmakers passed a large, mounted picture of President Leonid Brezhnev hung on the wall because of his resemblance, Jerry told the director, to his father. As they doubled back toward the front room, the international-themed décor continued: a vintage poster of a bull fight featuring Paco Camino, Manuel "El Cordobés" Benitez and Santiago "El Viti" Martín from Barcelona; a record sleeve of *The Wailing Wailers*; a black-and-white photograph of a local group posing in white vests; a collection of head masks; a postcard of Ken Dodd; and an original hand-painted artwork depicting a graphic scene of football violence. "This is our contract department," says Jerry, pulling out files of paper from a wooden cabinet, "and the contract from Bernie Rhodes," he adds, tossing it to the floor together with checkbooks, receipts and a slew of cassettes sent to 2 Tone from unsigned bands.

Crossing the room to show off the costume department, Jerry pulls at a suit precariously hung on a rail only for it to give way, bringing a row of secondhand suits tumbling down onto members of the group seated below. Hilarity fills the room as bandmates and friends keel over in recognition of Jerry's celebrated heavy-handedness. "He was all over the place," says Roddy. "He was struggling to deal with it. Neville passed him a spliff and he was talking away and suddenly realized, 'Cut! Cut! Cut!' When he dropped all the cassettes, people said he showed a lack of regard for the unsigned groups. It wasn't that. Jerry was clumsy. People used to laugh at him because of the way he looked, not realizing how cool and calculating he was behind all of that. When he wanted anything to do with the group, he was 100 percent. He'd argue the toss with anybody no matter how tough or businesslike they were. He'd fight every inch."

Recalling the evident comradeship in the room, Jeff Perks says the Specials were "a gang at ease with one another. They could take the piss out of each other and it was okay. The BBC didn't understand that the Specials were a mixed group and that antiracism was part of the 2 Tone ethos. When I said to Jerry that we should mention that in the program, he was strongly against it. He said it was on the stage and people could see it. I liked that. It was a good take on it."

Across the thirty-minute documentary, the Specials perform in front of a home crowd at Tiffany's. To the strains of *Where did you get that blank expression on your face?*, Horace Panter affects a frozen stare. "Gold!" cries Perks, zooming in for close-up. As they break into "Concrete Jungle," live footage intercuts with an image of an ill-lit underground walkway, a flash of a flick knife and a dramatized fight. "The song's about living in a rough part of town, going out and getting beaten up," explains Roddy to the camera, red-faced in front of a film crew and onlooking bandmates. "You write songs about what you've been through." Set upon by local youths, the staged scene ends with the guitarist lying trapped in a dark corner, cut from the glass of a broken bottle. "They went for it and were properly hitting me," says Roddy, "and then after, I noticed they'd stolen my wallet too."

In another sequence, a lone male throws a brick through a bathroom windowpane, smashing the glass. Cutting to a scene of a young, dejected woman trundling down a supermarket aisle, we then see her standing at an electric cooker preparing beans on toast to the soundtrack of "Stupid Marriage." The music segues to Neville Staple parading onstage garbed in a wig and gown. Taking inspiration from Prince Buster's "Judge Dread," Neville passes judgment over the rude boys. *I hereby sentence you to four hundred years.* "It was Jerry's idea," he says. Asked in the documentary about the meaning of "Stupid Marriage," Jerry says it was supposed to be humorous. "It was about somebody's girlfriend who got married to somebody else. He got jealous, broke a window, and ended up in court. He thought it was stupid to get married young."

Back at Albany Road, Jerry plays an original recording of "You're Wondering Now" by Andy & Joey on a Dansette, prompting spontaneous dancing from all concerned. Beautifully filmed in silhouette from the street, Jeff Perks says, "It was a great end to a film." To strengthen the narrative, Jerry suggested featuring the Selecter. "Don't just do us," he urged Perks, "show the whole thing." Heeding the advice, Perks filmed a performance of "Three Minute Hero" at Horizon Studios, but in hindsight, he says, it was the weakest part of the film. "They mimed, so it was static and too predictable." Relaxing on a long sofa surrounded by cans of beer, Adrian Thrills asks Charley Anderson to distinguish original ska from the Selecter. Pointing to a broader musical palette, Anderson says, "This is a 1980 sound. We have the old ska rhythm and we have reggae and there's a bit of blues and funk, and 'Jah' Neol playing his rock guitar on top of all that." Expanding the conversation to include the role of women, Pauline Black is quick to draw attention to the misogynist nature of sixties ska, citing Prince Buster's "10 Commandments" "as an obvious example," before assuring Thrills, "We're into a whole different scene."

Filming the *Rudies Come Back* documentary with the Selecter, Horizon Studio, 1979.

* * *

Broadcast on BBC Two on March 12 at 8:25 p.m., *Rudies Come Back or the Rise and Rise of 2-Tone* received little fanfare beyond perfunctory previews and the condescension of sniffy critics. "Whatever the intention, the gang-violence scene is more likely to be an incitement than a deterrent." "That was *Sounds*," says Jeff Perks, who prefers to focus on the positive aspects of the documentary. "The run-up to a program is usually quite a long time. You pitch an idea and six months later, you're maybe making it, by which time the moment's gone. We got the Specials at exactly the right moment in time: when it was happening. That's why I think it's a good film." Plans to extend the Selecter's involvement and to include the Beat were shelved due to the limitation of a thirty-five-minute running time. Nevertheless, the BBC film broadened the profile of 2 Tone and offered an incredible record of musicians in a provincial city commanding national attention.

The documentary coincided with the Specials hitting the top of the charts as 2 Tone mania continued to gather momentum. "It was amazing when 'Too Much Too Young' went to number one," says

Pauline Black. "It made you feel part of a movement." Likening the dramatic shift to going from "being an observer to the observed," Jerry says, "It was the biggest change in any of our lives and a lot to take in." The Specials were now bona fide rock stars. Roddy recalls Dick Cuthell suggesting that the band should move to London. "It'll do your heads in living in your hometown," the horn player advised. "We tried not to be pop stars," Roddy continues. "We still went to the same pubs. But it got harder and harder. Not everyone was a Specials fan or wanted to be your friend. People were more inclined to beat you up. Terry couldn't go out anywhere without getting bothered."

Perhaps benefiting Terry and Roddy's craving for anonymity, the broadcast of the Specials's live performance at the Colchester Institute for the BBC series *Rock Goes to College*, filmed on December 19 and scheduled to be aired on January 21, was postponed. Lizzie Soden recalls traveling to Essex with the band and a coach full of fans. "We arrived and there were all these National Front people that Jerry wouldn't let into the gig. They found a side door, got on the stage and were shouting. The BBC turned the cameras off and Jerry kicked one of the skinheads off the stage. When we were leaving, all the rude boys from Coventry wanted to get in there and Jerry was going, 'Just ignore them. Don't look at them.' Then a skinhead ran onto the coach and grabbed one kid's trilby. It was like, 'FUCK THAT!' They all piled off and there was a huge fight. The BBC was running up the road with cameras and Jerry going, 'FILM THIS! FILM THIS! THIS IS WHAT IT'S ALL ABOUT!'" In the ensuing melee, a brick smashed the front window of the coach. "We had to drive all the way back to Coventry with snow blowing in," says Jerry, somewhat skeptical of what he considers an exaggerated description of events, before confirming that the journey home "was absolutely freezing."

The footage of the Specials was sensational. Ripping off his cotton shirt to reveal a muscular, toned body, Neville acts like a man possessed. Dripping with sweat, he climbs over the amps, hangs from the balcony and jumps, falls, and runs across the stage in restless perpetual motion. "Neville couldn't keep still," grins Horace Panter. "He was just this dynamo. He'd get into the van for the next day's gig and say, 'Me not sleep yet, y'know.' He was so wired up. His energy was incredible. If you could climb it, he'd be up there. He was entertaining people, going wild, and having the most fun he'd ever had in his life."

Introducing "Monkey Man," Neville goads the audience with chimp noises. "Blacks were called 'monkey,'" says an unflinching Lynval Golding. "So Neville turned it back at the National Front. 'We're laughing at you because you paid to see us make monkey chants and we're throwing it right in your face.'" Whether intended literally or ironically, it was an incredible act of valor to see a Black man overtly confronting white prejudice. "I took on a persona. I'm an entertainer," says Neville. "I bring out whatever the song is to make people listen. 'Fuckin' hell! Look at him running across there . . . climbing up the speakers.' If you want to abuse me or call me a monkey, I'm up here . . . I didn't give a fuck. It was how I grew up. I didn't take shit. People would come up to me at school: 'Nev, this guy's fucking me around . . . can you help me?' I was the guy people came to. One day, somebody called me a wog. I nearly killed them. Once you do that, nobody approaches you or calls you names. I grew up not letting people get away with shit because they'll keep doing it. Nobody fucked with me." Pauline Black watched Neville in awe. "He seemed like a god at that time, on top of the PA stack singing 'Monkey Man' at them. To see a Black man do that was one of the bravest things I've ever seen. It needed to be done. That said more to me than any Rock Against Racism gig preaching to the converted. It was us taking them on."[82]

Midset at the Colchester Institute with the cameras still rolling, Terry Hall throws a tambourine at a bouncer. Activity explodes from all corners of the stage. But rage dissolves into merriment when tens of fans invade the stage for a stomping finale of the "Skinhead Symphony." Engulfed by a sea of Fred Perrys, braces and tonic suits, the Specials manage to clear a space and introduce the fittingly titled encore, "Madness." The lunacy continues, led by a boy half the size of Terry Hall showing off an array of dazzling dance steps. Young women are touchingly helped onto the stage and the Specials round off the performance with a rousing rendition of "You're Wondering Now." "It's a Christmas song even though this program is being broadcast in January," says Terry in a light monotone. "It's the thought that counts."

Crossing the Atlantic in late 1979, Madness introduced British ska to a US audience, and two months later, the Specials followed in their footsteps. It would be a defining moment in the group's history, one that would forever change them as a cohesive working unit. "America is so big it's like a lot of separate countries," explained Suggs to *Smash Hits* after a difficult tour. "The 2 Tone thing goes down well in 'hip' places like New York, Los Angeles and San Francisco, but go to Detroit or Cleveland and they have no idea. When we played in Portland, Oregon, the other band, who were some kind of heavy rockers, got so angry about our music they were telling us to get out of the country."[83] Conquering the US held great attraction, but it was a challenge that broke many groups who dreamed of replicating the success of the British invasion pioneered by the Beatles in the midsixties. Jerry contended that the Specials "were not ready and it would cause problems." After a short tour of Europe, playing club dates in France, Belgium, Germany and the Netherlands, the group arrived in New York on January 24, 1980. Shocked at the appearance of seven men dressed in uniform suits and short-cropped hair, the driver at the airport asked Rick Rogers if they were "inmates from a psychiatric hospital." Six weeks later, when the Specials returned to England crumpled and defeated, the innocuous wisecrack assumed an air of prophetic insight.

Reggae was no easy sell in America. In the past decade, there had been hits such as Paul Simon's "Mother and Child Reunion," Johnny Nash's "I Can See Clearly Now" and Eric Clapton's cover version of "I Shot the Sherriff." They may have paved the way for Bob Marley's global breakthrough but did little to convince record buyers that reggae was anything more than a novelty genre. In fact, when John Lennon appeared as a guest on *The Tomorrow Show* in 1975, he found himself having to define "reggae" to the host Tom Snyder. "It's great!" Lennon enthused. "It's been around for years under the disguise of ska and bluebeat." Five years later, *Reggae* opened on Broadway with theater producer Michael Butler attempting to do for reggae what *Hair* had done for rock in the late sixties. The story of the musical took place within a twenty-four-hour period in modern-day Jamaica, but despite a program which included a full-page insert of "Jamaican Patois and Rastafarian Terminology," the tale of a rude boy closed after twenty-one performances. Appraising its "exciting, multirhythmed, and infectious appeal" on *Good Morning America*, film and theater critic Joel Siegel said, "*Reggae* was none of the above."

On Saturday, January 26, at 1:15 a.m., the Specials stepped onto the stage at Hurrah nightclub, New York City, two hours late—after a five-hour soundcheck and, subsequently, a problem being discovered in the monitor system—to make their American debut. Such was the anticipation and so numerous the requests for interviews with the group that Chrysalis had called an afternoon press conference. "Such formalities are usually reserved for special occasions like the Rolling Stones's fifty-fifth tour of America, or Elvis Costello calling Ray Charles an 'old, blind nigger,'" observed the *New York Rocker*, making reference to Costello's ill-judged drunken slur aimed to shock US musical peers that led to a barroom brawl. Asked if they were looking forward to experiencing any particular aspect of American culture, Jerry replied, "No, not really, but I'd like to see Professor Longhair."[*][84]

Inside Hurrah, kids stacked up against the walls on top of one another in great anticipation. "This is our first gig in America," Terry said, introducing the band, "and we just can't say how pleased you must be to have us here." Like a firecracker in a shop window, the Specials burst into action. For an hour, they bounded around the stage with unstoppable energy, discharging discourses about life in Britain to a mixture of Jamaican and punk rhythms. "This, my little petals," continued Terry with trademark sarcastic overtones and playing on

* Jerry would see R&B pianist Longhair play one of his last gigs at the legendary New Orleans club Tipitina's a week later.

the fear of impending nuclear war, "is your last chance to dance before World War Three." Notwithstanding the menace he projected on the stage, the *New York Rocker* described Terry's performance as "nervous edgy stiffness" and "more than just a good foil for the loose-limbed, exploding frenzy of the Specials: it's the eye at the center of the hurricane." To a small contingent suitably attired in hats, natty suits and wraparound shades, Terry introduced the band's fourth encore with a final demonstration of homegrown, dry wit: "We'd like to thank you lot up front who're dancing, and the rest back there—shit to you!"

A fortnight into the tour, Lynval and Neville landed in their own proverbial mess when the Specials filled in for the Police in Portland after Sting lost his voice. "The night before, the Ku Klux Klan had murdered a Black man," explains Lynval, "and there's me and Neville: the only two Black guys. We went onstage and all the songs we done in like five seconds and then off. It was so scary." Snaking up through New Orleans, Denver, Salt Lake City, Seattle and Vancouver, the Specials doubled back to arrive in Los Angeles on February 8 to play eight shows in four days at the Whisky a Go Go. In honor of 2 Tone, the outside of the building was a newly painted vision of black-and-white checkers, while inside festive monochrome balloons decorated the walls. Terry was livid at the gimmick, comparing it to a "celebration of something they have no idea what they're doing it for."[85] Keeping shtum, Horace privately noted in his diary, "It looked cool."

As the enormity of the schedule stretched out before them, Roddy speculated, "Will the Specials break America or will America break us?" The guitarist's sense of foreboding deepened when a clutch of Chrysalis employees, dressed in office suits, ties and smoking cigars, turned up backstage requesting photographs and suggesting that the band put back on their hot and sweaty stage clothes. "One of them said to me, 'Oh, I love that song of yours "On My Radio."'" Hearing another ask if he could be "taught how to pogo," Jerry snapped and told them to fuck off. After that, says Roddy "they stopped pushing the record . . . But I must say it felt good."

Adding to the disquiet was an overwhelming feeling of physical fatigue—in part, a result of nonstop partying, but in the main a consequence of an unrelenting timetable. "It broke the spirit of the band," laments Jerry. Booked to play two shows a night, he compares the situation to a boxer knocked out in one bout only to discover he has to get up and fight a new opponent afresh. "It made no sense. We were completely exhausted. There was a horrible change and after that it suddenly became more like work." As tempers began to fray, an argument in Palo Alto, California, with local crew members ended with Jerry and Terry destroying the furniture, fixtures and fittings in the dressing room, and Neville requiring "four stitches in his head," noted Horace. "This is definitely the worst time of the band's career so far. There seems to be no point, no indication of whether we're progressing or not. This is 'barroom blues band' country, and I can't help feeling that we are achieving nothing playing here in the suburbs. The novelty has worn off. It's now a slog." Depressed, Terry and Horace concluded that "the band will burn out."

Back at home and oblivious to the darkening mood in the Specials camp, excitement was building at the British Rock & Pop Awards.* It was hosted at the Café Royal in London, with John Peel announcing the winner of the Radio 1 Disc Jockeys' Award for Outstanding Contribution to British Pop Music. Reading out Jerry Dammers's name, Peel pumped his fist in the air in celebration as copresenter Sue Lawley introduced a prerecorded film of the Specials receiving the award from DJ Andy Peebles in Washington, DC. Behind the scenes, the seemingly carefree presentation had in fact required a great act of diplomacy and engineering. Having insisted that he would only accept the award if the entire band were present, Jerry (and Horace) then missed their flight from Toronto to Washington. When they eventually arrived, Jerry appeared on the satellite link lost for words. As the rest of the group took pleasure in covering his face and generally larking about, Jerry was urged to make a speech. "What to say I do not know," he finally began, looking anywhere but into the camera. "It's really not that much to do with me . . . it's these chaps here," he

---

* A forerunner of the BRIT Awards.

said, laughing and spinning around. Asked collectively if they were enjoying the tour, there was a resounding, "No!" "We really want to go home, actually," added Jerry.

They were ground down but committed to struggling on, yet the positive responses received from audiences on the West and East coasts gave way to indifference in the Midwest. "Not so hip places didn't quite get it," recalls Roddy. "Everybody seemed to be into coke, something we hadn't really come across. We were mainly weed and beer boys, with a bit of mod whizz." As disagreements magnified, some of the band refused to wear "the same old suits." Interviewed by the *Los Angeles Times*, Jerry cracked: "I've had more fun on a school trip to Russia." "I've never felt like that before," he commented later in the year. "That's what it does to you. And if you're not enjoying it, then there isn't really much point in going on. I'm not sure if it would work out, but in the future, we might just do odd gigs instead of massive tours."

And still, more controversy plagued the tour.

On March 1 at the Diplomat Ballroom, New York, flyers appeared on the outside wall: one calling for a boycott of the show—"$10? Don't Go!"—and a second, decorated in black-and-white checkerboard and claiming to be "a message to you fans" offered 500 free tickets to the show on a first come, first served basis. It was a hoax.* Stepping up to the microphone, Jerry waved a flyer at the crowd and dedicated "Gangsters" to the club's promoter: "We found this on the way in, and I just want to say that we're getting $1,000 for this gig. [Promoter] Ron Delsener's gonna use the other $9,000 to build a new swimming pool, and this song's for him!" In the audience, the managing director of Chrysalis, Doug D'Arcy, watched on aghast—"Mick Jagger and Jerry Hall on one side of me and David Bowie on the other"—not knowing whether to laugh or cry. The Specials had become a celebrity success. The next evening, at Speaks Club, Long Island, Debbie Harry of Blondie introduced the band to a packed

---

* It was rumored to be the work of Madness, who played the venue a week earlier.

room. "All you rude boys and rude girls, skinheads, it's their last night in the US . . ." she began before a barrage of excited applause drowned her out. The Specials let loose and bedlam ensued. "We played like demons," Horace signed off in his tour diary, "destroyed the place. Incredible!"

The last-night hurrah was a welcome fillip but not enough to remedy the ills of touring. "It's been like gig, sleep, get up, travel, gig, sleep—nonstop," Terry complained, "and most of the time playing two gigs a night—it's hard to make much sense of it. Personally, I don't think 2 Tone will be as popular here as it is in England. Fashions don't tend to catch on in a big way over here, the country's too big."[86] Retrospectively, Terry would compare traveling to being "stuck in a mobile funeral parlor," further frustrated by the Specials being belittled as a "dance band" and their message diluted to wacky black-and-white graphics. Exacerbating the problem, the Specials were not a particularly tight-knit group. "We all have different lifestyles and different music tastes," remarked Roddy.

Adding to the internal differences, 2 Tone needed omnipresent management. Here, there were further anxieties as the group worked against a current of industry cynicism. "Regardless of the fact that there might be seven human beings playing it, and the fact that the lyrics might have some kind of social significance," Horace steamed, "they weren't really interested. It was, 'This album must be good because it's sold so many units.'" Outside of the UK, 2 Tone was subservient to the promotional whim of Chrysalis. "Europe and America were different markets," explains UK-based Roy Eldridge. "They got into the mindset selling a particular group and not a label identity. It was much easier for them to concentrate on the Specials or the Selecter but without having the time and the energy to develop a new label identity."

Resistant to 2 Tone's messaging, licensees in non-UK territories treated the label, and the groups, simply as a salable commodity. "They were selling the Chrysalis label," rationalizes Doug D'Arcy, "2 Tone was too subversive. It was not as well known internationally so therefore you were just literally selling a piece of music. The backup wasn't there. It was difficult to get people to accept 2 Tone as a label, as it was always difficult to sell new British music. Chrysalis in America was the same company, but it's a very big market so there would always be conflict." Adding to the frustration, records appeared without 2 Tone artwork, commonly replaced by a standard blue-and-white Chrysalis presentation and the ubiquitous butterfly logo. In the US, the publicity department advertised the Specials and the Selecter albums together, circulating a media campaign more appropriate to a high-school music quiz than a considered UK press release: "What's black and white and leading the reggae/rock 'n' roll movement? Two very unique English bands that have everyone . . . everywhere . . . moving to a brand-new beat. Their infectious music is more than just a good time . . . it's ultimately revolutionizing the sound of the 80s." "It was a dog's dinner," sighs D'Arcy, shuddering at the inadequacies of the international campaign. "I'm sure you can find some very strange overseas vinyl editions."

To conclude the US adventure, the Specials briefly returned to perform "Gangsters" and "Too Much Too Young" on *Saturday Night Live*, highly regarded for the variety of musical acts the show booked. Adding insult to injury, Horace Panter estimated the TV audience for the Specials was bigger than for the entire US tour. When it was broadcast on April 19, the Specials treated viewers to a rousing show of postpunk scowl, menace and aggression, ending the performance by dropping their instruments and marching offstage directly toward the camera and away into the audience. The exhilarating performance is repeatedly cited as a catalytic moment, akin to the Beatles appearing on the *Ed Sullivan Show* in 1964, prompting the third wave of ska that would later breathe new life into 2 Tone in the US in the early to midnineties. Yet, for the Specials, it would be fifteen months before they would cross the Atlantic again. By which time, the group would be dead in the water.

PART II
CONSOLIDATION

CHAPTER 19

BACKLASH

THREE MINUTE HERO. LET'S DO ROCK STEADY. ACCUSATION

2 Tone was sweeping the nation and beginning to make waves across the Atlantic. Nevertheless, on the home front the narrative of achievement and celebration was about to be challenged. For no overtly tangible or obvious reason, beyond perhaps creating conflict for conflict's sake, certain journalists within the British media readied themselves to knock 2 Tone off its pedestal. Futhermore, where previously musicians had embraced their meteoric rise to pop stardom, now some began to turn on their benefactors and succumb to greed and the gnawing destructiveness of in-group jealousy.

Pauline Black's first reaction to Neol Davies's new song—"Three Minute Hero," written after the success of "On My Radio"—was the sinking feeling that "it wasn't as good." Guitarist Compton Amanor thought otherwise. "I worked in a plating factory on a night shift for about a year. It was terrible. Tough, hard work. The drone of it. You wanted to be a three-minute hero." Bemoaning the hopelessness of working-class life—its inherent mundanity; going to and from work five days a week; the daily routine; clocking in and out—Davies wrote: *It's 5 p.m. and you're on your way home, just another day with that endless gray drone.* When writing the song on a bass guitar, Davies picked out three descending notes on the fretboard and, off the cuff, started singing, *It's too early in the morning—stupid job.* Then over staccato chords he lifted the key to its aspirational chorus: *I wanna be—a three-minute hero.*

Hearing a saxophone over the song's instrumental, Neol extended an invitation to Lee Thompson (from Madness) to play as a special guest on the track. Congregating at Horizon Studios, the Selecter eagerly awaited the woodwind player's arrival when news came of an unexpected hitch. "Neol rang me up and said Lee's sax is in for a repair," says local musician Joe Reynolds, "and would I lend him my instrument to do the session." A member of RU12—an underground gay reference—Reynolds had previously shared bills with both the Automatics and Terry Hall's former group, Squad. Of the latter, Reynolds says they were "a bunch of lads who wanted to be in a band but couldn't play an instrument," adding, "I didn't think much of Terry's singing either." Armed with his vintage Selmer Mk VI, Reynolds dropped around to Pauline Black's house and from there they made their way to the studio. "Lee never turned up," says Reynolds. "So they just sort of said to me, 'Go in there and do it.'" Somewhat apprehensively, Reynolds agreed. However, when he listened to a playback of the track, he heard a saxophone. Confused, he turned to Neol. It transpired that a musician named Jim Lang had recorded the part previously, but Neol wanted something "a little bit more streetwise." Relieved to discover mislaid handwritten notes on manuscript paper, Reynolds simply followed Lang's dots.

The song clocked in at exactly one hundred and eighty seconds. The announcement of "Three Minute Hero"—released on January 25, 1980—depicted 2 Tone man Walt Jabsco casually standing beside a factory time clock machine, card in hand. In contrast to the quirky ad and the bold song title, Joe Reynolds regarded the saxophone part as anything but heroic. "In the studio I was quite happy with the sound, but when it came out it sounded flat," he says. "Pauline said it sounded like a kazoo." Likewise unimpressed with the Selecter's new offering, *Sounds* described the record as "the least distinguished 2 Tone single so far," while *Melody Maker* labeled it "a big disappointment." "The shortcomings are all too obvious," wrote Ian Birch, "poor song, a cluttered arrangement and a threadbare chorus." Joining the choir of disapproval, bass player Charley Anderson commented, "It was a direct reflection on the time we didn't spend on it and choosing a poor song to follow up the hits we had before."[87]

However, it was declared the highest new entry on the UK chart; fans ignored the negative critical opinion and celebrated the song's jubilant pop stomp. Flying in from Brussels, the Selecter landed at *Top of the Pops* to register the fourth 2 Tone–related single presently gracing the top thirty, joining "Hands Off . . . She's Mine" (the Beat, number seventeen), "My Girl" (Madness, number three) and "Too Much Too Young" (the Specials, number one). Arriving at Television Centre, the Selecter became embroiled in a familiar hostile scene when a quarrel erupted at the entrance to the BBC bar. "There was a gentleman who sat on the door," explains Pauline. "It was his fiefdom and he took exception to Charley wearing a hat to cover his locks. We were all arguing that this was a religious thing. He didn't ask me to take my hat off." Denied entry to the bar, the group marched onto the studio floor, where their lack of decorum and general unruliness came face-to-face with the clean-cut professionalism of the Nolan Sisters. Sharing a soundstage with the five siblings from Dublin, Joe Reynolds watched on as they successfully performed their smash hit "I'm in the Mood for Dancing" live in two attempts. "The only reason that they needed a second take was because one of their dresses came undone while they were singing. Then because of union regulations, a wardrobe person had to come and do it up," says Reynolds in admiration. "We did three takes and we were miming."

Fresh from the BBC experience—and the welcome news that "Three Minute Hero" had jumped into the top twenty—the Selecter were featured on the front cover of *Melody Maker*. The photograph: Charley eating Pauline's hat.

"You've got to have an anthem," Gaz Mayall implored Rhoda Dakar.

The son of blues legend John Mayall, Gaz lived with his family in a large house on Bayswater Road. "Loads of people would go back to his and we'd sit in the basement round this massive bed and he'd just play tunes. That's where I first heard ska," says Rhoda Dakar. "When I got in the Bodysnatchers, Gaz said we had to have an anthem. So we wrote 'Ruder Than You,' Gaz on piano, and I was writing lyrics." Sending a missive to rude boys to take warning, *Watch out—long time now it is men-only scene*, Rhoda then addressed the nascent rude girl fraternity and enthused, *We have something to say!* "It was an anthem for rude girls," says guitarist Sarah-Jane Owen. "We had a message: we were females doing this kind of music and we were hardcore. It gave permission for other women to come forward in music."

As a concept and as a youth tribe, "rude girls" was new to 2 Tone. "We were the rude girls," asserts Penny Leyton. "We were dressing like the movement and getting the same influences as the people who came to see us were getting." Every weekend, saxophonist Miranda Joyce would venture to Gaz Mayall's stall in Kensington Market to look through the selection of Fred Perrys, mohair suits, button-down shirts and Harrington jackets. "I had short hair and looked like a little boy. I'd wear white Sta-Prest, a pair of red loafers with tassels from Freeman, Hardy and Willis, and lots of badges. We'd go to Gaz's Rockin' Blues club in Soho and there were fans dressing top to toe in black-and-white check and porkpie hats and Fred Perrys. It was all part of this wonderful feeling. It felt like a big family to me." For Rhoda, dressing in sixties clothing had been a teenage obsession: "1968: I'm backing Britain," she laughs, recalling the brief patriotic campaign aimed at boosting the British economy. "I was a little kid imagining what it would be like to be a grown-up wearing those clothes. Then suddenly I was an older kid dressed in those clothes. I'd see girls in the audience who looked like me. That was funny: seeing Black girls with white ribbons in their hair. I remember Gaz saying to me, 'It looks like fashion's catching up with you!'"

After they played their first gig in November, record companies had clamored to sign the Bodysnatchers. While they fielded offers from the likes of EMI, Stiff and Virgin, word arrived from America that Jerry was offering a two-single deal. The Bodysnatchers voted and unanimously elected 2 Tone. "It all happened in two weeks," says founding member Nicky Summers. "To make a decision, find a lawyer, record a single to coincide with the Selecter tour, and do all that and be thinking, *Shit! Am I being ripped off?* I was out of my depth."

Signed on February 12, 1980, the contract—agreed between the Bodysnatchers and the Selecter and *not* directly with 2 Tone, or indeed Chrysalis—confirmed the recording of a double-sided single entitled "Rock Steady" and "Ruder Than You." Itemizing seven key points, the two-page typed agreement confirmed that 2 Tone would arrange payment for the recording and decide on a suitable studio and producer. Referencing the Selecter's agreement with Chrysalis—signed on October 10, 1979—2 Tone further agreed to manufacture and distribute the recording throughout the world. Clause 5 stipulated the financial settlement: after recoupment of the recording costs the Bodysnatchers would receive a 10 percent royalty rate (9 percent in the US and 7.5 percent in Europe). Significantly, Clause 7 stated that in the event the record entered the Top 50 compiled by the BMRB (British Market Research Bureau), the group would agree to record another single for 2 Tone "at our request." The contract was signed by Iain Adam, acting solicitor on behalf of the Selecter. Identified as a minor, seventeen-year-old Miranda Joyce's signature was countersigned by her father.

"A fucking joke," says Rhoda of the legal document. Traveling to Queen's Park in northwest London to sign the contract, she says, Iain Adam, recommended by Madness as the named 2 Tone lawyer, advised the group: "The contract is fine. But I just want to know where the rest of it is." "He was a bit like an East End wide boy in a decent suit with better vowels. He said, 'This is all very well but what are you going to do for folding?' We go, 'You *what*? Folding?' 'I can see all the recording costs are covered in it, but how are you going to live?'" Adam clarified. Too young to care, Miranda says, the band skipped to Chrysalis to sign on the dotted line. "There was very little analysis. It was just, 'Whoa! Great!' like we were on some amazing roller-coaster ride. We were just in this whole kind of vortex of 2 Tone. It was just wonderful." Comparing the episode to a fairy tale, Penny says, "The whole thing was such an incredible buzz. We'd gone from being an idea to suddenly being a group with gigs with really big bands and making a record. It was like something you read about and you don't quite believe that it's happening to you. It was amazing."

Although today most of the group recall that recording the single was their first time in a studio, the Bodysnatchers, it seems, recorded a demo five days after they played their first live show at the Windsor Castle. An entry in Penny's diary on November 29, 1979, reads: "Bobby Recording Studio 45 Earlsfield Road, SW 18." This was a reference to Bobby Henry, a Scottish singer-songwriter who the Bodysnatchers supported on a couple of occasions in the lead-up to Christmas. Rhoda distinctly recalls going to a studio "up Tulse Hill where the Specials were recording a demo ['Sock It to 'Em J.B.']. We had a couple of hours after they'd finished on a Sunday afternoon," she says. "That was our first demo—in a twenty-four-track studio. I remember thinking this is the wrong way round. This is where you're supposed to end up, not where you're supposed to start."*

Sadly, any trace of the recording has been lost to history. And so, two days before embarking on a national tour with the Selecter, the Bodysnatchers traveled to Music Works on 23 Benwell Road, Finsbury Park, where over two days—February 12 (twelve p.m. to twelve a.m.) and February 13 (twelve p.m. to seven p.m.)—they recorded their debut single. On the way to the studio they passed a hearse, finding it "extremely funny, not to say ominous," they told one journalist. But as for the choice of single, Nicky says Chrysalis gave the group "no say whatsoever. We were discussing whether to release 'The Boiler.' However, the powers that be felt it was too challenging for the public, so against our feeling we agreed to 'Let's Do Rock Steady.'" Selected by 2 Tone as "the best song"—if not a way to replicate the

---

* An unexplained diary entry in Miranda Joyce's diary reads, "Sunday 6 January, Hillside Studios. Jerry Dammers recording."

success of other 2 Tone bands who'd had breakthrough success with cover versions—the Bodysnatchers considered it an "obvious choice." But as drummer Jane Summers informed *Smash Hits*, "We found that none of our other material was strong enough and that 'Rock Steady,' which has a catchy tune and simple words, had always gone down particularly well with audiences."

Originally recorded in 1967 by Dandy Livingstone, "(People Get Ready) Let's Do Rocksteady" represented a period in Jamaican music when ska morphed into a slower, more soulful rhythm. Shifting the accent from the second and fourth count, the new rhythm emphasized the kick drum and gave prominence to the third beat of the bar—known as "one-drop." Further characterized by expressive vocal parts and melodic basslines, rocksteady was a more pop-orientated sound. Where ska had been largely instrumental, now lyrics spoke of love and romance, and encouraged more sensual moves on the dance floor. Indeed, there is much evidence to suggest that the emergence of rocksteady helped to diffuse a dangerously volatile atmosphere in downtown Kingston. Reflecting on the original concept of the Bodysnatchers, Nicky says, "I wanted us to play bluebeat, but we couldn't play fast enough. It came out to be a modern take on rocksteady."

Before working with the Specials, Roger Lomas had never listened to ska. As for rocksteady, the producer simply heard it as an infectious rhythm perfect for making a modern pop record. Nonetheless, working with the Bodysnatchers, Lomas says, was "bloody hard work. They were a nice bunch of girls but they were a bit green, totally inexperienced. They could hardly tune up or anything. But I liked their attitude and enjoyed the session." Taking twenty-six attempts to record the backing track, Nicky says it was a torrid experience: "Roger kept saying, 'Play faster! Play faster!'" Enthusiastic and willing, the group responded and in gung-ho fashion fell in line with Lomas's live approach. Edited and mixed to sound as commercial as possible, Nicky felt the finished record was a compromise and the band were "losing credibility and authenticity."

Ad for the "Let's Do Rock Steady" single, March 1980. Courtesy of Chrysalis Records/
Jerry Dammers.

* * *

Cut at CBS Studios, "Let's Do Rock Steady" was released on March
7 and launched with an ad showing the Bodysnatchers being watched
over by a gender-altered Walt Jabsco. Illustrated by John Sims, "Walt's
girlfriend," as she was affectionately christened, stood hands-in-
pocket moody and coolly attired in a black knee-length dress, stock-
ings and white loafers. Keen to take control of their visual imagery,
Sarah-Jane and Penny designed a logo with jagged lettering and pen-
ciled "blobs" marking the angle of each letter of "Bodysnatchers," and
to accompany the typography a hand grabbing a dancing rude girl.

When "Let's Do Rock Steady" entered the top forty, the
Bodysnatchers accepted an invitation to appear on *Top of the Pops*.
When a limousine driver arrived to pick up Rhoda in Brixton, he discovered she was busy shopping. "I came back and the limo was outside
my flat. My dad was going, 'This poor man is waiting for you. Where
have you been?' I said, 'Firstly, this poor man is early, and secondly, I'm
paying for this poor man to sit here so don't you worry.'" Across town,
Stella Barker was catching a bus to Wood Green and using the brief
downtime to reflect on the band's meteoric rise to success. "Things

happened very quickly: we'd just got a set together; then we had a gig; then we were signed to 2 Tone and touring with the Selecter; then we're on *Top of the Pops*. You could hardly keep up. It was like a dream."

At the BBC, pop stardom met with the demands of prerecorded television. Left to sit around for hours, the group smelled the familiar odor of herbal jazz cigarettes floating freely down the corridor from UB40's dressing room. Eventually called to the soundstage, the Bodysnatchers stirred themselves. Stella says it was a challenge "to get the adrenaline going." Penny remembers that it was difficult to hear the playback, complaining that they played the music "so quietly you could hear yourself clumping around on the stage at almost the same volume." Job done, the group jumped in a limousine and sped north to support Bad Manners in Aylesbury.

Three weeks later and making a second appearance on *Top of the Pops*—"Let's Do Rock Steady" now at a healthier twenty-two in the charts—the Bodysnatchers relaxed. Positioned at the lip of the stage facing the studio audience, Jane spun around on her drum stool and began conducting her dancing bandmates with her sticks. It would be the last time they would appear on the show, but for now, the Bodysnatchers exhibited all the signs of a bona fide pop act.

The first seven 2 Tone singles had sold over a million copies between them. The Bodysnatchers's debut record was expected to do better, but as Jane reported to *Smash Hits*, "Strangely . . . we've had a lot of people tell us that they prefer the song that we wrote on the B-side, 'Ruder Than You.'" Still, if fans felt cheated of a rude girl anthem, a shopping trip to Portobello Road Market suggested otherwise. Passing by a bus stop, Penny and Miranda happened upon a group of boys singing "Let's Do Rock Steady." "It was like, 'Wow! How exciting!'"

Such is the vindictive nature of the British press that the success of 2 Tone, both commercially and as a social force for good, attracted a growing backlash. Sounding the warning, Dave Wakeling told *Melody Maker* in January 1980, "Every record company's going fucking mad over the 2 Tone thing: look at what's happening to the Bodysnatchers. They're gonna get killed 'cos they're just not ready for it. People are waiting for the 2 Tone mistake, and it won't be long."

Variously judging the label as "boring" (*Melody Maker*), "sickly exploitative" (*Sounds*) and the "rotting undergrowth of ska" (*NME*), music journalists felt the time was right to "explode the 2 Tone myth." Informing readers that he was resentful of having to interview the Beat in the first place, Mark Williams at *Melody Maker* wrote, "Another multiracial ska band currently plundering a temporary lapse in public taste," before gleefully executing character assassinations of each member of the band.[88] On February 23, Eric Fuller accused the Specials of "recycling other artists' inspiration and claiming it as their own." Writing in *Sounds* in an article spitefully headed "Who Really Wrote the Specials's Number One?," Fuller dismissed "Too Much Too Young" as "a slightly speeded up copy" of Lloydie & the Lowbites's "Birth Control." Begrudgingly acknowledging its Dammers/Chalmers cocredit, Fuller nevertheless asserted that this in itself implied "no compulsion for the 2 Toners to actually pay up hard cash in royalty form." Turning to the Selecter, Fuller condemned the group for retitling the Pioneers's original "Time Hard" and attempting to pass it off as their own composition, "Everyday." While having the good grace to acknowledge that inefficiency in Jamaica was the chief reason for nonpayment of royalties, Fuller concluded: "Hopefully the idealistic 2 Tone ethic of white and black working together in mutual coexistence will actually work in practice and not collapse back into the dubious R&B tradition of blacks getting screwed and whites getting all the profits."

Response to the accusation was righteous anger; and it came thick and fast. The Chrysalis press office branded Fuller an "elitist bigot" and a "nasty piece of work." Writing to *Sounds* to correct the "half-truths" and "downright lies," Chris Poole pointed to the fact that 2 Tone was not responsible for paying mechanical royalties. "The 6.25 percent of the record's selling price is allocated directly to the publishers of the songs concerned by Chrysalis." In the case of "Too Much Too Young," Poole conceded, the matter was more complicated, explaining that royalties had been suspended until a dispute over who owned the

original copyright to "Birth Control" was resolved by an independent body. Signing off with an "arithmetic lesson for Mr. Fuller," Poole wrote sarcastically, "There are fourteen people in the two bands on 2 Tone (the Specials and the Selecter), six of them are white—eight are black—another case of 'blacks getting screwed and whites getting all the profit'?"
Still there was more fury.

PAULINE BLACK (*Sounds*): What he's talking about is a totally just thing. Black people have been ripped off since the early twenties, but the way he's slanting it is just a way to get at 2 Tone. For example, our song "Everyday" turns out is really called "Time Hard" but we didn't change the name to rip anyone off. I only knew the song from discos and that's what I thought it was called, and the copyright people couldn't trace the song with that title. Our end's sorted out now; the rest depends on what the Specials and Madness do.[89]

LYNVAL GOLDING (*Sounds*): What amazes me about the whole thing is that Jerry has just got to be about the fairest person on earth. I've known him for years and if there's even a half-pence discrepancy with money, he ain't happy, it all has to be shared. When we put in the musical quotations from ska, like with "Too Much Too Young" and the others, he tried to make sure the money would get to the right person . . . as long as he's got his music, food and a place to eat, Jerry's happy.[90]

RICO RODRIGUEZ (*NME*): The Specials are a *vital group*, man. Some writers and men like this, they say that the Specials is stealing reggae or ska music from the black man. But this is just pure foolishness, just pure fuckery. I was playing this music and was a most loved and respected musician in Jamaica, so would I be playing with the Specials if these things that these people say are true? The Specials are truly a revolutionary group. This 2 Tone way of doing things is fantastic, man, for now it is the musicians who're running the music, not this pure thievery that goes on everywhere before.[91]

NEVILLE STAPLE (*Black Music*): Jerry has always been into black music, that's where his heart has been, and he's playing the music the same way me, as a black guy would play it. It's having the feel, and you get that through liking and listening to the music.[92]

LAUREL AITKEN (pioneering Jamaica-based ska singer): It was great for me to see Jerry Dammers and his posse doing what they were doing because a lot of black people weren't interested in playing ska. I don't know why. They want to play reggae. Reggae and ska are the same thing—except it's just a change of drumbeat or a different drop of the bass.[93]

LYNVAL GOLDING (*NME*): Me play Specials records to guys who is the strictest Rastas, and they don't complain. Not one has said to me that we shouldn't be playing this music. They just care about reggae music, not about whether it's black or white people playing it. Just the music, man.[94]

Nonetheless, the damage was done. Following complaints about overdue royalties, 2 Tone next found itself fielding renewed accusations of revivalism. "We've been labeled as this revival and that revival," responded Terry Hall in an interview with *Record Mirror*. "Revival is a word for people who haven't heard the word continuation."[95] Defending the Selecter's sound, Neol Davies said, "It's because of the media that there's such a revivalist/nostalgia tag attached to it. It's not like that at all. What we're doing is *now*. We're not regurgitating something that's been done before. We're creating something new. There's nothing like 2 Tone ever existed in the past."[96]

The great misconception about 2 Tone is that each of the original groups (the Specials, the Selecter and Madness—and later the Beat and the Bodysnatchers) committed to one genre. "Three completely different bands with a link in ska," says Mark Bedford. "It's everything," asserts Neol Davies, "the soul, the rock, the reggae, the ska, everything." On paper it should never have worked, such were the disparate influences. "Everyone thought they were in a different band," laughs Roddy Byers, contemplating the cross-genre influences of the Specials. "Lynval thought it was ska. Brad thought it was Tamla Motown. Neville thought he was U-Roy. Horace thought it was a funky-type Little Feat band. I thought I was in the Clash. Jerry thought he was in an avant-garde jazz group, and Terry thought he was in the Cure; his vocals were hardly Prince Buster or Desmond Dekker. That's what made the band what it was: all those different influences worked and made the sound of the Specials. Never mind what everyone else was doing. Ignore that! This is what we are."

Talking in October 1979, the Specials's drummer John Bradbury addressed the repeated accusation that reggae was music of and for Black musicians by arguing that ultimately music belonged to anybody. "Reggae, in its purest form, is very much part of Black people's culture and I think, in our case, they take exception to a bunch of white guys—well, bar a couple—messing about with what they consider to be their music. They have a very personal involvement with their music; it's very precious to them and has been for a long time. We don't get a lot of coverage in the Black press. In fact, we were slagged off recently by *Black Music* magazine, who take the view that people like Rico and other such luminaries have never got the break, whereas along come a bunch of white guys, take a few of the licks and riffs, and turn the whole thing into some sort of gold mine. I can understand that point of view, but it still sounds a little bit like sour grapes to me. Every individual has the capacity to get and do what they want, particularly in music, regardless of color. It's a shame, because we have got a very mixed audience, and it would be great if we could gain more credibility with the black audience—although I think we will, eventually."[97]

Conscious of the argument becoming too analytical, Jerry says, "Musicians are always going to imitate the music that they like. If you like reggae you're going to try and play it—it's just music."

CHAPTER 20

GO-FEET

THE BEAT LEAVE 2 TONE. SECOND 2 TONE TOUR. MISSING WORDS

By the new year, "Tears of a Clown" had sold a staggering 320,000 copies. Nevertheless, 2 Tone was spiraling out of control, as predicted by bass player David Steele. "It had more to do with the *Sun* and the *Daily Mirror* than the Specials," he told *Record Mirror* in September 1980. "It got so massive that Chrysalis had to step in and help run it. We had total faith in Jerry, and if it was totally down to him, we would have considered staying with 2 Tone." Suggesting that the label's success had been born out of naivety, Steele continues: "I think that was the reason that everybody pulled it off. Half its charm was that it came across as very spontaneous and very innocent."

Riding high with the success of "Tears of a Clown" and beneficiaries of 2 Tone's unstoppable momentum, the Beat nevertheless wanted out. "I'd be much more wary now of saying yes to 2 Tone because it is so big," guitarist Andy Cox told *Smash Hits* a year after signing with the label, "whereas it was perfect when we were asked to do it." Contractually free, the Beat courted the record industry to find a new label. "If the Specials and Selecter had not already had that arrangement with Chrysalis, they would have been one of my favorite labels to go with," says John Mostyn. "Rightly or wrongly, we felt that they had two bands already in a similar style and might we always be third? We wanted to be somewhere where we would be a high priority. We were happy to be associated with 2 Tone and be thought of as part of that movement. But from a long-term career perspective we needed a different arrangement with another major label."

Desperate to secure the Beat's signature, "Chrysalis," Dave Wakeling told *Melody Maker*, "had all these glamorous model types in our dressing room at the Lyceum. It was as though they were trying to tell us, 'Sign with us, lads, and all this can be yours.'" Skeptical of such base skulduggery, Chris Poole lets out a big sigh. "Oh, come on," he says. "I never remember Chrysalis using tactics like that to secure band signatures on record contracts. The nearest we came was when we had a Christmas party with naked mud wrestling. It made the front page of the *Sun*. My wife woke me up the next morning, threw the papers on the bed and said, 'So, you had a good time last night!'"

Attracting offers from Virgin, Island, EMI, Warner Bros. and Chrysalis, the Beat, wishing to emulate 2 Tone's autonomous arrangement with Chrysalis, held out for their own boutique label. "We want to maintain that allegiance to 2 Tone but having too many bands under the same umbrella could have allowed things to get sour," commented Dave Wakeling. "We thought we could work in a similar vein, come from a different angle with the same basic message."[98]

Investing in a Crombie and porkpie hat, A&R man Tarquin Gotch had first seen the Beat in the summer at the Electric Ballroom, and then at the Underworld Club in Birmingham in October 1979. Seizing the initiative on behalf of Arista, Gotch agreed to the creation of Go-Feet Records and offered the Beat a five-year contract and a £60,000 advance. "It was a continuation of Jerry's crazy, unheard-of idea," smiles Rick Rogers. "Other bigger labels were seeing the opportunities: 2 Tone worked and opened a lot of doors."

Bankrolled, marketed and distributed by Arista, Go-Feet offered the Beat a replica arrangement to the one that the Specials and 2 Tone had with Chrysalis. "We were influenced by their spirit," says David Steele. "It was a tribute. But in some ways, I wish we'd signed to 2 Tone. But we just thought we'd get submerged in the Specials's shadow." As Ranking Roger explains, "The Specials carried us at first but we all—Madness and Selecter—would have made it in our own right. We were on 2 Tone for one single. The next three years we spent all our time trying to get away from 2 Tone. 'You're 2 Tone?' 'No! We're Go-Feet. We've only got about two ska songs.' We didn't want to be curbed into a particular style. That's what kills bands. We did punk and reggae and soul and disco. 2 Tone was going backward with a forward message. It was a new type of music. We said, 'We're dance music. That's it.'"

Having agreed to terms with Arista, the Beat were disowned by Chrysalis, as Dave Wakeling claimed in an interview with *Melody Maker*, further objecting that the group only found out about a scheduled *Top of the Pops* appearance by accident. "They've totally ignored us. And look at all the money we're making for them. The way they come on when they're trying to sign you, it's hard to remember you're dealing with trained businessmen."[99] Skeptical of such malpractice, John Mostyn offers more considered analysis. "I don't know that Chrysalis pulled the promotion on the record. It got to number six. What else could they do? Maybe internationally they slowed down. But you would. If they didn't have an album, they were not going to pay lots of money taking the band to foreign TV shows. It was only natural for Chrysalis to lay off. Doug D'Arcy and Roy Eldridge were delightful to work with. Straightforward. You agreed something and that is what happened. But by Christmas I was starting to negotiate with other labels."

If there was any reservation that leaving 2 Tone would be to the Beat's detriment, the release of their first single on Go-Feet, "Hand's Off . . . She's Mine," and sales approaching a quarter of a million, put paid to any such lingering doubt. Three months later, "Mirror in the Bathroom" hurtled up the singles chart to number four. Next, the Beat planned a debut album and, in a display of independence, dropped out of a scheduled mouth-watering triple-bill tour with the Selecter and the Bodysnatchers. "The association with 2 Tone had been great," says Mostyn, "but did we really need a month on the road with the Selecter and the Bodysnatchers in terms of our long-term development? No, not really."

In search of a replacement for the Beat, Pauline Black had recently seen Holly & the Italians, a postpunk band sharing the bill
with the Selecter and Blondie at the Hammersmith Odeon. She suggested they come on board. It was billed as the second 2 Tone Tour to
promote the Selecter's newly released *Too Much Pressure*, and Holly
& the Italians gratefully accepted Black's offer to open the show.
Hailing from Los Angeles and led by Holly Beth Vincent, the trio
were an unusual musical choice for a 2 Tone package tour.* "I loved
the idea behind the tour," says Vincent, "mixing up the music and
a very strong representation of female musicians. But the audience
just wanted to hear the reggae rhythms vibe the whole night. We all
thought it would work but it just didn't." Holly & the Italians transmitted all the hallmarks of a new wave guitar band, audiences hoping
for a repeat of the first 2 Tone Tour and a night of ska-fueled dance
music vented their frustration at them. "The bigoted birdbrains down
front started up a set-long 'Fuck off' chorus while most people stared
apathetically," wrote Garry Bushell in *Sounds*. "Booed offstage for being different," he concluded.

Though Holly & the Italians were fresh from supporting Lene
Lovich and the Bodysnatchers at the Lyceum, Juliet de Vie says, introducing them to a partisan audience was a mistake. "They didn't
treat them well. The music was so different and Holly didn't have the
2 Tone look. But we thought what she was doing was great. She was
an accomplished guitarist. There weren't that many women around
with any real edge." Frustrated by the audience's intolerance, Pauline
Black admits the choice of support was misjudged. "It was too new
wave for our particular audience, let alone a female-fronting band."
But where a less sympathetic Chris Poole dismisses Holly & the Italians as "a second-rate Pretenders," Sarah-Jane Owen feels they were
perhaps "too sophisticated, somehow." Seeing it both ways, Miranda
Joyce—thankful for the tour falling during school half term—says,

---

* Steve Young was from Los Angeles, Mark Henry from Brighton. Vincent, at
the time, was dating Mark Knopfler of Dire Straits and was the Juliet in their
hit single "Romeo & Juliet."

"They were a good band but it was completely the wrong tour for them. The audience had come along to hear one thing and then they were confronted by something completely different halfway through. So it's not surprising they were given a hard time." Rhoda Dakar agrees: "If you come to see a 2 Tone band, you expect to see just that. You wouldn't expect or want to see Def Leppard, would you?"[100]

Defeated, Holly & the Italians left the tour. "We are appalled at the narrow-mindedness of a fashion-following audience," Holly informed *NME*, "and we apologize to those of our fans who were kicked and intimidated by a mindless few." Backed by a statement to the press, Trigger management expressed their disappointment at audiences unwilling "to give a different kind of music a chance. We think Holly & the Italians are a great band, which is why we invited them onto the package in the first place."* To take their spot on the tour, Neol Davies and Juliet de Vie invited the Swinging Cats, who they had recently seen at the Hope & Anchor in Coventry. "That was an amazing feeling," says guitar player and founding member John Shipley. "We'd only done about eight or ten gigs by then. But they wouldn't let us take our go-go dancers, Chris and Jane."

Debuting at the Cambridge Corn Exchange, the Swinging Cats made an immediate impact. Later noted for handling "her audience like a sarcastic schoolteacher" and "telling off the naughty boys, who chant quietly but consistently throughout every track," lead singer Val Webb asked, "Is there anyone in the audience called Dougal?" Met with predictable heckles, Webb then introduced the theme from the children's television program *The Magic Roundabout*. "It was amazing," says Shipley. "The whole place went mad. It lent itself to a ska rhythm. We also used to do a version of *The Avengers*." Mixing film soundtracks with childhood nostalgia proved a winning formula and, coupled with "an amazing sound system," bass player Steve Wynne

---

* In February 1981, Holly & the Italians released their only studio album, *The Right to Be Italian*, which was heralded by *Trouser Press* as "a new wave classic of romantic ups and downs, leather-jacket rebellion and kitsch culture, carried mightily on Vincent's tough-girl attitude, full-throated singing, gale-force Brill Building melodies and chunky rhythm guitar presence."

says, "For the first time you were hearing it full-on." However, off-stage, Shipley was not happy. Put off by Pauline Black who, he says, "used to sit at the front of the coach not having anything to do with anybody else," he discloses that Juliet de Vie tried to talk him into leaving the band. "We did a gig in Nottingham and she said that I would be better making music with other people. She could see it wasn't going very well. The drummer wasn't very good. He used to go on in swimming trunks. It was ridiculous."

Sidestepping interband politics, de Vie was busy organizing the Bodysnatchers. A week before the tour they signed to 2 Tone. "I did loads for them. They had no management and I helped them get their shit together. We were suddenly going, 'Come on tour,' but they'd barely played a handful of gigs. They had some gear but no flight cases. They didn't have a clue what they were doing. They needed an awful lot of help very quickly." Thrilled by the prospect of two months on the road and staying in hotels for the first time, Rhoda Dakar says, "I don't think we'd even done a gig outside London at that point."

When the house lights dimmed, a deep voice announced over the PA: "This is the invasion of the Bodysnatchers." On cue, Penny launched into the opening figure from a Bach prelude. Then, just as suddenly, the band sprang into action with "007." Off they went: Rhoda running from one side of the stage to the other, imploring the crowd to dance. "She really held it together," says Miranda. "She was such a great front person and had a good rapport with the audience. No one was a great musician. We were learning and getting better the more we played. If things went wrong or we were out of time, Rhoda would say, 'Oh, fucking hell! Come on, let's do it again.' Nothing fazed her. She rolled with it and carried all of us." At Leeds University on the third night on the tour, Garry Bushell reviewed a "Cocky Rhoda swaggering round the stage, grinning and cheeking the crowd. "'Ere you'll get what you're given and like it, mate.' When some wag shouted, 'Show us yer minge,' she turned on him and cut him down to about two centimeters high with an ace selection of South London abuse."[101]

Struggling to keep it together, the group attempted "Mule Jerk" five times and still failed to move beyond the introduction. "It started with the bass and drums on an offbeat," says Penny, "and in the end Rhoda asked the audience if they wanted us to skip to the next song or have another go. They said they wanted us to have another go." Frustrated, Rhoda says, "We weren't good enough. There wasn't any leap of imagination. If it hadn't been for Penny, we wouldn't have been able to write any songs. She was the one who could say, 'We're playing in this key. This is where you need to play . . . these are the notes.' Nobody had a clue. It was a baptism of fire." Adamant that they were a product of punk as much as ska, Nicky Summers argues, "It wasn't the point to be a proficient musician. It was about getting your thoughts across or your attitude or your energy or your fury or whatever it was. That was a large feature of the Bodysnatchers."

Happening across graffiti that read, "The Bodysnatchers are a true punk band," Penny says, "In those days women weren't picking up a guitar at the age of thirteen. They didn't have years of experience playing an instrument like the guys did. We didn't have musical confidence. We couldn't jam onstage. Our songs were the same all the time, whereas the Selecter had musical sophistication. I was in awe of that. They were totally in control of everything they did. At that point, I was still suffering a lot from stage fright. It was inevitable that playing six nights a week we were going to get better. It's like they say, 'How do you get to Carnegie Hall? Practice, practice, practice.'" Yet, all around there was a barrage of disparaging comments. Men mocked the novelty of an all-woman group. "Whenever we did a soundcheck there was a lot of expectation that we would not be able to play our instruments," continues Penny. "Roadies on the side of the stage with their arms folded going, 'This is going to be a laugh!' Sexism was a hurdle that we came up against often. 'Oh, you play good for a girl.' We were determined to keep going. We were doing music that had a strong message. There was a sense of accomplishment and joy being part of a movement that was exciting and different. We demanded respect."

Night by night, the Bodysnatchers studied the stagecraft of the Selecter, noting how they handled situations; how they got from one song to the next until "slowly and surely we got tight," says Penny. "The lighting crews and roadies changed their tune and realized we weren't just a bunch of girls to be laughed at." "By the end of the tour," adds Sarah-Jane, "we were a different band."

Backstage a different set of challenges faced the band, as Penny explains: "The dressing rooms were awful. Stinky. Slobby. Cigarette burns in the carpet. They'd never had a woman in these places. There'd be seven women all trying to get dressed and look okay to go on-stage and not one mirror in the place. We learned quickly to bring our own. I don't know how Pauline coped. She was with an all-male band."

The touring party of near a dozen women were at the forefront of an industry that would take decades to evolve. Progress was slow. Nevertheless, Juliet de Vie makes the case that the tour represented women "answering back. It was their turn," she says. "It felt like we were getting some momentum with the 2 Tone idea. There were cool women out there doing stuff. It wasn't 'the girls having a go.' They were delivering. It was women being supportive and having a great time. Strong women. Women with views. Women who didn't have domestic ambitions. We weren't being strident feminists either. We were on a mission to show the boys, we can do it too." Confronted by obstacles and bigotry at every turn, the Bodysnatchers tackled endless rounds of stock questions. "Do you share makeup?" "Do you share your clothes?" "Have you got boyfriends?" "How relevant is that to us as a band and what we were doing?" asks Stella Barker, firmly pointing her finger at easily titillated rock journalists. "It was very annoying, and it happened often."

Brushing aside their grievances, the band got down to hard partying and innocent fun: making apple-pie beds (preventing anyone stretching full length between the sheets) to welcome late-night revelers, knitting on the tour bus, and if in doubt, starting a water fight. "We were like schoolkids," laughs Rhoda. "We all had water pistols and soaked journalists whose questions we didn't like." Armed with their aquatic weaponry, Sarah-Jane, Rhoda and Miranda graced the front cover of *Record Mirror*, pistols cocked in their mouths. Physically exhausted, Penny says by the end of the tour she was throwing up. "I don't think we ever went to bed before three in the morning. It was nuts."

Food and drink rider on the second 2 Tone Tour, March 6, 1980.

Rooming list on the second 2 Tone Tour, February 1980.

* * *

On March 4, the party mood was abruptly silenced when a fight in the middle of the dance floor in Guildford forced innocent fans to cower on the edges of the auditorium. "People would be dancing, then somebody would push somebody or want to get in front and then a fight would break out," says Sarah-Jane. "It just seemed that is what men did on a Saturday night. There was such a lot of unrest with audiences in general and the music seemed to stir all that up." Rhoda was incensed. "How dare you!" she shouted at the perpetrators. "What do you think you're playing at? I'm going to sort you out." Forced to stop playing, the Bodysnatchers left the stage. But Rhoda was not finished. "I came back on and had a go at everybody: 'Why do you spend your money to come in and ruin it for other people? You're not going to change anybody's mind. You're wasting your time.' I shouted until they stopped. I was absolutely fuming." Then, on March 15, during a show at Whitla Hall, Belfast, two stewards, aged twenty-one and twenty-three, were stabbed in the back and admitted to the city hospital in serious condition. Reported in the *Belfast Telegraph*, a police spokesperson said that a fight developed after a group was refused admission and that the two youths were helping with their inquiries into the incident. Watching on horror-struck as fighting cleared the room, Miranda now says stabbings were a common occurrence. "Many skinheads carried knives. They were like, 'Cut ya.' It was nasty. National Front supporters would dance merrily to Black-influenced music played by Black musicians. I was too young and naive to make sense of it all. Nobody can." Attributing their actions to "herd behavior," Penny says, "Part of 2 Tone was to educate the audience and say Black people invented this music. You need to accept that the world is two tone. It was trying to make people aware of equality and to stop racism."

Trouble then reached a boiling point within the Selecter camp. Constantly having to put up with members of the band willfully being late, Pauline Black sat at the front of the bus seething. Climbing up the stairwell, Desmond took one look at Pauline and, lunging at her, began strangling her, shouting, "YOU AIN'T NO FUCKING

QUEEN!" Dragged off by Charley Anderson, "Desmond," says Pauline, "was self-medicating with a bottle of whiskey a day and taking pills for a sexually transmitted disease. It was shocking but I didn't make a big deal out of it. The man was ill. He needed treatment. But nobody was going to listen to me. It was new for me to work with Black people, particularly Black men. Male musicians don't like women being around, and being the lead singer made no difference. I was a provincial Black girl who originated from Essex. That was a very different thing from somebody like Siouxsie Sioux, Rhoda, Debbie Harry or Chrissie Hynde. They were either from London or America and had been involved with club scenes from an early age. It was a different sensibility."

Horrified by the unexpected show of aggression, John Shipley describes Desmond Brown as a "scary big guy who completely lost the plot. It was horrible to witness." Demanding that the driver stop immediately, Shipley refused to stay on board and for the remainder of the tour traveled in the roadies' van. "There was a lot of friction," admits Neol Davies. "The guys weren't used to a woman like Pauline: how she talked to people. She wasn't West Indian but she was Black. It threw them. She was coarse and it upset people." Perhaps. But Desmond's behavior was nonetheless inexcusable.

There were often people in the audiences who ignored pleas for calm from the stage, and an air of violence followed the tour when it crossed the Irish Sea back to England. At Friars Aylesbury, opposing gangs clashed on either side of a gaping hole in the crowd. "You can't play when people are fighting," reasons Penny Leyton, "and sometimes it would be women." In Middlesbrough, violence spilled onto the street when an angry mob smashed the windows of the Bodysnatchers's van. Taking it upon themselves to challenge the inherent contradiction between supporting 2 Tone and having racist attitudes, members of the band questioned the agitators. "Yeah, but we like the music." "What about Rhoda then?" one of the girls asked. "She's alright," came the oblique response. "She's a tart, ain't she?"

Committed to winning over so-called "undesirables" intent on sabotaging the shows, Charley Anderson proposed staging a mock fight to highlight the absurdity of unbridled violence. Midway through "Too Much Pressure," strobe lighting would suddenly engulf the stage, the music would falter, and, dropping their instruments, the band would seemingly attack one another. "Most people used to think we were actually doing it for real," laughs Pauline, "and sometimes we were, depending on how much dissension was going on in the band at the time. It was a way of offsetting fights in the crowd, and saying, 'This is what it looks like when you don't get along. Is this what you want?' It must have been quite a thing to behold to see a group of Black folk all lamping each other."

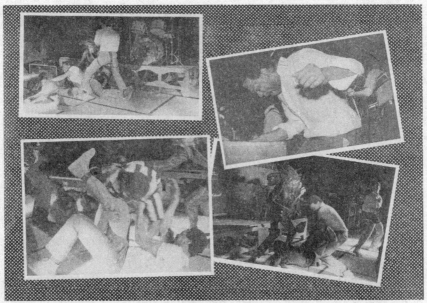

Filming of the Selecter stage-fighting for *Dance Craze*, Lee Studios, London 1980.

Having limped offstage often covered in blood, Compton Amanor says Pauline was vicious. "She'd lay into Charley, or Desmond would jump on top of Gaps and start punching him in the ribs. We would all let off our tensions. It was exactly what those songs used to say, *Every day they make me mad; too much pressure.* The point wasn't that violence is not the way. It was saying that violence is part of every-day life." Reviewing for *Sounds*, Garry Bushell watched on wide-eyed as Desmond's organ cut out, and losing his cool, he kicked it over and stormed offstage. "He's so fuming, so angry, that once again I'm fooled by the fight scene 'cos it looks so real and how the hell do I know he ain't using it as an excuse to beat shit out of his fellows?"

The juxtaposition of stage play and realism resonated with Juliet de Vie, who argues that alongside the ambition and originality of the idea, the mock fighting held a mirror to the audience and made them question mindless antagonism. "Violence only makes sense when you're in it and fueled by the anger," she says. "Just watching it becomes ludicrous. People were like, 'Fucking hell! Look what's going on up there.' It was a distraction: it took the aggression out of the audience. By the time they picked up their instruments again, people had forgotten where they were at."

Fortunately, so had the press, who, much to the delight of the Selecter, focused their opinions on the music. "Watching the band is like watching a hornet's nest after you've thrown rocks at it," wrote Garry Bushell. "They're up and down, in and out, jiving and dancing all over the shop." Reviewing a performance at the Hammersmith Palais, *Melody Maker* was similarly enthused: "Pauline Black's natural effervescence puts her well above other 2 Tone vocalists. The Selecter satisfy almost every musical craving, throwing in a little social com-mentary as a bonus. They're yet to let us down." To capitalize on the success of the tour, the Selecter prepared to release a third single. To his surprise, the job of remixing "Missing Words" was offered to Roger Lomas. "They realized they'd made a mistake as soon as the album came out and knew 'Missing Words' wasn't up to it as a single. I listened to the multitrack and said, 'This doesn't want remixing. It wants *rerecording*!'" Reluctantly accepting the task of reinvigorating the song, Lomas began by isolating each individual instrument on the multitrack only to discover layers of unwelcome noise spillage. "I had a hell of a job filtering it out," he says. "It was all wrong but I had to go along with it."

245 ♪ Daniel Rachel

Remixing the song over two consecutive evenings, Lomas freshened the arrangement by introducing a chorus immediately after the first verse, deleting an unnecessary repeated bridge and adding an extra chorus as the song played out. Released on March 14, "Missing Words"—backed by a live version of "Carry Go Bring Come" recorded at Tiffany's during the 2 Tone Tour—divided opinion. While *Record Mirror* claimed it "their most successful yet . . . a record that gets better with each hearing," *NME* complained about "another 2 Tone, not unlike all the other 2 Tone records . . . 'Missing Words' lacks the easy grace that characterizes the best of the genre, and generally sounds just a little too pompous for its own good. To be brutally frank, it bores the balls off me."

Stalling just outside of the top twenty, "Missing Words"—memorably misprinted as "Nissing Words" on later pressings—did little to invigorate a group caught between the forward thrust of their 2 Tone peers and ailing chart positions. Nonetheless, the Selecter once again graced the *Top of the Pops* studio and, much to the delight of eagle-eyed fans, poked fun at the demands of television miming. Swapping instruments, Desmond pranced around the stage with Charley's bass as his bandmate swung his golden dreads and danced exuberantly behind the keyboards: the Selecter 1, BBC 0.

CHAPTER 21

WORKING AT YOUR LEISURE

RAT RACE. MORE SPECIALS

By spring 1980, 2 Tone had launched five new bands—the Specials, Madness, the Selecter, the Beat and the Bodysnatchers—each one of them enjoying hit singles and a flurry of media attention. In April, a search began to find a suitable location for a 2 Tone studio, including a request submitted to West Midlands County Council to purchase the iconic Paris Cinema in Far Gosford Street. Celebrated for its decorative façade and giant crown topping the building, the premises, first opened in 1912 as the Crown Theatre, boasted a large wooden sprung dance floor. Valued in 1980 at £25,000, Neol Davies says the former cinema was "big enough to have a venue, a huge studio and office space." Short of investors, the dream of a 2 Tone power base fell through. "We never got our own studio, and sadly Coventry didn't shape up to be the next Memphis," commented a rueful Jerry Dammers.

Attention turned to the next Specials album and a new single to follow the all-conquering success of "Too Much Too Young." In 1973, Bob Marley sang of captivity, linking the urban hardness of a pervasive "Concrete Jungle" to a theme of unrequited love and longing for sweet caresses. Three years later, he offered "Rat Race" as a comment on political violence and an alleged CIA-backed Rasta militancy in Kingston. In the same year, 1976, Roddy Byers discovered the music of Marley and subsequently wrote two songs: "Concrete

Jungle" and "Rat Race." "Titles were always my big problem," laughs Roddy. "I always picked ones that had been used before. Whether I'd heard 'Rat Race' I don't know, but I didn't think, *Oh, I'll use that for the next Specials single.*"

The inspiration behind "Rat Race" traces back to a rejection of art college in favor of what Roddy describes as "three years of learning to bum around and play guitar." One night, benefitting from the cheap beer on tap at the Lanchester Polytechnic bar, Roddy overheard some well-to-do students discussing career opportunities lined up by their parents after graduation. Provoked by a perceived injustice and his own personal regret at snubbing college life, Roddy went home and created "Rat Race." "It struck me that their places would be better used by students of a less wealthy background," he says, cognizant that the lyrics chastising students for *learning the things you don't need* and *wasting your time* are open to misinterpretation. "It wasn't anti-education," he insists. "It was about privilege and people wasting their time at university when their places could have been taken by people who are poor and deserved those places better."

Amplifying the polemical content of the song, the Specials filmed a promotional video for "Rat Race" in the student union building at Lanchester Polytechnic. Performing in front of a row of students taking exams, the group were dressed in various educational guises: Lynval as a PE teacher, Neville in gown and mortarboard, Jerry as a school ma'am in tweed jacket and Dr. Martens, and Brad and Roddy as science and art teachers respectively. Lured away from an enticing FA Cup Final televised clash between West Ham and Arsenal, students were encouraged to participate in the filming in exchange for a free signed copy of the new single.

Recorded to bridge the gap between the band's first and second albums, "Rat Race" saw the group returning to Horizon Studios, where a little over a year earlier "Gangsters" had been made. As an homage to Linton Kwesi Johnson, the rhythm section conjured a backing track indebted to the poet's agitprop album *Forces of Victory*. "It was like, 'Let's have "Want fi Goh Rave" in the back of our mind,'" says

Horace Panter. The cyclical arrangement perfectly complemented a bass, drum and percussive rhythm track, infusing the backing with a subtle, infectious offbeat. Adorning the introduction, Jerry lifted three notes from the guitar solo and plucked them on the exposed strings of a grand piano to create a distinctive opening riff. Lastly, sheets of corrugated iron, assembled to create a "shantytown-style" vocal booth, helped to enhance Terry's melodious warbling and brighten the overall sound of the record.

During the session, the BBC arrived to film a short feature for the early evening news program *Nationwide*. For the benefit of uninitiated viewers, a cut-glass English voice-over reported, "When the executives of 2 Tone Records gather for a subcommittee meeting, you might be forgiven for failing to notice the similarity between their quiet gatherings and those of the Young Conservatives. Yet these earnest young Midland entrepreneurs are the epitome of free enterprise in Margaret Thatcher's brave new Britain." Described as one of the most successful record labels of the past twenty years, with sales of over three million since its inception, 2 Tone was credited as a small firm setting up "in a deprived area of high youth unemployment" and becoming "a thriving international concern." Downplaying its nonexistent legal framework, Jerry set the record straight: "It's more of an anarchist commune than a business. It has no managing director, no written partnership." Further revealing plans to rent an office and employ a secretary to cope with the deluge of letters and tapes, Jerry reaffirmed that 2 Tone would continue to be run "by ourselves." Then, keen to shift the conversation from business to music, Jerry gave a demonstration of the R&B style which inspired the original ska sound. Playing an upright piano, his "tribute to Professor Longhair" neatly segued into the backing of "Rude Boys Outa Jail" and footage of the Specials adding handclaps to the flip side of their new single.

To promote the release—championed by *Record Mirror* as "another winner . . . the best since 'Gangsters'"—Chrysalis advertised the double-sided single with a sixties-styled office woman wearing a black-and-white patterned blouse, her hands imitating the paws of a rat hanging suspended above the keys of a typewriter. This earned John Sims the 1981 Design & Art Direction Award.

Ad for the "Rat Race" single, May 1980. Courtesy of Chrysalis Records/Jerry Dammers.

In May, Terry Hall peered into a camera lens on the front cover of *Smash Hits* dressed in a red jacket and matching shirt, while on page twelve, the rest of the Specials gathered around the plinth of Lady Godiva. "Today Coventry, Tomorrow . . . Coventry" ran the headline at the top of the article. Beneath, David Hepworth offered a short course in "Two Tonics" and how to keep out of the rat race. "[The Specials] lit a match under the year 1979," enthused the twenty-nine-year-old journalist, "plugged into the mains electricity of Jamaican rhythm" and "made nothing but records you could dance to." After declaring 2 Tone the "most consistently successful record label in Britain (and probably the world)," Terry is asked about his status as a teen idol. "I don't want to be on a big stage with bright lights and kids gawping at me," he replies, deflecting the responsibility of pop stardom. "I'd much prefer them to turn their backs on me and just dance."

The call for less exposure received unexpected support when *Top of the Pops* took offense to "Rat Race" and refused to broadcast its accompanying film. Unmoved by what Jerry described as his "impression of a headmistress straight from the shower scene of *Psycho*," the BBC asserted their "moral obligation to protect young viewers from anything that might be considered offensive." Thriving on the adverse publicity, Chris Poole confided, "We used to play up stories like that. It was part of the game." Indeed, it was. The following week, and clearly unharmed by circulated images of Jerry dressed up in drag grinning inanely, "Rat Race" leaped into the top five.

Jerry Dammers on set filming the video for "Rat Race," Lanchester Polytechnic, Coventry, 1980.

* * *

"I'd really like to destroy people's ideas of good and bad music, so that eventually people will hear a record and they won't even know if they like it or not," said Jerry Dammers in June 1980. Four months later, the Specials would release their second album. If fans were hoping for more of the same, Jerry had one more message to communicate: "My ambition is to make background music." Acknowledging that songs like "Too Much Too Young" and "Concrete Jungle" had become a soundtrack for a generation, now Jerry introduced a new expression: "Muzak." It was a concept first raised in December 1979, when Jerry explained to *NME* that "Muzak" belonged "in city rail bars" and played "with an absurd mixture of instruments." Further informing readers that a lot of original ska had a very strong movie-theme influence, Jerry offered an enigmatic vision of the Specials: "We want to use the source and mix it with ska . . . like going from an accordion to a really fuzzed guitar or something."

There is a fine line between carrying an audience forward and holding on to the present. Bands have to progress and evolve. The challenge is to remain true to the spirit of creativity while repaying loyalty: introducing something new but not burying the past. Historically, the Beatles perfected the art of progression, innovating and pioneering sounds that transported the group and their fan base together into the future. It was a blueprint Jerry Dammers admired and wished to replicate. In America, he discovered the new direction for the Specials in the unlikely surroundings of hotel and shopping mall elevators. Loosely fitting the description of ambient music, Jerry says of the music he heard, "It was all sorts of vibraphones, just very, very strange, and it suited my mood of being out of touch, because we'd been out on the road so much. So I was getting into all these different types of music that had previously been regarded as just rubbish."

Prior to the US tour, Jerry had taken advantage of a trip to Paris to rummage through bargain bins. The search uncovered records with titles like "A Touch of Velvet—A Sting of Bass" by the Mood-Mosaic—an instrumental track from 1966 and later adopted by Dave Lee Travis as the theme for his Radio 1 show—and *Super Stereo Party Vol. II*, a compilation of cha-cha, rumba and marimba songs. "I think it's time for the 2 Tone bands to start getting a bit more experimental," Jerry told the newly launched *Face* in May 1980.* "Some of it has really started becoming a big cliché. Really, we've got to go back and start all over again. It's back to square one."

---

* Jerry was the front-cover star with a photograph taken by Chalkie Davies.

The new Specials record would experiment with exotica and the ironic use of bossa nova and calypso "home organ" drum machine rhythms. It would feature complex chord structures and a sense of "wallpaper music" familiar from supermarkets or heard in Chinese restaurants. "Jerry wanted to break away from the identity of the first Specials album musically and visually," Terry Hall told the BBC in 2009. "I was fascinated. Stuff like 'International Jet Set' and 'Stereotypes' was brilliant. I was really happy to go along. I trusted Jerry musically. He's a genius."[102] And so, in April 1980, slightly battered from their exhausting tour of the US, the Specials reconvened at Horizon Studios and settled down to two months of recording and experimentation. "We were all looking at each other going, 'He's lost the bloody plot!'" says Roddy. "Jerry had been hanging out with John Shipley, who was really into soundtrack music: Mantovani, John Barry and all things Muzak!" With talk of a radical change, drum machines, lounge music and very little ska, Roddy concluded somewhat disingenuously, "It was basically what the Swinging Cats were doing."

Jerry and Roddy had once been drinking partners with a shared sense of humor, but their relationship was beginning to crumble. "My first disagreement with Jerry was over 'Hey, Little Rich Girl,' a song I'd written about a girlfriend I went out with in the early seventies who came from a posh area just outside Coventry. Jerry's new sound included the use of robotic drum machines and I thought this would ruin my ska-billy–rock 'n' roll song." Disagreement over the direction of the track resulted in an ugly argument and Roddy producing a weapon. "I let Jerry admire my new James Dean flick knife," he says, "and drove it in the top of my amp to make a point." Rightly feeling violated, Jerry says the incident was "deeply upsetting." It also revealed a disturbing side to Roddy's increasingly unpredictable character.

On another occasion, Roddy presented a new song called "We're Only Monsters." Jerry was far from impressed. "The lyrics went something like, *We're not the boys next door, we're the werewolves down your street*. It was not right for the album, so I told Roddy to go and write something else." It did little to help the situation. Matters spiraled further out of control when Roddy pinned another new composition—"Why Argue with Fate"—on the studio wall. The words questioned *false prophets* and putting faith in leaders *with a heart as cold as ice*. "It was essentially saying, 'Jerry Dammers is a heartless bastard.' It was a bit much to expect me to play on a song which was blatantly trying to insult me," bristles Jerry.*

Forty years on from the album sessions, it is clear how damaged and hurt both parties remain by the experience. "I had ideas," says Roddy, "and to be told some of them weren't good enough and then to be told note-to-note what to play, it was almost like Jerry wanted session players. It was like, 'No, I want you to play this. This note, this note . . . no, not that note.' Neville was being told what to ad-lib. Terry was being told what to sing and how to sing it: 'Sound more pissed off.' 'I *am* pissed off.' 'Sound even more pissed off!' It was Jerry's baby. He had the final say. He'd tell us what was going on or just whine and moan until he got us to agree to whatever he wanted." Pressed to answer such accusations, Jerry reluctantly points to Roddy's in- creasingly drunken and abusive behavior. Further pointing out that the guitar had to be recorded separately because of repeated "bum notes," Jerry says more sophisticated chord changes and the move away from the trashy punk of the first album exposed Roddy's limita- tions. "You couldn't tell him anything," he reasons. Rattled by the sur- rounding negativity, Jerry lashed out: "Beethoven's musicians never questioned him." Whispering in his ear, Roddy retorted, "Thou art mortal, Caesar."

Wishing to avoid additional confrontation, the group began to splinter in an attempt to avoid one another's company. "You'd get to the studio and Horace would be there, and you'd go, 'I'll come back later,'" says Roddy. "Then someone else would come in, 'Who else is here?' People wouldn't turn up for three days because you knew it was going to be a nightmare. The spark had gone," he sighs. Frustrated by such juvenile behavior, Lynval attributes Roddy's belligerent conduct

---

* Recorded as an instrumental, the song was subsequently titled "Holiday Fortnight."

to being abused by his father when he was young: "It's like Roddy stopped at a certain age," Lynval hypothesizes. "He said to me once, 'I can't feel older than twenty-one.' Anybody who's in authority he hates. He had all these gripes with Jerry. And as soon as he had a drink, he became a twelve-year-old kid again. It was painful . . . a nightmare. Every day there was a fight and someone left the band. It was a tough record to make." Simpatico with Lynval, Horace says recording the album was "horrendous . . . it almost killed us."

To lift the negative mist descending over the session, Jerry invited a small coterie of guests to contribute to the record. Following a show at Tiffany's on April 24—headlined by Madness and supported by the Go-Go's—Lee Thompson dropped by to add saxophone to "Hey, Little Rich Girl." When they were accompanied by Belinda Carlisle, Charlotte Caffey and Jane Wiedlin, the three Go-Go's walked into a "blazing row" between Jerry and John Bradbury. Calm restored, backing vocals were added to a revamped version of the 1949 Herb Magidson and Carl Sigman standard "Enjoy Yourself (It's Later Than You Think)." Next, the Bodysnatchers's Rhoda Dakar popped by to duet with Terry on "I Can't Stand It," a song predating the formation of the Specials. "We did it at Wessex Studio in Highbury," says Rhoda. "I was there for one day and I did two vocals. Terry and I sang together in the booth. Then, on 'Pearl's Café,' I joined in the sing-along chorus, *It's all a load of bollocks and bollocks to it all.*"

Recently split from his wife, Roddy was living in a hotel in London, succumbing to depression, finding solace in Hank Williams and Johnny Cash records, and dating an American model. When Roddy suggested he add laid-back jazzy blues guitar to "I Can't Stand It," Jerry instead asked for a screaming rock guitar. "So I did," says Roddy. "You can almost hear me having a breakdown on the record. It was a great song, but if I'd said to Jerry, 'I'll play some screaming rock guitar,' he would have said, 'No, I want you to play quiet jazzy blues.' Jerry was the genius in the press. But I think that went to his head." In his memoir, *Original Rude Boy*, Neville observed, "Hatred was beginning to bubble to the surface."

Since joining the Specials, Terry Hall had not contributed as a songwriter. In his previous band, Squad, his lyrics had covered themes such as unwanted children ("Berlin") and *groups who have no right to exist because they are so bad* ("Wrong Attitude"). Now, Terry offered "Man at C&A" (with additional lyrics written by Jerry), addressing a generation's fear of impending nuclear war. *Warning! Warning! Nuclear attack!* Neville bellowed as Terry spat out verses about men in gray suits driving their *ballpoint views*. Switching from the latest *Moscow news*, there are references to Mickey Mouse and Ayatollah Khomeini, who in 1979 banned all music from Iranian media outlets, believing it stupefied the listener and "made their brain inactive and frivolous." Justifying his remarks in a radio interview, the political and religious leader decreed that "a youth who spends his time listening to music can no longer appreciate realities, just as a drug addict cannot."

Charting the musical course of the Specials, Jerry admitted that after "Gangsters" he was uncertain what the band would do next. "For quite a long time I thought we should just go into this total Northern Soul thing. We were going to totally change direction. In the end we didn't, obviously, but that's how 'Sock It to 'Em J.B.' ended up on the album."[103] Dating back to 1966, the Rex Garvin & the Mighty Cravers's original had been a soul mod anthem. In December 1979, members of the Specials, including Rico and Dick Cuthell, recorded the track in a small studio in south London. It was earmarked by 2 Tone for release—credited to the JB All Stars—and John Bradbury informed the *Face*, "I've always been heavily into the soul thing, probably more so than ska. But from the point of view of a drummer, there's no difference when it comes down to it. There are a lot of similarities and it is very easy to slip from a ska drum pattern to a soul one." Further revealing that "once the ska thing was established, phase two of 2 Tone was always planned as a diversification," he added, "Sticking to the same thing could be dangerous for the label."

Bradbury had in fact held a long-standing ambition to stage an on-the-road musical revue along the lines of the Stax/Volt tours of the 1960s. Along with a house backing band, Bradbury imagined a stream of guest vocalists including Laverne Brown from Red Beans & Rice, Pauline Black from the Selecter, and Terry and Neville from the Specials. "You could change the tempo and feel for each vocalist and mix the ska and soul things and take it all on the road for six weeks." It was a mouthwatering idea and matched an earlier discussion among the 2 Tone musicians, where the Beat's Ranking Roger would have toasted between the bands on the first 2 Tone Tour, and even included the suggestion that Madness's Chas Smash and Roger record a track in a competitive sound clash.

The Specials: (L–R) Roddy Byers, Neville Staple, Terry Hall, Horace Panter, Lynval Golding, John Bradbury, Jerry Dammers. Performing "Gangsters" on *Top of the Pops*, August 30, 1979.

The Specials performing at the Hammersmith Palais, August 21, 1979.

Madness: (L–R) Mark Bedford, Suggs, Chas Smash, Chris Foreman, Mike Barson, at the Lyceum, London, August 26, 1979.

The Selecter, 1980.

The Selecter: (L–R) Neol Davies, Pauline Black, Charley Anderson, Gaps Hendrickson, Compton Amanor, Aitch, Desmond Brown. On set filming the video for "Missing Words," November 1979.

Ranking Roger performing with the Beat, circa 1980.

The Beat: (L–R) Ranking Roger, Andy Cox, David Steele, circa 1980.

(L–R) Pauline Black, Suggs, Neville Staple, in front of the 2 Tone tour bus, October 1979.

Members of the Selecter, the Bodysnatchers and Holly & the Italians, February 16, 1980.

Members of the Specials, Selecter and Madness, Blue Boar service station, Northamptonshire, October 1979.

Rico Rodriguez backstage with the Specials, Spa Centre, Leamington, April 15, 1981.

Rhoda Dakar dancing, Barrow-in-Furness, June 9, 1980.

Sarah-Jane Owen and Miranda Joyce dancing, Barrow-in-Furness, June 9, 1980.

The Bodysnatchers: (L–R) Stella Barker, Nicky Summers, Rhoda Dakar, Miranda Joyce, Sarah-Jane Owen, Penny Leyton, at the 101 Club, Clapham, London, December 13, 1979.

Fans onstage with the Specials, Hammersmith Palais, August 21, 1979.

Fans of the Specials dancing at "A Peaceful Protest Against Racism," Butts Stadium Coventry, June 20, 1981.

Fans watching the Specials at the Northern Carnival Against Racism, Potternewton Park, Leeds, July 4, 1981.

Pauline Black on tour in the US, April 1980.

Gaps Hendrickson onstage with the Selecter, circa April 1980.

The Selecter playing live on *The Old Grey Whistle Test*, February 19, 1980.

Members of the Bodysnatchers, the Go-Go's and Specials on the Seaside Tour, June 1980.

Sean Carasov and Miranda Joyce on the Seaside Tour, June 1980.

Nicky Summers and Sarah-Jane Owen with Gaz Mayall (top right) and Sarah-Jane's boyfriend at her flat, London, 1980.

Jerry Dammers on the Seaside Tour coach, June 1980.

(L–R) Sean Carasov, Lynval Golding, Miranda Joyce, Jane Summers, Rhoda Dakar, on the Seaside Tour, June 1980.

Rhoda Dakar on the Seaside Tour coach, June 1980.

The Specials at the Rainbow Theatre, London, May 1, 1981.

The Specials at the Top Rank, Brighton, October 10, 1980.

Page from the diary of Miranda Joyce,
October 1980.

A Specials album shoot, Regent Hotel,
Leamington Spa, 1980.

The Selecter on tour in the US, 1980.

Northern Carnival Against Racism poster, July 4, 1981.

Storyboard for the Special AKA's "The Boiler" video, January 1982.

Storyboard for Rico Rodriguez's "Jungle Music" video, February 1982.

The Specials on location for the "Ghost Town" video, London, 1981.

The Specials on location for the "Ghost Town" video, Tower Bridge, London, 1981.

CHAPTER 22

BRAVO DELTA 80

SEASIDE TOUR. COPYCAT BANDS. FASHION

In June 1980, the Specials set out on a new British tour, albeit one with a key difference. Unusual for a rock 'n' roll tour, women outnumbered men. Traveling with the Specials, the Bodysnatchers and the Go-Go's gave rise to an unprecedented gender imbalance. "There was much less bullshit and nonsense," says singer Rhoda Dakar. "Women get up, get their breakfast. They can pack their suitcase and be on the coach at the time you're supposed to. You wouldn't have to go looking for them: 'Oh, sorry, we just went off into town.' Most male musicians are hopeless. If they know where their passport is you're in luck."

The Seaside Tour was a novel idea: the Specials would circumnavigate the British mainland on a sailboat, anchor offshore and land ahoy courtesy of a speedboat. Taking inspiration from Ronnie Lane's circus-style Passing Show in the midseventies, when the former member of the Faces together with a troupe of minstrels and animals traveled the country in buses and caravans taking music back to the people, Jerry Dammers romanticized breaking with rock 'n' roll convention. Ambitious: yes. Practical: no.

Developing the theme to do a tour of neglected coastal towns, Rick Rogers suggested a more economical approach: traveling in a bog-standard coach. To announce the summer sojourn, ads appeared in the music press of a police officer wearing a pair of dark sunglasses and a square black-and-white cravat with a miniature Walt Jabsco, and a *Rude Girl* badge pinned to her blouse. Above her right shoulder, a walkie-talkie blared out the typed message: "BRAVO DELTA 80. SEASIDE SPECIALS TOUR IS IN TOWN. OVER!" "I liked the way 2 Tone stole the black-and-white checkerboard from the police," says the Beat's front man Dave Wakeling. "It was taking icons back from the opposition."

Poster for the Seaside Tour, June 1980. Courtesy of Chrysalis Records/Jerry Dammers.

Then, on the first day, as the trucks got loaded, the tickets sold out, and the roller coaster rattled up the track, Jerry announced that he was feeling anxious about potential fighting among increasingly violent audiences. To cries of despair, Roddy piped up, "Oh, bugger him! Why don't we get Paul Heskett [from the Swinging Cats] and go without him?" Jerry, who had recently split up from his long-term girlfriend, Val Webb, who he'd been with since 1973, was "coming apart before our eyes." Roddy alleges, "Jerry was prescribed pills to help him sort out his breakdown."

The tour was back on. But friction between Roddy and Jerry encircled the band. Yet, rather than two grown adults sorting out their differences amicably, they resorted to playground-style tit-for-tat squabbles. "Jerry would throw wobblers if he didn't get his own way," claims Roddy, as if being asked to justify his behavior in a head teacher's office. "So to get my material or input noticed, I had to throw as big a wobbler as him, which wasn't always the best thing to do."[104] After a soundcheck at Blackpool Tiffany's, the group crossed over to the waterfront for a photo session. Unhappy with how the band were dressed, Jerry turned on Horace. "You're not wearing the right clothes," he berated the bass player. "You'll have to go back to the hotel and get changed. In fact, everybody ought to get changed." "What he meant was," interprets Roddy, "we'd all stopped wearing the band identity."

Following a conversation in which the group mutually agreed to wear the 2 Tone look to meet audience expectation, everybody complied. Except Roddy. Stubbornly keeping on his leather jacket to beat off the unseasonally cold summer rain, he stood sullenly by the seawall. Meanwhile, dressed in red tartan trousers and matching Harrington jacket, Jerry decided to mount the railings on the seafront wall and began to clown around. Stepping forward, Roddy pretended to push him. "You all saw that!" screamed Jerry, clinging to a lamppost to avoid a thirty-foot drop. "He tried to kill me! You're all witnesses." Stone-faced, Roddy countered, "Jerry, if I meant to kill you, I'd have killed you."

Having covered the tour on behalf of *Melody Maker*, Paolo Hewitt says the interband antagonism was shocking. Submitting his copy, he reported overheard phrases like, "This band's falling apart at the seams and it's all because of your egos," and, "Our best work in the studio has always been done when Jerry hasn't been there." At one point, Hewitt listened to Roddy and Jerry argue for half an hour until eventually Roddy struggled to his feet and, as he made his way to the stairs, caught a snippet of conversation about someone's "head being kicked in." Turning around, Roddy shouted back to the room: "Yeah, it's a shame it's not Jerry Dammers."[105]

Today, Roddy admits he was experiencing personal problems and was increasingly turning to alcohol for solace. "I always rebelled against authority and Jerry started to become an authority figure to me. I saw him as the guy who was telling me what I could and couldn't do."[106] Matters escalated when a confrontation onstage came close to blows. "Jerry kept screaming at me across the stage, 'Play the notes I told you to play.' I was like, 'Fuck off!' I lost it, ran over, smashed my guitar down on his keyboard, and just missed his hands. It took the neck off my 1958 Les Paul Special vintage guitar." Outraged by the violent burst of anger, Jerry froze, shocked, if not scared. He had one thought, *Roddy has gone mad*. Unapologetic, Roddy skulked into the hotel lounge after the gig and, reflecting on damaging Jerry's instrument, coldly pronounced, "Better than over his head."

Still. Twenty-plus musicians on the road and the tour soon succumbed to a riotous roving party of revelry and merrymaking. "To get everyone on the bus would take forever. Then you'd get on and there'd be no seats left because Jerry had invited twenty skinheads, so you'd have to stand," chuckles Miranda Joyce, who midtour had to race back to London to sit an A level exam. "There was a lot of drinking and fun to be had. Just doing ridiculous things. Then there was the night a foot came through the bedroom ceiling," she says, laughing at the memory of Jerry unsuccessfully attempting to smuggle a group of fans into his hotel room via the attic.

Seventeen, and secure in the knowledge she had a place at Hornsey School of Art, Miranda persuaded her mother to dash off a note to the headmistress: "Miranda's gone on tour," it read. "She's not coming back." Miranda and some school friends soon found themselves wrapped up in pop star affairs. "It was a bit of a free-for-all really," she says. "My boyfriend [Mark from Madness] was doing the same. I had a fling with Dave Jordan, the Specials's soundman. He was quite cheeky and married. It was mad!"

And so the antics carried on: chucking people into swimming pools, throwing drinks out of hotel windows, fans sleeping in the foyer, inflated Durex onstage.

Wowed by the fast Go-Go's pop songs onstage, Miranda says that offstage they had a penchant for Newcastle Brown Ale and Black Russians. When the tour arrived in Scarborough, a drinking contest was organized: boys versus girls. "I took one look at Margo [Go-Go's]," says Rhoda, "and thought, *She's got this!*" Her judgment proved right when Sean Carasov [a merchandise seller] was carried back to his hotel room unconscious.

"We were all young and excited," says Miranda, giggling. "It was like a big office party or some kind of weird sitcom. You can imagine! There were lots of affairs!" One night, incessant banging from an adjoining room awoke Miranda and keyboardist Penny Leyton. "It was obviously someone shagging. We could hear the headboard going," blushes Miranda. "We rang down to reception and said, 'Who's in the room next to us?' They said, 'Umm . . . Mr. Radiation.'"

Along the corridor, Stella Barker was sharing a room with Sarah-Jane Owen when they heard continuous tapping at the door. "Don't answer it," implored Sarah-Jane, cowering under a nylon quilt. "Then we heard scraping and we were both terrified. In the morning we opened the door and Roddy had carved 'I love SJ' with a heart through it on the doorframe with a penknife."

Romance blossomed. Hitching along for the ride, John Shipley recalls, "Sarah-Jane had her hand in Roddy's pocket and he was smiling all the way down the motorway. It was the only time I saw him happy." Along the aisle, amid the "beehive of conversation and girly pop tapes" playing, Stella and Neville fell in love, and Terry and Jane [Wiedlin] seduced each other with words, writing verses like conversation: "Can you hear them? They talk about us, telling lies." Choosing *silence* as a weapon of defense, they whispered, "It doesn't matter what they say in the jealous games people play."*

On previous tours, the Specials had slept two to a room. Now, says bass player Nicky Summers, "They all chose single rooms with a double bed." Noting the change, Roddy says, "Some of the guys started to shave, comb their hair and get all dressed up in the morning." But where you might suppose women were fending off unsolicited male advances from audience members, Miranda says, "Men behaved differently to women in terms of adoration." Rather than the conduct of traditional rock groupies, she says, admiring fans would be "carrying your flight case or tuning up your guitar for you."

The three-band bill entertained audiences in a variety of rickety seaside pavilions, often located at the ends of piers neither built for nor accustomed to thousands of people dancing en masse. With steam rising off the crowd and buildings shaking, Jerry would actively encourage stage invasions by inviting fans to dance alongside the group. "The energy was absolutely unbelievable," he says, bringing to mind the sight of fans stomping and jumping up and down all around. "It was total chaos. A kind of contained riot. I felt like I was floating above and then sort of coming down to touch the stage. I don't think there have ever been gigs like that in Britain before or afterward."

Over two weeks, the Seaside Tour breathed life into desolate resorts: Great Yarmouth, Bridlington, Barrow-in-Furness, Colwyn Bay and Margate. "It wasn't the usual coastal venues like Brighton or Bournemouth" says Stella. "We went quite far to reach fans that couldn't afford to get to gigs. It was amazing. At one venue, the Specials came on and we could see the pier going up and down. We were thinking, *It's going to collapse any minute.*" In Hastings, the band could see the wooden slats of the pier and, between the cracks, waves crashing on the rocks beneath. "I really thought the audience might

---

* In 1981, the resulting song, "Our Lips Are Sealed," was a US top twenty hit for the Go-Go's, and a UK top ten hit for the Fun Boy Three, with amended lyrics.

go through the floor!" hollers Jerry. "In fact, in Southend they did. You could just see huge holes appearing in the floor and kids were falling into the cellar below because the crowd was stomping so much. It was bonkers! The PA stacks were literally swaying. That was the injection of the African rhythm. Ska is very energetic music. It really lifts off and is relentless. You've got two rhythms going on at once: the drums playing at half the speed; and the guitars doing a double speed. It just gives this extraordinary rhythm." When the stage collapsed in Skegness, Jerry appealed to fans in an interview with *Melody Maker*: "We don't mind people getting on the stage, but if anyone's reading this, it's just if there's a lot of people on, don't get on, because it really is dangerous, someone could get killed."[107]

Behind the mayhem lay a deep-rooted desire to break down the barrier between audience and band. "We'd done that tour with the Clash where Joe [Strummer] would let the kids in through the windows and help the ones who didn't have the money to get in," recalls Roddy. "We'd carried on from that, but it got out of hand. Jerry would say, 'Roddy, can you have these couple of guys sleep on your floor?' Jerry once had about fourteen people staying in his room. Some of the kids would literally leave home and join the tour. They'd be on the bus and at the hotel fighting among themselves, drinking, partying and crying. A couple of times I'd give these kids money: 'Go home! Go back to school.' We started with all those ideals, but it was almost impossible to carry on treating people like we had. When you're tired, you don't want umpteen kids sleeping in your room. In the end we had to get a bigger tour bus so there was room for them all."

Talk to Horace Panter or Lynval Golding and they will share similar tales of skinheads taking over their hotel room or having to give up backstage passes. "It was another thing that caused rifts within the band," suggests Horace. As tour manager, Frank Murray says, the situation was impossible. "It was a nightmare because you can't control those kind of kids. If they get lippy, some band member will always stand up and defend them when you're trying to keep order in all the chaos. After a gig, people were full of it."

Pumped up by their growing popularity, the musicians had every reason to be "full of it." In June, John Peel devoted his late-night radio program to 2 Tone. Replaying sessions by the Specials, the Selecter, Madness, the Beat and the Bodysnatchers, Peel introduced "Gangsters" by telling listeners, "[It's] one of those records that really changes your life. I mean it actually does, rather like I suppose the Damned's first single, where you wake up the next day and nothing's ever really quite the same again."

Such was the impact of 2 Tone nationwide that by the summer, any band with a vaguely ska-sounding rhythm was attracting record company interest. New wave forerunners the Ruts, no strangers to mixing punk and reggae in the late seventies, released the antagonistic dance-floor anthem "Staring at the Rude Boys." Brighton-based Piranhas hit lucky with an updated version of the kwela instrumental "Tom Hark," known to millions from the reggae compilation album *Tighten Up Volume 2.* The Lambrettas also breached the top ten with a version of Leiber & Stoller's "Poison Ivy," presented in a mock 2 Tone sleeve—rebranded Two-Stroke Records—with a monochrome mod attired in loafers and a parka. In a similar vein, "The Ballad of Robin Hood" by the Charlie Parkas posed Walt Jabsco with a feather in his trilby. Even newcomer Kim Wilde injected "2-6-5-8-0" with a Jamaican-influenced backbeat. Stirred by the sudden interest in Jamaica's past, ska veteran Laurel Aitken teamed up with the Ruts and enjoyed chart success with "Rudi Got Married." Similarly, Desmond Dekker signed to Stiff Records and, backed by the Rumour, rerecorded a selection of past early reggae classics, including "Israelites," "It Mek" and "007."

Deluged with demo tapes, Jerry says, there was an incredible pressure to find more acts for the label. "Everybody was on my case, day and night. I was sent literally hundreds and hundreds of cassettes. Some of them were quite threatening. There was an Oi! band in Coventry called Criminal Class who more or less demanded I put out a record on 2 Tone. It started idealistically but it became completely impracticable. It was just crazy. Prefab Sprout was the only one that

I was aware of that might have been worth signing, and it's possible Desmond Dekker got lost in all that too."

2 Tone had been established to help groups kickstart their career, and many of the bands felt that to get a deal with the label, they had to play a certain way. "You're getting just a load of clone bands who feel obliged to make a certain type of music," observed Pauline Black. The answer, according to Horace Panter, was to change. Safe in the knowledge that the Specials were soon to unveil a new album with an innovative direction, he cautioned against continually churning out the same music while criticizing bands for playing similar stuff. "I think that's even more reason to change," he told *Melody Maker*. "I think that Jerry has the right idea of using Muzak as the new basis. It's like starting again, which is great. I had this mad idea of going out and playing a completely new set under a different name. Then we could get back to the Sheffield Limit club and the Fusion in Chesterfield where we had our best times."[108]

Supposedly managed by fourteen people, 2 Tone, according to Neville Staple, had become ridiculous. "Jerry used to go to Chrysalis and say, 'I like this band.' It wasn't all of us going, 'Let's have them.'" As far as Horace was concerned, 2 Tone belonged to Jerry. "I can think of no time when we all sat down together and said, 'Let's do this, everybody.' Jerry would go, 'We'll do this and then we'll do that . . .'" In reality, the dream of an independent record label, imagined and planned by Jerry since he was ten years old, was beginning to take its toll. He told *NME*, "It's just a logo. That doesn't mean a thing. It's the music that counts. And how can you own music? All these people are starting to come to me asking for something from 2 Tone—people who feel they've contributed and now want some sort of divvy. I say divvy of what? 2 Tone? That doesn't exist. It's in them. They're 2 Tone, not some daft design."[109]

With the label increasingly viewed as a marketable brand stretching beyond his control, Jerry snapped. "2 Tone has become a monster," he told *Melody Maker*, "like Frankenstein's monster. It's just mind-boggling." Further complaining that he had seen cartoons of the Specials in kung fu battle with Madness and 2 Tone cash-in cigarettes, Jerry fumed at the meaninglessness of it all. "It's purely on a fashion level. There's such a great danger of it becoming too commercialized."

Such was the potency of the Specials's rapid rise to popularity, 2 Tone became the dominant youth culture in Britain. "I've never seen the momentum behind a group move so quickly," enthuses Roy Eldridge. "It had this pace and energy that was unstoppable and quite scary in its intensity." Where once the bands had trawled secondhand shops in the hope of finding old pairs of Dr. Martens and tonic suits, suddenly city centers teemed with young teenagers dressed in the style of their heroes. "It was incredible," commented Terry Hall. "I can't really weigh it up. I don't really understand it." Not knowing whether to be appalled or flattered, Charley Anderson says, "Everything changed. The fashion became commercial and manufacturers began to make clothes and sell them with the 2 Tone logo on it without permission."[110] Walking down Oxford Street, Pauline Black says, "It seemed like every single window display was black-and-white, HMV, even Evans the outsize shop for ladies. And the music newspapers were full of it."

Suggs recalls feeling depressed at the sight of mass-produced clothing styles and hordes of kids dressed identically. "I remember horrible see-though Harrington jackets. It became a travesty of the original thing. The new gear was made from nylon; and what was it with those cardboard porkpie hats? It was unfortunate because we were sort of preaching individuality, which is not what it became." Flipping the argument, Dave Wakeling contended that clothing was the critical factor in Black people coming to 2 Tone concerts. Suggesting that the requisite look was not restricted to one racial group, he told NME that many Black people were now coming to Beat gigs as opposed to the traditional white rock audience when they started out. "Now we get dreads and Black beat girls, 2 Tone girls or whatever. It's easy to get into it 'cos it's the same fashion for the Blacks and the whites. They all come as rude boys, so it's not half as weird as some of them coming as punks and some as Rastas."

CHAPTER 23

TOO EXPERIENCED

THE SPECIALS IN JAPAN. EASY LIFE

In the summer, *Record Mirror* exclusively revealed a proposed open-air free festival featuring the Specials, the Selecter and the Bodysnatchers. Planned for mid-July on Clapham Common, the event was far from definite. Permission was required from the Greater London Council (GLC), so local traders and residents pointed to noise pollution and the huge numbers likely to attend the event. On June 10, at an open meeting at County Hall, both the Lambeth Council and the police approved the idea, only for the GLC to refuse to grant a music license. Disappointed, the Specials prepared to make their first visit to Japan. "We were getting burned out near the end of the first album," said Neville, foreseeing trouble ahead. "We were a high-energy band and touring like nobody's business. Then we went to Japan to do the same thing we'd done in America. That's what kind of screwed us up."[111]

Scheduled to play eight shows in seven days—five in Tokyo, two in Osaka and one in Kyoto—the Specials delivered characteristic high-octane sets. To control the crowd, a squad of military police stood at the front of the stage. "Yes, alright, they can do that," agreed Jerry reluctantly before the show, "but they've all got to kneel down and wear Specials T-shirts." Though some were amused at the sight of a squad "hard as fuck" kowtowing at the foot of the stage, the mood turned when exuberant fans were pushed back into their seats when they stood up to dance. Launching into the final song, "Gangsters," Neville exploded. Bare-chested and with sweat pouring down his brow, he smashed up a set of congas and wantonly threw microphone stands across the stage as he flailed and screamed, "Don't call me Ska-Face!" Intoxicated by the show of bravado, fans invaded the stage, damaging instruments, and flagrantly ignored instructions to return to their seats. Freaked out, the promoter fell to his knees. "Please, Jerry," he said, "do not ruin my life." News of the eventful tour reached the offices of the *Daily Mirror* and, under the banner heading "POP GROUP FACES BOOT FROM JAPAN AFTER FANS RIOT," the British tabloid reported the group "were being detained at their hotel after a wild stampede by fans at their show in the city."

Returning to England, there was further anxiety when Lynval Golding was the victim of a racially motivated attack. Leaving the Moonlight Club in West Hampstead after watching a show by the Mo-dettes, Juliet de Vie describes what happened next. "Lynval and I heard somebody shout. We turned round and there was three skinheads running down the road toward us. Lynval immediately reacted and said, 'Run.' There was some work being done on the flats where I lived and as we ran toward the stairs, Lynval picked up a long piece of scaffolding, in self-defense."

Frightened and forced to protect himself, Lynval says, "It was just horrible. I thought, *This is it. They're going to kill me. If there's a heaven, there's a hell. I'm not sure where I'm going but you're gonna come with me.* I had to fight to get out. I got away and rushed into this stranger's flat by mistake."

Armed with a knife, Lynval suddenly reappeared on the upper walkway. Urging him to run toward her, Juliet says, they managed to get inside her flat and wedge a broom under the door handle. "I had an old decorative sword on the wall and Lynval grabbed that and was brandishing it. The next thing I know there's a lynch mob outside. Lynval was injured but I didn't know how or when. Then the manager of the Mo-dettes unexpectedly turned up and he was able to calm everybody down. I was the subject of a fanatical hate campaign for quite a long time afterward: horrible notes were pushed through my door, and more than once human shit was left on the door handle of my car. I don't know if the skinheads recognized Lynval, they'd been at the Moonlight, or if it was that classic thing of a Black guy with a white girl, which racist skinheads didn't like."

Taken to hospital, Lynval suffered a concussion, cracked ribs and severe bruising. The next day and under heavy sedation, he flew out to the fourteenth Montreux Jazz Festival to perform with the Specials. Injected before going onstage and wearing sunglasses to hide his swollen face, Lynval stood undefeated in a magnificent show of defiance.

Such boldness of mind had taken the Bodysnatchers from blowing away the mystique surrounding rock 'n' roll to courting the attention of the music business. But when amateurism mixed with professionalism, there was little give. Taking to the stage one night, Nicky Summers plugged into Horace Panter's bass amplifier, turned up the volume, and blew the rig. Accidents happen. But a drummer who could not keep time proved too much. Writing in her diary after a show at Hastings Pier Pavilion, Penny Leyton noted, "Miranda and I discuss Jane with Rob Gambino [tour manager] who says she's crap and band won't last three months—band agree to get rid of her." The following day, Nicky delivered the news and Jane graciously agreed to stay for the rest of the tour.

Never one to mince her words, Rhoda Dakar says that Jane was not only a "terrible drummer" but "a cow. She had a little plastic kit with a razor blade and a straw that she used to carry about with her. I just thought, *You're pathetic.* I once asked Paul Cook [Sex Pistols] to try to teach her how to play reggae. He came to the rehearsal studio, but it was a pointless exercise. A band stands or falls by its drummer. When we had a decent drummer, suddenly the possibilities opened up." Sarah-Jane agrees: "Jane couldn't cut it as a drummer. There was timing issues: slowing down, speeding up. We needed someone that was tighter and could keep time." Warming to the theme, Sarah-Jane then adds, perhaps a little hypocritically considering the general behavior of the band, "There was drinking issues too."*

At the Electric Ballroom, Jane suddenly stopped playing, got up from the drum kit and threw water over Buster Bloodvessel from Bad Manners. Recalling indulgences of a darker kind, Miranda says, "She was into whips and S&M. She said she had a dungeon. But I have no idea why she left." In 2023, Jane Summers had an elusive online presence, but one might imagine her reaction to reading the comments of her former bandmates chiming with a quirky song she wrote to spice up the Bodysnatchers's set in spring 1980: "What's This!"

Next, the Bodysnatchers sacked Frank Murray. Having managed the group since returning to England after the ill-fated Specials tour of America, Murray says, "From the time you met them they were looking at you going, 'I hope you're not going to try and change us and tell us what to do.' They were very defensive and weren't prepared to listen. There was this sense of noncooperation and they were suspicious of everything. It was impossible." Having employed him on a trial basis since April Fool's Day, Rhoda crows, "That's about fucking right! Frank was a nice guy but he was rubbish as a manager. We all had the same sense of innocence. If someone said this can't be done, we'd ask why. As seven women, we had a pack mentality—if we couldn't get what we wanted, we'd all shout at once and get it. We all supported each other." Miranda Joyce remembers Frank on occasion giving the band speed before gigs. "I was so young, I had no idea if that was right or wrong," she says. "I've got 'Sack Frank' literally every week in my diary." Stella Barker says, "We thought we knew it all. It's all very well saying Frank was busy snorting coke and that's where all the profits went. We weren't all squeaky clean. Most of the band was doing drugs. It was a very difficult role and our lack of experience meant that we made wrong decisions that Frank advised against." Plotting their future, the Bodysnatchers decided everything by vote.

---

* In March, *Record Mirror* reported that Jane Summers "was forcibly ejected from a Selecter party at Legends nightclub when she fell over onto some tables and rather upset a few diners."

"That was the problem," decries Rhoda. "We didn't have a leader. It was a democracy. Somebody would be phoned, a meeting would be arranged, and all seven of us would go: lawyer, record company; we all went and shouted until we got what we wanted."

In the short term, the group needed a new drummer. They asked Chrysalis to help. *Record Mirror* ran a news item: "The Bodysnatchers, that attractive bunch of girls, are desperate for a drummer (to be honest, I don't think anyone should settle for anything less than a lead singer, but still). If you fancy the job, call the suave Chris Poole at Chrysalis Records (what do these people think this is? A situations vacant column?)." An immediate response came from a percussionist known to all as Carla Mad Dog. After an impressive audition, a gig in Oxford, and a £100 advance for expenses, Carla was never seen again.

Next up was a scientist working at a government hydraulics research station in Wallingford. Twenty-eight at the time, Judy Parsons now says, "I'd been slogging around Oxfordshire getting nowhere. I saw an advert in *Melody Maker* and got my husband to phone them up. I got home from work and he said, 'You've got an audition tomorrow morning.' I was like, 'No! I didn't want an audition. I just wanted to know who they were.' It was all completely unintended." Having driven down to Mornington Crescent in a minivan, Judy says the rehearsal room—Barry Sullivan's Studio 9—was "a shithole. There was a tiny staircase going down to a terrible basement where the band played. At a certain point, they all stopped playing and said, 'We've got a photo shoot.' They all got their powder puffs and lipsticks out. I thought, *That's a bit unfeminist!* I was aware of 2 Tone but I'd never bought a record. The rumor was Nicky thought that you plugged a bass guitar into an electric socket. It was quite a weak band to play with. You had to do the same thing all the time because the band was liable to collapse if I did a drum fill. It was a fragile feeling. We just about kept it together, but in a way, that was part of the excitement: *Are they going to blow it? Phew, they got through another song.*"

Judy had previously played in a feminist band called Mistakes with the sister of comedian Victoria Wood, but she was new to reggae. "Lynval Golding gave me a lesson. Then I went to John Reynolds who later produced and played on Sinead O'Connor records. He showed me the fundamentals. Then someone taught me a fill from 'On My Radio' and it became a major part of my repertoire. We did a lot of listening to cassettes of the gig of the night before. You think you're doing really well: you listen to it and it's shit. At the end of the tour they said, 'Will you join us full-time?' There were loads of reasons against it, but I was like, 'Okay! Yeah. I'll join.'"

Parsons was never contractually signed to 2 Tone, and her first engagement was to promote a record she had not drummed on. Two months earlier, the Bodysnatchers had played their first headline tour, performing in eighteen cities in twenty-four days. During a weekend break, between shows in Manchester and Edinburgh, the group traveled to Wessex Studios in north London to record their second single, "Easy Life." The song addressed parity in working wages and society's expectation for women to procreate. "The good thing about twenty-year-olds writing songs," says Rhoda, "is that their ideas are pure and unfettered with complications like, 'How the fuck are we going to achieve that then?' It's like saying, 'Let's go to the moon.' 'Yeah, let's do it.' There's no notion of we actually have to build the rocket. At twenty, I thought motherhood was a thing that dragged you down. It was doing what everyone else did. But with the genius of hindsight, I now know that it's a very empowering role."

In what would prove to be one of his last acts as manager, Frank Murray persuaded Jerry Dammers to produce the record. "I had to twist his arm. It took awhile and all the time the girls were going, 'When are we going in? Is Jerry doing it?'" In the studio, "Easy Life" transformed. "It came across as an anthem," smiles Nicky. "It became this very slick production. We were taken aback by how it sounded. The riff came forward and it had this catch line. Lyrically, it was about not taking the easy option. It was about girls doing something more creative than leaving school, being a typist, meeting a bloke, marrying and giving everything up. It was about inspiring younger girls to do more with their life, or at least to think about things."

For the B-side, the Bodysnatchers recorded "Too Experienced." Written by Jamaican singer Bob Andy on a bus journey to a recording studio, the soulful rocksteady song recounted the rejection of a woman by a man not wanting *to be taken for a ride*. In the modern hands of the Bodysnatchers, the gender of the song was flipped and presented a compelling feminist narrative with a radical production to match. "The Specials were experimenting and getting away from the classic 2 Tone sound," says Penny Leyton, "and Jerry wanted it to sound like a Phil Spector 'Wall of Sound' production." Stripped of guitars, the arrangement gave prominence to the bass and drums, endowing the track with a mysterious feel. "It was wonderful," raves Nicky. "It was the closest thing to the original sound I had in my head for the band. *NME* said we sounded like a cross between Public Image Limited and the Supremes recorded in an aircraft hangar. That was the coolest compliment."

The band were filled with optimism and able to overcome Jerry's sudden fixation about the meter of the song—studio rebooked, song remixed, and a tambourine overdubbed ahead of the offbeat while members of the band made use of a nearby launderette—the single was released on July 11. "Another successful horse bolting from the 2 Tone stable," neighed *Melody Maker* a week later. Drawing attention to the record's "fiendish rhythm and wonderful feel of contemporary relevance," Martyn Sutton continued the riding analogy with a two-way prediction: "Can't fail unless it falls at the first fence (airplay). Are our nation's broadcasting gurus getting tired of 2 Tone? Wait and see." A stablemate at Chrysalis, Leo Sayer felt no compunction toward loyalty and told BBC Radio 1 *Roundtable*, "I don't like it." More damning was *Record Mirror*'s review: "Not as good as 'Rock Steady' but then nothing they do is. Tedious bleating from the least talented of the current crop of all-girl skankers."

Then an industrial dispute over the BBC's decision to axe five of its eleven house orchestras resulted in the cancellation of *Top of the Pops*. Just weeks before, producer Michael Hurll had made the unusual decision to give records outside of the official Top 40 a slot on

the program. One immediate beneficiary had been Orchestral Ma-
noeuvres in the Dark, who performed "Messages" when the record
sat at number fifty-three. Timing counts for much in pop, and when
"Easy Life" stalled at number fifty, *Top of the Pops* was still off-air.
"We thought that the trajectory [of the band] would continue in the
same direction at the same speed," says Penny. "People were pretty
depressed that 'Easy Life' didn't do anything. There were recrimina-
tions that it should have been a different song, or it wasn't promoted
properly."

Ad for the "Easy Life" single, July 1980. Courtesy of Chrysalis Records/Jerry Dammers.

Worse still, talk of a Bodysnatchers album crashed with the single's failure to impact. Only recently, Richard Branson had been desperate to sign the group, "offering the earth," according to Nicky, "but
the rest of the band wouldn't meet him. I met this woman in Notting
Hill. She bought us pancakes in Asterisk's and said Branson wanted
to take us to Memphis with Aretha Franklin's producer. Five people
refused to play ball. I don't know why. It was like, 'Aaarrggh! How can
you let that go?'"

Adding to their woes, the Bodysnatchers were broke. With the
band facing the prospect of "sinking back into obscurity," Pauline

Black asked, "Do they try and use Chrysalis as a means to an end in providing money for them to go out on tour and get together their next single?" As they mulled over their precarious status, Penny says, "We were a novelty and novelty sells: an all-girl group playing ska; people were seeing great profit potential in us. We wanted to stick with 2 Tone but the fairy tale had come to an end." By the autumn Rhoda concluded, "We'd sacked the manager. We didn't have a deal and we didn't have a plan."

The situation gave rise to accusations that Chrysalis was using 2 Tone as an informal scouting unit. According to a report by Vivien Goldman in *Melody Maker*, "While Jerry Dammers continues with his magical talent-spotting and hit-creating, Chrysalis is only too happy to have 2 Tone as a kind of unofficial or unpaid A&R department." Speculating that if the Bodysnatchers received a £4,000 advance and only made £3,000 back, "then 2 Tone is in debt for a grand to Chrysalis," Goldman concluded: "2 Tone carries the financial can, *not* Chrysalis."

Making his own calculations, Jerry determined, "If a 2 Tone record sells 100,000, which gets it into the top ten, I stand to make a maximum of £250 out of it. 2 Tone gets a 2 percent royalty and that's cut between eight people. That doesn't even pay the costs of running the 2 Tone office." Nevertheless, and keen to assure readers of *New Musical Express* that it wasn't a "lousy deal," Jerry reminded naysayers that Chrysalis had been the only label to offer the Specials a deal on their own terms, including the establishment of 2 Tone. "Like I say, I am not trying to become some sort of big record business mogul or anything like that. It's just there doesn't seem any other way of doing it, that's all."

CHAPTER 24

JUST A WHISPER

THE SELECTER LEAVE 2 TONE. SPLIT

Following in the footsteps of Madness and the Specials, the Selecter embarked on a six-week tour of North America, starting in Vancouver on April 18, 1980, and ending in Connecticut on May 29. Writing for the *New York Rocker*, Richard Grabel praised Pauline Black for stealing the show. "She is simply one of the best female front persons I've ever seen. Her stage manner defines the word 'presence'—she's totally in command, striking that elusive and perfect balance between doing too much and not doing enough." Flattered, but ever a realist, Pauline says, "We didn't mean jack shit there except maybe in some of the major cities. That was quite a leveler. We went to the South Fork Ranch in Texas [home of television series *Dallas*] and these people came up and said, 'Get the niggers out of here.' After that, we didn't feel as gung-ho as we were in New York or when we played four shows at the Whisky a Go Go in LA. We did an interview with Marsha Hunt [actress/musician] and the first thing Desmond said to her was, 'I've always wanted to fuck you.' I constantly had to hear crap like this. 2 Tone paid lip service to antiracism and antisexism but it was pure tokenism. It really got to me after a while. I was suffering from laryngitis and I felt terribly lonely. When we came back all our problems kicked in."

Shortly after returning to England, the Selecter announced they were leaving 2 Tone. Initially proposing that the label should dissolve while it was a success, the group then decided they were being held back and straightjacketed by the media. In a statement issued to the press in July, they set out their grievances: "Every 2 Tone single has reached the charts. This is a situation which the Selecter feels is ultimately stifling new talent, leading bands to feel that they need to stereotype themselves into what they believe to be the 2 Tone sound. Plonking a new group into the Top 20 is not enough. A band needs much more basic help than that. Originally, we wanted to stop 2 Tone completely but that proved impossible so now we feel caught in a cleft stick. On the one hand, we have certain ideals about the music industry/process, which could have been put into practice—in fact, some of them were. But because of the success of 2 Tone, many of the ideals have been hampered and we are led to the choice of leaving or staying and living with it."

Further condemning a proliferation of counterfeit merchandise flooding the market, the Selecter concluded that 2 Tone had established itself officially and become a "big business in order to combat unsanctioned product." Sounding an ironic note—"At least a lot of sharks will be stuck with a load of 2 Tone/Selecter badges and ties etc., that we hope no one will buy"—the statement concluded with a summation of the label's founding ambitions. "2 Tone was intended to be an alternative to the music industry, a label that took risks and, we hope, injected some energy into what had become a stale music scene. The time has come when we want to take risks again."

Evaluating the failed relationship between the Specials and the Selecter, Rick Rogers says, "By the time the Specials were making their first album things had exploded. It was so fast it was insane. To actually try and get fourteen people in a room together to sit down and have an A&R meeting was just impossible." Founding member of the Selecter Neol Davies says the limited contact between the bands broke the spirit of 2 Tone. "We were always in different places," he says, "so you lose the understanding you start out with. It was one-way traffic. The Specials were so busy that communication became less and less. We felt it was better to establish our own identity."

Agreeing that there was a feeling of playing a secondary role to the Specials, Pauline addresses what perhaps was at the core of the Selecter's decision-making: money. "We were never going to get as good advances [with 2 Tone]. At the end of the day, you're selling records. The Beat and Madness had jumped ship, signed lucrative deals, and were doing a great deal better than we were. There was also an element of fear in our camp. Jerry was voicing the concern that 2 Tone had become commercialized and it wasn't how he'd envisioned things. He was trying to regain control of something that he felt had slipped through his fingers. In retrospect, we threw the baby out with the bathwater. We moved far too fast and far too quickly."

Responding to the announcement, 2 Tone issued a brief statement: "We are sorry that Selecter have decided to leave the label, but 2 Tone will definitely continue, with the main objective of helping new bands."

If there was an end to phase one of 2 Tone, this was it. Of the five acts originally signed to 2 Tone, three had moved on—Madness, the Beat and the Selecter—and now the Bodysnatchers were hurtling toward an unsavory demise. "The problem is Jerry doesn't trust no one," Lynval Golding told Jon Swift in an interview for *Smash Hits*. "If Jerry doesn't do it himself, it's never done right as far as he's concerned. He just took too many things on. We didn't do anything bad. The Selecter had the freedom to do anything they wanted to do. But the actual running of the label has got completely out of hand. The worst thing was when they [the Selecter] got a better deal out of Chrysalis than we did."

The Selecter had in fact first entertained the idea of leaving 2 Tone four months earlier. With the rationale that the band would receive more attention signing to a separate label, on March 28, Roger Lomas accompanied them to see the head of A&R at WEA. "We all went down and straight after the band said, 'We don't want to be with them. They're a racist company.' I said, 'How the hell do you work that out?' They said, 'We didn't see any Black people working in the offices.' What kind of logic was that? I couldn't understand it. I felt like a twat because I'd set it all up. I said, 'Don't be ridiculous. If they were racist, why would they want to sign you?' They would have got a massive deal. Warners would have made them ten times bigger than Chrysalis ever would have done."

Today, Neol Davies regards the decision as his "biggest mistake. Moira Bellas at WEA desperately wanted to sign us. It was an incredible deal, but I was convinced it was best to sign with Chrysalis and keep 2 Tone together." The choice would prove costly. "We didn't get proper record company support," laments Neol. "When we looked at what the Beat were getting from Arista and Madness from Stiff, nobody at Chrysalis was that interested. They looked at it as selling itself: 'We don't have to do anything.' Usually they have to create an image for artists—we supplied it all." Alarm bells ringing, the stark realization of their folly came when the band visited the record company to discuss a new contract. Welcomed upstairs, the group listened to the label's latest acquisition, Spandau Ballet. Hearing "To Cut a Long Story Short"—a song heralding the arrival of New Romanticism. Pauline Black remembers thinking, *This is going to be a tricky meeting.*

"Totally!" shrieks Chrysalis press officer Julia Marcus recalling the abrupt change from 2 Tone to foppish fashion. "Pauline is 100 percent right. Hilarious: pantaloons, frilly shirts, makeup, floppy fringes. Not me, I hasten to add. I stayed very faithful to my 1950s look. But Sue Winter [promotions] overnight went from looking like a little skinhead girl to frills and dandy clothes. It was a natural progression," she says, charting pop's easy-come, easy-go transitions. "A year and a half before 2 Tone, you would have had people wearing ripped jeans and Seditionaries T-shirts, Vivienne Westwood . . ."

Fashion was a movable feast. As one movement showed signs of ebbing, so an alternative sprung up to breathe air into the vacuum. Not only was competition a driving force between rival companies, it was a critical factor within interlabel departments. Making the point that Chrysalis was more than just 2 Tone, Chris Poole says, "In 1980, Blondie was still a big force at the label. Then Ultravox and Spandau

Ballet. We had some big-selling acts: Stiff had come out of punk but even they went commercial. Labels had to develop because movements died off. Something else replaced them. That's the history of pop music."

In an instant, legions of 2 Tone fans ditched their Fred Perrys and tonic suits and embraced the flamboyant colors of New Romanticism and the all-conquering Adam & the Ants. Photographed without her trademark trilby, Pauline Black untied her hair in a celebration of femininity and refreshed her wardrobe with red and white accoutrements. The new look was backed in August by the Selecter's first single for Chrysalis. Written by Neol Davies, "The Whisper" was an older song based around a New Orleans blues riff and a tango offbeat. The twist in rhythm, as Compton Amanor observes, gave it a different quality to their previous releases. "We were bringing in calypso and it also had a sixties R&B feel. We wanted to diversify and break away from following that machine backbeat ska."

"The Whisper" would spend five weeks on the UK chart but climb no higher than number thirty-five. It is tempting to attribute the relative failure of the record to a change in the musical climate, but a cursory glance at their peers suggests otherwise. During the same period, Bad Manners ("Lip Up Fatty"), the Piranhas ("Tom Hark"), the Beat ("Best Friend"), the Clash ("Bankrobber"), Madness ("Baggy Trousers") and the Specials ("Stereotype") would all enjoy significantly greater success with reggae-influenced backbeats. There was an overwhelming sense of disappointment. "Often fans want more of the same and maybe they thought that we'd turned our back on them," muses Compton. "Released at the right time, 'The Whisper' could have been as big as 'On My Radio.' Perhaps the record company didn't support it."

Blunt and concise, Gaps Hendrickson simply says, "Chrysalis had given up on us." Doug D'Arcy scoffs at the idea. "There's usually a fair amount of friction between a record company and the artist. Maybe there's something about the pressure of what we're doing: creating and getting it out there. It's the way the business works. No careers are bulletproof. There are always stages, even for the most successful acts. There's always been the theory in the business of overkill. People have too much of a good thing and they get bored of it. The Selecter were the architects of their own downfall."

On Monday, August 21, the Selecter reconvened at Horizon Studios to commence work on a second album. Twenty-four hours earlier, Desmond Brown had visited Neol Davies at his flat in Hillfields and told him he was leaving the band. Neol was stunned. "We had a ridiculous conversation for an hour or two. I said, 'You can't. Please. Don't leave.' I knew it would be catastrophic. But he wouldn't tell me why." After Desmond agreed to come to the studio, the resulting three weeks collapsed into a series of ongoing arguments. "It was very emotional and difficult," reflects Neol. "Desmond was all over the place. But despite all my efforts, I couldn't change his mind." When an argument erupted with Charley Anderson, Desmond exploded like a volcano and walked out shouting, "I'm done with the band!"

Two days later, Pauline informed Charley that he was out too. When Charley was reproached for underperforming and refusing to contribute to a new song, "Celebrate the Bullet"—believing it was not the "the right direction for the band"—the ongoing power struggle between him and Neol divided the group. "We had two leaders," says Compton, "and Charley was spending too much attention on that rather than the actual music. Tensions built up. Charley was under a lot of pressure and wasn't performing—dropping bass notes in the wrong places—and people started laying into him." Talking to *NME* in April 1981, Charley acknowledged an ongoing feud but insisted the issue centered on Neol receiving all the songwriting royalties despite the fact that the band had come off tour in debt. "It just seemed like everyone else was just a session musician, helping him [Neol] make money. I told him that he ought to divide it equally with the rest of the group. He didn't agree."

Accused of "running off with the money," Neol counters that he always encouraged everybody in the Selecter to write. "We needed as many songs as we could get, but that perception that I was greedy grew and was the source of many arguments." Neol had written the majority of the group's original songs, including four successful singles—"The Selecter," "On My Radio"—coupled with "Too Much Pressure"—"Three Minute Hero" and "Missing Words." Yet, during the recording of *Too Much Pressure*, Charley designed a mock sleeve and cocredited all of the tracks to the Selecter. "That's how it should be," he declared. Neol was furious. "'No, Charley! That's not how it should be. *I* wrote the songs. My name goes on them. Like it or not. That's it.' I had written these fantastic songs that were hits," Neol says, venomously. "It was enabling us to do what we'd always wanted to do. But as soon as the band was successful, everybody tried to tear it down."

As relationships rapidly deteriorated over the summer, Charley campaigned for the Selecter to pursue a more reggae-influenced direction. Neol argued against it. "It would have been a mistake. For us to be a reggae band would have taken anything original from us and made us a Jamaican copy. We were better than that. We played our version of reggae mixed with everything else and came up with something new. Charley made this conflict between us. It wasn't coming from me. I had wanted Charley in the band from the beginning and told him we'd run it together. That's how it was set up, but after a while he started working against me."

Seeing no way forward, Neol issued an ultimatum: "It's me or him." The band chose Neol. Distraught, Compton visited Desmond and told him he was making a mistake, and that he and Charley should both come back. Desmond called a band meeting and told the band, "I want to come back." "The mood lifted," says Compton. Then Desmond added, "But Charley has to come back too." "WHAT!" cried Neol. "You did that to us and then you say *that*?"

It was an impossible situation. "I'm still not clear to this day why Desmond left," says Neol. With Desmond suffering from a fragile mental state, few were surprised by his postband decline. "He could get really fucking scary," says Juliet de Vie. "He was a big man and you didn't want him to turn on you." Saddened by his deteriorating health, Neol says, "There were signs of what was to come. The pressure of touring may well have made it worse. Desmond used to call us a manufactured band. He would get steamed up and say it was artificial. 'It's not real,' he'd say. 'It's plastic, man!'"

Heading toward an inevitable crash, Juliet de Vie says, arguments within the Selecter became synonymous with their very existence. "On the whole they didn't take to the degree of discipline needed in a band," she says, "or to be challenged, advised or navigated by anyone. They were a band with huge potential for self-sabotage. Looking back, I think Neol felt the weight of white guilt very keenly. It was a struggle for him. Band arguments over ownership are as old as the industry itself, but they don't usually have to address it through the distorting prism of racism, which made it difficult for all of them." Pointing to a tempestuous relationship between Pauline and Neol, Aitch suggests that the breakdown was related to misunderstanding and lack of communication. "You could just say three words and the next thing it was an argument. The two of them would just take things literally and wind each other up and it just got worse and worse." Compton agrees: "We'd get into all kinds of petty arguments. We took what we had for granted. We were acting like we were still playing small bars, and finding any little thing to argue about."

Having only recently found acceptance as a woman of color, Pauline now asks, "Why does anyone imagine that just because Black and white people are suddenly in a band together that everyone's going to get along like a house on fire? This is some white middle-class utopia: wouldn't it be nice if everyone loved each other? It wasn't a Pepsi-Cola advert. It was real life. Outside on the street, people weren't getting along with each other. Our main objective was to demonstrate that: we're here; we're Black and white people in the same band; isn't that amazing? Music wasn't worth doing if you weren't dissenting about something. You didn't waste your time doing love songs and crap like that. If you were going to write a song, make it about something. Racism was rife. Working-class rights were being decimated. Thatcher had just come to power out of the turmoil of the seventies: the three-day week; the Winter of Discontent. The country was in recession. We weren't going to stand around with our arms around each other being happy. We were a microcosm of society. But then you're faced with being creative, trying to do music, touring schedules, people's pettiness going on. It was very hard, but it was also very exciting. We bought into the ethos of 2 Tone: of unity, celebrating the things that unite you rather than divide you, but we were subjective animals. It was hard to do on a 24/7 basis. We were our own worst enemy. We were continually arguing. I don't think that's a terrible thing, but there was a lot of destructiveness within the band. We were an incredibly angry band. We went out onstage as though we were going to rip the head off everyone as soon as we opened our mouths and played the music. But it didn't make for a good day-to-day working life."[112]

Defying anyone to have managed the Selecter, Juliet de Vie is equally forthright, recognizing that relationships within the Selecter were both complicated and constantly shifting. "It got to the point where you thought anything we do is sabotaged by seeing racism in everything we encounter. They were outspoken and hard work: always late, always arguing, always changing plans. Everything was 'Soon come.' There was a classic on a ferry crossing where Neol and Pauline managed to get a sleeping berth and everybody else slept on chairs and sofas. It became a raging argument. Desmond got very angry. I was like, 'But I'm sleeping here too.' It was horrible. There were Black and white minefields everywhere you went, in everything you did. None of it was simple."

"It was a very intense experience," concurs Neol. "There were seven really strong personalities. We treated each other badly. We saw ourselves as a political expression. Just in our existence. I was white. Pauline was female and from African heritage. Compton was African. The other guys were either from Jamaica or St. Kitts: the Caribbean islands. The common experience there is that, aged eleven, twelve, thirteen, people were told they were leaving to go to England. Bang! It happened. All of a sudden, you're with your parents who are a completely different generation and have a different experience of being here, going through all the racism of the fifties. The Selecter was a prime expression of that cultural trauma. The anger that they felt. The everyday racism they received. It wasn't overt. It was under-the-counter racism: day-to-day, walking down the street, going into shops. It was corrosive and it was everywhere. We struggled being with each other. We weren't nice to each other. You can't just say, 'People should get on. Black and white unite.' Yeah, how? We were saying, 'Look, we're finding it difficult. But we're doing it.' We weren't presenting ourselves as a perfect example of harmony. We were putting ourselves forward as a political statement. 'We're trying, why can't you?' We were an extremely dysfunctional band, our own worst enemy, but that was what made us what we were. We argued a lot and took it out on each other. But what we accomplished in that short time is extraordinary."

Reduced to a five-piece after the departure of Charley and Desmond, the Selecter made their final appearance on *Top of the Pops* on August 28, 1980, performing "The Whisper" with Gaps miming from behind the keyboards and Compton playing bass. The new record was backed by "Train to Skaville," originally recorded by the Ethiopians and fittingly one of the last ska records of the original Jamaican genre. "The Selecter make a valiant attempt to get away from the 2 Tone stamp with a single that seems to owe more to the Coasters than ska," read a review in *Record Mirror*, "and manages to confirm the impression that they are still among the best equipped to survive the downturn in interest in things black and white and Blue Beat."

It was not to be. The original lineup of the Selecter had lasted less than a year. In September, a terse statement sounded a note of finality: "The culmination of personal and musical differences that have been around for some time." In fact, the Selecter did regroup, aided by two new members, but a resulting second album—*Celebrate the Bullet*—in the early months of 1981 did little to reignite the zest and swagger of the original lineup. With an underperforming long player and no hit single, the Selecter crumbled.

CHAPTER 25

UNO, DUE, TRE, QUATTRO

THE SWINGING CATS

The Swinging Cats may have been the first 2 Tone act to have the misfortune of not charting, but they would not be the last. Neither a one-hit wonder nor a group revered with posthumous cool underground credentials, the Swinging Cats have simply been lost to the dustbin of musical history. Yet, in their brief time together, barely twelve months, they filled a musical biography tight with stories of heart-wrenching possibility and tales of woe worthy of bands twice the value in weight.

"We were like the band that never existed," says founding member John Shipley. "We formed in Billy Gough's garage, and his mum used to come in with chocolate spread sandwiches. There were all these canoes and moose heads hanging up. We squeezed in and somebody said, 'There's not enough room to swing a cat in here!' That's how we became the Swinging Cats."

Born in Highgate, north London, Shipley moved to Coventry in 1965. Earning a scholarship at Henry VIII Grammar School, he befriended Jerry Dammers. "I left with one art O level," smirks John, quoting from Roddy Byers's condemnation of education in the Specials's "Rat Race," "but it did nothing for me! I met Roddy on the David Bowie scene. There were only about two or three pubs in Coventry you could be safe in. To go through the precinct in stack heels and shaved eyebrows you'd get chased by skinheads." Developing a taste for ska, John lent Jerry some Prince Buster albums, which he had bought for his older sister Linda for Christmas. By the summer of 1978, John and Jerry were sharing a house in Burnaby Road. "I was working for a wine merchant driving a van, so I kept us stocked up with crates of Beaujolais."

Inspired by the dramatic transformation of the Automatics to the Specials, John left his group, the Urge, and formed the Swinging Cats. "John had a simple plan," says bass player Steve Wynne. "'We'll put this band together. Put it into this battle-of-the-bands competition and get a single on 2 Tone.' That was our motivation."

For singer Jane Bayley, it was the most exciting thing that had ever happened. "Until then I'd only sung other people's songs at folk clubs. John asked if I fancied singing a couple of his songs, so I introduced him to Toby [Lyons] who played keyboards and, like me, liked playing old Latin and rumba-inspired numbers. I felt a bit out of my depth because I couldn't jam, but I managed to put melodies and words to some of the songs. The result was a kind of dancy ska with a tongue-in-cheek Latin flavor and some fun cover versions like the theme from *The Avengers*, 'The Magic Roundabout' and a Mantovani tribute tune."

Making their debut supporting the Mo-dettes at Lanchester Polytechnic, the Swinging Cats entered the regional battle-of-the-bands competition. "The others played me a tape of my singing and it sounded awful," says Jane, "so they replaced me with a better singer—Jerry's girlfriend."

Valerie Webb had been engaged to Jerry Dammers since 1973.* "I was lucky enough to be there at the very birth of 2 Tone," she says, "and live at Albany Road during its hectic heyday!" Working then as a life model by day at the polytechnic, Val says, "I used to know who was in the room by people's shoes because I never looked up." Describing Val as "small, really pretty and a terrible flirt," Neol Davies recalls her teasing him one night when he was touring with Nite Train. "We were on one of these workingman's club stages with

---

* After a brief correspondence, Val chose not to contribute further to this book for personal reasons.

curtains at the side, and Val was standing in the wings so the audience couldn't see her," he says grinning, "and she was lifting her skirt up, showing her stocking tops."

Dashing off an identifying theme, "The Swinging Cats Song"— *The walls are too high, the ceilings are too near, there's not enough room to swing a cat in here . . . meow*—the group invited Val to sing at the final of the competition. "I had less than a week to learn the songs and rehearse," she says. But just as John Shipley predicted, the Swinging Cats won and bagged a two-day recording session at Woodbine Studios with Jerry Dammers producing. "People thought it was a fix," says Steve Wynne. "But Trevor Horn [member of the Buggles, producer] was on the judging panel and he was impartial. He wanted to sign the band at one point but we kept splitting up."

Ahead of the recording session, the Swinging Cats secured a slot on the local BBC arts show *Look! Hear!* Fearful of earning money while claiming unemployment benefit, the band decided to adopt rock 'n' roll pseudonyms. Thus, John Shipley became Vaughan Truevoice. Toby Lyons donned a red fez and became Toni El Dorko. Saxophonist Paul Heskett, later of the Specials, became Vince Le Rado. Steve Wynne—Wayne Riff. Billy Gough—Troy Corner. Val Webb— Pussy Purrfect. Excited to be making their television debut, the group were shocked to hear presenter John Holmes introduce their performance with a quote from a disgruntled correspondent: "Some people didn't agree with the final decision," Holmes read. "Like the writer of this letter who chose to remain anonymous so we can't take your criticism any further. But," he signed off, "for everyone else, here are the winners . . . the Swinging Cats!"

They performed "Never on a Sunday," which John describes as "an old song from a fantastic Greek film about a prostitute. She says, 'You can kiss me on a Monday, Tuesday, Wednesday, Thursday, Friday, Saturday, but Sunday is the day of rest.' It was one of Toby's mum's records."* Wearing a glittery blue dress and a pink crocheted coat, Val

---

* Released in 1960, *Ta Pediá tou Pireá* (Τα Παιδιά του Πειραιά) was a romantic comedy written and directed by and starring Jules Dassin.

doggedly avoided the lens of the camera. "As soon as it came toward her face she looked away," recalls Neol Davies. "She did it in such a brilliant way. She was really different and looked great on camera."

Then, unexpectedly, Val quit. "She couldn't take the pressure," opines John. "I wasn't that keen anyway because she was Jerry's girlfriend and the press were gonna think it was incestuous."

Booked to play a series of club dates, the Swinging Cats determined to carry on. Making use of the 2 Tone Fan Club, they rehearsed in the front room of a terraced house. "People would stand outside watching us," says John. Among them was Jane Bayley, who was invited to rejoin the band on the promise that "they'd get foldback" so she could hear her voice in the monitor speakers. On April 12, the group traveled to London to support Bad Manners and the Bodysnatchers at the Electric Ballroom. Playing to a hostile audience, heavily ranked with neo-Nazis, former dancer and now co-singer Chris Long introduced the first song. "I hear there's a lot of skinheads tonight," he said, determined and unintimidated. "Well, we're going to play 'Magic Roundabout' because you like those moronic little ditties."

Shortly after, the Swinging Cats received their first national feature in *NME*. Posing the question, "Who else is there to kick new life into what had become the withered old ska horse?" journalist Adrian Thrills answered his own question with the suggestion, "Maybe we should look to the Swinging Cats?" Quick-witted, John Shipley responded, "We want to make the sort of music you'd listen to while waiting for an ice cream in a cinema or in a dentist's waiting room. Having your teeth out needn't be so painful with the Swinging Cats."[113]

Teeth, maybe not, but the interpersonal dynamics within the group were proving to be equally sore. First Toby Lyons left—"because he didn't get on with Steve [Wynne]," says John—and then Billy Gough, who according to Wynne "didn't like the experience of being on telly and thought if he carried on it would get even worse. He wanted a quiet life as a carpenter."

When they were booked to record in Leamington and now without a keyboard player and drummer, fortune favored the Swinging Cats. By chance, the Specials were photographing the cover for their second album barely half a mile away. With the shoot complete, John Bradbury agreed to play drums on the session.

Such was the group's ad hoc approach, the Swinging Cats made a last-minute choice to record an instrumental track called "Mantovani." Although an original, the music incorporated passages from two older songs, "Hear My Song, Violetta" and "Speak to Me of Love," both featured on the album *Mantovani Love Songs*. "I used to hear them as a child, from my mother's record collection," explains Shipley.

Under-rehearsed, the group readied to record, uncertain what to do. Introducing "Mantovani" with an Italian count-in—*Uno, due, tre, quattro*—saxophonist Paul Heskett was unaware that Steve had broken a bass string. "I couldn't believe it," says Steve, shuddering at the memory. "So I played with three strings." Attempting to negotiate a sequence of tricky bass runs, Wynne inevitably slipped up. "We decided to leave the mistakes in," he says, "because it proved we were human." Behind the control desk, Jerry Dammers encouraged a relaxed atmosphere. Relatively inexperienced as a producer, Shipley rechristened the band the Swinging Guinea Pigs.

As Jane Bayley prepared to sing on the second track, "Away," Wynne was not happy. "Jane sang on the record but Val had won the battle-of-the-bands competition and done the television appearance. She should have recorded it but she didn't want the spotlight. I tried to persuade her but she wouldn't." To complete the track, Toby Lyons agreed to put differences to one side and return to the fold to overdub an organ part directly onto the eight-track master. However, for John Shipley, who had written the song to evoke the type of music heard at a fairground, the result was disappointing. "We used to do 'Away' in Urge," he says, "and it was a lot better!"

The Swinging Cats outside Noel's Cafe, Coventry, July 19, 1980.

* * *

One week after the Selecter walked out, the Swinging Cats signed to 2 Tone. "We could have signed with Chiswick, but I wanted to stay loyal to Jerry," says Shipley. "I said to him, 'Never mind the royalties, where's your loyalties?'"

When "Mantovani" was issued as a double A-side single in August 1980, the first 20,000 copies of it sold at fifty pence to entice buyers. The marketing tactic failed. "Fifty pence was the price of a pint at Mr George," says Steve Wynne, measuring the public's preference for liquid refreshment over vinyl satisfaction. "There wasn't a band to promote it: the one on the telly wasn't the one on the record; and the one on the record wasn't the one on tour. There was no solid base."

Described by Jerry as "quirky, melancholic exotica" and labeled by Terry Hall as "three brothers and an auntie," the Swinging Cats were subject to critical review on BBC Radio 1's weekly edition of *Roundtable*. Joined by special guests Shakin' Stevens and Harry Nilsson, presenter Andy Peebles whipped "Mantovani" off the turntable, declaring it "probably the worst record I've ever heard in my life." Listening in during a soundcheck at the Fulham Greyhound, John Shipley's face was one of "absolute horror," much to Paul Heskett's amusement. "I was crying with laughter," he counters.

"This was the era when Radio 1 was everything," says Julia Marcus, press officer at Chrysalis. "If you didn't get your record on the playlist, you were screwed. Radio 1 was still mullets and middle-of-the-road. Obviously records like 'On My Radio' and 'Too Much Too Young' were hugely commercial, but the Swinging Cats were too left-field and not mainstream enough." Nevertheless, Harry Nilsson loved it. And furthermore, he had a message for 2 Tone. "He was staying at the Dorchester Hotel," says Paul Heskett, "and a taxi arrived with this handwritten letter addressed to Jerry Danners [sic]. I opened it and it said, 'Dear Jerry, Dr. John really likes what you do and wants to make a record.' I called Jerry and he just said, 'Fine.'"

Discussing 2 Tone's first flop, Horace Panter informed journalist Chris Salewicz, "Jerry said to me that it seemed a bit unfair that if a factory turns out a duff model of a car, then at least it can be recalled and repaired, yet of course you can never do that with a record. I think it's a huge strain for him feeling that he has to be in charge of all the quality control of 2 Tone records and all the hustling that's necessary for it. He's been in a pretty bad state."

In December 1977, *Investors Review* nominated the Sex Pistols as "Young Businessmen of the Year" for accruing £115,000 from record company deals and featured a photograph of Johnny Rotten and co. on its front cover. As far as financiers and entrepreneurs were concerned, 2 Tone merited similar commendation. "Actually, I'm not very good at all at hustling," squirmed Jerry. "But it just seemed that no one else was going to do it, so I had to. Someone made me out as being like Young Businessman of the Year. But I hate all that. I really hate capitalism. 2 Tone is just about music."

Jerry was renowned for his dislike of interviews, and Julia Marcus says the process would cause him physical pain. "He'd work himself up into a terrible state. He overthought everything. He was worried he'd say something and it'd come out as something else and it would upset somebody. Maybe the problem with the press was he couldn't control it. He worried a lot about the way he'd be perceived and if he would be misinterpreted or misquoted. He wanted the music to do the talking. He didn't want to have to justify and explain the thought process behind things."

Uncomfortable with its elevated status as an iconic brand, Jerry downplayed the significance of 2 Tone. Yet, in order to maintain artistic control, he continued to manage its visual presentation with meticulous attention to detail. "Jerry was a total control freak," continues Marcus. "Every single thing that went out—musically, the artwork, the videos—had to be approved." The autocratic tendency is one that the Selecter's manager, Juliet de Vie, recalls all too well. "Jerry found it difficult to share responsibility. Consequently, if Jerry got stuck on something, everything got stuck. It could make it difficult trying to meet deadlines and move things forward for the band."

While nobody doubted his unique artistic vision and hands-on approach, it was the cause of much frustration. "Jerry was never great at delegating," says Terry Hall. "That's always been his problem, about trusting, especially members of your band to do jobs and to share the responsibility. He couldn't do that. Unless you've got somebody, not even with the business head, just somebody with a better sense, you need someone to look after it because there are too many checks coming in and out, just real basic things and you've got to deal with VAT and we didn't do that at all. It was a bit of a nightmare."[114]

To remedy perceived procrastination, Chrysalis would call Jerry's bluff. "A record was never finished," says Chris Poole. "He was constantly, 'No, no, I want to remix it. I want to do this. I want to do that.' In the end, it was like, 'Okay, it's being released next week.' Jerry wanted the impossible. If he had an idea in his mind, he wouldn't accept it wasn't doable. If you said, 'Sorry, I can't do that,' he'd take it as a personal insult or see it as defeatism. 2 Tone caught the zeitgeist and Jerry rode that wave spectacularly well. But in the end, he couldn't deal with it."

As the first autumn leaves began to fall, 2 Tone greeted the winds of change with dramatic reinvention. Gone was the commercial shop front of ska and its accompanying rude boy imagery, and in its place a Specials record of incredible imagination and concept. The statement was one of progression and survival, but the question was whether the audience was ready to make the transition.

CHAPTER 26

INTERNATIONAL JET SET

STEREOTYPE. MORE SPECIALS TOUR. AUDIENCE VIOLENCE

On September 20, 1980, the Specials issued their third single of the year, "Stereotype." It was an audacious statement and introduced record buyers to the group's radical new sound. Talking to the fanzine *Ded Yampy*, Jerry Dammers explained the theme behind the song: "We couldn't decide whether it should be *I'm just a stereotype* or *We're just a stereotype* 'cos most of it is true. It's about me. The song's just about getting pissed and driving home at night." To accompany the release, full-page ads in the music papers showed a black-and-white image of a mangled, upturned car—its license plate sensitively erased to protect the possibility that its occupants may have died in a road accident—beneath a full set of song lyrics. "People seem to miss the humor of what we're doing," Jerry told *NME*. "They don't seem to realize we're taking the piss a lot of the time. On the new single, I'm taking the piss out of myself. If it's all going over people's heads then I'm not sure what the point is. All good rock 'n' roll's meant to be funny. We just write about ourselves and hope they'll see how that relates to themselves, too."

Making light of recent sexual encounters—contracting a venereal disease during the US tour—"Stereotype" originally opened with the line, *The last girl you went with, she gave you VD.** "Jerry picked up a

---

* The first draft of lyrics also has a crossed-out stanza describing queuing for a football match: *You couldn't be bothered who loses or wins.*

bad dose," claims Roddy Byers, suppressing a smile, "and because he wouldn't stop drinking, he couldn't get rid of it." Channeling the experience into song, "Stereotype" tells the tale of a seventeen-year-old who after *seventeen weeks* alcohol free, *drinks his age in pints* and *ends up in a fight*. Driving home *pissed* through a dark rainy night and chased by a *fluorescent jam sandwich with flashing blue light*, the saga ends with the protagonist *wrapped round a lamppost on Saturday night*.

Ad for the "Stereotype" single, September 1980. Courtesy of Chrysalis Records/Jerry Dammers.

Taking offense at the use of the word "pissed," the BBC banned the song. It was a reactionary and futile gesture. The single rocketed to number six on the national chart. A relieved Chrysalis quieted down, having argued that coupling the single with the more agreeable ska-inflected album track "Enjoy Yourself" would be to the group's benefit. "In retrospect it might have made it a Christmas number one," mused Jerry in an interview with *Record Collector*, "but art won out over commerce."

While Horace Panter declared it "the best song the Specials have ever made," Terry Hall shared some of the musical influences behind the record, and its accompanying B-side, telling *Smash Hits* that they had been listening to a John Barry album and his current favorite track, "The Third Man Theme." "Jerry's written a song called 'The International Jet Set,' which stems from our touring America and all the crap that we went through, and he's just given that odd feel to it—it's spooky."

Written as a reaction to breaking up with his long-standing girlfriend—"She couldn't handle that new element," opined Jerry, "seamen are about the only other people who have comparable stresses placed on their relationships"—"International Jet Set" also captured the pressures of pop stardom. Set on a DC-10 cruising at 25,000 feet, the song addresses a passenger on flight 1313 reflecting on losing touch with reality and spreading *the disease from the South China seas to the beach Hotel Malibu*, surrounded by businessmen *like well-dressed chimpanzees*. According to Chalkie Davies, Terry had a nervous breakdown on a flight to Seattle, inspiring the lyric *downer pills make me feel ill*. "Somebody had to give him Valium," recalls the photographer. Allegorically, "International Jet Set" can be read as a suicide note forecasting the death of the Specials, revealed at the end of the song when an in-flight announcement turns out to be a prerecorded message as the unmanned plane attempts an emergency landing.

Not knowing whether to laugh or cry, John Shipley says that there were "things on *More Specials* that had quite a Swinging Cats influence. The chord sequence on 'International Jet Set' is the same as

'The Magic Roundabout' and the passage *the businessmen are having fun* is 'The Sun Has Got It's Hat On'—I always thought Jerry would end up at the Old Bailey!" teases Shipley, playfully undermining the originality of the songwriting.

While lyrically macabre, the new double-sided single was musically years ahead of its contemporaries. Both songs on *More Specials* defined its impact. Progressive. Radical. Enlightened. Psychotic. Advanced. They are all fitting adjectives. Added to which, both tracks—"International Jet Set" (five minutes thirty-nine seconds) and "Stereotype" (seven minutes twenty-five seconds)—accounted for over thirteen minutes of playing time. Asked to toast over the extended instrumental passage of the latter, Neville Staple responded in one take. "I made it up as I went along," he said. "I can't write words down in advance and then read them out, that wouldn't seem very natural to me. So I just did it off the top of my head."[115] In the control room, Jerry was in hysterics: "Neville was fuckin' brilliant at misunderstanding everything. He thought 'Stereotype' was about someone that owned a stereo!"

Reflecting on the evolved sound of *More Specials*, Jerry argues that the natural desire for a musician is to progress. "I'd always thought the band should be experimental. To me, albums are a place for experiments and then you hone the best of it for a single. You have to move on, otherwise people get fed up. It's just the next step. It wouldn't occur to me to do the same thing twice. The first side is sort of similar to the first album, but the second side has moved on. It's all overdubs. We built it up like a jigsaw. No one, except me, knew what it was going to sound like." Sharing his thoughts with *Record Mirror* in 1980, Jerry admitted to being "a very devious person" and trying things "just to be different." Asked whether he thought "Stereotype"—and the new album—would be successful, he replied, "I don't know whether it will be a hit. It certainly wasn't intended to be. In a way it was supposed to be something different to try to get the cult thing going again."

To sweeten the pill, the first 100,000 copies of *More Specials* came with a free poster—an outtake of the band from the front cover shoot—and a seven-inch single. Although having fewer tracks on the long-playing record meant that the needle was less likely to jump on a turntable and it could be played louder, Roddy says, "The free single seemed like an apology to me." Recorded during the album sessions, "Braggin' and Tryin' Not to Lie" (credited to "Roddy Radiation & the Specials") and "Rude Boys Outa Jail" (credited to "Neville Staple AKA Judge Roughneck") stretched the sound palette to exaggerated ska theater and Roddy's newly found infatuation with rockabilly. "It became my religion," he says. "It was about a very early Specials gig where the band thought I'd scored with a lady. I hadn't but no one would believe me."

More Specials presented the group sitting around a Formica table in a sixties-style bar drinking beer behind a multicolored glass dividing wall. Dressed in a range of colored clothing—from a white shirt and dickie bow (John Bradbury) to a chunky yellow knitted cardigan (Jerry)—the group revealed a disparate array of fashion influences adorned with gold chains and dark sunglasses. Seated in the corner of the image is a Black girl dressed in leather trousers and a collarless black-and-white checkered blouse—a friend of Jerry's, Pat Bailey, sat in for the unavailable Rhoda Dakar to complement the "James Bond vibe" of the sleeve—listening passively to the group banter. Shot deliberately out of focus on a Polaroid SX70—to look like a King Tubby sleeve, at Jerry's request—Chalkie Davies picked up his Hasselblad camera and cheerily instructed, "And now *in* focus for the Americans!" Basing it on retro-style sleeves from the late fifties, Davies says that when he showed Chrysalis the completed design, they asked where the real picture was.

"I remember very specifically," he continues, "the record was going to be called *Specials Enjoy Themselves*. But I felt that it was too close to *Get Happy* by Elvis Costello and that it also could be misinterpreted in a sexual way. The second Monkees album was called *More of the Monkees,* so I said to Jerry, 'I think we should call it *More Specials.*'" As a final touch, an embedded sticker was printed over the

"E" of "MORE" as a satire on "middle-of-the-road" music (MOR). "Chrysalis took it off after a few years," adds Davies. "I forget why."

When the album reached the desk of *Sounds*, Garry Bushell gave it a five-star review: "*More Specials* is a massively successful gamble, wider, warmer, weirder and as good if not better in its own way than its predecessor." At Chrysalis, Julia Marcus, tasked with promoting the album, likewise lauded its greatness. "It's a work of absolute genius," she says. "It's a perfect album. The way it starts with an upbeat version of 'Enjoy Yourself' and then a melancholic version at the end. It's like a concept album. It has a flow. There were loads of problems going on when they were making it, but it doesn't come out in the music. The reviews waxed lyrical about it. It was miles ahead of its time and really brave to do off the back of the first album."

Released in September, *More Specials* achieved gold status within a matter of weeks. Unimpressed, Roddy threw his BPI Award against the wall. "I can't bear to listen to the album," he says. "It just makes me feel ill."

To promote the record, the Specials set out on a twenty-five-date British tour. After two weeks in rehearsal, on Thursday, September 11, the group traveled to Cornwall in a new coach co-opted from the Coventry City Football Club, in crisis, with talk of canceling the tour. Troubled by Jerry's deteriorating health, trombonist Rico Rodriguez shared his concerns with Chris Salewicz: "Jerry has to take better care of himself, otherwise he could cause himself some harm. He has to work fantastically hard, making sure everything runs as it should. But he must look after himself better, that's all."[116]

The following morning, the Specials trekked to the beachside entertainment complex in St. Austell to run through their set, only to discover that the PA was not yet set up. Complaining that he was not feeling well, Jerry requested a doctor. "I thought I had glandular fever," he told Chris Salewicz two days later. "I've had it before and it's really horrible: I knew that if I had got it, I wouldn't be able to go on the tour. I think I was just trying to think myself into it because if I had it, all I'd be able to do would be just to stay in bed." Diagnosed "overworked," Roddy made his own assessment: "Jerry had a break-down. He had been burning the candle at both ends. It didn't help," he adds with a devilish grin, "that I suggested for a second time, 'Let's get Paul Heskett to play keys instead.'"

After a successful opening night, however, Jerry boarded the coach the next day and loudly announced, "Right! I had my nervous breakdown yesterday. Whose turn is it today?" Thoughts moved to the support act. Having recently played a series of club dates across London, the Midlands and Yorkshire, the Swinging Cats were on the verge of collapse. Amid persistent rancor and acrimony, Jane Bayley stepped down. "We only lasted about a year," she says. "Chris [Long] wanted to sing, so once again I was out. I was floored because I loved being in the band and playing such great music." Meanwhile, be-lieving John Shipley was having "a sort of breakdown," Toby Lyons planned a coup d'état with Paul Heskett. "You take over keyboards and I'll play guitar. Keep Jane in the band and we'll tell John we're not having it." Heskett hesitated: "It just wouldn't work." Alerted to the plot, Shipley pounced. "Paul used to play over everything whether it was needed or not. It used to really get on my wick. The day before we went on tour with the Specials, I said, 'I'm not going with Paul or Jane.' I didn't like Jane's singing. It sounded too much like a cat. I sacked them, so Chris Long had to sing." "There was all this madness going on, squabbling," remembers Steve Wynne. "It was like little catfights—bloody bunch of bitches!"

In fact, the Swinging Cats had been an unexpected late addition to the tour after newcomers the Stray Cats dropped out to promote their upcoming debut single, "Runaway Boys." Hastily organizing a warm-up at the Hope & Anchor, the Swinging Cats celebrated post-gig at a nearby nightclub, only to discover in the early hours that their equipment had been stolen from their van. Arriving in St. Austell, Lynval Golding loaned John Shipley a guitar. "It didn't have a trem-olo arm, so I was really miserable," bemoans Shipley.

Taking to the stage in front of 3,000 people, recalled Chris Long, was a nerve-wracking experience. "I thought, *What have I let myself in for?*" Presented with a band playing easy listening, Latin and film soundtracks, and a front man tooting "Whistling Song" and versions of Captain Scarlett and Sandie Shaw's "Long Live Love," the audience became abusive, throwing objects and spitting at the stage. "We weren't a true hard-core 2 Tone band, if there was such a thing," Long told author Paul Eddington. "We were a bit lightweight in that sense. So the hard-core rude boys didn't take too kindly to us, which made it really difficult."[117]

Ad for the *More Specials* tour, September 1980.

By the time the tour reached Coventry, Steve Wynne says, the band was "falling to bits." The atmosphere in the Specials camp was little better. "They didn't get on at all," maintains Shipley, "especially Roddy and Jerry. Roddy used to smash up his guitar during 'Enjoy Yourself,' going, 'Destroy yourself.'" Looking on in dismay, Wynne says, "People were biting each other's heads off. It was like watching a slow-motion car crash." Fueling the mood was a dramatic increase in alcohol intake. "Way too much," confirms Rick Rogers, who would happily drink to oblivion. Where the band had once traveled with a wardrobe full of stage outfits, it now bulged with bottles of beer and spirits—a touring bar. "Jerry had a bottle of vodka on top of his keyboard," recalls John Shipley. "He'd be knocking it back dressed in his tartan suit."

Preferring the comfort of a hotel room with "my weed and women," Neville Staple says: "When they were pissed, that was when their inhibitions came out. That's when it all became: 'I hate you.'"[118] Stimulated by a proliferation of cocaine and amphetamines, the spiraling behavior is best illustrated by the appearance of 2 Tone mirrors branded with a Walt Jabsco logo and, as Horace Panter described, "a three-inch groove cut out of them on one side, from where you snorted your 2 Tone cocaine . . . I made sure they were binned at the earliest opportunity."[119]

Attempting to lift the mood, Chas Smash arrived with a box of Madness's new album, *Absolutely*. Meanwhile, Paul Heskett—invited to join the Specials after being kicked out of the Swinging Cats—entertained the touring entourage backstage with ragtime renditions of "The Entertainer" and "Lovers Concerto" accompanied by another new recruit, Rhoda Dakar from the Bodysnatchers, improvising dance routines. Earning a reputation as the tour court jester, Heskett proudly took to showboating. "During 'Nite Klub,'" he hoots, "I'd play with my saxophone upside down, a trick I'd seen Andy Mackay do in Roxy Music, or Jerry would be dragging me by my braces. Horace once said to me, 'You must stop upstaging everyone, Paul,' but because my role was limited, I thought, *I'm going to be the clown.* One time we were doing 'Sock It to 'Em J.B.' and, with all the James Bond references, I walked onstage with this old Roger Moore suit with wide lapels, big flared trousers and a shirt with a flowery tie and sunglasses. The whole band was laughing their heads off." Exacting revenge, members of the Specials surreptitiously stuffed a pineapple down the horn of Heskett's saxophone. "The next night he couldn't get a note out of it," laughs John Shipley.

After more than year on the road, the Specials were firing on all cylinders. Older songs like "Too Much Too Young" and "Gangsters" were transformed and delivered at breakneck speed. "Stereotype" roused audiences to hold their hands aloft and clap in unison to its attention-grabbing backbeat as Terry punctuated Neville's extended toasting with an infectious choral chant: *Stereo, stereo, stereo.* During "Holiday Fortnight," he added the sing-along refrain, *We're all fucking mental.*

"Terry was lovely but quite angry about a lot of things," says Julia Marcus. "He could appear quite rude and brusque with people." Put in front of an audience, he stood stock still, seemingly emotionless. "I had that from about the age of four," Terry explained. "My friends' mums would say, 'Why are you looking so miserable, what's wrong with you?' I gave up explaining when I was about eight. I was like, 'Okay, I'm miserable. I'm happy with that. It's cool. With the gigs, it felt like a kindred spirit. It's fantastic when you get 1,000, 2,000 people all dancing and you can actually feel the building move. It was brilliant."[120] In his element, Terry honed the art of the introductory wisecrack, more often than not leaving members of the audience cut down to size.

"This is about the feeble excuses racist groups give you for violence. They can't face up to the fact that they're shitheads." (Potternewton Park, Leeds)

"A lot of you have been very naughty tonight. You've fought, you've

spat at us and generally shat on us . . . but we've enjoyed ourselves. Goodnight!" (Pavillon Baltard, Paris)

"If any of you under-sixteens are planning to make love later on, get hold of your dad's dictionary and look under the word 'contraception' and under the word 'fun,' and under these two words you'll find four words . . . 'too much too young.'" (Paris Theatre, London)

"The next song's for all you students who are going to walk out of here missing your mothers and fathers, but you're going to have a little degree tucked under your arm. It's called 'Rat Race.'" (Colchester Institute, Essex)

"I've got a disturbing story to tell you. When we tried to get in the club tonight there was this little picaninny chap who tried to hurt us. This song's for you, if you're still on the door, you little cunt. It's called 'Doesn't Make It Alright.'" (Paradiso, Amsterdam)

"Now, little girls, we nearly had a little upset with a little fight down there . . . [Interrupted] . . . It's no use telling me to fuck off because if you start fighting, we'll all fuck off." (Long Island, New York)

"Music is for your feet, not for your fucking head." (Long Island, New York)

"These people have got the mentality of a house brick; they don't think twice about belting you with one of those bars, so just leave the fence alone. It's not worth it." (Pinkpop Festival, Holland)

"This next song's dedicated to Ronald Reagan, who gave up riding on horseback to ride on a neutron bomb. It's called 'Man at C&A.'" (Liberty Bell Park, Philadelphia)

"This is dedicated to my sex life, and no doubt to a great many others'. It's called 'I Can't Stand It.'" (Hammersmith Palais, London)

On September 27, the Specials were featured on the front cover of *NME*, captured by seasoned photographer Adrian Boot onstage in Brighton. Where the audience ends and the stage begins is near impossible to identify. With the band mobbed by a sea of rabid fans, the caption aptly reads: "Spot the Special." It is an incredible image. In a later frame, Terry Hall presides over the assembled masses, swaying unsteadily on the shoulders of a clutch of zealous admirers.

Inviting the audience onto the stage had started in the summer of 1979 as a measure to protect traveling fans from intercity rivals. In July, at Eric's in Liverpool, a contingent from Coventry used the stage as a safe haven. When they were hassled by locals, Jerry beckoned the nervous throng onto the wooden risers. The sympathetic act became a statement of solidarity uniting the audience and the group. "The previous punk statement had been gobbing on the band," says Jerry. "Inviting fans onto the stage was stating that the band weren't superior to the audience." To make the point, the chant *Nobody is special* was incorporated into the "Skinhead Symphony" medley.* "It was saying, we're all in this together," explains Jerry. Rejecting student talk of a violent or fantasy revolution, Jerry says he wanted a revolution that involved all people: a radical change in society and attitude that made life fairer, adding, "Music was part of that."

Stage invasions were not new to 2 Tone. In the past, Chuck Berry would invite Teds onto the stage, step aside, and let them dance. However, as the success of the Specials attracted audiences in ever greater numbers, says Rick Rogers, that inclusivity went from stage invasions to fans on the coach to coming back to the hotel to being

---

* The chant served a second purpose, says Jerry: "Some people took the name—the Specials—literally and thought we thought we were something, so I put *Nobody is special* into 'Liquidator' to make it clear."

put up in people's rooms. "This was very much Jerry's agenda of: 'Just because we're pop stars and we're in a band, that doesn't make us any more special than you.'"

Initially, fans waited until the end of the set. "But then," says Jerry, "they wanted to get on by the third number." Forced to retreat, the group requested additional risers. "The stage would be invaded halfway through," recalls Horace. "You'd have to stop for five minutes. 'Can you get off, please?'" Amid the melee there was a lot of unruliness, says Frank Murray. "The fans that got on the stage were totally exhilarated, just dancing their arses off, knocking over microphones, equipment getting damaged. It used to drive me mad. Jerry loved breaking down the barriers and the bouncers were told to stay away. But I just saw it as fucking hassle letting all these clowns on the stage."

"Come on, everybody," Terry implored the audience in St. Austell. "Get off the stage, please. You can all come back on at the end and have a nice little dance." In Bristol, he told the crowd, "This stage is our prison. We don't want you to have to become prisoners of the record industry, so please clear the stage." Unwilling to accept the traditional divide between performer and audience, Terry calculated, "Who am I to say the kids can't come up? Do they say I can't come down into the audience? They've paid the £3. They can do what they like for that as far as I'm concerned. They have wrecked the equipment sometimes, but it's only equipment, isn't it? That can be replaced."

Shifting his ire to unrestrained bouncers meting out indiscriminate violence, Terry complained, "They're supposed to stop the trouble, not start it. It really pisses me off when they've got nothing to do so they decide to kick the shit out of a group of kids in the front row and then blame them for causing the trouble. It not only spoils it for the kids, but it spoils it for us."[121] For Neville, sticking up for fans against unruly bouncers not only endeared them to the band but livened up the gig. "It was brilliant! It only affected the music by making us more into it, more involved with the audience and closer to them. That way we knew they were getting off on it. Which was getting *us* off on it."

"Youthful enthusiasm," surmised Jerry. "They're not really causing any problems. They just want to be part of it. They're all really good kids. But if it goes on like this someone's going to get really badly hurt."

At the Locarno in Bristol, fear became reality when a stack of speakers fell fifteen feet from the stage into the audience, causing minor injuries to two girls. Jerry urged fans to curb their behavior. "The audience might destroy 2 Tone anyway," he confided. "Cardiff and Newcastle was just chaos. I think a lot of people didn't enjoy it. There would be five-minute gaps between numbers so that we could clear enough space to play. If the audience does destroy it, then it's just sad. I hope they see sense."

Adding to the hazardous live experience and the unwelcome increase in audience violence, Jerry was keen to make a distinction between genuine fans, skinheads and troublemakers. "I just wanted 2 Tone to be like a little club, and if you liked the music then you became part of it—that's all," he told *Melody Maker*. "As it is, it just gets a bit worrying. But there's nothing I can do about it. The skinheads aren't a problem at all. They're discriminated against, really. They just look intimidating." Pressed about reported skinhead association with far-right political groups, Jerry was forthright: "It's just not true at all that if you're a skinhead you've gotta be in the National Front. But even so, you can tell anybody that if they're into the NF or the British Movement that if they want to come to our gigs, we don't want them there. They're not welcome."

Despite the plea, troublesome incidents flared in Newcastle—"If one more glass hits me we're fucking off for good," Terry told the audience. One did and the band left the stage—and in Leeds and Glasgow, fighting broke out between bouncers and fans. Then on October 8, an ugly scene at Brunel University resulted in an incredible act of defiance by the Specials. Having paid the £2.50 ticket price, a small group of agitators set about disrupting the concert and throwing sharpened coins at Lynval and Neville. Losing his temper, Neville jumped into the audience, backed up by Jerry, Lynval, Terry and then Roddy. "I misjudged the height of the stage and fell flat on my face. I started swinging my guitar round me head and the good skinheads said, 'The fight's over there, Roddy.' I was like, 'Okay! Do I really want to get involved in this?' Neville was shouting, 'Roddy, give me your guitar!' He broke someone's arm with it. The neck was split and bits hanging off it." Chasing the culprits out of the building, a victorious Jerry now exclaims, "Imagine that! *Top of the Pops* coming to life and running toward you."

If pockets of the tour were in danger of hijacking by acts of mindless violence, events in Cambridge the following day led the band to question their very existence. As 3,500 fans wedged themselves into a tent set up on Cambridge Common, rival football fans clashed in anticipation of a fourth-round League Cup tie between Coventry City and Cambridge United scheduled for October 28. Anticipating trouble and miffed at having already failed in their attempt to cancel the gig, the police sent a squad of uniformed officers to stand guard around the edges of the tent. Inside, as the Swinging Cats took to the stage, the atmosphere was riotous. "It was like rent-a-mob," says John Shipley. "The crowd were just chanting, 'Specials, Specials.' We stopped playing and Chris said, 'No, no, we're not them.' It was hilarious."

The playful banter soon took on a more sinister tone when Long saw a gang of about twenty football fans wading through the crowd. "You could hear them chanting before you could even see them."[122] Fighting broke out, forcing the band to halt their set on several occasions. Exasperated, Dick Burrows got up from behind his drum kit and lashed out at a group of skinheads with his sticks as Long begged for calm. "Why do you want to fight? It's probably the last chance to see the Specials in Cambridge." Suddenly, out of nowhere, an assailant climbed onto the stage and launched himself at the singer. "[He] was coming for me but thankfully one of our roadies saved my bacon by chinning the twat, sending him flying in a reverse swallow dive back into the audience."[123]

When the Specials eventually took to the stage, all hell broke loose. "I walked on and some guy's going, 'COME ON THEN,'" says Roddy. "I was going, 'YOU COME HERE!' We got through two or three songs and a big fight started. Terry and Jerry were trying to calm it down." Opening the set with characteristic confrontational sarcasm—"We got any students here?" (Big cheer.) "We think you're all a bunch of wankers."—Terry became embroiled in a tit-for-tat argument with the crowd. Incensed at their spitting, Jerry joined in. "You're not doing anything new—we've got hot and cold running gob in our showers at home." More fights broke out. Fans clambered onto the stage. Bottles were thrown. There were chants of "United" and "Coventry, where are you?" And on three separate occasions, the Specials walked offstage. "YOU BLOODCLAATS HAVE SPOILT THIS EVENING FOR EVERYONE!" Terry shouted at a group of troublemakers. "WE'RE GOING DOWN THE PUB." Livid, he turned on a bouncer who was indiscriminately picking on people, threatening him with a microphone stand, yelling, "YOU'RE JUST AS BAD!"

After Terry was told to "shut his mouth," the band restrained him and marched offstage in disgust. When they returned, a cluster of the audience making Nazi salutes inflamed the volatile mood further. Security attempted to constrain the agitators but failed. With patience in short supply, bouncers threw arbitrary punches at members of the audience. "You could check your watch from when it was going to kick off," says John Shipley. "It was always during the chant to intro-duce 'Concrete Jungle': *You're going home in a fucking ambulance*. It was like the audience was programmed: 'This is where you go mad,' cue: skinheads go mad."

At the end of the night, neo-Nazi skinheads invaded the stage, brazenly saluting. Backstage the rumpus amplified. First, the police arrived and arrested Jerry when he told them to fuck off. "There was collusion between the bouncers and the local police," alleges Paul Heskett. "The band had done their utmost to prevent trouble. Then to be accused of doing the exact opposite, I was aghast. Rico had a giant bag of ganja and I remember thinking, *Oh, fuck!* I took my jacket off and put it over the stash, hoping they hadn't seen it." Next, the police arrested Terry and charged him with behavior likely to lead to a breach of the peace. "Why would we want to start a riot?" asked Roddy, gobsmacked. As the situation escalated, Chris Poole received a phone call from the Parkside police station. "It was Rick saying, 'Help!'"

Investigating the story, *NME* collared Superintendent Murden to challenge the conduct of his officers. "It was normal police work," he informed the paper. "Good police work, making the arrest. It's not a news item." Refusing to discuss the incident in detail, Murden was irked at the suggestion that the Specials should be described as "a band": "A *what* did you call them?" he asked. "A band? Well, they weren't a band as defined in the *Oxford English Dictionary*. I don't know how you can call a row like that a band!" A council organizer expressed further antipathy toward the Specials, telling a local journalist, "Shouting and swearing at the audience are all part of the group's set. They do it everywhere they go and take along a group of hecklers to excite the audience and warm them up. They also storm off the stage regularly as part of their set to excite the crowd."

Though thankful to leave Cambridge the following morning, the touring party was uncertain whether Terry and Jerry would make the next date in Brighton. Steve Wynne recalls being in the van listening to a news report on Radio 1. "They were saying, 'Big riot at the Specials last night,' and we were going, 'Ha! Bloody hell!' Requested to appear at the Cambridge Magistrates' Court in November, Terry and Jerry rejoined the tour after a night in a police cell, to great cheers and a heroes' welcome.

Still, the resurgence of fascist activity was taking its toll. Terry advocated not playing for a year. "I didn't want to be a part of that," he reflected in 2009. "It became a bit of a trend. And the more you played the more likely it was to happen. I thought we should just shut down shop for a year or something and it would go away."[124] In an attempt to take control at gigs, Terry singled out and attempted to humiliate ringleaders. "They were made to look like idiots," says Paul Heskett. "To get the opprobrium of everybody else in the audience and to show the band are not going to tolerate this and have absolute contempt for that kind of behavior. No one could have done it better."

Contrary to how it may sound, disturbances at 2 Tone gigs were actually infrequent, or, more exactly, typical of the period, happening not only at live events but regularly at football matches, local discos and pubs where macho posturing and base bigotry targeted innocent victims. Still, it is worth repeating that overall, 2 Tone concerts were joyful, exuberant celebrations hyping audiences into an ecstatic frenzy powered by the blistering display of music and energy coming from the stage. But with Sieg heil-ing and swastikas on show, the tabloids circled. Desperate to distance themselves from a suggested "epidemic," Chrysalis blacklisted offending journalists and publications. "They were not given access to the bands and to records or given tickets to concerts," says Julia Marcus. While acknowledging that isolated incidents were "blown out of all proportion by the media," Rick Rogers viewed the disorder as a natural consequence of the Specials's social stance. "They were doing something powerful and challenging a racist agenda; racists are going to try and infiltrate and protest. On top of that, the music and the dress took from right-wing culture. It was reappropriating signs and symbols and some people got confused."

Shocked to see people making Nazi salutes, Juliet de Vie says the same people would then "be going nuts during the songs—we just couldn't fathom it." Sickened by the ugly scenes, Jerry commented, "It just shows that they haven't understood what we're trying to put across at all." In Brighton, Jerry invited one troublemaker onto the stage and asked him to explain to the audience why he was doing it. "When he started speaking, I pushed him off to a huge cheer from the rest of the audience. Any violence was too much violence for me. I hated it." Then, at the Hammersmith Palais, when trouble flared up during "Gangsters," Jerry stopped the song and addressed a small faction in the audience: "Hey you, Sieg heil-ing, go and do it outside." Ignored, he added, "I hope you get stabbed."

As the front person of the Selecter, Pauline Black says, "You felt obliged to say something. If it persisted, you'd try to shame them: 'Right! If all these people here are doing this and the rest of you are having fun, what's your feeling about that?' If they put the lights up, the perpetrators could be identified and bouncers would get rid of them, often by sinking their teeth into a person's ear to immobilize them. If there was a fight, we'd down tools and go offstage until the troublemakers were thrown out." Trying to remain calm to show control, Gaps Hendrickson maintains, "You didn't want to pour oil on the flame. Most people came having paid their hard-earned money, not for some idiot to spoil it."

Chris Foreman says there were "a few very nasty incidents" at Madness gigs. "We'd stop the show, get the spots shone on them and sling them out." Quoted while on tour in America, Lee Thompson threatened to call time on the band, commenting, "We're only in this game for a laugh, and if we are forced to drop out then none of us would have any regrets at all. We don't want anything to do with the National Front. As far as I'm concerned, if they start venting their political feelings at our gigs, then we can call it a day."[125]

Outside the venues, the National Front actively recruited for members and sold copies of *Bulldog*. Edited by sixteen-year-old Joe Pearce, the four-sided pamphlet sold for three pence and featured stories about the "Paki Army," "blacks mugging and stabbing whites," "Asians raping women" and "learning to hate multiracialism." Attempting to make sense of the nationalistic bile, Suggs joked, uncomfortably, "There was a period where you thought, *Jesus! It's happened. We've been taken over by the Nazis.*" Further expressing his abhorrence of racism, he told a BBC reporter, "It started off like a fashion for a lot of kids. It was like football teams and then it was Nazis. It died off a bit, which is why we didn't take it seriously in the beginning. But now I think it *is* serious. I think everyone should do as much as possible to put 'em down." Clearly upset by the association, drummer Woody added, "It's got to the extent where we want it to end. We just want everyone to know positively and clearly that we have got nothing to do with any racist movements."[126]

Having purloined the melody from the aptly titled "Free Love" by Prince Buster, Lee Thompson says he is the one who wrote "Embarrassment." It was a clever vignette telling a true story about his sister, who, expecting a mixed-race child, is disowned by her family: "Don't come round here no more," say her parents. "What will the neighbors think?" says her aunt. "You're a disgrace to the human race," says her uncle. Set to a sprightly melody and an infectious Motown beat, Thompson's ironic nonjudgmental reportage ends with the damning line: "You're an embarrassment." It took the issue of interracial marriage into the top five of the UK singles chart, albeit with a video in which Mike Barson performs in blackface.

As a protest against racism the message was clear, but within months the Centre for Contemporary Studies published a report on the role of fascist groups in music, reporting neo-Nazi activists recruiting at Madness concerts. When it was picked up by the BBC current affairs program *Newsnight*—in a feature called "The Rock and the Right"—Madness were publicly challenged. In response, the band issued a statement read by presenter Joan Bakewell categorically denying support for "any political group which has racial politics." Drawing attention to their first-ever hit, "The Prince"—"Dedicated to a Jamaican, Prince Buster, who is the godfather of ska and reggae"— the declaration reminded readers that "the record was released on a label belonging to the Specials, who have both Black and white members." Reiterating their abhorrence of racism, Madness signed off with the hope that "fans of all ages and all nationalities do likewise."

In a letter sent to the Beat Club newsletter *The Noise in This World*, Rosalind from Falmer, Sussex, wrote of her experience seeing the Beat at the Brighton Top Rank. "Halfway through the set a wave of skinheads formed into a solid line and pushed the crowd back against the wall chanting 'Sieg heil.'" Citing "a few sporadic attacks against individuals,"

Rosalind described how "bloody violence" had come to be expected at gigs. In response, Dave Wakeling condemned the violence, adding, "Although we now have our own label, we still believe what 2 Tone stands for in terms of racial integration." Further arguing that drawing attention to unwelcome factions gives "the thugs" a greater platform, Wakeling urged positivity: "Even if it's just dancing the night away."

As a boy, Ranking Roger became aware of the National Front when racist pamphlets appeared through his mailbox in Birmingham. Stechford was the home of the National Front headquarters and Roger would regularly see skinheads march past his house shouting discriminatory slogans. "We never understood why our gigs attracted that crowd," he says. "I remember once a group of about ten skinheads making Nazi salutes and throwing coins. I opened my mouth to speak out and one of them spat at me. I was raging mad and jumped off the stage. The band stopped playing and Dave Wakeling and David Steele had their guitars up above their heads ready to whack them. The skinheads backed off and we got on with the music. I got a lot of abuse onstage. You'd have 2,000 people who'd come to enjoy themselves and a small minority disturbing the show. A couple of times it got out of hand. One time there were half a dozen or so skinheads shouting 'Sieg heil' and National Front slogans. I remember screaming, 'Stop your fuckin' fighting. Have you come here to fight or dance? Look! I'm a Black man.' I ripped off my hat and jacket and said, 'See, I'm Black! So what you here for?' My blood was boiling. Suddenly, from nowhere, the audience started chanting, 'Black and white unite.' Deanne Pearson reviewed the gig in the *New Musical Express* and said I was 'almost hysterical with rage and emotion.' The fighting and abuse at gigs cemented my mission to promote a message of peace, love and unity."

The potent synthesis of racism and macho male aggression caused Dave Wakeling much concern. "It always struck me as deeply ironic that the skinheads were dancing to ska, but it was also the place where the National Front and British Movement were recruiting. In London, they were shouting, 'We hate spades.' Roger said, 'It's funny how much you like the music, then,' and they shut up. You're in a strong position to ridicule the Front and get away with it, but then they razor someone in the toilets on the way out and you've accomplished nothing."[127] The simple but surprisingly successful solution was the Beat Girl. "As soon as the rucks started, I said, 'We should have a dancing girl as our emblem because Walt Jabsco needs somebody to behave with.' We thought if the 2 Tone man was dancing with a girl, he'd be more like a real person rather than like some super-stud."

Flicking through a back issue of *Melody Maker*, artist Hunt Emerson happened upon a black-and-white photograph of Prince Buster dancing with a cool-looking modette dressed in black heels, skirt, white long-sleeved blouse rolled below the elbow and a feathered fringe. Poised asymmetrically, the young woman dances with her knees and waist angled one way and her arms and upper body facing the other. It was a breathtaking image. Keeping the basic outline, Emerson sketched a caricature of the girl and colored her clothing in shades of pink.*

The Beat Girl holding an image of Prince Buster dancing with Brigitte Bond.

* The young woman in the photograph was identified as Brigitte Bond, who in 1964—billed with the Bluebeats—recorded the ska single "Blue Beat Baby." Bond achieved much media notoriety over the succeeding years, not least for the claim that she was transgender.

Adopted for ads and record sleeves, the Beat Girl softened the image and pitched the Beat as an antisexist, antiracist dance band. "At 2 Tone gigs the audience would be 80, 90 percent male," says Ranking Roger. "Then the malevolence began to subside and our audience broadened." According to Dave Wakeling, "Within a month the fights started to diminish, and within three months it was a thing of the past. Dancing uses up the same energy as punching somebody in the mouth. After an hour's dancing, you're in a much stronger position to think positively on what you're going to do with your life.[128] We'd have loads of girls at the front dressed as the Beat Girl and the boys seemed to behave themselves a lot better." Acknowledging its success, John Mostyn postulates, "I'm sure you could find a lot of people who came to those first gigs as angry skinheads and ended up being permanent fans of 2 Tone and leaving their past behind." Expressing her gratitude in a letter to the Beat's fan club, Rebecca from Chorlton, Leeds, wrote, "You and the Specials etc. have done a lot to stop the racism in schools, uniting us all together whatever the color."

Pointing to the generation too young to attend 2 Tone concerts who only heard the music on the radio and on record, Rick Rogers adds, "That's where the difference was."

CHAPTER 27

GHOST OF THE VOX CONTINENTAL

THE BODYSNATCHERS SPLIT

Back in February 1980, Horace Panter questioned the suitability of certain artists signed to 2 Tone, telling *Record Mirror*, "I'm not sure if it's too early for some of the groups. Sometimes I get a bit worried. Like if we sign the Bodysnatchers, what are we letting them in for?" By autumn, the question had an answer: infighting, a flop single and a premature end to the group's existence.

Memory plays extraordinary tricks on the mind. We like to place ourselves at the center of dramatic situations, cast as the heroic pro- tagonist. Distorting the true nature of events, the passage of time— unwittingly or not—enables us to restage episodes from the past to our mutual benefit. The breakup of the Bodysnatchers is a case in point. Four decades after the event, Penny Leyton singles out a key moment where she remembers singer Rhoda Dakar throttling guitarist Sarah-Jane Owen. Then, locating her diary from 1980, she is shocked at what she reads: "Friday 10 October, Edinburgh Uni [Freshers' Ball]. Rhoda upset because she had to get up at 4 p.m. for soundcheck which she didn't have until 5:30 p.m. Causes hysterical scene, shouts at SJ and Miranda, tries to strangle me ... I decide defi- nitely things can't continue this way ..."

"It was *me*!" screams Penny, stunned. "Obviously I put that out of my memory and transferred it to SJ." On hearing this, Rhoda also cries out. "What! I had her by her throat? Nah!" she says. "Penny was a fruit loop. Somebody said something that really annoyed me, so I had a go at them. Then Simon, our roadie, jumped in the middle and started having a go at me. Then my brother jumped in and basically said, 'You hurt my sister and I'll kill you.'"

"Ugly," "nasty" and "physical" are three words repeatedly used by band members when retelling the breakup of the Bodysnatchers. The exact details are hard to ascertain. Penny receives a lot of criticism. "Opinionated," says bassist Nicky Summers. "Difficult," says drummer Judy Parsons. "Irritating," says guitarist Stella Barker, adding, "I suspect Penny was goading Rhoda or contradicting her. I could see it was going to explode. It was awful to witness. Penny was difficult, but Rhoda and Nicky could be as well."

Young and innocent, saxophonist Miranda Joyce now says she tried to avoid arguments and generally got along well with everybody. Nevertheless, having shared a room together, she says Penny was "very uptight. She was classically trained and liked things to be right and in time. I remember her going, 'It goes like THIS!' Telling everybody. She used to lie on the floor and scream and shout after gigs because she was so annoyed that we'd gone out of time."

For her part, Penny compares the dynamic within the band to a blossoming romantic relationship. "In the early stages people are on their best behavior, but as you get to know each other you feel freer and resentments come out. I was not emotionally or mentally prepared for the whole experience. That probably contributed to the wrangling in the band. It was hard to spend that much time with people. It's ironic, since the whole idea of 2 Tone was to put differences aside and come together to promote a better society, that we couldn't overcome our own differences. It says something very sad about humans: that we have good intentions but we're all victims of our own shortcomings."

While not wholly absolving herself of blame, Penny points to other factors that ultimately split the band. "Rhoda had meltdowns," she says. "She would just sit in a chair and scream. There was a lot of pent-up frustration in her. She had problems with me and SJ. She felt that we were privileged middle-class white girls who didn't understand how things were." "White, privileged, middle-class kids?" repeats Miranda with a wry smile. "That was me, Stella and Penny."

Yes, the Bodysnatchers had diverse backgrounds and enjoyed varying degrees of parental affluence. The social differences are what make the group such a fascinating study. Nicky's parents owned a market stall in Soho. Rhoda's father grew up surrounded by servants and worked in the music business. "My parents behaved as if they lived in a big house," she says. "I was brought up to think of myself as someone who could expect everything and anything. I didn't have the psychological or cultural restrictions of being working class." Sarah-Jane compares herself and Stella to Posh Spice (Victoria Beckham). "We came from very well-educated backgrounds," she says, "whereas Nicky and Jane were what I call street kids."

Identifying a clear class divide, Rhoda postulates, "It was about: should we upset the neighbors or shouldn't we? I slotted into the working-class 'Let's rock the boat.' For instance, there was talk of releasing 'The Boiler'—an unremittingly chilling spoken-word piece describing a harrowing story of sexual assault—as a single: 'No! We can't release that! Oh my God!' Two or three members of the band wanted to release it, and the people that wanted to be 'pop stars' didn't." Rhoda then says education blurs class distinctions. "Your frame of reference shifts. You've maybe experienced more of the world. It changes who are you, what you think you can do, and where you fit in. Life had been good to them. We played Jesus College Ball [Oxford] and Penny's dad came because he was a professor there.* It was like, 'What do you need to change, particularly?' There was no reason to swim against the tide. They were all fucking ridiculously rich. Stella's dad owned a plane. We stopped off at her mum and dad's farmhouse

---

* Penny says her father did teach at Oxford but never as a professor. "It's a high distinction that my father never gained. He was a member of a very small and not very well-known college, mainly for foreign students. He would not have had any influence at all with Jesus College and he himself had a hard time at Oxford being a working-class lad from the north of England."

in Yorkshire on the way back from a gig at St. Andrews in Scotland. It was fucking enormous and had a double staircase. I remember Miranda in the games room taking the piss by saying, 'Is there a toilet near here?' How they treated me was neither here nor there. It was where I wanted to be. I didn't think any further ahead than getting on *Top of the Pops*. Once I'd done that, I didn't really know what else to do. I kind of lost momentum. When they treated me badly or it was apparent that it wasn't going to improve, I was gone."

Nicky complained that they rarely had time off. She urged the band to take a break, regroup, reevaluate and write new material. "There was a point toward the end where motivation changed. I felt I was losing the original intention of why I had formed the band. There was a lot of pressure on us to 'perform,' keep up a certain image, and churn out hits. We had gigged solidly for the best part of a year. It was tiring." But at twenty-one, Nicky struggled to explain her ideas eloquently. It was "more of a whine at people," she admits with refreshing candor. In the face of a wave of public recognition and an opportunity to capitalize on a more overt, pop-orientated path, Nicky argued for saying something different. "Not 'Have I got the right T-shirt?' or 'Do I look good in a photo shoot?' but creating a great piece of music. It was clear that the band was going in two different musical directions," she says in resignation.

If musical compatibility is the perennial pop minefield, for the Bodysnatchers add irreconcilable differences. "Maybe Nicky wanted something more purist," ponders Miranda. It is a view shared by Stella: "The five of us wanted to evolve and not just play reggae. 2 Tone was coming to a natural conclusion. It couldn't sustain itself. We wanted to expand our musical repertoire." Rhoda dismisses such ambition. "They wanted to be pop tarts," she states.

After the disturbing backstage altercation in Edinburgh, the Bodysnatchers lurched into further arguments and undignified division. As they traveled through Scotland toward a final appearance in London, Penny's diary reveals an unedifying demise:

*Saturday 11 October: Strathclyde: We tell Nicky we will not work
with Rhoda anymore. She says she wants to stay with R. Is this
the end of the band?*

*Sunday 12: St. Andrews University: No more discussed, we just
are definite about R leaving. Judy dithers and tries to be nice to
everyone.*

*Thursday 16: Goldsmith's College [London]. Nicky tells us that
band is splitting up after 31st.*

*Saturday 18: Leicester Poly: Nicky threatens to punch me between
the eyes because she won't play "Monkey Spanner" although everyone else wants to.*

"All the 2 Tone bands used to scrap and squabble," says Rhoda
with an air of sanguinity. "Just because you're in a band didn't mean
you got on with them personally. You were thrown together in this
cramped goldfish-bowl space. You let off all your steam onstage, came
off and you have all this energy. Inevitably people are going to argue,
they have a drink, and sometimes it's all going to go horribly wrong."
Appearing to stoke the flames of division was Rhoda's brother, Clive.
"He was always there," sighs Judy. "It was like, 'What's he doing
hanging around?'" Penny remembers Clive—who had a tattoo of the
Bodysnatchers on his upper arm—expressing his opinion at band
meetings and having no qualms telling all and sundry that his sister
couldn't sing. Rhoda denies it. "I wouldn't put up with that. I would
have told him to fuck off!" she says. Then, after a pause, she adds
softly, "Clive wasn't on my side. I didn't have a say because my mum
would have a go at me if he couldn't do what he wanted."

On Halloween night, October 31, the Bodysnatchers performed
for the last time. It had been eleven months since their debut at the
Windsor Castle in November 1979. Penny says that two hundred–
plus gigs later, "We were all mentally exhausted. It felt more like three

years than eleven months. It had been super intense." When the band played a set consisting almost entirely of original songs, *Record Mirror* described the farewell appearance at the Music Machine as celebratory. "It's quite obvious that most of the band are in the party mood. The Bodysnatchers certainly went out in a blaze of glory, buried under a sea of confetti, streamers, rubber string from a spray can, and Doc Martens, as the skinheads invaded the stage."[129]

"And that was the band over," says Judy. Answering her own question—why did it end?—Miranda cuts to the quick: "Nicky left and Rhoda got wooed away to do stuff with the Specials. We then morphed into the Belle Stars, so it didn't feel like it was an end. We just adapted to the people leaving." Ever ready to offer the final word, Rhoda sums up the experience with blunt analysis: "I'd played with the Specials. Then you come back to the Bodysnatchers and you think, *They're so shit*. It was a relief."

CHAPTER 28

BLANKET COVERAGE

DO NOTHING. COURT SENTENCE. IRISH TOUR

W ithin a year of the Conservatives's election victory in May 1979, unemployment had doubled, reaching two million for the first time in forty years. Most of those out of work were between nineteen and twenty-four. Joining the ranks of the "great unwashed" were the Bodysnatchers, members of the Selecter, and the Swinging Cats, who had fallen apart with ungracious and inexorable firmness after the *More Specials* support tour. 2 Tone had lost the Midas touch. Like the king of Phrygia, whose finger turned all things to gold, and to whom Apollo gave ass's ears as a punishment for not appreciating his music, Jerry Dammers conceded in September 1980 that 2 Tone no longer helped bands' careers. "But," he hastened to add to anybody who might consider his loss from a business perspective, "2 Tone was never commercially orientated in the first place; it was always just friends of the band. I'm not a capitalist. I don't want to make money from other people's music."

There had been talk of the Swinging Cats recording a second single, "Greek Tragedy," and revered reggae producer Dennis Bovell producing an album. Sadly, both ideas fell by the wayside. Lynval Golding was not surprised. "Take the Specials," he volunteered in an interview for *Smash Hits*. "We went from pleading with bands for a support slot [to the] whole road. We didn't form the band one month and suddenly we were a hit. With the Bodysnatchers and the Swinging Cats, they didn't have to go through it really. To me, I think the Swinging Cats were just lazy anyway."[130] Pondering the rapid decline of the Selecter, the Bodysnatchers and the Swinging Cats, Jerry says that each of the bands "came together because of the Specials," but none had "a clear vision of what it was they were supposed to be doing, and that would almost inevitably have led to arguments."

Though shorn of all three bands, the upside was a welcome ease on 2 Tone's finances. Rick Rogers had estimated that the Specials would make £60,000 on the *More Specials* tour, but costs of £80,000 left the band in debt. Still, this was a label run by musicians not businessmen. And so, in October, 2 Tone gave a platform to Jamaican trombone player Rico Rodriguez, who released an instrumental take on the R&B Frankie Ford classic "Sea Cruise," backed with "Carolina," a song first recorded by the Folkes Brothers in 1960. In its original version, producer Prince Buster invited Rastafarian bandleader Count Ossie and his drummers from the Wareika Hills to play on the recording. The result was one of the first proto "ska" records to incorporate religious beliefs and political philosophy, and it gave voice to the poor of downtown Kingston.

In 1958, Rico lived at Renock Lodge in the Wareika Hills among a Rastafarian musical community presided over by Count Ossie. "They're more developed, mentally and musically, than the average musician," Rico explained to Richard Williams. "When you play with them you can really explore. Most of what I know I learned from playing with them." Yet, despite the Specials performing "Sea Cruise" with Rico on their British tour and recording the track for a John Peel session—alongside "Stereotype" and "Raquel"—the single failed to make an impression on the British charts.

On October 30, the Specials returned to London's Hope & Anchor to open a fortnight of charity gigs to raise money for the homeless in Islington. Under the banner "Blanket Coverage," the festival featured headline sets by the Skids, the Only Ones, the Damned, Madness, Bad Manners, the Rezillos, the Rumour, and Ian Dury & the Blockheads. "It was a great gig," remarked Lynval Golding. "Everyone was so enthusiastic. We'd not performed better." Taking to the stage, the Specials introduced themselves with an impromptu round of *It's all a load of bollocks*, variously spoken, slurred or shouted in overlapping ad hoc timings by anyone in close proximity to a microphone. The comic revelry crescendoed with a keyboard riff and an energetic rendition of "Pearl's Café." Adding vocals to the musical melee, special guest Rhoda Dakar then collapsed in hysterics as Jerry pounded at the keyboards with his fists, emitting atonal chords, discordant notes and swirling avant-garde figures over "I Can't Stand It." Twenty-eight minutes of amateur film footage, shared on YouTube in 2021, reveals an impenetrable Terry Hall performing deadpan behind a pair of large dark sunglasses and wearing a green paisley shirt, insouciantly chewing gum throughout until he traps his foot in a beer crate at the lip of the stage.

Six weeks later, the Specials released a new single, "Do Nothing." In order to invoke reggae records of the late sixties and early seventies, such as Bob & Marcia's "Young, Gifted and Black" and "Love of the Common People" by Nicky Thomas, which were sweetened with orchestration to appeal to a broader British audience, Jerry Dammers softened the sound of the Specials's sixth consecutive top ten single with an Italian-made Elka Rhapsody string synthesizer, ambiguously billed as the "Ice Rink String Sounds" and described by Horace Panter as Paul Heskett's "dodgy string synth."

Although credited as a Lynval Golding composition, the songwriting origin of "Do Nothing" suggests otherwise. Before moving to Coventry in the midseventies, Charles "Aitch" Bembridge lived in a flat on Cromwell Street, Gloucester.* Friends from school, Aitch and Lynval played in a band, Keith & the JBs. One day, singer Herman Squires visited Aitch after having just split up with his girlfriend. "He came round," explains Aitch, "and said, 'Man, I'm feeling so down. I just feel like I'm living in a life without meaning.'" Ignoring his heartache, Aitch seized on the unintended lyricism of the singer's speech. "Wow!" he exclaimed, "let's do something with that!" After hastily

---

* The house was a few doors from 25 Cromwell Street where, between 1967 and 1987, Fred and Rosemary West committed twelve murders.

fashioning a song structure on a keyboard, the idea was recorded on cassette. Then, using a second tape machine, they began multilayering additional instrumentation to complete the song.

In September 1978, a demo of the track, titled "Living in a Life Without Meaning," was recorded at Woodbine Studios in Leamington. "I sang harmony on the track," recalls Gaps Hendrickson. "We recorded it with a guy called Don Mayers, who was in a male vocal trio called True Expression and came second on *New Faces* in 1976." The song was then stored and, in time, left forgotten.

Then, in 1980, as the Selecter toured the UK, much to Aitch's surprise, "Do Nothing" came on the radio. "Lyrically it had changed but the chorus and melody was the same. When I spoke to Lynval, he said, 'Oh, I don't know anything about that, Aitch.'" If the chorus of "Do Nothing" had been appropriated from an existing song, Horace Panter believes, "at least two of the verses" were written by Jerry.* "*Fashion is my only culture* and *policeman come and smack me in the teeth; I can't complain it's not my function* are very much Jerry lines," Horace says, further asserting that Jerry also added an extra chord.[131]

"A truly excellent single," gushed Ronnie Gurr in *Smash Hits*. "Flip over and find a horrendous cocktail lounge calypso cover of Dylan's 'Maggie's Farm.' Excusable only if it's a political statement." The reinvention of "Maggie's Farm" (originally recorded by Bob Dylan in 1965[†]) served as blistering attack on Margaret Thatcher and the incumbent government. This new version featured a radical percussive arrangement drawn from Brad's bias for the Burundi drum rhythm heard on recent Bow Wow Wow and Adam & the Ants records. Horace, nonetheless, says he detested the Specials's version. "I felt we didn't have a great deal of say in the matter. Jerry said, 'We're going to do this.' 'Oh, alright then.' I was very unhappy with it." Adding to the grievance was a contentious picture sleeve. With the group

---

* The first pressing of "Do Nothing" is credited to Golding/Dammers.

† Shortly after Dylan's version, soul singer Solomon Burke recorded "Maggie's Farm." In July 1980, Paul Jones—formerly of Manfred Mann—had a minor hit with "Maggie's Farm" as part of the *Blues Band* EP.

sporting a new image, Horace was styled as a Miami Beach–type American tourist surrounded by a group wearing tartan, open-neck shirts and moccasins. Roddy was not impressed: "I was like, 'Fuck off, I ain't wearing a pink straw hat, check trousers and white loafers,'" instead opting to don a black Teddy Boy jacket, cowboy shirt and creepers. More surprisingly, Brad leaned into the group shot flouting a white shirt and black dickie bow.

Terry Hall (L) and Jerry Dammers, Cambridge City Magistrates' Court, January 9, 1981.

Sartorial humor at a premium, the Specials made a festive return to *Top of the Pops* dressed in Christmas knitted jumpers. However, on closer inspection, all was not as it appeared. A plan hatched in the dressing room resulted in David Steele performing with the Specials and Horace playing bass on "Too Nice to Talk to" with the Beat, having learned one another's respective basslines during rehearsal. "That was just trying to mess with BBC heads," laughs Steele, "because they didn't know who the hell these bands were." Backstage, fresh from putting one over on Auntie and no doubt intoxicated with the festive spirit, the two bands agreed to do a mini-tour of Ireland in the new year.

First, there was the small matter of an impending court case and answering to charges of inciting a riot. On Friday, January 9, 1981—postponed from November—Terry Hall, Jerry Dammers, Rick Rogers and tour manager Pete Hadfield appeared at Cambridge City Magistrates' Court. Recalling the events at the Specials concert on Midsummer Common three months earlier, PC Mark Mills told prosecutor David Beal, "The lead singer and the organist were calling the bouncers a load of wankers and telling them to fuck off. They made the atmosphere very tense. The group were constantly inviting the audience to come onto the stage if they wanted to fight." Next to give evidence, Chief Steward Harry Sparks testified, "They started singing a record in which the lyrics were, 'It's a load of bollocks.' Then they started f-ing and blinding and saying that the tent was a pigsty. It was just one big melee. The lead singer and the organist were singing, 'Cambridge United are a load of wankers.' The lead singer said, 'If you want to come up here and fight me.' Then he picked up a mic stand and tried to hit a steward with it." Third on the stand, Police Sergeant Ronald Pearce added, "They said the bouncers were a load of wankers and if they wanted to cause trouble they should come outside. This sort of language served to aggravate the unruly elements."

Acting on behalf of Terry and Jerry, Tom Culver defended his clients' actions, telling the magistrate, John Hall, "These young men were in an almost impossible situation. They were going onstage when there had already been a lot of trouble. It was football trouble. The group had come to play music, not cause fights." Invited to give his account of events, Terry insisted, "We had to stop singing, and just told them how ridiculous they looked singing football songs in the circus tent when we were playing. When more trouble started at the back of the tent, the only way I could see us stopping the fighting was to call them wankers, which I thought they were, for fighting. I just told them to get out if they wanted to fight. I was more concerned about the people around them. It was only like thirty people fighting out of 3,000. When I said, 'If you want to fight, come up here,' what I meant was for them to come up onto the stage so the whole audience could see what sort of fools they are."

Found guilty of inciting violence and using words likely to cause a breach of the peace, Terry and Jerry received fines of £400 and were ordered to pay £265 court costs. After the six-hour hearing, Jerry commented outside the court, "It was horrible. I know I'm biased, but to me the evidence against us just didn't stand up. The 3,000 people at the concert will see the injustice of this decision. We detest violence at our concerts." Then, attempting to lighten the mood, he quipped, "This ain't a town. It's a trained-dog act! That's a quote from an old film by the way."

Foreseeing the consequences of the court decision, Rick Rogers was incensed. "It looks to me as if they're setting a precedent which makes bands accountable for the behavior of their audiences." The following morning, the *Daily Mirror* led with the headline: "Swearing Specials Fined for Concert Uproar." Reporting Terry's and Jerry's denials, the 140-word article accused the group of "substituting four-letter words for the original lyrics of a song" and suggesting that Jerry, "swigging from a whiskey bottle, started abusing the fans who replied by throwing beer cans."

Mulling over the event, Terry issued a shocking ultimatum. "It was stupid . . . everyone was out for a good time, but you'll always get your odd moron wherever you go. The people who went home are the ones I felt sorry for. They paid their money; they were entitled to a good night out. As a group, we're now thinking whether to carry on or not to carry on doing tours. We don't like violence at our concerts; we've made that clear from the outset. We offer music as an alternative to fighting. If the fighting doesn't stop, there's only one way to make it stop. We either stop gigging or call it a day."

Determined to reignite a sense of communion, the Beat and the Specials set off for their mini-tour of Ireland. Four dates in four days. Both bands traveling together on one coach. "At first, we sat at the back and the Specials were in the middle and up front," says Ranking Roger, "but we soon mingled: the Specials were going, 'The Beat are our heroes', and we were going, 'You're *our* heroes!'" Arriving in Belfast, Dave Wakeling says, "We were terrified." They were booked to stay at the infamous Europa Hotel—the most bombed hotel in Europe—where guests looked out over a barbed-wire perimeter fence and armed soldiers patrolling the area in Land Rovers. The opening date at Ulster Hall had been organized as a benefit for Corrymeela, an interdenominational group offering holidays for deprived children on the west coast of Ireland.*

Inside the venue, the atmosphere was electric. "We hadn't realized how much the fans wanted to see us," says Roger. "They were starved of music. We were the biggest thing since Jimi Hendrix as far as they were concerned. Before we went onstage, I walked through the audience to get a feel for the mood, and one skinhead said, 'All the Catholics have to sit upstairs.' I didn't like it. It would have been the equivalent of separating Black and white people. During our set there was a lot of shouting, and I could see Catholic kids flicking cigarette butts over the top of the balcony onto the Protestants below."

"It worked well," counters Dave Wakeling, "there were no fights. But afterward we were told stories about how nobody in the balcony had used the bathroom; they just pissed over the top." It was presented as a double bill, and the Specials insisted they play first. "It was the scariest thing we ever did," says David Steele. "I thought

---

* The event raised over £2,000.

everybody's gonna walk out after they'd been on. It was like, 'We can't follow them.' There's hardly a band I've seen as good as the Specials at their peak. It was one of my favorite tours ever." The Beat held their own, and Roger says, "None of us had ever been to Ireland before and it was absolutely fucking brilliant. The audience was probably better than most of the audiences we'd played to in England." To cement the union of the bands, at the end of the Beat's set Rico joined saxophonist Saxa onstage. "You couldn't stop them," continues Roger. "I remember thinking, *It's caught fire here!* It was like a great jam!"

Back at the hotel, fellow guest and comedian Frank Carson entertained the touring entourage with an endless roll of jokes and tall tales. "I had to leave about three o'clock in the morning because my stomach hurt so much from laughing," recalls John Mostyn. "You couldn't have a better introduction to Belfast. It was brilliant."

The following day, January 15, the party traveled south to the Stardust Ballroom, Dublin. "By seven o'clock there were a couple of thousand people crammed into the venue," says Mostyn, adding with a note of caution that "half of them were totally pissed. I thought, *Oh shit.*" Alternating the headline slot, the Beat opened the show. "We went down a storm," boasts Roger. "Toward the end of the set some kids started doing Nazi salutes but there wasn't any real trouble." Bursting onto the stage, the Specials managed half of "Concrete Jungle" before "the blockheads at the front started to beat seven bales of shit out of one another," reported Simon Ludgate.[132] Forced to stop halfway through "Gangsters," for the first of many interruptions, Terry Hall appealed to reason. "We hate violence!" he screamed, to little effect. As tension mounted, a section of the audience started berating Jerry, accusing him of allowing fans in England onto the stage but not in Ireland. "There were no risers for the drum kit so it was too dangerous," says Jerry. Matters escalated when bouncers waded into the audience wielding truncheons and rubber hoses filled with lead shot.

As security oscillated between incitement and containment of two rival gangs, the Coolock Boot Boys and the Edenmore Dragons from

Raheny, a stack of speakers on the left side of the PA system collapsed during "Sock It to 'Em J.B.," narrowly missing a cluster of young fans. "I knew it was going to happen," says Roger, deflated. "There were too many people, pushing and shoving forward." To shrieks of "I told you so!" from Neville, chaos ensued. Fights broke out and a gang of skin-heads clambered onto the stage, smashing up equipment and sending sections of the drum kit flying everywhere. "One skinhead punched a roadie," says Roddy. "I was trying to stop the fight and I got punched in the face. I was like, 'Okay, carry on fighting.'"

Desperate to escape the intensifying scene, Ranking Roger and a roadie fled backstage and attempted to break open the fire exit only to discover a pile of randomly stacked chairs blocking a set of padlocked doors. "I was kicking at full brute but we couldn't unlock them," says Roger, reliving the panic of the moment. "Skinheads got back and there were fights in the dressing room. We ended up barricading our-selves with sofas in a room."

Behind the locked door, John Mostyn called the police as fans tried to escape the escalating violence and hand-to-hand fighting. "When the fire brigade arrived, we somehow formed a kind of rugby scrum with Neville and a couple of handy roadies. We were all shell-shocked." Convinced that the venue was not safe to host a gig, Jerry now says, "It was an absolute shithole. It had a crappy little stage which was completely unsuitable: it came up out of the floor on pneu-matics and it was obviously dangerous, let alone allowing a stomping audience onstage."

When the bands emerged from their backstage hideout, they confronted a gruesome scene: blood up the walls and broken glass everywhere. A month later, the Stardust Ballroom burned down.* "That could have been us," muses Roger. "There were three times as many people in there when we played—we would have all died. It was a lucky escape. People tried to get out through the fire exits but

---

* Despite rumors of an electrical fault and a tribunal verdict of "probable arson," an independent examination in 2009 concluded that there was no evidence the fire was started deliberately.

couldn't break through the padlocked doors. My heart goes out to the forty-eight people who died that night."

In a somber mood, the entourage crossed to the west of Ireland where the arrival of English pop stars was big news. They performed at Leisureland, Galway, and then UCC in Cork, and Roger remembers "the whole city" being there. "Fans were thanking us and saying, 'Nobody ever comes to play for us.'" Yet, despite Rick Rogers feeling that "if there was a serious contender to the Specials's crown it was the Beat," such generosity was in short supply when the two bands attempted to leave the country. As they passed through the airport departure lounge, officials confronted the Specials's manager and without charge frog-marched him to customs. Requested to open his briefcase, Rogers revealed £10,000. "You can't leave with that," he was informed, unaware of Irish currency laws. "Well, I'm not leaving it here," objected Rogers. Then, turning to the onlooking musicians, he pleaded, "Lads, help me!" He was greeted with laughter-tears, cheeks flushed crimson with mirth and parting shouts of, "See you, Rick!"

CHAPTER 29

A LOOK AT LIFE

DANCE CRAZE

I n December 1979, American filmmaker Joe Massot was staying at the Tropicana Motel on Santa Monica Boulevard, Los Angeles, a popular haven for English touring bands, when his attention was drawn to a group of seven men "messing around" by the pool. Discovering it was a band called Madness and that they were due to play the first of four nights at the Whisky a Go Go (with the Go-Go's) that evening, an intrigued Massot went along. "They were amazing," he said. "Their music was so different from anything I had been hearing at that time." At the gig, Massot heard the word "ska" for the first time and discovered that something interesting was happening in the music scene in the UK.

Traveling to England shortly thereafter, Massot contacted their management with a proposal to make a film about the group. Greeted with enthusiasm, Massot then told his fourteen-year-old son Jason about the plan. The boy's reaction came as a surprise. "You can't just film Madness!" the 2 Tone–obsessed teenager scolded his father. "What about the other bands?" Home from Winchester Boys School for the Christmas holidays, Jason wrote out a list of all the groups on 2 Tone. Explaining the importance of Jerry Dammers and rude boy fashion, from porkpie hats to "two-tone suits," "Jason wrote all the songs down," says the older Massot, "and I filmed every one of them."

Describing his estranged father, Jason says, "He was always quite hard to pin down. He was here today, gone tomorrow. You never quite knew what he was doing. He was very sixties in that way: a hustler, never did anything by the book—'That's just boring bullshit. Why do you have to keep receipts?' He was always trying to make films quick and fast: 'Let's get going!' He was totally chaotic, sleeping on people's floors and living a bohemian life. If you want to get a sense of my dad, when Oasis released 'Wonderwall' [1996], I went round to his flat in Chelsea and played it to him. He immediately called Creation Records and said, 'My name is Joe Massot. I directed *Wonderwall.** I want some tickets to Oasis.' The next night we were in Southampton backstage meeting Liam and Noel [Gallagher] and he was pitching a film to them. It happened within thirty-six hours of him hearing the song!"

As a younger man, Massot claimed he was associated with the CIA. But his then wife, Felicity Fairhurst, insists he did not work for them.† "He was much too mad for that . . . you have to take Joe with a pinch of salt. He was a great hustler, had great ideas, putting things together, but he couldn't really contain them properly." Raising an eyebrow, Jason says, "Maybe . . . he spent a lot of time in Cuba. He used to tell me stories about people in the pay of the CIA bringing up drugs from Colombia or Mexico, fomenting an anti-Marxist movement in Latin America. I'm sure he was involved on some level."

Nefarious tales aside, Massot focused his attention on making a film about 2 Tone. At Dingwalls, he saw the Bodysnatchers, where he says fans were "packed wall-to-wall, dancing almost on top of each other." At a photo session in Covent Garden, he met the Beat and allowed Saxa to regale him with stories about Jamaica and Prince Buster. In Leicester, he witnessed the "amazing energy" of the Selecter— "Pauline never stopped," he noted, "she was like a tiger." In Bradford, "the pounding of dancing feet" during a Madness concert made "the

---

* In 1968, Massot directed the film *Wonderwall* with a soundtrack by George Harrison.

† Fairhurst was Massot's third wife. "We had separated for a short period. Joe went to the States and when he came back, he wanted to put together this 2 Tone film. I got drawn into it and went to a lot of the gigs with him."

whole building vibrate" and the stage shake "as if it was being blown by a strong wind." And at the Electric Ballroom, "the heat of the audience dancing" and "creating mist" intoxicated him during a Bad Manners show.

(L–R) Mike Barson, Daniel Woodgate and Suggs discussing the *Dance Craze* shoot with Joe Massot, April 1980.

Massot recalls venturing to Coventry and Jerry Dammers waking at nine in the morning "wearing a dressing gown that he must have worn at school." Seeing the "so-called" 2 Tone office, which "consisted of records strewn all over the floor," Massot says, he and the cameraman were offered a cup of tea only for Jerry to discover "he didn't have any after all." Painting a picture of Massot, a "big guy" with "curly hair" and "quite nervous," Horace Panter recalls the 2 Tone bands crammed into Jerry's front room to hear the film director's pitch. "He told us about this groundbreaking technique using the latest cameras so the cameraman could be onstage with the bands and there'd be no wobble in the film."[133]

The central concept of the proposed film was to reproduce the atmosphere of a 2 Tone concert for kids too young to attend live shows. Further drawn to the simple idea of "all the bands together for the price of a movie ticket," Massot enlisted the help of an old friend. Born in Camden, Joe Dunton's background included sound credits for the first *Glastonbury Fayre* and *The Who Live at Kilburn*. Establishing his own film company, Dunton was an early advocate of the Steadicam. In 1976, American inventor Garrett Brown used the Steadicam during the filming of *Bound for Glory*, enabling him to operate a camera on foot by means of a gyroscopic harness with a counterbalance. "It's like having a tripod attached to your body so that the camera stays steady," says producer Gavrik Losey, who describes Dunton as a very creative, original character. "To use it for a music film and to shoot on Super 16 [later enlarged to 70mm] was an innovation."

(L–R) Rhoda Dakar, Miranda Joyce, Ranking Roger and Joe Dunton, 1980.

And so, on February 28, 1980, armed with cameras and celluloid stock, Joe Dunton and his team traveled to the south coast in a minibus to shoot the Selecter at Portsmouth Guildhall.* Filming onstage, Dunton either moved in time with the musicians or held the moment until somebody came into the picture. Caught up by the energy onstage, Dunton collided with Pauline Black. "She gave me a

---

* The Selecter were filmed performing "On My Radio," "Too Much Pressure," "Missing Words" and "Three Minute Hero," and on March 22 "James Bond" at the Pavilion, Hemel Hempstead.

dirty look, so I backed off and hid behind Charley." Immediately after the performance, the film stock was raced to a local laboratory to be processed. The following day, Dunton invited the Selecter to watch the rushes at a cinema in Southampton. Although it was screened without sound, Felicity Fairhurst says, "They were selling the fact that Steadicam was a unique way of filming and for the band to see the visuals on a big screen." Much to their surprise, members of the Selecter started singing along to the images. "Once that happened," says Dunton, "the word went round the other bands."

In March, the Bodysnatchers were filmed at Hemel Hempstead on the second 2 Tone Tour, and then again five days later supporting Bad Manners at the Electric Ballroom. While Bad Manners was not officially a 2 Tone band, Jerry Dammers had offered them a one-single deal. Lead singer Doug Trendle, known to all as Buster Bloodvessel, remembers "this toothless man" coming to see the band at Dingwalls and saying, "'You've got to do more ska in your set.' We thought, *Who's he talking to, us?*"[134] Having formed in a bedroom in 1976 by Trendle, bass player Dave Farren and guitarist Louis Alphonso (née Cook), six of the nine original members of Bad Manners went to the same school in Stoke Newington, forming a collective of Black, white and Jewish members. "We didn't have a demo tape or anything," says Trendle, "so we got one together, and by the time 2 Tone came back to us there were other companies after us. And because we thought 2 Tone was more of a stepping stone for groups who couldn't get a good contract . . . we let it pass."[135]

Signing a five-album deal with Magnet, Bad Manners enjoyed instant success with a run of hit singles, including a cover version of Dicky Doo & the Don'ts instrumental track, "Nee Nee Na Na Na Na Nu Nu," "Lip Up Fatty" and "Special Brew," and then a trio of commercially successful albums all produced by Roger Lomas.* Reviewing their debut album *Ska'n'B* for *Smash Hits*, Mark Ellen made it crystal clear that Bad Manners "are about having fun, dressing up,

---

* Bad Manners spent more weeks on the UK charts in 1980 (forty-five) than anyone bar Madness.

snappy dancing, getting pissed, making an unholy din and very little else besides. It can't be denied that for the newer ska-based bands ploughing through the exhaust fumes of the ever accelerating 2 Tone tank, sympathy is starting to wear thin. Bad Manners, to their credit, don't attempt to wave the checkered flag but offload any political sentiment and simply assume the basic position, a ska backbeat, to make this logical diversion: *Ska'n'B*. Sure, there's a lot of porkpie hats and shades in evidence, but otherwise 2 Tone references are indirect and unobtrusive. Bad Manners set their sights down low and win outright."

Bad Manners onstage, 1980.

Invited to partake in the film as "honorary members of 2 Tone," Bad Manners were recorded at London's Electric Ballroom, and then at Aylesbury Friars. Renting lights and special effects for the occasion, Joe Dunton says, "I knew there was going to be an explosion, but I didn't know where it was going to go off. I was petrified that I was going to step on it." Avoiding smoke bombs was one thing, but of greater concern was the unsavoury trouble that followed Bad Manners. Felicity Fairhurst recalls the gigs as "violent," with Union Jacks held aloft embroidered with the word "SKINS" and being surrounded by acts of "drunken aggression" more familiar to football terraces. Watching Bad Manners support Madness, Jason Massot's abiding memory is of a large National Front presence: "I was up on the balcony looking down and it was terrifying. There was an air of intimidation."

Filmed in April at St. George's Hall, Bradford, and the Mayfair, Sunderland, Madness clashed with director Joe Massot. "He was a lovely man," says Joe Dunton, "but when you come from Camden Town to have an American to deal with was very difficult. He rubbed them up the wrong way and Suggs refused to work with him. So I was the communicator. I had a way of talking to the bands. They trusted me." Short on diplomacy and the required social skills to carry the film forward, Massot's overbearance threatened to derail the project. Before long, he had fallen out with Jerry and was arguing with Dunton. "Stupid. Ego stuff," says Fairhurst.

The situation was poorly organized, chaotic and in danger of falling apart; Chrysalis turned to seasoned film producer Gavrik Losey, son of acclaimed director Joseph Losey, to rescue the film. With a career pedigree involving the Beatles, David Essex and Slade, Losey had most recently produced the film *Babylon*, depicting young Black British kids organizing a sound clash in Brixton. "Terry Connolly at Chrysalis called me in and said, 'Massot is crazy. He's as nutty as bat shit. He's running all over with these mad ideas. Money's streaming out the door.' Desperate to have sanity restored, Losey's first task was to sack Massot. 'He was an incredibly arrogant individual: he was fired because he kept insisting, 'I'm the man, you can't do anything to me,' all that sort of thing. Chrysalis said, 'This is not a black hole into which we will throw money so you can make a movie. We want to know what it's going to cost, and why it's going to cost it.' It was running out of control."

Furthermore, the Specials were not yet on board. Fairhurst points to the standoff between Massot and Dammers. "Jerry was very troublesome during the filming," she says. "He'd set up 2 Tone and didn't want anyone else having any say in anything. He wanted to know where he stood and what the deal was. To be fair to him, he was right. Joe [Massot] was trying to jump in and film everyone before they realized what was going on." When a meeting was organized at Chrysalis, Massot arrived with a lawyer. "He could see the writing on the wall," says Losey. "Connolly said, 'I cannot take a meeting where you're represented by a lawyer and I am not. We will have to reset this meeting or you'll have to ask the lawyer to leave.' That was the end of the meeting. And the last time I saw Joe Massot."*

Opting to "manage without appearing to manage," Losey explains that his favored tactic was to use other people to do his bidding. "In other words," he says, "Dunton had a good relationship with the musicians, so he was my man for the bands. Other people were good at transport, etc. You made it function. The shoots were no more difficult than working with any other set of artists. They would want to do this and not that. It's a constant battle of diplomacy to keep egos from clashing. Your main function is to keep the thing from blowing up in your face." To Losey's dismay, Dunton then revealed he did not have the finances to complete the picture. As a result, "Chrysalis got in deeper than they thought they should," says Losey.

Another band disheartened by Joe Massot's brusque style was the Beat. Dredging his memory, John Mostyn says, "There was something, a kerfuffle." But with Massot now out of the picture, Losey arranged to film the Beat in New Jersey. "He got the tickets and everything," says Mostyn. "We all flew out on Freddie Laker airways." Offering his services, the originator of the Steadicam, Garrett Brown,

* Jason Massot says this was not the first time his father had been sacked: "He was fired off *The Song Remains the Same*. Led Zeppelin say it was because he didn't shoot enough close-ups of their live gigs, and my dad said Peter Grant accused him of making Robert Plant look gay. It got out of hand. They hadn't paid him, so he was like, 'Right, I'll hide the film and then they have to pay me.' They sent people to break into his house to get it."

joined the crew and helped to capture the group at their live prime. Illuminated by neon lighting, the Beat's performance was a bundle of energy, heightened by David Steele's idiosyncratic "shuffle"—surely the only man in rock 'n' roll history capable of dancing out of time while playing the bass in time—and Ranking Roger skanking and ceaselessly running across the width of the stage to the delight of a packed auditorium. "It was a great gig," enthuses Roger. "We finished off by playing 'Click Click' and 'Jackpot' as an encore, but the audience kept on clapping and shouting for more. We'd already played for an hour, so we went back on and played 'Big Shot' and 'Twist and Crawl' again." Dave Wakeling says that seeing the audience bounce "was wonderful. It was the feeling of mass consciousness in action; one of the best feelings you'd ever had. You get this emotional connection between the audience, the band, and the song."

To complete the film, cameras rolled when the Specials played in September at De Montfort Hall, Leicester,* and three weeks later at Rotters, Liverpool. The footage was sensational. Toward the end of the set, Jerry was forced to climb on top of his organ and direct proceedings from up high as fans engulfed the stage. "You didn't know what was going to happen," grins Dunton. "All these people kept coming up. One of the audience got turned upside down. There's a boot in the bottom of the picture with a kid's head downward where he can't get up."

Calculating the thousands of minutes shot by four cameras over one or two hours at over ten gigs, Gavrik Losey determines, "You're suddenly looking at six or seven thousand hours of film. With digital all that doesn't matter because there's no stock, but this was film." Edited by Tony Sloman, the first reel opens with archive footage of London's West End taken from the documentary series *Look at Life*. Neon lights flicker with the words "Dancing" and "Majestic Ballroom" as an accompanying narration informs us: "All over Britain, signs like

---

* Filmed supporting the Specials, the Bodysnatchers performed with their newest member, drummer Judy Parsons.

this flash their nightly invitation and in response more than half a million people go dancing every week all the year round." Abruptly, the action cuts and we hear the Specials performing "Nite Klub." As Terry Hall encourages the audience to "dance" and "stamp your feet," the voice-over continues: "Today they turned off the wireless and turned on the musical heat in the nation's dance halls. Beneath the neon lights, youth resolved its differences. It's an offbeat, toe-tapping sound, a rhythm for their feet that takes high-spirited youngsters off the street and into a music that speaks to them. It's been called ska; it's even been called bluebeat and rocksteady. But when these bands start swinging, our young people are in total agreement; the only word for it is . . . fun."

The camera pans across Neville Staple dancing frenetically and freezes on Jerry Dammers staring into the lens. "That was there to cut to full stereo sound for Madness," informs Joe Dunton. "Up to that point it was mono." On cue, Suggs sings, *Buster, he sold the heat,* as Madness rip into the rocksteady beat of "The Prince." The tone of the film is set. Over eighty-six minutes, the best of British ska plays out in a succession of continuous live performances and unstoppable rhythm and movement. When Jerry came up with the title *Dance Craze,* Joe Dunton says it gave him an idea. Unearthing a selection of postwar Pathé News footage—the latest "dance craze," showgirls, Lady Lewisham opining on enthusiastic teenagers, Syncopating Sandy setting a world record for continuous piano endurance (134 hours), the Shadows performing at the *NME* Awards and images of Le Macabre coffee house, Soho, which Dunton and his wife used to frequent in their youth—the extracts were collated as a spoof news-reel at the midpoint in the film between "Too Much Too Young" and "On My Radio." "I would have found it difficult to sustain eight-six minutes of nonstop music," says Dunton.*

---

* In the film's original showing, Dunton staged a technical fault. The music cut to an old-fashioned Pathé countdown: *10, 9, 8, 7, 6* . . . suggesting the projector had broken down. "Everyone started throwing things at the screen and shouting," says Dunton, "but the Rank Organisation cut the countdown out." Egged on by Bad Manners's playfulness, Dunton further reveals that his

To complement the distraction, Dunton filmed two additional sequences at Lee Studios, Wembley Park. The first featured *Swan Lake* intercut with slow-motion footage of Madness wearing Dr. Martens and loafers doing a "boot ballet" on a staircase. "They'd just made a shoe commercial," says Dunton, "and the steps were left over from the shoot." The second outtake was a staged fight shot in black-and-white to dramatize "Too Much Pressure." "Desmond Brown goes mad," says Dunton. "He'd got real anger in his face. You can see it." Jason Massot remembers the day with mixed emotions. Arriving on set in a newly made tweed jacket fit by his mother, Jason spent the day trailing Pauline Black. "I had a crazy crush on her. I was following her around until my friend Paul said, 'Jason, you need to stop. It's weird.'" Later, he shared a cigarette with Charley Anderson at the back of the studio. "I'd just bought 'Going Underground' by the Jam and I told Charley this really proudly, and he said, 'The Jam are shit.' I felt awful. I was like, 'Fuck the Jam!'"

Having bled dry £30,000 of company money, Dunton sold the footage to Chrysalis to pay for the music rights. "We more or less gave it to them so I could finish the film," says Dunton, who maintains that the record company subsequently shafted him. "I was offered 10 percent by Chrysalis and then got a Telex saying 1 percent. I said, 'You left the nought off.' I wanted to shut the film down because they reneged on the deal." Further still, the final reel credited Joe Massot as "director" and Dunton as "visual concept & photography." It was a compromise, judges Gavrik Losey. "Massot had a reasonable contribution to the ideas and the way it was going to be cut up until the firing."

In a final frame, a caption reads: "DEDICATION. To our keenest fan, Martin Allen, who disappeared from King's Cross Station 5th November 1979 and others like him." "Martin worked for me,"

---

original idea for "Inner London Violence" was to sound a police siren. "Imagine the screen goes black," he explains, "and you see blue light and the sound of a siren from the back speakers in the auditorium. Then you slam the doors, and a voice says, 'Let's get him,' and the audience hears the sound of footsteps running to the front of the cinema."

says Dunton. "He used to come in Saturday mornings and clean my vans with his brother, Kevin. He was never found. He was fourteen. I walked round King's Cross looking for him. All my vans had pictures of him to say we'd lost him. The memory of Martin drove me on to make the film."

On January 26 and 27, 1981, an entourage, including members of Madness, the Specials and Chrysalis Records attended a premiere of *Dance Craze* at the Cannes Film Festival. "It was the first time I'd been," says Chris Poole. "It rained the whole time." Less salubrious but perhaps more fitting was a London premiere at the Sundown Disco on Tottenham Court Road. Seven hundred guests from residential homes, schools and youth clubs responded to an invitation advertised in the *Daily Mirror* for a Saturday afternoon under-eighteen screening. Welcomed by Richard Skinner, the BBC Radio 1 DJ played a selection of 2 Tone records and ran various competitions—such as who can jump the highest—to win records, badges and posters. While many happily danced and eyed the prizes, a contingent of less disciplined kids simply ripped posters off the walls.

Outside, Madness arrived in a Bentley, dressed in black tuxedos. Lee Thompson remembers driving through the streets throwing eggs out of the window and shouting, "Down with capitalism!" While Chris Foreman says, "We got Alan Winstanley, our engineer, to dress as a chauffeur and then we threw eggs at his car." Joining the nutty boys and Suggs's mother on the red carpet, an array of 2 Tone stars frolicked into the theater to party in the upper balcony—among them, six of the Bodysnatchers, five of the Selecter, three of the Specials, and Ranking Roger representing the Beat. "It was fun—lots of drinking," recalls Gavrik Losey. "All the seats had been taken out and everybody danced while the press stood in the background being cynical and getting pissed."

Typifying the media reaction, Chris Salewicz asked how "a charismatic vital scene had been transformed on celluloid into a listless, one-dimensional affair."[136] Disappointed that *Dance Craze* was not a history of the movement, Suggs complained, "The kids who are into 2 Tone but haven't seen the bands might enjoy it. Otherwise, it's no great benefit to mankind—it would be alright as a B movie, I suppose." Suggesting that the film would have profited from more variety and an exploration of the history of each group, Suggs revealed that Jerry had walked out of the premiere and wanted nothing further to do with it. "Dammers phoned us up and said how much he hated it, which is a bit odd considering he'd been up to the editing every day. I just think it's down to Chrysalis following their last chance to make a bundle before 2 Tone becomes totally forgotten about."[137]

Dance Craze album sleeve, February 1981. Courtesy of Chrysalis Records.

Likewise drawing attention to the film's supposed shortcomings, Pauline Black commented, "There were no interviews, no insights into what the people were like. The image was of all these people in 2 Tone bands, Black and white, living and working together in total harmony. But of course, it wasn't always like that. We were angry young people." Neville labeled the film "disappointing" while the *2 Tone Club Newsletter* dismissed it as a "bad film." "It represented the exact moment of ska overkill and exhaustion," says Jerry. "It was actually a bit boring." Agreeing with the analysis, Juliet de Vie suggests, "*Dance Craze* felt a bit fag end. As soon as you've got Bad Manners, it was game over. The other bands earned it, and meant it. It was the end. *Dance Craze* should have been a celebration, but by 1981 most people weren't speaking to each other."

Playing to its original ambition—for children too young to see 2 Tone bands live—the release of *Dance Craze* coincided with the half-term school holidays. An original soundtrack, with a front cover announcing, "THE BEST OF BRITISH SKA . . . LIVE!" enjoyed a six-week run in the UK top ten album chart and swiftly achieved gold status with supported film screenings in more than thirty cities across the country.* "The film was completely underrated," insists Joe Dunton. "When I was there I experienced something really special: of seeing Black and white musicians playing together; and the kids loved it. I realized then I had to make the film for the future. 2 Tone brought Black and white together. You'd never seen a concert movie like that before. It was as if you were at the concert. Everybody shows the audience and what I call the 'third row' shot. I didn't want that. You were in amongst it! You were there! To appreciate the full experience of the film you have to play it loud; I wrote that as an instruction on the film canister boxes."

Dance Craze enjoyed a brief video release in the late eighties but soon succumbed to obscurity. It was a great shame. The film is an incredible document of 2 Tone. The sensational onstage footage captures

---

* It was mixed and produced by Clive Langer and Alan Winstanley. The latter says, "We did a bit of patching up and got people in to rerecord bits where they made mistakes." According to Neol Davies, audio of the Selecter—and Bad Manners—was "not good enough" and was substituted with a recording from the Hope & Anchor in November 1980. "I refused to accept the gold disc because I was ashamed of the whole project. It was false. It wasn't the real live recordings. It was a masquerade." Responsible for the sound of the Selecter, Bad Manners and the Bodysnatchers, Roger Lomas doctored the audience to make it sound like a recording from a bigger venue. "When there was a vocal that wasn't up to it, I put up the multitrack and get them to sing along with it."

the wild, frenetic energy of the groups in their prime and preserves for posterity an incredible collection of high-octane musical intensity. More recently, the original master of *Dance Craze* was recovered, digitally restored and, in March 2023, given a theatrical release. It offered not only its first mainstream availability in forty years but an expanded box set of previously inaccessible soundtrack outtakes. Today, Jerry describes the film as "the definitive 2 Tone document."

CHAPTER 30
BANDS WON'T PLAY NO MORE
GHOST TOWN

Far had we traveled. The distance between 1979 and 1981 was immense. Gone were the last vestiges of punk and do-it-yourself typescript, and in came the Sinclair ZX81 home computer and the high-speed Advanced Passenger Train. It was the year of the inaugural London Marathon and, for horticulturists, the opportunity to shop at the first garden superstore, Homebase. Bucks Fizz won the Eurovision Song Contest and New Romanticism broke out from the clubs of Birmingham and London. Suddenly the charts were awash with the synthesizer, with Soft Cell, Ultravox and the Human League, fronted by a singer with an asymmetric haircut and two backing vocalists plucked from the dance floor of a Sheffield nightclub. Dandyism and bold makeup were all the rage as 1981 handed itself to Adam & the Ants and Aneka's "Japanese Boy."

The new colorful pop world provided an escape from a country deeply divided by record unemployment. Now at three million. They had a name: "Maggie's millions." One in ten of the British workforce was out of work. In Coventry, the rate was 20 percent. An oppressive climate of social and economic unrest pervaded as the effects of monetarism seemingly favored the "haves" over the "have-nots." "Thatcher was putting more air in ice cream and taking out the fucking cream," thunders Chas Smash. "There was nothing left in there but a load of fluff. They turned the lights off. Surely, the purpose of life is to feel better, to express oneself better, to live better in harmony. If profit isn't giving something to everyone then not everyone can get what they should be getting. It was inherently wrong."

In the Specials's camp, a self-imposed six-month sabbatical had done little to revive the deflated septet. "Working in music totally divorces you from what life's all about," opined John Bradbury in the *New Musical Express*, suggesting that he was considering working on a building site for a few weeks. "You know why: because amongst blokes working on sites you really find out what's going on and you don't get any bullshit and you do get real communication." But then, against all expectation, Jerry Dammers pulled out of the bag one of the greatest endgames in rock 'n' roll history. He named it "Ghost Town."

Its arrival came when relations between the Specials were at an all-time low. "People weren't happy," says Jerry. "But nobody would explain to me what the problem was. If they had grievances, they didn't tell me." Convinced of "plotting and scheming" behind the scenes, Jerry says the bad vibes got "quite nasty." Channeling his frustration from a state of "complete depression," Jerry wrote "Ghost Town." "It was about disillusionment with rock 'n' roll and the alienation and paranoia that success brings: all the demands people make on you, they become very frightening, ghostlike figures."

The song was written on a Yamaha home organ bought from a factory showroom in Milton Keynes. Jerry recalls walking in on a Japanese salesman holding a class on keyboard technique. Sitting at the back of the room and increasingly feeling agitated, he started playing one of the instruments on display and inadvertently disrupted the session. Making a hasty purchase, he spent the following months experimenting with the organ's prerecorded rhythms and built-in woodwind settings. Daringly switching between flat and minor notes—using "weird Japanese fake clarinet sounds"—Jerry created a haunting melody with a distinct Eastern feel. Acknowledging that the riff was common to Prince Buster and "embarrassingly" the organ solo in "In-A-Gadda-Da-Vida" by Iron Butterfly, Jerry elucidated,

"The little motif denotes Arabic snake charmers. Musically, I wanted an atmosphere of seedy, decaying poverty, but on an international scale, with schmaltzy Latin Muzak chord changes and an Eastern flavor, which, in my mind, conjured up the idea of the third world rising up."

With the song revolving around a repeating verse, Jerry's creativity faltered: "I spent a year trying to find the third chord. I was going crazy. Eventually I just gave up and stayed on the E major. That was eureka!"

Reflecting on the steadily deteriorating social conditions in Britain—and taking the song title from a Nips song—Jerry sat in the studio with a pen and an exercise book and summoned images of inner-city anger and alienation. "Once I got the idea, the lyrics came pretty quickly." Describing Coventry as a *boom town*, "Ghost Town" interconnected a multitude of once-prosperous industrial towns and cities now in rapid decline. Shocked by the extremes of poverty and the impact unemployment was having on towns in northern England and Scotland, Jerry conveyed his view of touring in 1980. "In Liverpool all the shops had cast-iron shutters, and in Glasgow there were these little old ladies on the streets selling all their household goods, their cups and saucers. It was unbelievable. It was clear that something was very, very wrong. You could see the anger and frustration in the audience. The country was falling apart." Infused with a mood of dread and decay, "Ghost Town" was an attempt to link personal feelings to the political situation. "It was about the state of the nation," says Jerry, "and the state of the Specials."

Shortly after the Specials reconvened for rehearsals in Coventry, relations within the band spiraled. "People weren't cooperating," says Jerry, who on more than one occasion stormed out virtually in tears. Adding to the brooding mood, bass player Horace Panter had recently discovered a path to personal enlightenment and transformation through the self-religious group Exegesis. "I was full of *it* and self-assertion," he says. "It must have been hell for Jerry." Citing his conversion as a "contributing factor" in the group's decline, Horace says that "everybody was stood in different parts of the room with their equipment, no one talking. It was a nightmare.[138] I just felt like I was being sucked into a black hole of depression."

In a rapidly disintegrating situation, salvation came from an unexpected source. Listening to *Roundtable* in March 1981, Jerry found himself enamored by a new release by Victor Romero Evans called "At the Club."* Discovering that the song had been recorded in the front room of a flat in Tottenham, Jerry contacted the record's producer. "It must have been one o'clock in the morning when the phone rang and got me out of bed," John Collins told *Sound on Sound* in 2011. "A tired-sounding voice said, 'This is Jerry of the Specials. I've heard your record. Will you produce us?' I thought it must be a joke. I said, 'Do you know what time it is?' So he apologized and said he'd call me back the next day, which he did."

It transpired that several months earlier, Collins had in fact sent a tape to 2 Tone. "It was going to be released," recalled Terry Hall, "but like quite a lot of tapes, it just didn't happen." Undeterred, Collins traveled to Coventry to meet the group during rehearsals at the General Woolf on the Foleshill Road. Surprised to discover that he was white, Lynval and Neville later told Collins over a pint, "We were expecting someone like Lee Perry: a wild Rasta smoking ganja." Contracts signed—two points and an advance of £1,500: "A good deal for an unknown producer," says Collins—studio time was booked at Woodbine in Leamington Spa. Having previously worked on twenty-four track, Jerry had taken the unusual decision to revert to eight-track to impose discipline and encourage decision-making at every stage of the recording. For Collins, who to this point was used to working on four-track, the upgrade was "a luxury." After Rick Rogers said they would have unlimited time in the studio, sessions commenced on Friday, April 3, and continued through to Thursday of the following week.

---

* Talking in 2011, producer John Collins said, "Jerry subsequently wanted 'At the Club' on 2 Tone with 'Robber Dub' as the B-side. However, Victor was not keen because 2 Tone wasn't a proper reggae label."

At this point "Ghost Town" still had no words, and Collins said the instrumental version had "a good groove but the intro and ending still hadn't been worked out." Opting to layer one instrument at a time, Collins asked John Bradbury to set up a simple kit of bass drum, snare and hi-hat—like a human drum machine—and bass player Horace Panter to plug directly into the mixer. "I tried to simplify it and make it more like a Sly & Robbie–sounding record," says Collins, referencing the revered Jamaican rhythm section and production duo. Instructing Bradbury to omit drum rolls, Collins emphasized the song's heavy dub groove in stark contrast to the energetic sounds of previous 2 Tone releases.

Terry Hall would later comment that using Collins gave the Specials "something fresh," adding ruefully, "That's what we needed." But as more ganja was smoked and drink consumed, a mood of paranoia set in. Attempting to overdub a two-handed organ shuffle, Jerry became frustrated, convinced that the track was slowing down. "I'll get a stopwatch," suggested engineer John Rivers before declaring that the tempo was "solid." "It nearly all ended there," said Collins. "John saved the day!" Worse still, Jerry was playing an unpopular C minor diminished chord, known in the Middle Ages as the "devil's interval." Lynval Golding rushed into the control room. "NO! NO! NO!" the guitarist screamed. "IT SOUNDS WRONG! WRONG! WRONG! WRONG! WHY ARE YOU DOING THIS?"

Convinced that the chord sequence didn't fit the song and furthermore sounded disjointed, Lynval was horrified when Jerry shared his idea for Arabic wailing. "It didn't make any sense to me," he admits. "I said, 'I can't hear what the melody is. It sounds horrible.'" The "Arabic wailing" referred to a vocal chant intended for the middle passage. John Rivers recalls, "Everyone thought Jerry'd finally gone mad." But if comprehending a musical visionary was problem enough, the collapse of Roddy and Jerry's working relationship sent the session into freefall.

Refusing to be shown how to play the diminished chord and indeed the song structure, Roddy resolutely played only what he thought sounded right. Angry and fueled by drink, the guitarist later compared the experience to military stalemate. "The Specials was like the Spanish Civil War by that time," he promulgated. "If we were confronted by fascists like the National Front, we pulled together. Otherwise, we formed our own factions."[139]

Resistant to Jerry's alleged dictatorial approach, Roddy resorted to kicking holes in the control room wall. "That's right, Roddy," piped up Terry, "if you don't understand it, kick it!" Accounting for his increasing belligerent behavior, Roddy reasons, "I was trying to come up with something to play and Jerry was like, 'No, I don't want you to play that. I want you to play this.' I was like, '*Jawohl, mein Führer,*' and somehow got it together to play what he wanted me to. It was a bloody nightmare. I was almost suicidal, close to cutting my wrists. There was a nice little pub down the road. I used to go there, get totally off my head, and then stagger back and try and play guitar."

At wits' end, Jerry declared, "It's him [Roddy] or me." "He was crazy," says Jerry, remembering the guitar player's unpredictable manner during the recording of their previous album. Putting it to the band that Roddy "has to go," Jerry says, "Everyone more or less agreed, except Brad. And then . . ." he adds in a tone of disbelief, "Neville turned on me."

While full of energy and charisma onstage, "Neville was a loose cannon offstage," Stella Barker says of her then boyfriend. "He smoked a lot of weed and was unpredictable. You didn't know how he was going to be when he walked into a room." In the strained studio atmosphere, Neville insisted on toasting on the record and, in Jerry's words, "adding his own little bits . . . I was going, 'Look, I don't want you to toast on this particular song.'"* Exasperated, Jerry walked out. "It was really difficult to get certain people to cooperate. They'd reached a point where they didn't seem to want to take my ad-

---

* Talking to *NME* (February 13, 1982), Neville claimed that the idea of a "ghost town" came from a trip he and Lynval Golding had taken to Kingston, Jamaica. "Kingston is a real ghost town. The place is a complete wreck," he said, before sensationally adding, "I wrote most of the lyrics to 'Ghost Town.' Jerry did most of the music."

vice anymore. It all got very unpleasant. The band turned against my creative leadership, which was exhausting." Such was the animosity that John Rivers threatened to terminate the session. "No! No!" Jerry pleaded. "This is the greatest record that's ever been made in the history of anything! You can't stop now!"

When everyone agreed to complete the track, attention turned to Rico and an extended trombone passage dramatically stretching the song past the six-minute count. "I think I did everything in that solo," Rico told the BBC in 2012. "It was talking about suffering. It was talking about goodness. It speaks for all those who cannot speak, and I had the opportunity to be there because I knew oppression very well." The final ingredient in the recording was a flute, as Paul Heskett explains: "Almost as an afterthought, Jerry said, 'No offense, I don't like saxophone, or at least the way you play it. Do you play anything else?'" Stung by the criticism, Heskett nevertheless suggested a woodwind part. Set up in the hallway with a microphone at the top of the stairs to absorb natural reverb from the stairwell, Heskett recorded over a guide organ part with a riff taken from the second part of the C harmonic minor scale. "I heard it once and then had to go straight in and record," complains Heskett. "I had to put a piece of tissue under my chin because sweat was dripping off my face."

Amid the pervasive rancor and growing mistrust, the Specials surprisingly recorded two more songs at Woodbine. "Friday Night, Saturday Morning" recounted Terry's misspent youth drinking and fighting in a poetic litany of flashing lights, hen parties and drunken stags, comically ending in a taxi queue standing in vomit, wishing he had lipstick on his shirt *instead of piss stains on my shoes*. "I was saying, what's the point in me going out and doing all of that?" Terry told *NME* in 1982. "That's what I used to do every weekend. I was always getting turfed out of clubs and chased and beaten up. Then I got to twenty-one and began to think, *Fuck it. I don't want to get beaten up anymore.* It's a mundane song about a mundane lifestyle."

Although solely credited to Terry Hall, the song's backing track dated back to a film Jerry made while studying animation at

Lanchester Polytechnic, as he explained in an accompanying pamphlet when the short—*Far Gosford Street*—was shown at a 2 Tone exhibition in 2021. "The main soundtrack was recorded on the art college's new EMS suitcase synthesizer and eventually became the musical basis of the verses in 'Friday Night, Saturday Morning'—but with the three semitone figures played 'upside down.'" With the song supported by a double-tracked vocal and, as Horace recalls, chorus lyrics written by Jerry, its author dismissed the arrangement as a compromise to accommodate the band. Imagining a simpler approach, Terry suggested recording the song with just piano and vocals "as if it were being sung by a bloke in a pub."

Dick Cuthell (L) and Jerry Dammers recording "Ghost Town," Woodbine Studios, Leamington Spa, April 1981.

Expressing similar dissatisfaction, Lynval says the production of the second track, "Why?," was lousy. Having recorded a demo of the song at TW Studio with producer Dave Jordan, Lynval says, "Jerry wasn't on the original recording so we had to redo it. The whole feel of the music was the way I did it first. Things really got to a head but we had to do it Jerry's way. He never understood how I *feel* the song." It had been written in response to the racist attack he suffered outside the Moonlight Club a year earlier, and Lynval says the idea of "Why?" came to him on a train journey between Birmingham and Gloucester. Conjuring the spirit of Burning Spear, he began humming a melody and writing down lyric ideas: *Why did you try to hurt me, tell me why . . . did you really want to kill me?* Singling out the British Movement, the Ku Klux Klan and the National Front for cowardly behavior and hiding behind police protection, *too scared to make a speech*, Lynval castigated racist supporters who *follow like sheep in a wolf's clothes.* Although the words were cut from the final version, Neville Staple backed the song's plea for racial unity and a wish *to live in peace* by calling to men of all creeds and colors—*Irish man, Welsh man, Indian man, Jamaican, Canadian, Iranian, Nigerian and Cuban man*—in an extended celebration of immigrant diversity.

Mixing the three-track EP over three days in London, John Collins added ghostly sound effects (played on a Transcendent 2000 synthesizer) to the lead track, additional harmonies and a sixteen-line rap written by Terry describing a waiter in a curry house who is racially abused for not serving a chapati with the main course. "It was too busy and broke the mood," says Collins, who made the executive decision to expunge the extraneous narrative.

To complete the "Ghost Town" package, assistant art director David Storey and John Sims rummaged through an assortment of boxes marked "ghosts," "towns," and "poverty and hardship" in an upstairs room of Barnaby's, a picture library housed behind a Georgian shop front just off Oxford Street. When Storey discovered a postcard of two skeletons—one upright at a piano and the other slumped on a chair beside it—Jerry immediately interpreted the image as himself and Terry. All that remained was to commission Barney Bubbles, whose extensive résumé included Madness's schoolyard classic "Baggy Trousers," to direct a promotional video. The result was an iconic film with the band driving around a deserted London in a vintage 1962 Vauxhall Cresta attired in zoot suits and double-breasted jackets. "As dawn broke, we wound up on the banks of the Thames just east of Tower Bridge," recalls Chalkie Davies. Wide-eyed and speeding, "The band walked to the edge of the water and started throwing stones into the river. I grabbed about three frames before they dispersed and moved away from each other."

It was a symbolic moment: not only did it represent the detaching of relationships within the group, but it was also the last official shot of the Specials. Making the record had been very stressful, says Lynval Golding: "We were all on different levels. It wasn't a together band." Matters intensified when Chrysalis refused to issue "Ghost Town" as the group's next single. "I got a call from Roy Eldridge," reveals Chris Poole. "He said, 'We've got a battle on our hands. Chris [Wright] doesn't want to release it.'" Convinced the song was "too political" and critical of the government, Wright argued it would never be a hit. Underlying his concerns, Poole suggests, "Wright wanted a gong." When "Ghost Town" was sanctioned for release on June 12, Radio 1 refused to add it to the daytime playlist.

Half a million sales later, and the song widely lauded as one of the greatest singles ever made, Chrysalis's fears and the BBC's lack of judgment had the distinct air of humiliation.

CHAPTER 31

PEOPLE GETTING ANGRY

RIOTS. NORTHERN CARNIVAL AGAINST RACISM. THE SPECIALS SPLIT

On the evening of April 11, 1981, Brixton erupted. More than 200 vehicles damaged or burned out, 150 buildings defaced, 450 injuries. Open warfare between the local population and the police. CS gas used for the first time. Riot helmets and plastic shields. This was youth despair, inner-city anger and an uprising dictating national news. "More than a hundred white and colored youths fought a pitched battle against the police," reported the BBC. "The trouble started about midnight and still the bricks, stones and lumps of iron were thrown, worst of all the petrol bombs." The chief constable of the Metropolitan Police went on the record: the vicious attack on the police was not racial, he concluded.

Against a backdrop of government spending cuts, the introduction of "stop and search" and the reinvoked "SUS" laws—empowering the police to arrest any reputed thief or suspected person found loitering with intent to commit an arrestable offense—Operation Swamp 81 was launched.

So named after a comment on *World in Action* to mark the third anniversary of Margaret Thatcher's election as party leader, suggesting that unrestricted immigration quotas would leave the country "swamped by people with a different culture." She added, "[And] if there is any fear . . . people are going to react and be rather hostile to those coming in." This was read as a direct attempt to lure right-wing support to the Conservative Party, and opponents branded the speech as state-sanctioned racism. By 1981, with the Conservatives now firmly rooted in power, plainclothes police conducted indiscriminate, aggressive tactics to combat "muggings"—their main target: Black people.

"We'd been to America during the riots in Miami in May 1980, triggered by a Black Marine Corps veteran being viciously beaten to death by the police," says Pauline Black. "It was only a month after the St. Pauls riot in Bristol, triggered by a police raid on the Black and White Café. The sense of unease and continued lack of Black people's empowerment in society was international. It could have been any city. Riots were happening here and in the US. It was racism on two different continents. And in South Africa, there was apartheid. Pretty much wherever there was a Black person there was some degree of turmoil."

In the UK, antagonism toward the police erupted nationwide. Suddenly there were disturbances in Aldershot, Birmingham, Birkenhead, Blackburn, Bradford, Chester, Derby, Halifax, High Wycombe, Hull, Huddersfield, Leeds, Leicester, Luton, Maidstone, Manchester, Newcastle, Nottingham, Preston, Sheffield, Stoke, Shrewsbury, Stockport, Southampton—the list went on. On July 8, Margaret Thatcher made a party political broadcast to address the nation. Commenting on events in Liverpool—after making a secret visit to Toxteth—she said, "What happened there horrified us all. A thousand policemen embattled in one of our great cities. Two hundred injured. Riot shields and CS gas needed to defend the very men to whom we all turn for protection. Nothing can justify, nothing can excuse and no one can condone the appalling violence we've all seen on television which some of our people have actually experienced and so many fear." Addressing the House of Commons, Home Secretary William Whitelaw denied it was a race riot. It was a confrontation with the police, he declared.

Three days later, "Ghost Town" topped the UK singles chart. The record would become the emblematic soundtrack of the era. "It encapsulated a feeling of despair when, economically, everyone was under siege," says Pauline Black. "When you heard the wind blowing at the beginning of the song, you knew instantly what it was about." As far as Rick Rogers was concerned, "Ghost Town" was the best track the Specials ever recorded. "It's an absolute masterpiece," he exalts, "a most beautiful piece of music. I'm quoted as saying that it was going to be the Specials's 'Vienna'—terribly embarrassing."

With the song spending the first of three weeks at number one, Terry Hall received a phone call at ten a.m. with the news. "I sang, *Oh, what a beautiful morning*," he glibly noted in a diary entry for a feature in *Flexipop*. Two decades on, Hall's comic flippancy gave way to deep despair. "I wasn't prepared to go and celebrate a number one single when I had aunties and uncles who were literally losing their jobs," he told the BBC in 2009. "They worked in car factories and it was all being closed down. I really didn't want to be a part of it anymore."

In "Ghost Town's" final week at number one, 700 million viewers, the highest in global television history at the time, watched the wedding of Prince Charles to Lady Diana Spencer. Skillfully avoiding direct reference to the continuing instability across the country, a BBC news reporter informed viewers, "It is as though a whole nation is gathering in front of Buckingham Palace and saying, 'Yes, we do respect law and order. Yes, we can be happy. Yes, we do like each other, and we do like being British.'" Soon after, the secretary of state for employment, Norman Tebbit, addressed the annual Conservative Party Conference: "I grew up in the thirties with an unemployed father. He didn't riot; he got on his bike and looked for work and he kept looking till he found it."

At every turn, the country was in conflict. Class, race, gender, culture. "I'd planned a band from the age of ten that was going to cause a revolution," says Jerry Dammers, "and when it actually happened, I suppose you're entitled to think, *Oh my God!* It was scary because I'm not a person who likes violence in any way." In the public eye, the Specials were at their zenith. Yet, exacerbated by violence and right-wing elements at their shows, the band were permeated by a feeling of disillusionment. As far as Jerry was concerned, the music scene in

England was "dead," with touring bands reluctant to perform because of fighting at concerts. "That's part of what we're saying in 'Ghost Town,'" he told Richard Cromelin of the *Los Angeles Times*. "We're not going to play if you're going to cause trouble."

Ad for the "Ghost Town" single, June 1981. Courtesy of Chrysalis Records/ Jerry Dammers.

Taking a single-minded view, the Specials approached 1981 as a year to promote worthwhile causes. In April, a Rock Against Racism show in Leamington Spa was advertised with an accompanying flyer and a quote from Jerry: "You can tell anyone you like, the NF and the BM are not welcome at our gigs. We just don't want them there." In May, a People's March benefit at the Rainbow. In June, a 2 Tone reunion featuring the Specials, the Selecter, Madness and the Beat at the St. Lucia Carnival of Caribbean Arts. After signing on to participate in a coordinated effort to help the economy after a hurricane devastated the island in August 1980, the groups eventually pulled out due to "organizational chaos." And on June 20, a hometown, all-day benefit in solidarity with Coventry's Asian population of 22,000 after a spate of horrifying racist assaults.

In early April 1981, Susan Cheema, the daughter of a local grocery store owner, lost a finger after being attacked with a scythe. Then, a fortnight later, on April 18, a twenty-year-old student, Satnam Singh Gill, was beaten, kicked and stabbed to death by a group of white youths four years his junior in broad daylight in the city center. The appalling act prompted the establishment of the Coventry Committee Against Racism. However, when protestors marched on May 23, a large group of National Front supporters shouted abuse and threw objects from behind a protective police cordon. Among the seventy-four arrests, one Asian youth claimed he was beaten in an unprovoked attack by a police officer. Barely a week earlier, on May 17, there had been an attempted arson attack at a Krishna temple and the Indian and Commonwealth clubs. And still there was more: an attack on a fifty-year-old woman and a bus driver; the rape of a young Caribbean woman; a Jandu family home set on fire; and on June 7, Dr. Amal Dharry was fatally stabbed outside a chip shop in Earlsdon. The assailant: a seventeen-year-old skinhead, who later admitted that he had carried out the attack for a £15 bet to "get a Paki that night."

"It was a really terrible time," says Jerry, still visibly shaken by the devastating acts of violence that swept through Coventry four decades earlier. "Racism was still there. The National Front was still there." Close friend Lizzie Soden recalls Jerry questioning the validity of 2 Tone and its "Black and white unite" slogan. "One night there'd be skinheads beating up Indian kids and the next night the Indian kids would beat up white people," decries Soden. "But some of the white skinheads would be Specials fans. One of our [white] friends, Andy, got beaten up by some Asian kids. I remember Jerry saying, '2 Tone is causing more division. It's actually highlighting a racial view of people. We're inadvertently saying, 'Black people are different from white people—and there's racism both ways.' I remember arguing with him, going, 'Black people can't be racist.' He went, 'Of course they can. They're judging all white people to be the same by virtue of their skin color, so what's not racist about that?'"

Having similar doubts, Terry expressed his thoughts in an interview with the *Face*. "There's so many foolish people around that put on things like Union Jacks just to impress people. It's just gone totally mad. Actions speak louder than words, and it's no use saying you believe in something in a music paper and not doing anything about it. We might have been a successful pop band touring America in LA, man, but there's still an Indian kid getting murdered in the city where you've always lived, so really, what *is* the point?"

In a show of solidarity, the Specials announced "A Peaceful Protest Against Racism" at the Butts Stadium, Coventry. On the morning of the concert, the National Front marched through Hillfields, a predominantly Black and Asian area. At one o'clock, the newly formed Ship's Crew, featuring former Swinging Cats members John Shipley and Paul Heskett, launched the all-day event. "The only people in the audience were my dad and Jerry standing in the middle of this athletics track," says Shipley. "We were doing a version of 'Z-Cars' and these policemen walked in while we were doing it." Further sets followed from local artists, including the People (featuring former Selecter members Charley Anderson and Desmond Brown), Reluctant Stereotypes, the Bureau, and Hazel O'Connor. During the Specials's performance, a white victim of a racially based attack took to the stage and told the crowd, "I understand why they did it." "It was heartbreaking," says Lynval Golding, who then introduced his own riposte to a vicious racist attack. "The next song is about why you're all here," he told the audience. "I'm asking the question: why do people have to fight? Why?"

Reviewing the show, one local reporter wrote, "Perhaps the high point of the whole [Specials] set was a guest appearance by Rhoda Dakar." Introduced as a song about another kind of violence, "The Boiler" was described as "the most chilling, shaming song I've heard . . . it was a necessary reminder of the sexual dimension to violence that antiracist campaigns can lull us into forgetting. The audience stood transfixed; her message went right home."

The benefit had cost £13,000, with all profits donated to local antiracist groups. At the event, the Specials took a loss. "It's been a disappointment that there weren't more people prepared to stand up and be counted," tour mananger Pete Hadfield told the *Leveller*. "But there had been a National Front rumor campaign to scare people off. The press haven't helped either—all their reports have linked the festival with racist attacks and people are genuinely worried about walking into a race fight. But let's hope it does something to get the message across."

A week later, the Specials and UB40 played a free concert at Herringthorpe Playing Fields in south Yorkshire. Again, skinheads and rival football supporters from Rotherham and Sheffield clashed. Amid the fighting, a senior police officer took to the stage and threatened to cancel the concert unless order prevailed. Calm restored, the Specials kicked off proceedings with "Concrete Jungle" and the incendiary chant: *You're gonna get your fucking head kicked in.* Whether aimed at the police or the audience, it was difficult to tell. Nevertheless, here was a band at the top of the charts acting as a sort of cutural clarion call; simultaneously singing about social and political division in the country while uniting people of all races and creeds in a celebration of joyous music. Yes, there were minority factions intent on crushing the spirit of unity, but the Specials rose above it, delivering jubilation and infectious dance music of the highest caliber.

On Saturday, July 4, determined in their ideological stance, the Specials headlined the Northern Carnival Against Racism. Staged at Potternewton Park in Leeds, it was the last event Rock Against Racism would organize before rupturing in acrimony. Since the antiracist movement's inception in 1976, the majority of 2 Tone artists had supported it by either attending gigs or carnivals, or in later years playing at events.* "When you saw 2 Tone, you went, 'Job done—that's it!'" says RAR founding member Red Saunders. "Their music, their spirit—and what Jerry went on to do for Nelson Mandela—trumped the whole fucking lot of us."

The day after the farewell carnival, Terry was interviewed by *Temporary Hoarding*, telling the political broadsheet that there were a "lot of racial problems [in Leeds], so we thought it was the ideal place to play. We do a lot of Rock Against Racism gigs. They unite people for a day at least. We played with Rico the night before. I got up at 7:30 and traveled to Coventry, had a bath and drove to Leeds. We arrived only half an hour before we went onstage. We would have liked to have gone on the march, but we didn't have time."

As the Specials had neared the concert park, they drove head-on into a counterdemonstration staged by the National Front. "It was very sinister looking with lots of nationalist flags and mostly older blokes in grubby coats," recalls Jerry, who likened it to "a giant red, white and blue slug creeping through the center bristling with Union Jacks. There was a strong atmosphere in the town, but the carnival outnumbered them by a hundred to one." Seated in Neville's car, Rhoda now remembers an intimidating mass of people waving flags. "We were low down so people looked taller. It was like, 'Woah! This is all a bit scary.'"

Traveling on a coach with the rest of the band, Paul Heskett seized the opportunity to speak with a local radio journalist. Asked why he thought the Specials had gone from "strength to strength,"

---

* The exception was the Selecter. "We didn't believe in Rock Against Racism," says Neol Davies. Critical of its effectiveness, Davies argues that any money the organization raised was "sliced off" for administration. "By simply doing what we do and being who we are: we *are* rock against racism."

Heskett replied, "That's a very good question and thank you for ask-ing me. You're absolutely right, over recent months the band has gone from strength to strength. It's extraordinary . . ." Then, sensing he had the attention of the band, Heskett delivered his punch line: ". . . and remarkably, it's been ever since I joined!" The rest of the group burst into roars of laughter, but on a day when joviality balanced precar-iously with despondency, the Specials soon found themselves back-stage confronted by a blast of anger.

"One of them came into the dressing room," recalls Rick Rog-ers, "and said, 'Misty in Roots are accusing of us of stealing their heritage.'" Reproaching Rico for "playing with Babylon," the west London–based reggae band urged the Jamaican trombone player to sever his ties with the heathen Specials. "They were all, 'Nah, dread,'" says Rhoda. "I thought, *What's that all about? We're here trying to get everyone together and you're busy trying to split the Specials up.* It really pissed me off. It was a load of bollocks." Adding to the frustration, the Specials went onstage at six o'clock without their sound engineer, who mistakenly thought it was an evening performance. Neverthe-less, Jerry says, the atmosphere was incredible and one of the most exciting concerts the Specials ever played. "It was shit," insists Horace Panter. "The worst gig we ever did. We hated one another. We didn't care. There was no cohesion. It wasn't a band at all. We just went through the motions. The band was falling apart. I felt ashamed."

In front of the largest audience the Specials had ever played to in the UK—39,000—a scuffle broke out at the foot of the stage. Forced to stop on two separate occasions, Terry screamed at the front row, "There are about fifteen people down here spoiling it. Yes, you're to blame—this is about racial harmony, remember." "You're a disgrace," added Lynval. Ten minutes later, Neville vented his frustration and the group's growing dismay, shouting, "You big boys don't prove any-thing to us up here by fighting, or to the tens of thousands of peo-ple out there!" As they launched into the climatic set closer, "Ghost Town," Jerry says, "it came to the solo and Rico didn't play. Asking him why not, Rico replied, 'Me nah feel for play, Jerry.' I think Misty had put a bit of pressure on him and made him feel bad about playing with us." What should have been a defining moment in the group's history crumbled, sabotaged by petty jealousies and mounting personal discord. Then, five days later, Terry, Lynval and Neville quit the Specials.

Booked to appear on the 900th edition of *Top of the Pops*, the Specials gathered backstage only to fall despairingly into arguments. "We were at each other's throats," says Terry. "But you look at us on that program and the tension between the band was fantastic."[140] Brandishing a walking stick, Terry later remarked, "[It was] in case one of them came near me, I was going to twat them." Staring down the barrel of the camera lens, Terry knowingly sang, *Bands won't play no more*. Then, casting his eyes to the skies, he joyfully grinned, *Can't go on no more.* As the song reached its eerie finale, Terry, Lynval and Neville grouped together in a tight huddle, their three faces filling the screen, and delivered the song's denouement, *This town is coming like a ghost town.* In case the message was not yet abundantly clear, the trio confronted Jerry in the dressing room and announced, "We're out."

Stunned by the news, Jerry supposedly bawled, "You're not allowed to leave. You have to stay." As far as Lynval was concerned, it further illustrated Jerry's authoritarianism. "We were never allowed to express ideas or simply just be ourselves. You had to be what Jerry wanted you to be. It worked up to a certain stage, but after that, individuals are going to want to throw some ideas in." Incensed by the betrayal, Jerry counters, "I don't think I would have said, 'You're not allowed to leave,' except possibly as a joke. Lynval had missed the point so completely by that time that even me wanting them in the band would have been seen as evidence of me being a 'dictator.' It was crazy. Terry, Neville and Lynval had no justification or reason to leave the band. They've never been able to give a reason that was true. I'd spent four years trying to convince everyone that we were a good combination of people with something to offer. It just didn't seem to matter what happened, some of them were never going to get that."

Disagreeing, Terry told the BBC in 2009: "Jerry had a real problem about us leaving but I had a big problem with us staying. Things had got so bad that it couldn't continue, and we all knew it. It's like you can tolerate all the stuff going on outside the band, like the problems at gigs, problems with record labels, if the band is united. But if the band is not united then it's pointless. We were arguing too much with each other. Do you want to spend the whole of your life arguing with everyone all night? I didn't want to do that. I thought we left on the perfect note. 'Ghost Town' was the perfect song to split that band up with. It said it all."

Such conviction was nevertheless prone to uncertainty. Having resolved to leave the Specials, Terry later revealed, "Originally our last gig was going to be the Campaign for Jobs at the Rainbow [May 1, 1981], but the three of us decided to stay on for 'Ghost Town' and an American tour, just to see if there was any way that we could hold on."

On July 24, the Specials played at the Royal Court in Liverpool. It would be their last UK gig. Then, somewhat surprisingly, they honored an outstanding commitment to do a second tour of the US, postponed from January. Prior to the first date in New York on August 12, Terry answered rumors about an imminent split. "We've all been writing songs that might go on a third Specials album," he told Robert Palmer of the *New York Times*, "but right now we're thinking about Wednesday night's concert, which we've been looking forward to for a long time. When we get back to England, we'll decide what to do next. We learned long ago that planning things far in advance doesn't work for us; we have to plan things from day to day."

Traveling between East and West coasts, the band watched *One Flew over the Cuckoo's Nest*, a film in which Randle McMurphy, played by Jack Nicholson, is convinced he is the only sane patient in an institute for the mentally ill. "That was like how it was in the Specials," sniggers Roddy. "We often said amongst ourselves that we looked like lunatics from the asylum."

"Mental health," "friction," "fragmenting," "strained," "pressure," "exhaustion," "disillusioned" and "unpleasant" are words frequently used to express the decaying mood in the Specials camp in autumn 1981. "People are not told how to deal with success," says Paul Heskett. "It can be incredibly challenging. Egos become incredibly fragile. You've got to be tough and tenacious, but it takes its toll. Many of us have had mental health problems: depression in one form or another." Nonetheless, Heskett is keen to emphasize that he spent "some of the most glorious moments of my life" onstage with the Specials, none more so than when Terry Hall would introduce the band during "Nite Klub." "Then, with a spotlight on you, you hear a big cheer from thousands of people. It was exquisite joy."

After the emotionally damaging US tour eighteen months earlier, the Specials followed a more relaxed schedule, including guest spots supporting the Police to audiences of 30,000 and more. Gone were the frantic blasts of punk-ska and in came the deep reggae grooves of "Ghost Town," "Why?" and the instrumental "Chiang Kai Shek" featuring Rico. It did little to placate Terry. "I just felt like I had to get away from it for a bit," he told *Uncut*, "and Lynval and Neville felt the same way. I didn't think it was a permanent thing." Reiterating the claim that Jerry discouraged creative input from within the group, Terry surprisingly added, "I was cool with that because it was Jerry's band. And what he needed was this beautiful mouthpiece. The music was great. My problems with Jerry were political. We had different roots, hearts in different places."[141]

Reeling at the affront, Jerry spits, "I couldn't believe that some people could be as destructive and disloyal to leave when we were doing such great stuff. We were at the top of our game: universal critical acclaim, commercial success, one of the top bands in the country, on the verge of really establishing ourselves internationally." Taking it out on Rick Rogers for not trying to persuade Terry, Neville and Lynval to stay—not least stopping the planned formation of a new group, the Fun Boy Three—Jerry sacked the manager. "I didn't understand or recognize the rot that was going on," admits Rogers. Blunt to the point of discomfort, Roddy says, "Rick was off his head on cocaine

and vodka. 'Where's Rick?' 'He's lying on the floor, crying, drunk.'"
Standing by her former business partner, Juliet de Vie says he had
"issues which he fought a lot. But that's oddly what made him a very
decent and nonjudgmental person." Accepting the accusation that he
was probably "too soft," Rogers adds, "I had my faults but when I
played to my strengths it worked well. My faults were made bigger
by the situation."

On August 27, 1981, the Specials played their last concert at the
Bradford Ballroom, Boston. A month later, on October 1, the British
press announced that the Specials had officially split up. "A lot of
people thought we were like the Monkees and lived in a house all
together, like in the *Arena* documentary: dancing on the tables to ska
all night long," says Roddy. "It wasn't the case. None of us were particularly good friends. We never hung out together unless we had to.
As soon as we had a chance, we went in our own directions with our
own friends. We all thought we were big boys and could manage to
do it on our own, without Jerry's guidance."

The exact reason why the Specials split up is confusing and frus-
tratingly distorted by the foggy prism of time. Forty years after the
event, deciphering reality from myth and fabrication is a conundrum.
Giving scant value to differences in class or education, Rick Rogers points to the unedifying influences of fame, pressure and money.
"When anybody becomes hugely famous in a very short period of
time, you get surrounded by people telling you that everything you
do is the right thing to do. All of us, to some extent, were seduced by
fame and the money. Jerry saw that and wanted to bring it back down
to earth a little bit."

Since the Specials's first visit to the US, Jerry had cautioned against
unnecessary expenditures and the temptations of pop star privilege.
"We'd often have to move out of a hotel because Jerry would walk in
and there'd be a chandelier in the foyer," says Roddy. "Or they'd send
a limo to pick the band up from the airport and he'd refuse to go in it.
The first time we went to New York, I could see Jerry in the foyer of
this hotel looking stressed. I said, 'What's up?' He said, 'Neville's just

moved himself up to the penthouse.' Whatever was going, Neville would take it. But there's Jerry, 'No, you can't do that. It's wrong. You shouldn't want those things.' You start off fighting the system, but to fight the system you have to join the system. And by the time you've joined the system, you've become as bad as the people you were fighting against."

For those from a working-class background, success offered a chance to escape. Terry wanted to buy a house. Lynval and Neville wanted to own BMWs. "Who the hell wants to live in a council house all their life with an outside loo or frozen pipes?" questions Horace Panter. Pointing to class as the cause of "a lot of tension within the band," he adds, "When you become famous, what you were before becomes exaggerated. If you were a bully, you're going to be an even bigger bully. If you're a drunk, you're going to be an even bigger drunk. If you're shy, you're going to be even shyer. You are not the person you were two and half years ago." Discovering many years later that Jerry's father was an environmentalist in favor of recycling waste, Horace ruminates, "I can see that in Jerry. He hated that money would be spent on champagne or expensive hotels."

Frank Murray believes the problem within the group stemmed from class differences. "Jerry was trying to banish his middle-class roots," says the Specials's tour manager. "You can't rid yourself of your background no matter how hard you try. It doesn't mean you don't know what a working-class kid is about, or they won't like your music." Claiming that such criticisms were not expressed at the time and, rather, have been exaggerated over the ensuing years, Jerry retaliates: "In America we were staying in Holiday Inns. They were really quite posh hotels. But I wasn't keen on limousines. I came up through the era of Rod Stewart. It was a big thing when he appeared on TV with Britt Ekland buying ludicrous art deco lamps and being really flash. A lot of his fans were disappointed. Punk was going to be a new start. When we supported the Clash, they were staying in these massive hotels. I was really disappointed. I didn't want to put kids through the disillusionment that I'd felt with them and Rod Stewart. It's as simple as that. Plus there was a very sound financial reason for being sensible, in that ultimately, we had to pay for everything out of our royalties. If Neville or whoever wanted to buy a flash car, the best way was not to waste an absolute fortune touring. I had no fucking interest in what they spent their personal money on. I was trying to make sure they got as much money as possible. It was just common sense."

Adding to the growing unease, Rick Rogers says, "All these weird pressures started attacking our little bubble. People talk in ears. Jealousies start to arise: 'Why d'you do everything Jerry tells you to do?' 'Shouldn't you be getting more money?' It was outside sources, some of whom were very close to the core circle. It's not unusual. 'We can do better for you.' My relative inexperience and naivety in the steering position did not recognize certain things that were happening. I was partly to blame, but we are all to blame."

Since signing to Chrysalis, each of the Specials had been on a monthly wage. However, when songwriting royalty statements started to arrive, there was a wave of incredulity. According to Roddy, "Brad got a seven grand check, I got twenty and Jerry one hundred and fifty." Money suddenly became the source of jealousy and recrimination. People turned against Jerry, says Rogers: "Demands were being made of him to share equally his publishing income." Yet, since "Gangsters"—credited to all seven members of the band—Rogers insists songwriting acknowledgments were generous to a fault. "Even to the point that there was a percentage of the publishing put into the pot to share equally, whoever wrote the stuff." In fact, when other writers began to emerge within the band—"all of whom, including Roddy, were far less competent songwriters—Jerry worked with them, contributing words and melody and arrangements but never asking for a cowriting credit."

As far as Brad was concerned, Jerry was the leader of the Specials and the main songwriter. "But when you have a bunch of egos, particularly singers, there's bound to be a bit of 'I want my own songs in' tension. No one could deal with each other in the end."[142] During the dying months of the group's existence, Terry, Neville and Lynval confronted Jerry and insisted that songwriting royalties should be shared equally among the whole band. If not, they were leaving. "I said no," explains Jerry, "and that was the end of that."

Speaking on Canadian television in 1981, Neville Staple defended his position: "We were preaching equality for everyone and yet in the band, near the end, we weren't getting none of that at all.* It got to the stage where we didn't all have a say in what the Specials were doing. People can't be yes-men all the time. That's what split the Specials up: everybody think they're it. We were crumbling away. That's fame. Everybody thinks they're better than one person. 'I need to say something now,' 'I need to do this,' 'I need to do that.' So the three of us didn't like it or want it and wanted out."

Money, class and songwriting all play their part, but history is multilayered and laced with nuances, and, as so often in the 2 Tone story, everyone has a different explanation. Talk to Paul Heskett and he is convinced that drugs took "a severe toll on people." Limiting his own indulgence of cocaine to "a handful of occasions," he says, "Others were less discriminate and fell prey to suppliers who quickly circled around the band." Elsewhere, Rhoda Dakar, having "popped down to see the Specials" at the Hope & Anchor in November, had ended up as a backing vocalist. "I didn't ever expect her to fully join the band," says Jerry in his inimitable bemused manner, "she was just there. It did get silly. She was on *Top of the Pops* for 'Ghost Town' when she didn't even sing on the record. That was my fault. Terry was not happy at all. Rhoda was good company when some of the Specials were being shitty toward me, so she probably became attached to the band more than she maybe should have. I was sticking my neck out trying to help after the Bodysnatchers."

Resentment festered, confirms Horace: "Terry didn't like Rhoda. There was no outright hostility, but there was this, 'Okay, well, it's

---

* It is worth noting that Madness employed a formula to distribute songwriting royalties as follows: 50 percent to the writer(s) and 50 percent shared between all seven members of the band. Thus, the writer(s) gets half plus a seventh. In the Beat, although Dave Wakeling and David Steele wrote the lion's share of the songs, the writing credits were shared equally. In the Selecter, Neol Davies and Pauline Black claimed a full share of their songs.

what Jerry wants.'" Matters came to a head in one of the band's final arguments. "I was the buffer, so in the end it meant that everything could be my fault," intones Rhoda. "I don't know if that was intentional. It appeared from the outside that the Specials was a democracy. The Specials was not a democracy. One person took a decision and everybody just had to lump it. I think that was a problem. Jerry has since told me, 'If I didn't want you in the band then the Specials wouldn't have split up.' It was true. But it wasn't my fault."

Having been privy to the Specials's inner sanctum, Chas Smash observes, "Madness was a very democratic process. That's why we lasted and the Specials only lasted two years. The Specials weren't friendly. They had no mutual respect. There was jealousy, anger, frustration, a lack of fucking gratitude for each other's existence. The fuckers couldn't stop arguing. It was sad."

"Show me a group that doesn't argue," disputed Terry, ruminating over the split in 1982. "In fact, the reason we were so good was because of all that tension. The split didn't come out of any mass fight or anything. Nothing nasty happened. I just got really bored of being part of the same organization for two and a half years. Jerry was drafting people into the band and the first we'd know about it was when they turned up onstage. And then you'd have people walking offstage during sets. I'd be doing my compere bit, introducing the members of the band, and when I looked around, half of them weren't there. By the time we got back from the tour, there was no way. The Specials had become one big joke."

Initially, Jerry felt a wave of relief that it was finally over. Fed up trying to guide a band and a label, he was simply exhausted. "But a couple of months later it kicked in what had happened," he says, "and I was devastated." Like Jerry, Roddy experienced an initial sense of liberation. "The future suddenly seemed so much brighter and happier," he says. In fact, Roddy had been tipped off in June when Lynval alleged that Jerry wanted Roddy sacked. "I didn't care," asserts Roddy. "They never got in touch with me and I never got in touch with them." But freedom soon turned to despair when Chrysalis gave the guitarist four days to record new material to justify a solo record deal.

"I had plenty of new songs, but so little time," he grumbles. "Then I heard Jerry was angry that I had been dropped so I asked him at a party in Coventry if he would put out my 'ska-billy' on 2 Tone. He turned around and headbutted the wall!"

On October 26, 1981, a booby-trapped improvised explosive device was discovered in the basement bathroom of a Wimpy burger restaurant on Oxford Street, planted by the IRA. While attempting to defuse the bomb, Metropolitan Police Officer Kenneth Howarth was killed. The reverberation shook the nearby Chrysalis office, where only weeks earlier, news of the Specials's breakup had reached a distraught Roy Eldridge. Accused by Jerry of being compliant in the carving up of the original Specials and facilitating the formation of the Fun Boy Three—within weeks of "Ghost Town" dropping off the chart—Doug D'Arcy defends the honor of Chrysalis. "We were presented with a fait accompli: Pete Hadfield came in and said, 'That's it.' There was no discussion. What influence do you think I could reasonably have? People are so busy building up the notion of record companies as big human-crushing monsters, but they're just people shifting vinyl around really."

On November 7, 1981, "The Lunatics (Have Taken Over the Asylum)" entered the British chart. It would be the first of seven successful Fun Boy Three singles released by Chrysalis over the next eighteen months. It was written and recorded at TW Studios in January 1981 when, as Jerry explains, "Everyone was supposed to go off and write songs for the next Specials album. Fun Boy Three thought the first thing they came up with was so utterly fantastic that they didn't need us anymore and they could make more money on their own. It's as simple as that. 'The Lunatics' could have been a worthy follow-up to 'Ghost Town.' It had a huge amount of potential, but it wasn't really fully realized. The irony of Lynval, Neville and Terry singing that after what they'd done seemed completely lost on them. Like John Peel said, 'The lunatics have taken over the asylum? I think you'll find that's stale news, lads!'"

PART III
TRANSITION

CHAPTER 32

THAT MAN IS FORWARD

RICO. THE BOILER

2 Tone had formed as a vehicle for the Specials and like-minded bands to establish themselves independently and, in doing so, provide an alternative to standard music industry practice. But now, with the lead protagonists no more, the question was: did 2 Tone have a future? Having achieved incredible success, not only in fulfilling his ambition to be a pop star—principles still intact—and having overseen an awe-inspiring catalog of hits, Jerry Dammers was widely regarded as a visionary and the mastermind behind one of the greatest and most widely acclaimed songs in UK pop history—"Ghost Town." The answer was simple: keep moving forward.

In 1981, there was no precedent for a group splitting after having just achieved a number one single. In 1970, the England World Cup Squad netted the top spot with "Back Home," and a decade later Dexys Midnight Runners splintered soon after the glorious success of "Geno." Neither offer satisfactory comparison. However, here, in October 1981, were the Specials, minus two front men and a rhythm guitarist. It was an incredible situation. Oscillating between anger and disbelief, Jerry, John Bradbury and Horace Panter (billed as the Special AKA and accompanied by horn player Dick Cuthell) set off on a three-week club tour of Germany and Switzerland to back trombonist Rico Rodriguez. "It was like, 'Gosh, I'm a musician. I don't have to worry about half of Swansea's skinheads onstage," recalls Horace. "I could just play." Reviewing the show at Rheinterrassen, Bonn, Olaf Karnik observed "six gentlemen on the stage who were probably more interested in spreading happiness and fun among the crowd than getting rid of any political or religious slogans . . . The clear highlight of the concert was Rico's version of the old jazz piece 'Take 5.'"[143]

Jazz was never far from Rico's influence. "I like to do different music every night," he explained, "but we have never been a trendy style of musician who leaves the roots for money or whatever. The kind of musician I am, I do a lot of research . . . you need ideas, new inspiration. Music is an exploratory thing. I can't stop that." On his first album for 2 Tone, *That Man Is Forward*—released on March 1, 1981—the primary influence of jazz was evident on a cover of Charlie Parker's "Fiesta"—first recorded in 1951—and Lionel Hampton's "Red Top." Recorded at Joe Gibbs's studio in Jamaica and backed by a sterling ensemble of musicians—including Sly Dunbar, Robbie Shakespeare, Ansell Collins and Jah Jerry (guitarist with the Skatalites)—the album connected 2 Tone to its birthplace, exemplified by the inclusion of the pioneering ska track "Easy Snappin'." Revisiting his contribution to Theophilus Beckford's 1957 recording, Rico ingeniously bridged British ska to its founding roots. It was augmented by four original cuts—"Chang Kai Shek" (named after the former president of the Republic of China, 1950–75) "X," "Ganja" and the album title track—and the accompanying sleeve notes, written by Richard Williams, drew attention to the disproportionate influence reggae had exerted on rock music despite Jamaica's meager population of two million people. Further recognizing 2 Tone's impact in revealing aspects of the country's undiscovered treasure trove, Williams wrote, "A great deal of [Jamaica's] postwar popular music remains obscure."

Lightening the mood, the album's paper label depicted Walt Jabsco blowing on a trombone. The subtle touch of joviality was again evident on a new single, "Jungle Music." Based on lyrics by Stevie Wonder, written during a jam onstage in Jamaica, Rico's adaption of "Whatcha Talkin' Bout" was recorded in a live session at the new Woodbine Studio in Leamington Spa. Joined by Jerry, Brad, Horace,

Dick Cuthell and John Shipley on guitar, Rico was then persuaded to appear in a promotional video directed by Barney Bubbles. Filmed at Noel's Cafe in Coventry, the cast was made up of regulars and friends from the local music scene. "The idea," explained Lizzie Soden, who helped to develop the storyboard, "was that the band drew up in this big car and then took over the café, singing. It ends up with Ken, who ran the General Wolf pub up the road, and one of Jerry's mum's friends complaining about the noise. It was like, *What you talkin' bout, you say you don't like the jungle beat.* They come in and end up joining in the dancing."

Ad for *That Man Is Forward*, March 1981. Courtesy of Chrysalis Records/Jerry Dammers.

Arriving in a green Buick, owned by keyboard player Jools Holland, Jerry enters the café wearing a giant sombrero while Rico sings to the camera. "He was off his head smoking sensimilla, this really strong weed," laughs Soden. "Trying to get him to mime to the song was a nightmare. We were filming it in a different order and Rico couldn't get his head round the fact there were different parts of the song at different times. The clip of him miming, *You must be crazy,* was the nearest we could get him to sync up."

Among a throng of dancers, including Chris Long (the Swinging

Cats) and Simon Kirk (the Apollinaires), and Brad serving drinks dressed in spotted dickie bow and waistcoat, Rico leads the revelers out onto the street. "There were about eight arcade games in the café and the local kids were all playing *Frogger* and *Phoenix*," says Soden. "So we said to these lads, 'Can you move out because we're making this pop video?' They were like, 'We're not moving anywhere.' Jerry said, 'Oh, they can just stay there.' They ended up joining in the conga and dancing outside. It was really spontaneous."

In the summer, Rico recorded a second album for 2 Tone, mixed and coproduced by Dick Cuthell and Jerry Dammers. *Jama* was a delightful and worthy successor to *That Man Is Forward* but made no chart impact. "Playing with the Specials was a good atmosphere," Rico explained to David Katz in 1991. "It was very good to be with a band that was so successful. But after they broke up, I went [back] to Jamaica [for nine years]."[144]

Welcoming the opportunity to write new material and to plot a new direction for the remaining Specials, Jerry says he was loath to "just churn out the same thing . . . If we do something else as a band after this, it will be totally different." Prior to recording "Ghost Town," Jerry had spent downtime working on a former Bodysnatchers song with Rhoda Dakar, previously only heard live and on a John Peel session in April 1980.

The song had been written as an instrumental track and built around a sixties-influenced keyboard riff. Nicky Summers remembers leaving Gaz Mayall's club (Gaz's Rockin' Blues) one night and asking Rhoda to put lyrics to it. "She wrote it on the tube up to the next rehearsal and improvised over the music." Taking its title from an expression used by the manager of the Nips, Howard Cohen, who would dismissively refer to aging women as "boilers," Rhoda used the first person to recount a friend's rape. "I suppose the character is how I see a *typical* girl," Rhoda explained to *Record Mirror* in January 1982. "She's maybe how I could have been. A lot of women seem to see themselves in terms of the blokes they know and are or aren't going out with. You're only as important as your bloke. Most of the women I went to school with are married. And I went to a so-called *good* school, a grammar school."

Rape has always been an uncomfortable topic of conversation, not least in 1980s Britain. The attitude of "girls asking for it" in the way they dressed or walked alone late at night permeated public opinion. "We are almost conditioned to think that if a girl is raped, then it's her own fault, which is ridiculous," Rhoda scoffed.[145]

Performed onstage, "The Boiler" was as daring as its unflinching delivery. Backed by a jaunty twelve-bar offbeat, Rhoda tells the tale of meeting a guy while out shopping on a Saturday and being flattered when he offers to buy her new clothes. Reluctant to think of herself as anything but *an old boiler*, she agrees to go to a club with him. Dancing all night *to a nice steady beat*, they leave the club *hot and sweaty*. But when an invitation to go back *to his place* is politely declined, an argument ensues. As the music quiets down, the situation intensifies. Her arm is grabbed. She is taken up an alleyway. She is hit. Her clothes are torn. She is raped. *There was nothing I could do*, she laments as the music plays hard, *all I could do was scream . . . NO!* With Rhoda shrieking and yelling incessantly, the remainder of the song is almost unbearable to listen to.

"Rhoda used to really go for it," says her former bandmate Miranda Joyce, shuddering at the memory. "You'd see people's faces going, *Fuck!* The whole thing turned. It was really powerful and a great song. I loved playing it: just because of the change in tone. You'd get everybody dancing along thinking it's a fun night at the club and then something hideous happens. Rhoda used to literally scream full force down her microphone as if she was being raped. It was hard-core. At that age, you don't share personal stuff. You're trying to get away from all of that in a way and music helps you do that. But 'The Boiler' was about as honest as it gets."

More often than not "The Boiler" was greeted by stunned silence. Penny Leyton says the band "thought it was an important song to do." She was right. It was powerful, challenging and spectacularly radical. "There's nothing that I've heard before or since that was like that," says

Frank Murray. "It was unique and peerless. The way Rhoda acted it was chilling. To scream for the last minute on a song was revolutionary." Sarah-Jane Owen says, "It almost became a favorite. People wanted to hear it." It is no surprise to Pauline Black, who regards the former Bodysnatchers front woman as nothing short of extraordinary. "Rhoda had a commanding presence onstage, a whole style completely of her own. 'The Boiler' left the audience totally and utterly perplexed."

Asked how she approached performing "The Boiler," Rhoda refers to the seminal Russian theater practitioner Konstantin Stanislavski, who developed a technique called emotional memory. "You take something that's terrified you and you reuse that feeling using the words you've got to speak. That's what I did. It was theater. The rape didn't happen to me. It was a performance piece. You had to be inside the performance in order to make it work."

Stunned by the song's unforgiving stance, Jerry wanted "The Boiler" to be the Bodysnatchers's first single. The band resisted. "Some of them felt it was too hard-line and it wouldn't help us commercially," decries its author. Asked to join the Specials on tour, Rhoda came with "The Boiler." "The first time we heard it, Jerry played it to the band and a couple of the guys were acting it out in bad taste," says Roddy Byers. "We were all gobsmacked. Like you do when you're horrified: you try to make light to deal with it. The Specials had been this happy-go-lucky ska punk band and the next time we went back to America we're suddenly playing all this weird jazzy stuff which you can't dance to, and we're doing 'The Boiler.'"

Initially making a rough demo at his flat with John Shipley on guitar, Jerry then produced a version of "The Boiler" at Horizon Studios in a single day in January 1981. "That was the first thing we did as the Special AKA," says Shipley. The backing track featured a padded electronic drum kit—recently purchased by John Bradbury—and a new bassline rewritten and played by Nicky Summers. "Jerry wrote this music specially," Rhoda told *Record Mirror* a year later. "We just kept the piano riff, which was stolen from somewhere anyway. Jerry's music sounds like a soundtrack from a film." In its original extended version, the song featured Dick Cuthell impersonating a police officer interviewing the survivor of a sexual attack. "The idea was that he was victim-blaming," says Paul Heskett. "I think Dick had mixed feelings about it, and the idea was cut."

The Special AKA's "The Boiler" sleeve bag, January 1982.
Courtesy of Chrysalis Records/Jerry Dammers.

To visualize its harrowing content, Jerry invited Lizzie Soden to make a video of "The Boiler." Working at the Super 8 Workshop in Leicester, Soden devised a storyboard with Steve Binnion. "We wanted to explore that rape was fundamentally about violence against women as opposed to sex, and to use images of passive women and violent men from mainstream media as a metaphor." Largely inexperienced and with a budget of £500, Soden recalls the embarrassment when the crew asked for a shooting script. "I was like, 'It's all in my head!'" Admitting to "making it up" as she went along, Soden corralled friends to participate in an opening nightclub scene. "It was very homemade," she says. "Everyone we knew was in it." Notable for the absence of the perpetrator in the reconstruction, the video offered images from the point of view of the female protagonist: walking the empty streets, *no cars, not even the occasional stray animal*. At the song's climax, the screen fills with a random selection of juxtaposed images of violent men and passive women—recorded off the television—depicting misogyny in its wider social context.

When the video was broadcast, 2 Tone received a letter from a "Mother and Baby" campaign group threatening to sue the label for use of unlicensed footage. Pete Hadfield directed the complaint to Soden. "That was a good move," she laughs, "because I was a student and I didn't have any money!" A second airing on Tyne Tees TV resulted in the end collage sequence being replaced by a silhouette of a man raping a woman, in this instance much to the anger of Soden: "It was against everything we wanted."

Affronted by its amateurism, Rhoda bluntly declares, "The video was shit. It was Jerry's fucking stupid idea to get an art student to do a film who doesn't know anything." Rhoda's opinion of the single sleeve was little better. Based on an illustration showing the survivor of the song screaming—"loosely based on Rhoda," says Jerry—it was offset by "flowery" typography. "It was a hateful cover," spits Rhoda. "It was a white woman and I wasn't. I really objected to that. It was going to be a painting by Magritte called *The Rape* but his widow wouldn't agree to it being used, so it could have been a lot worse. At least it was quirky." The song was credited on the sleeve as "Based on an original by the Bodysnatchers," and Nicky Summers is similarly indignant: "It was *written* by the Bodysnatchers!"

As uncompromising and profoundly disturbing as "The Boiler" was, Doug D'Arcy says, "To be honest, I didn't get the importance of what Rhoda was saying at the time. The change in feminism and women's rights since then has been extraordinary. It's because of records like 'The Boiler' that started it moving along. It was a good thing to have done but I didn't get the relevance of the record as much as I would now." Reflecting on Chrysalis's willingness to issue such a controversial record, Julia Marcus argues that Jerry had a "huge amount of creative freedom . . . you weren't about to turn around and say to somebody who had been involved in one of the most successful singles in the company's history ['Ghost Town'], 'We can't release that.'"

Incredibly, "The Boiler" climbed the UK pop chart over three successive weeks and nestled in the top forty. Accused of banning the record, BBC Radio 1 issued a statement to the contrary, pointing to two plays on John Peel's evening show, and two on Richard Skinner's early evening program, including Saturday's *Rock On* review slot. "But it is unlikely that it will get future plays unless it crops up in some other context," the BBC stated, adding that the record "is unsuitable for normal radio play."

This was an era where women featured in the charts typically as backing vocalists or duetting with men. The subject of songs ranged from the escapism of Buck's Fizz ("The Land of Make Believe") and the chirpy Altered Images ("I Could Be Happy") to the romantic sagas of Dollar ("Mirror, Mirror [Mon Amour]"), Abba ("One of Us") and Anna Maria leading the Mobiles through the synth fairground pop and lyrically vapid "Drowning in Berlin." To their credit, Chrysalis backed "The Boiler," unlike their rivals Polydor who only months earlier deleted "Spasticus Autisticus" by physically impaired Ian Dury in the International Year of Disabled People when the BBC deemed the record "offensive."

When "The Boiler" was released on January 8, 1982, Jerry described it as a new concept: the "listen once only" single. Performing a live vocal over a prerecorded backing track on the *Oxford Road Show* while struggling to read the lyrics scrolling on a monitor out of sight of the audience, Rhoda danced uncomfortably. There followed a panel discussion where Rhoda sat beside Carolyn Schofield (lawyer for the Rape Crisis Centre) and presenter Jackie Spreckley on a red sofa. Making reference to a recent trial in which John Allen had been convicted of rape at Ipswich Crown Court and Judge Bertrand Richards found the seventeen-year-old "victim . . . guilty of a great deal of contributing negligence," Rhoda sighed heavily. After she recounted another recent case of a guardsman not convicted of rape because "it might ruin his career . . . never mind the girl's life," the discussion ended with two young girls demonstrating karate moves as a means of self-defense against male violence.

CHAPTER 33
THE FEELING'S GONE
THE APOLLINAIRES

By 1982, 2 Tone was operating out of a rented two-room office under the arches of a business park in Spon End, Coventry. But where three years earlier the ad hoc running of the label had an endearing charm—effectively operating out of Jerry's bedroom in Coventry and a small office in London—its standing in the heady days of eighties pop excess was almost embarrassing "They used to send you headed notepaper with a label over the old address and the new one typed on," recalls Rhoda Dakar. "It was so shit."

A former entertainment secretary and president of the student union at Lanchester Polytechnic, Pete Hadfield had made his name locally by organizing a disco night playing new wave, punk and reggae. After agreeing to look after the Swinging Cats, his foray into management had barely lasted a fortnight before he accepted an invitation to become the Specials's tour manager. "Pete was great," says Roddy Byers, "a real working-class socialist. Jerry would tell him what he wanted and then Pete would have to talk to club owners or management or hotels and try to explain it in terms that they could understand."

Known not to suffer fools gladly, Hadfield was militantly protective of his artists. Straightforward, no nonsense: "You do it for this amount of money; get it done in this time." His long-term partner, Kate Butler, who was a fervent feminist with a fiery reputation, assisted him. "Pete and Kate had a very open relationship and very open arguments," says Tim Strickland, who since leaving the Automatics in 1978 had learned the basic art of bookkeeping. "They were a pretty volatile pair and Kate did the administration and ran the office when it was a cottage industry."

One day, talking to Jerry Dammers, Lizzie Soden suggested two groups he might be interested in listening to and handed him a couple of cassette tapes. The first contained the music of a band from Manchester called the Frantic Elevators, led by a flame-haired young soul singer. Jerry took no further action. "Years later, he joked that he could have made loads of money," says Soden, "if only he'd signed the band and the future front man of Simply Red, Mick Hucknall."

Soden's second recommendation was a soul/funk outfit from Leicester called the Apollinaires. Formerly known as Il Y A Volkswagen, the group had released a single on Rough Trade in 1981. Its solitary review contained a memorable put-down in *Sounds*. "'I'm Going to Kill Myself,'" wrote the reviewer, "morose Midlander's promise to do us all a favor."

The Apollinaires: (L–R) James Hunt, Tom Brown, Paul Tickle, Kraig Thornber (sitting), Francis Brown, Simon Kirk, circa 1982.

On Prince Charles and Diana's royal wedding day, July 29, 1981, the group renamed themselves the Volkswagens, before settling on the Apollinaires,* around the nucleus of Leicester Polytechnic art students Paul Tickle and brothers Francis and Tom Brown. Having left school and failed an audition to get into the Royal Academy of Dramatic Art, Kraig Thornber was working in a supermarket, uncertain of his future. "I used to go and watch the gigs. They had a drum machine. I said, 'Well, I've always wanted to be a drummer.' They said, 'Come along to a rehearsal.' I turned up and all I had was a pair of drumsticks."

Celebrated as the industrial center of socks and hosiery, Leicester was also infamous as the birthplace of the National Front. In 1976, more than 14,000 people voted for the right-wing party in the city's local elections, winning 18.5 percent of the poll and, in some areas, finishing third above Labour. The immigrant population in Leicester—estimated at 40,000 (20 percent of the population)—was mainly Asian and refugees from Uganda. Leicester had never been an epicenter for musical awakenings until the early seventies, when the city gave rise to the progressive rock band Family, and soon after the invincible fifties revival act Showaddywaddy. In 1982, ripples of a burgeoning scene prompted *Melody Maker* to suggest a resurgence of Leicester groups. "They tried to build it up that there was a happening scene," says bass player James Hunt. "There wasn't." Nevertheless, on Monday, January 25, Jerry Dammers and Pete Hadfield went to see the Apollinaires play at the Horsefair in the city center. Liking what they saw, Jerry organized a gig a month later at Guys in Coventry, described as "an old gay club with walls like a cave" by Kraig Thornber.

Keen to see how they fared in front of a less partisan audience, the band, dressed in checkered shirts, passed the audition. "We went down well so Jerry got us in the studio," marvels Tom Brown. Not quite, recalls James Hunt. "We played a disastrous gig at Lanchester Poly," he

---

* They took their name from their favorite French cubist poet, Guillaume Apollinaire. The moniker was also a subtle reference to Elvis Presley's vocal backing harmony group, the Jordanaires.

insists, "but Jerry really liked 'The Feeling's Gone' and agreed to do something." In their favor, manager John Kehoe and Pete Hadfield had been students together in Coventry. "We had quite some enmity," says Kehoe of his former Socialist Workers Party comrade. "Pete was good at talking and getting results. He went from being a Trotskyist to a grade one capitalist." Comanager Tony "Curly" Cheetham remembers Hadfield as "quite thin" with a "pointy face, quite vulpine, like a fox. He was a proper businessperson with a proper business head. He wore button-down shirts, smart trousers and loafers, as I recall."

The Apollinaires were far from rude boys. Indeed, far from ska. It was to their advantage. "We were a bit scared that it might go against us because of their old image," noted singer Paul Tickle. He need not have worried. 2 Tone was changing. It required a fresh, contemporary sound to reinvigorate the label. "We went to 2 Tone because they were genuinely interested in us and we liked the label," guitarist Francis Brown told *NME*'s Adrian Thrills. "We never really thought about the image. Neither Jerry or Pete seemed particularly keen to push that aspect of 2 Tone."[146] Sealing the deal at the bizarrely named Elastic Inn, the band convened at Jerry's house on Albany Road. "I went in the downstairs front room and on the mantelpiece were uncashed checks lying on top," recalls James Hunt. "There was one for £650,000. Pete said, 'Oh! That's just the royalties from Japan for 'Ghost Town.' There was all this money just lying there. Pete opened this cupboard and there were boxes of 2 Tone singles by Elvis Costello."

Leaving the band to discuss music matters, Hadfield took Tony Cheetham aside to address practicalities. "He started talking to me about being a manager and what I needed to do and how I needed to get myself organized: 'This is what a manager ought to do; these are the kind of people you need to contact. You need to think about setting up gigs. Make sure you mention that you've just signed to 2 Tone and you're going to be making a single.' Then he said, 'And what's your phone number?' I go, 'I don't have a phone.' He said, 'Right. We need to organize that, too.'" Known to most as Curly, on account of his unmanageable locks, Tony Cheetham had attended the same school as singer Paul Tickle and shared a large Victorian house where the band rehearsed in the basement. "Paul and Frank were very ambitious. They'd got a vision about what they wanted to do. I had no idea. I wasn't very organized or particularly employable. I'd worked as a laborer in factories since I'd left school, and as a gardener. I was just a street kid really, a bit airy-fairy. I wasn't an ambitious or business-minded person but I was obsessed with music."

The six core members of the Apollinaires signed a two-single deal with an option on a third. Under the agreement, 2 Tone would pay for the recording sessions, packing and distribution, and costs would be recoupable. "That was the ethos with a lot of the smaller record labels," says Curly. "Send us a tape and if we think it's okay and good enough quality, we'll put it onto a disc."

Using the meager advance (about £5,000) to buy new equipment, the band readied themselves to record at Horizon. Then, after hearing the shocking announcement of an offer to play and tour with the Thompson Twins, Kraig Thornber says, "I had to go to the band and say, 'Sorry, guys, but I'm just going to fuck off for six weeks.'" Spotted playing percussion and dancing in a previous band, Thornber had joined a program of movement training organized by the pop duo. "There were three of us. It wasn't eyes, tits and teeth dancing, it was more like performance art with masks, martial arts and animal movements. Then this actor came up to work with us called Tim Roth. He arrived in Leicester with about six quid to his name. Stayed in our house for two weeks. We fed him. Bought him beer. Then he fucked off to do *Metamorphosis* in London. Everyone was like, 'What a fucking cunt!'"

Obligation fulfilled, including a last date at the Hammersmith Palais on April 12, Thornber rejoined the Apollinaires a week before a six-day session was booked at Woodbine. "I was so excited," he says, recalling his first time in a recording studio. "I turned up with the cheapest Premier Olympic drum kit that I'd bought secondhand out of the newspaper and somehow Jerry managed to get a reasonable sound out of it." Slow to find the groove, James Hunt freely admits that he was not a very good bass player. "I must have smoked about ten packets of cigarettes. I was trying to slap pathetically. They gave me so many chances to do it. And the more I couldn't do it, the more nervous I got. Eventually, Jerry came in, de-tuned my bass down an octave on the bottom E string, and said, 'Do this, *boom, boom*, in time.' You can hear it on the single. I'm amazed they didn't kick me out the group after that."

Written by Francis Brown, "The Feeling's Gone" was a live favorite. "It was about a girlfriend he'd had since he was thirteen," says his brother Tom, who arranged the structure of the music. "She'd gone to Warwick University and keeping the relationship at a distance proved impossible." The basic track recorded, John Barrow, Gaz Birtles and Dean Sergeant of the Swinging Laurels added complementary brass. Alto sax player Birtles remembers Jerry wearing a tweed suit jacket with a five-inch round badge of the pope on his lapel. "We had to do the brass over and over again. There's a part where it's stabbing on the offbeat in different weird places and Jerry was there, pointing, 'NOW . . . NOW . . . NOW!' We were like, 'Fucking hell!' tripping over ourselves. I remember thinking, *Are we ever going to get this?* We were there for hours trying to do the whole sequence in this strange time signature that Jerry had just made up off the top of his head."

Agreeing that it was by no means an easy session, John Barrow says, "Jerry was a pedantic perfectionist. He got us jumping through hoops." At one point, Jerry positioned an ambient microphone inside a grand piano and asked each of the musicians to play phrases into the open lid. "It was a clever idea," says Barrow. "The sound was bouncing onto the harp of the piano and creating this resonance." Less experienced, saxophonist Peter Millen was in awe recording in a professional studio for the first time. "Two months earlier, I'd been playing the sax in my bedroom and then I was in a studio with Jerry Dammers. Woodbine had the most amazing sound system so everything sounded fantastic. I remember thinking, *We are the best group ever!*"

During the session, Jerry asked Millen if he knew anybody who played the flute. "I said, 'My best mate Stephen. He lives upstairs in our house.'" Studying for his last year at college to be a silversmith and shocked when asked to play on the session, Stephen Leonard-Williams says he met Jerry and was alarmed. "He had no front teeth," he laughs. "He was the most laid-back person ever. He didn't give me any clues what I was supposed to do. I was like a rabbit in the head-lights. I did it a few times and at the end he said, 'If I'd met you earlier you could have done the flute on 'Ghost Town.'"

To add a final touch to the track, Jerry invited Dick Cuthell to play cornet and Rhoda Dakar to add backing vocals on the chorus. "Jerry was like an artist seeing the canvas: 'We just need a touch of this or a little touch of that,'" says Thornber, who also recalls Rico arriving from London on the train. "He added some trombone, and we were laughing because he doesn't say, 'I want a tea or a coffee,' he goes, 'Me want coffee tea.'"

Speak to any member of the Apollinaires and very soon an anecdote about Jerry arises. "He was dead quirky," the band told journalist Jim Reid. "He'd always turn up late and with no money. We came down to London with him once and we had to keep paying for him on the tube 'cos he'd left all his money at home. In the studio, he'd close his eyes for ages. I always thought he'd dropped off, but he was only thinking because all of a sudden he'd jump up and shout out some new ideas."

While Jerry mixed the track, the Swinging Laurels departed for a prior engagement with the Fun Boy Three. "I heard you've been working with Dammers?" Terry Hall asked John Barrow. "It was how he said it. I thought, *I hope this isn't going to sour the session.** But he never said anything else."

---

* The Swinging Laurels added brass to "The Telephone Always Rings" on Thursday, March 18, along with a cameo by Sean Carasov, who utters the immortal line, "Hello," at the beginning of the song. According to Horace Panter, the opening verse—*It must be wonderful to live like you do*—was written about Jerry Dammers.

Prior to its release in July, "The Feeling's Gone" began to attract the attention of the media. Chastening any doubters, *Smash Hits* advised, "If you thought that 2 Tone had slipped out the back door recently, you'd be mistaken . . . The Apollinaires have whipped up a rich, supple and furiously energetic brew. My copy's already glued to the music center." Spinning the record on his late-night show, John Peel mused over its "interesting cacophony." A less-enamored scribe described it as a "mess from start to finish," deriding Dammers's production and "an empty shell of a song."

Perhaps nervous about securing a debut hit, Stephen Leonard-Williams now confesses to some old-fashioned record company malpractice. "We were told where to buy copies from the shops that were doing the chart count. We bought loads of them from Revolver by the market in Leicester. It looked like it was going to do well." This was not to be. The record failed to chart. "I think we got to 112," scoffs Thornber. "I remember going, 'That's pretty good!'"

Reeling at the disappointment, the band fired Tony Cheetham and replaced him with John Kehoe. Six feet tall, 250 pounds and with his head shaved, Kehoe was an imposing character. He describes himself as "a strange skinhead, communist punk . . . I used to wear a boiler suit, *Clockwork Orange* style, and eighteen-hole cherry-red Docs." Variously described as "humorous," "eloquent," "charismatic" and "a truly larger-than-life character," Kehoe was well read, had a passion for old maps and was acquainted with the less-than-legal life of the underworld. "John had run businesses," insinuates Cheetham. "He was much more of an entrepreneurial type. He'd got a drive which is not something I've ever had. I'll sit in a chair, me, and just look out the window and have a sandwich. I was a crap manager. I had no idea what I was doing. They rightly decided, 'We've had enough of this idiot.'"

CHAPTER 34

TEAR THE WHOLE THING DOWN

THE HIGSONS

In 1981, the Higsons traveled from Norwich to Bristol. When they arrived, they discovered the gig they had been booked to play did not have a suitable PA and would have to be canceled. In search of alternative entertainment for the evening, guitarist Stuart Mc-Geachin and drummer Simon Charterton located the legendary Dug Out club on Park Row. Inside they were surprised to see Jerry Dammers. Introducing himself, Stuart launched into an anecdote about Jerry's father, the dean of Bristol Cathedral, whom he had known as a schoolboy. Blustering into the conversation, Simon suddenly blurted out, "Why don't you produce our next single?" To his surprise, Jerry agreed. "That had been the way we had gone about everything," snuffles Simon. "Jerry was a legend as far as we were concerned. But we were out on a limb in Norwich and thought we were too distant from the trendy London/2 Tone scene."

The story of the Higsons begins four years earlier when, in 1977, Charlie Higson, a student at the University of East Anglia (UEA), formed a punk band with his wannabe-comedian friend Paul White-house. They called themselves the Right Hand Lovers, and any notions of pop stardom proved premature and the band soon flopped. Determined to start afresh, Charlie recruited Simon Charterton (a former member of the Alex Harvey Band), Colin Williams (of Wah! Heat), guitar player Dave Cummings and talented multi-instrumentalist Terry

Edwards. Combining the spirit of punk with a shared love of funk, the newly named Higsons released their debut single on the independent label Romans in Britain. In the *NME* end-of-year polls, Jerry Dammers voted the Higsons "Best New Act" while in the glossier pages of *Smash Hits*, Terry Hall elected "I Don't Want to Live with Monkeys" among his all-time top ten favorites singles. "It makes me laugh," he commented.

Shortly after, Terry Edwards spotted Hall at a Higsons gig in Victoria, London, and mustered up the courage to say hello and thank him for the recent accolade. Yet, despite its infectious banality and jaunty sing-along quality, the neatly wrapped two-minute single made little headway. It left the Higsons languishing in a state of flux, unable to make the step up from university funksters to pop star contenders. "Punk came and went pretty quickly so there was a definite sense of, 'What's the next movement?' opines Charlie Higson. "In the late seventies/early eighties, hip people got into dance music: ska, funk and white soul with a punk ethic behind it. That was the crossover we were doing: a scratchy urban white version of funk using a punk approach but probably slightly too fast to dance to."

Two further single releases followed—"The Lost and the Lonely" and "Conspiracy."* Then, on June 21, 1982, Jerry saw the Higsons play at the Holy City Zoo Club in Birmingham. Soon after, he offered the band a two-single deal with 2 Tone.† "We had a very loose arrangement," explains Simon Charterton, "where Jerry would produce one song and might do another one." The band had replaced guitarist Dave Cummings two years earlier, and Stuart McGeachin says it was exciting to be on 2 Tone: "We always had the sense that they all lived in a big house together. The Higsons were very much an indie band trying not to be. We wanted to step out and this was our chance."

Proposing they record the gloriously titled "Burn the Shit House

---

* Terry Edwards: "There was an after-a-few-drinks idea for Jerry Dammers to play keyboards on 'Touchdown' [B-side of 'Conspiracy'], but I think it was near to being done so it couldn't possibly have happened."

† The Higsons would be the first band signed to 2 Tone, with the exception of Rico, to have previously released records on another label.

Down (Before the Yanks Do)," Charlie Higson now explains it was a "protest song" commenting on the Cold War. "Reagan was president and was coming out with a lot of anti-Russian statements. It felt like America was trying to stir up trouble and maybe start another war. There was a feeling of, 'Well, let's smash everything to pieces before we get bombed by the Russians.'" Uncomfortable with the jingoistic sentiment, Jerry suggested the band change the song title. "He saw, quite rightfully," continues Charlie, "that we were not anarchist revolutionaries. We were a bunch of nice middle-class boys who had met at university and weren't about to start burning things down."

Furthermore, Terry Edwards was finding the whole experience "very strange. Without discussion, it seemed to have been decided that 'Tear the Whole Thing Down' was going to be the single. I could never hear it as a single. It was a solid thumping groove that was fun to play live but it didn't really have a hook. But Jerry thought he could make something of it; something of these five cats in a bag making a noise."

And so, in late summer, the Higsons traveled cross-country to Leamington Spa and, over two days, laid down their first recording for 2 Tone. Working with a recognized producer for the first time, Charlie says, there was a lot of excitement and the expectation that Jerry might do for the Higsons "what Langer and Winstanley had done for Madness, and say, 'If you do this, this and this, you're going to have a big hit.'"

Instead, the group stepped into an environment that was "chaotic and shambolic," recalls Stuart McGeachin. "Jerry was drinking and was a bit odd." To emphasize the Northern Soul backbeat and give the song a kick, Jerry attached a brass section to the introduction. "It was a bit piecemeal," complains Terry Edwards, who not only double-tracked all of the horn parts—trumpet, saxophone and trombone—but also added a plucked guitar melody over the opening bars as a guide. "When we heard the rough mix," titters Charlie, "Jerry had left the guitar mixed in with the brass. It sounded like a tinny Casio brass sound. Jerry could get fixated on details: he was meticulous about tuning and timing. We spent a bit of time cutting the song down to make it single length."

Midsong, a tremendous roar of thunder spectacularly announces itself over the rewritten chorus refrain, *Turn the whole thing down before the storm breaks.* The effect had been recorded on a cassette player held by Jerry outside his front room window and, by doing so, fulfilled a long-held ambition to replicate the thunderclap heard on the Doors's atmospheric 1971 hit "Riders on the Storm."

A rumble of pounding, high-pitched concert toms and a repetitive brass motif introduce the second track recorded by the Higsons.* Spirited by a deft, tongue-twisting roll call, "Ylang Ylang" called up poets and film icons—*Bob Dylan and Dylan Thomas, Man Ray and The Man with the X-Ray Eyes*—alongside writers and pin-ups—*Henry James, James Dean and Dean Martin.* The clever wordplay then summons *Martin Luther King* and the addendum *Kong; I'm climbing up the walls*, conjuring images of Hollywood's fictional furred beast scaling the Empire State Building. Such verbal dexterity perfectly suited the song's title, which to this day continues to elude definition among the various members of the band:

TERRY: "Ylang Ylang" was the name of a takeaway in Streatham that did a really good curry. The Higsons's van would stop there on the way to wherever. We just thought it was a funny name.

SIMON: It was an answer in the *Guardian*'s cryptic crossword which we used to do in the back of the van.

STUART: It was some sort of essential oil. Charlie came up with it.

---

* The Higsons toured in 1981 with Bow Wow Wow, who, like Adam & the Ants before them, used a similar rhythm. "We all got it from 'Burundi Black' [Burundi Steiphenson Black, 1971]," says Simon Charterton. "There was also John Kongos's 'He's Gonna Step on You Again' and 'Neanderthal Man' by Hot Legs. The beat is really in your face."

CHARLIE: Ylang is some kind of tree or a shrub from Asia with a distinctive scent. It was Colin's idea. He liked the sound of it. It has no meaning beyond, and had nothing to do with the song.

Recording completed, the group headed back to Norwich where Colin, Simon and Terry were studying for their finals. Weeks passed without word from Jerry. "We were thinking, 'He's put a lot of work into this! This is going to be amazing,'" says Charlie. "We eventually got his mix and it sounded exactly the same as what we'd heard before we left."

The band were still keen to press ahead with the record, but there was further consternation when Chrysalis took umbrage with the multicolored illustration designed by Charlie for the artwork. Credited to the nom de plume René Parapap, the vivid, two-foot-square painting presented images of nuclear warheads branded with fatalistic warnings, "Death," "USA" and "USSR," surrounded by a cast of skeletal figures, a caricatured soldier brandishing a machine gun, and ambiguous slogans declaring, "Riot," "Slum" and "Entropy." "It's like a schoolboy's idea of an agitprop poster," explains Charlie. "I tried to make it look colorful and fun." Balking at the expensive reproduction costs, Chrysalis subtracted the additional outlay from the band's royalties. Furthermore, in a subtle attempt to progress the identity of 2 Tone, the inner printed label changed from black-and-white checker squares to a brown and gold imprint and disposed of the rude boy figure, Walt Jabsco.

Released on October 29, 1982, "Tear the Whole Thing Down" was the Higsons's first overt attempt to register a pop hit. "Jerry saw that," says Stuart McGeachin, "but as it turned out, it wasn't a great record, and it wasn't a hit." Expressing disappointment, Charles Shaar Murray singled out, mistakenly, "synth brass instead of steam-powered brass and a vocal instead of solos," and informed *NME* readers that the Higsons's live sound had translated poorly to vinyl. "The song is virtually nonexistent, the rhythms sound flustered and nervously hectic, and the production is simultaneously cluttered and unvarnished. Everyone concerned could do better."

Ad for the "Tear the Whole Thing Down" single, October 1982. Courtesy of Chrysalis Records/Jerry Dammers.

Elsewhere, *Melody Maker*, while praising the record's production, "which at times sounds lovely," condemned the lead vocal: "It slightly spoils it when you've got some bloke whining away who has *not the foggiest idea* of how to sing." Already self-conscious and susceptible to criticism, not least from the band "taking the piss" all the time, Charlie cut the review out and kept it in his wallet for many years to come. "I'm technically not a good singer," he says with touching self-deprecation. "My singing was mostly high-pitch grunting. It worked live but it was hard to record. It was a reminder to self, *Don't get ideas above your station.*"

Breaking ranks to criticize the record's "cold" production, Charlie told *Record Mirror* that the BBC were refusing to play their new single on daytime radio. "They say it's too political. We decided to tone down the title and chorus of the song so we could get radio play. It makes you wonder how bland, stupid and inoffensive you've got to be to get played on the radio." Privately, the band admitted that "Tear the Whole Thing Down" was not strong enough to be a hit, but nonetheless felt entitled to whinge about the lack of record company promotion. "Chrysalis probably thought, 'Are they going to make any money for us?'" says Stuart. "Is it worth us throwing money at?' They talked about doing a video and then they didn't." Doug D'Arcy answers the charge with a metaphor: "It's like gardening: you plant things and sometimes they grow up nicely and sometimes they don't. There's a lot of trying things in different directions to see if it can grow." Roy Eldridge remembers, "We were prepared to back them. But we didn't A&R 2 Tone signings. Jerry had artists that he wanted to help and put records out by, and we were happy to go along with that."

As Christmas decorations began to appear in the Chrysalis office, "Tear the Whole Thing Down" topped the Independent Labels Airplay chart. It provided some brief but welcome cheer.

CHAPTER 35

PUT PEOPLE FIRST

ENVY THE LOVE. RUN ME DOWN

With a single now out on 2 Tone, the Apollinaires were confronted by audiences bedecked in faded Fred Perrys and dog-eared trilby hats. "We were booked to play in the Isle of Dogs and it was full of skinheads," recalls John Kehoe. "They were expecting ska and an eleven-piece jazz funk band gets up. The boss was in a dinner suit with white pumps. I went to get paid and there was a bad feeling. He sat down with these two fucking huge guys standing behind him, and said to me, 'Right, you cunt. Do I really have to explain why I'm not going to pay you? Fuck off!'"

Spotted at an Apollinaires gig in London, Terry Hall and David Byrne (Talking Heads) watched impassively as the brass section teased the audience with the opening riff from "Gangsters." With a view to rekindling the tours of the past, 2 Tone raised the possibility of a US double headline featuring the Higsons and the Apollinaires to introduce the label's new signings. "I don't know how serious it was," considers saxophonist Laurence Wood, conscious of the fierce rivalry between the two bands. "People were saying, 'Wouldn't it be great if we could do this?' The Higsons were a few steps beyond us, but everybody thought they were going to do really well."

On December 15, 1982, the two bands appeared together at a doubleheader at London Polytechnic in Aldgate East. Remembering the evening for perhaps the wrong reasons, Stuart McGeachin says, "England were playing a Euro qualifier against Luxembourg, which we won 9–0. We were watching the match in the pub next to the college and were a bit late, so we missed the Apollinaires." But where Terry Edwards insists it was the only time both bands played together, John Kehoe recalls a mini-tour of four or five dates coupled with a distinct lack of stablemate camaraderie. "It was trying to update the first 2 Tone Tour with a 1982 flavor. We were like, 'Why are you putting us with them?' We didn't see any kudos in playing with the Higsons. I'm sure the feeling was mutual."

Interviewed by *NME* in 1982, singer Paul Tickle discussed the Apollinaires's relationship with their record label. "As a band, I think we're all quite happy to be on 2 Tone. We don't feel a great deal of pressure because of the label's past history. We're certainly not a ska band, even if we do still get people turning up at our gigs in rude boy clothes and ska T-shirts. What 2 Tone are looking for now are groups like us and the Higsons who can establish our own identity. At the same time, I think we can help change the way that people look at 2 Tone."[147]

On August 25, the Apollinaires gave a taste of what they had to offer when they secured a coveted John Peel session. Recording four songs, including "The Feeling's Gone" and their new single "Envy the Love," the band were joined by Dick Cuthell on cornet and Paul Heskett on saxophone. Three days in the making, "Envy the Love" had been a challenging experience, leaving the band unhappy with the cleaner and more radio-friendly production. "It was slick but lacked some of the grit and soul of our live sound," says alto sax player Pete Millen. "It was too sanitized."

Ahead of the song's release in October, James Hunt says, a few members of the band thought the B-side, "Give It Up," should have been the lead track. "Definitely not," said Pete Hadfield. "It's an open goal for reviewers to say, '"Give It Up": yeah, why don't they?'"* Nonetheless, expectations were riding high when Radio 1 DJ Dave

---

* A few months later, KC & the Sunshine Band scored a monster hit with their own song called "Give It Up." "It was a far catchier tune," says Hunt.

Lee Travis made "Envy the Love"* pick of the week on his popular morning show. True to form, the self-anointed "Hairy Cornflake" saw mileage in parody and took to interjecting, *Fish, fish, fish and chips,* in a rap style over the more tasteful and original lyrics, *Shake, shake, shift the shaft.* Whether people were put off by the unwelcome lampooning or simply unmoved by the track itself, sales slumped. "It's all about timing," muses John Kehoe. "Somebody told us—either the girl at Chrysalis or Pete Hadfield—'Another week of good sales and the plugger will go to work and you'll be Record of the Week.' It never happened. It was all jam tomorrow. Chrysalis was having problems because Blondie's 'War Child' had bombed. Apparently, there was some corruption involved with money, cocaine and a DJ at Radio 1." Though the band had been led to believe the single was selling 10,000, possibly 20,000, it was later discovered it had sold 3,700 copies. They were shattered.

By 1982, 2 Tone was hemorrhaging money and Chrysalis was rapidly losing interest. "It was a weird half relationship," says John Kehoe. "We were on 2 Tone but had to deal with Chrysalis. Who do you talk to? Chrysalis had had enough of Jerry. When you've had enough of the breadwinner, it drizzles out. We said to 2 Tone, 'Is there a third single?' 'Wait and see.' Nobody shat on us: they just forgot us." Bass player James Hunt says he has no recollection of collective disappointment. "We weren't massively ambitious or driven. Maybe that was part of our downfall. We were quite amateur, which was part of the postpunk thing: anyone can do it; design your record yourselves. At the end of the day, we didn't want it badly enough. All the music was hammered together by people pratting around. 'Oh, that sounds interesting'; hours fucking around in a recording studio and the art-student vibe of, 'Oh, just let it happen.'"

In time-honored fashion, the group turned on one another. Ac-

---

* The artwork for both of the Apollinaires's singles was based on cigarette packets: "The Feeling's Gone" (designed by Paul), John Player Special; and "Envy the Love" (designed by Frank), Rothmans.

cused of being overly ambitious, Kraig Thornber prefers to see it as people misreading what they perceived as nagging. "I'd always be telling people what to do, 'Can you be here for this?' 'Can you do this?' 'Can you help me load up?'" Matters came to a head during an ill-fated excursion to Paris. It came after an argument at a freshers' ball at the University of East London when a fight between Kraig and percussionist Simon Kirk left the former hospitalized: the result of Simon throwing a cowbell at Kraig's face, splitting his lip open and smashing his front tooth in half. Driving to France, the band bombarded Kraig with balls of paper. Stressed at having to negotiate the Paris one-way system, Kraig then discovered Simon had smuggled a lump of hash through customs. "I was furious because he'd hidden it in our equipment. So later, to wind him up, I banged on his door and shouted, 'OPEN UP! POLICE!' I went in and shouted, 'Arrrggh. Got you!'" Terrified, Simon swallowed his drug supply. "We headed back to England," says Kraig, "and everything went south."

Dropped by 2 Tone, the band cut a final single. "'Put People First' was the first trade union–commissioned single," says Tom Brown. "This guy from NALGO [National and Local Government Officers' Association] came along to the recording desperate to get his voice on it. The record didn't do well but it got a lot of national coverage. Paul did an interview on the *Nine O'Clock News*. It was one of those designed-by-committee singles where you had to have a bit of everything in it; trying to please everybody but pleasing nobody." It was a fitting epitaph to the Apollinaires's short-lived career.

In a brazen attempt to be played on the radio and replace the regular introductory theme ("Picking the Blues" by Grinderswitch), the Higsons named their new instrumental track "John Peel's New Signature Tune" and posted a copy to the influential BBC Radio 1 DJ. The plan failed. Rejected by Peel, but ever resourceful, the Higsons duly tagged the instrumental onto the latter part of a new song called "Put the Punk Back into Funk."

Introducing the song with a high-pitched *1, 2, 3, 4*, Charlie Higson channels the squawked rolled vowels of Johnny Rotten—*Here we go now*—and sets in motion a manic psychobilly funk blast of punk fury. *Sell your soul*, he squeals like a rabid animal, *'cause all you need is money to buy your way into the charts*. Ending in a cacophony of spontaneous feedback, played by multiple guitarists, "Put the Punk Back into Funk" suddenly gives way to the sober and measured tones of the aforementioned "Part Two." Augmenting the ad hoc recording approach, inebriated members of the band gathered around a microphone and "chattered." "There was a Kool & the Gang record, 'Funky Stuff,' which was a big influence on the Higsons," explains Stuart McGeachin. "There's a bit where they all go *Paaaarrrtyy*. We were doing that, but we hadn't rehearsed it and everyone was doing it at a different time. It was meant to be chaotic."

Live, "Put the Punk Back into Funk" proved to be a popular set closer, often inciting fans to invade the stage clutching percussive instruments purloined from domestic kitchens and surreptitiously sneaked past unobservant security checks at venue entrances. "It was that attitude of, 'We're all the same,'" says Terry Edwards, proudly linking stage invasions at the Higsons's gigs to their predecessors, the Specials.

The B-side of their second 2 Tone single in the bag, there was much anticipation for the lead track, "Run Me Down." Taking over duties from Jerry Dammers, producer Warne Livesey recorded the Higsons in a twenty-four-track basement studio at Wave Recording in Hoxton Square (later the home of Blue Note). "Run Me Down" is described by Charlie as "more of a step forward into what we wanted to sound like. It was technically more proficient but with a funk edge." And with an eye on its potential commercial appeal, a Motown-influenced guitar figure reminiscent of the Supremes's "You Keep Me Hanging On" was added and complemented by a bank of seductive pop harmonies courtesy of session vocalist Tessa Niles, later seen sharing a stage with David Bowie at Live Aid.

Thrilled with the results, the band invited an outside designer to produce a "classy-looking record cover" in full color, presenting a young woman robed in a patterned flowered dress, dark sunglasses and a headscarf, invitingly stepping out of a fifties automobile.

The Higsons: (L–R) Charlie Higson, Colin Williams, Simon Charterton, Terry Edwards, Stuart McGeachin, July 1983.

Expectations were high. Then came the crushing reviews. Comparing the music to "a Land Rover revving in the mud," *NME* decreed: "The Higsons have sounded careless and superficial in the past, and now seem to be in a terminal stupor." *Melody Maker* labeled it "the same old boring Higsons song," snidely determining, "They deserve to be remembered—if remembered at all—as the Freddie & the Dreamers of the Brit-funk revival." Joining the queue of dissenters, *Smash Hits* poured scorn over their "scratchy sound," memorably stating that "Run Me Down" was "as funky as beef tea." "There were some bad ones," concedes Simon Charterton, "almost *Spinal Tap* style: 'The only thing I've got against the Higsons is them daring to exist in the same century as I do.' It might as well have said, 'Shit sandwich.'"

Worse was to come when fellow students at UEA, Haircut 100, made a guest appearance on Radio 1's *Roundtable*. "We thought we were quid's in," says Charlie, "then they slagged us off. They were scathing and said, 'If you're going to do a record like this, you really do need to keep it in time.' I thought, *Thanks, mate.* They were caught up in the excitement of being music critics for a day."

On the upside, "Run Me Down" unexpectedly attracted American college radio attention. Although only available on import, the extended version sold a healthy 5,000 copies, leading to an invite to play in the States. "It was impressive," reflects Terry Edwards. "I remember talking to Jerry after and he said, 'You kept that one ['Run Me Down'] from me!'" But back in England, the record stalled outside the Top 100. Once again, fingers pointed at Chrysalis and to the lack of promotion. But as Charlie astutely observed, "It felt like as long as Jerry was releasing records, we had a relationship with the label." The trouble was, Jerry was living on borrowed time.

And so, in 1984, the Higsons released their debut album, *The Curse of the Higsons*, on Upright Records, including "Run Me Down." It did little to ignite a flagging career. "That would have been the 2 Tone album," reflects Terry. "Everyone, including ourselves, thought we were going to be the next big thing. But standing back from it all, I just wonder if the band was good enough. Peel said the reason he really liked us was because we had 'a nice sense of the unimportance of it all.' There were certain people who said, 'You've got to take this a bit more seriously.' I was always a serious musician, but I didn't see any reason not to don a Hawaiian shirt, put the punk back into funk and be very jolly. It was said that we were looking for a party that wasn't there."

"It was really exciting to be on 2 Tone," concludes Charlie. "We thought, 'At last, we're going to be big stars.' But 'Tear the Whole Thing Down' and 'Run Me Down' didn't have any more impact than any of our other singles. Like the fact that punk was only vital for a couple of years, the whole 2 Tone/ska thing within two or three years was seen as passé. The Higsons were an attempt by 2 Tone to say: 'Can we try a different direction?' Instead, we were the final nail in their coffin."

CHAPTER 36

THE LONG SUICIDE

SPECIAL AKA. IN THE STUDIO

In 1983, the Labour Party's election manifesto promised unilateral disarmament and renationalization. To the mainstream electorate it was a socialist program at the dustbin end of the Thatcher revolution. Shadow Home Secretary Gerald Kaufman famously dubbed it the "longest suicide note in history." He was not wrong. On June 9, the Conservative Party romped home to a second successive landslide, surfing a wave of popularity reignited by victory over Argentina in the Falklands. Almost half of those under twenty-six did not vote. Apathy was the new buzz word. In the three years between the release of "Ghost Town" and what would become the Specials's next album, *In the Studio*, the Fun Boy Three would release two top twenty albums and notch up a plethora of hit singles, including the hugely successful "Tunnel of Love" and "Our Lips Are Sealed." In the same period, Jerry Dammers was the equivalent of a dead man walking: incarcerated in the studio, and constrained by the amateurism of a newly revived band. "The Special AKA," he says, "was a nightmare."

Coming to terms with Terry, Neville and Lynval's departure, and shortly after Roddy's and Horace's resignations, Jerry says it was like "everyone abandoning ship. We'd already started on some rhythm tracks that were intended for the old band, so then we were left with the choice of abandoning it completely or carrying on."* After taking the difficult decision to enlist new members and move forward, it soon became apparent that the recent recruits had "different talents." Reflecting on the two-year growth that led to the first Specials album, Jerry bemoaned the difficulty breaking in a new lineup. "It's hard," he told *Jamming!* in 1984, "because you can't just go down the local pub and do gigs and develop naturally because there's so much attention.[148] Suddenly I was expected to find a whole new band, write a whole new album of songs, make songs out of Brad's and John Shipley's rhythm tracks, and neither of the singers could sing consistently in tune."

Determined to retain the political ideals of the original Specials, Jerry revived the moniker Special AKA as a link to the group's inaugural release, "Gangsters." If not defined by a written manifesto, the Special AKA stood for racial unity and a left-wing ideological stance. Pop for pop's sake, this was not. At twenty-seven, Jerry Dammers was maturing. "Some of the things you thought were great when you were younger you realize aren't. The whole rude boy thing got to be a pain, and with right-wing elements, it just got worse. Then in Dublin at the Stardust when there was loads of fights, I'd just had enough; I've tried to put all that behind me. I've never seen the Specials as a pop group. If you say pop, it automatically implies what you're doing is in order

---

* Shortly after recording "The Boiler," the Special AKA recorded two possible follow-up releases: The first was a former Swinging Cats song, known as "Greek Tragedy." "John Shipley's guitar sound was like a cross between the Shadows and Blondie's 'Atomic,'" recalls Paul Heskett. "It was an extraordinary song, but it didn't see the light of day." The second was a rap written by Rhoda, "Female Chauvinist Pig," described by John Shipley as "like a funky Isley Brothers thing." "It was bloody awful," insists Jerry Dammers. "The lyrics were directed at former members of the Bodysnatchers: *Liberated ladies curse male chauvinist pigs but does man realize there's a feminine version, she's it, FCP.* I didn't want to know. I was like, 'What is the point of that? It's not going to achieve anything at all.'" Asked by *Record Mirror* in 1982 to define her position on female chauvinism, Rhoda offered, "I'm more antisexist than definitely feminist. I don't know who this superwoman I believe in is but she's not this manipulative woman nor this separatist woman. I wouldn't presume to say separatism is wrong or anything. It's just not for me." Also scrapped was talk of backing poet John Cooper Clarke. "We were going to do one track," says John Shipley. "I'm not sure why it didn't happen."

to be popular and successful, it's basically the American Dream. But what the Specials have supposedly been about is working together for something better than personal success. A pop group is not going to do that. It would be nice to think that music wasn't particularly aimed at a teenage market, that it involved wider issues."[149]

Not a band in the traditional sense, the Special AKA were in effect a collective. While Jerry and John Bradbury were contractually obliged to Chrysalis, other musicians came and went or were paid on a retainer. Added to which, the strong sense of visual identity and musical purpose that had defined the original Specials was now in danger of becoming a millstone. "2 Tone had become so associated with a certain sound and a certain style of music that it was very hard to break out of that mold," Jerry said in 2008. "I made the mistake of going straight into the next album rather than going away and writing some songs. We went in there a bit unprepared, and it just went from bad to worse really."[150]

The first casualty was Horace Panter, who had committed to the Exegesis program. He says Jerry was "unbearable to be around." Further judging that Jerry was in the "process of falling to bits by this stage, trying to run the record label on top of everything else," Horace attempted to persuade him to take time off. "No," protested Jerry, "my frustrations have to come out in the music." Offering his own analysis, Jerry points to the destructive extent of Horace's new influence. "People don't understand just how dangerous Exegesis was and how completely it changed Horace."

As they worked on half-finished songs, the recording process descended into labored work practices and tit-for-tat gameplay. "I would arrive in good time," says Horace. "Brad would arrive at half past twelve [from London], accompanied as often as not by a bottle of vodka. Jerry would appear at about three o'clock and then want to go for breakfast. We'd start work around five." Urging him to stop the sessions and address the suffocating malaise, Horace says Jerry refused and subsequently watched in despair as his determination to continue turned into tunnel vision. "I was saying, 'Jerry, take a break.

Stop. Just leave it alone. Go away for six months and we'll start this again.' 'No, no, just fight through it.' It was unbearable, like going to a funeral every day. I was on £100 a week. I would have paid £100 a week *not* to be here." Deflated, he quit. "Horace's newfound impatience!" decries Jerry. "He had joined a really nasty self-assertiveness business cult. He was like a totally different person. The new Horace demands exactly what he wants and exactly when he wants it. It was disturbing and very stressful trying to either rescue him from the cult or relate to this new person. I couldn't do either."

Having played on three instrumental tracks—"War Crimes," "What I Like Most About You Is Your Girlfriend" and "Alcohol"— Horace was replaced by Gary McManus from new wave band School Meals, and latterly the Defendants, who Jerry coproduced a track for in March 1981. The new intake joined the band of semiprofessional musicians and soon added to Jerry's increasing frustration. Tempers flared. In vain, Jerry appealed to Chrysalis to release just singles for a year. They refused, insisting the contract stipulated an album. On they ploughed. Making a comparison to "painting the Forth Bridge," Jerry considered throwing in the towel. But convinced that there were ideas that would be "a shame to sling out," he told Gavin Martin, in an *NME* cover story appropriately titled "26,732 Hours in the Studio with Jerry Dammers," "It's just the fact that it was started . . . it had to be finished."[151]

With the band entrenched in the recording process, Chrysalis moved them to Wessex Studios in north London, owned by the record company. "They were just taking the money out of one pocket and paying it into another," protests Jerry. Not so, objects Roy Eldridge. Labeling him as a "control freak," Eldridge says, "Jerry had a vision and unfortunately it took forever for him to be happy with what he was doing. We had faith in him. He'd had incredible success with the Specials and the other hits we had on 2 Tone. He'd earned the right to continue being creative. We backed him."

Rhoda Dakar says that when she joined the group, all the backing tracks, apart from "Break Down the Door" and "(Free) Nelson

Mandela," were already recorded. "So that was the entire budget used up and then some. The album was called *In the Studio* because it took two years just to do all the overdubs." With relatively little previous studio experience, Rhoda recorded her vocals line by line. After the musicians arrived at the studio sometime in the afternoon, sessions would run regularly into the early hours. Recalling her contribution to "Alcohol," Rhoda says the session ran across three or four different studios. "Jerry would say, 'Can you just come in and do one line?' You'd do that and he'd say, 'Oh, that's really good. Do you think you could do this as well?' Then at three a.m., you would say, 'Look, I really can't sing anymore,' and he would say, 'You always give up.' I used to go home in tears. Many of us came out of that record with mental health problems. It was just awful. We were spending five days a week in the studio, in the dark, singing the same thing over and over. We were in a catatonic heap. It was a nightmare. Jerry was clearly ill. He was like the dead hand on it. My last day in the studio was sitting on the floor crying, rocking backwards and forwards. They had to call me a cab and take me home. It was a horrendous experience."

Reluctantly drawn into the debate, Jerry claims that Rhoda struggled to hold a melody. "We'd do loads of takes until one line was in tune and then move on to the next," he says, recalling a process that was stressful for both parties. "By the time we got to the end of the song, her voice had changed so we had to start all over again. It was a really bad situation." Jerry's mental fragility lay exposed; he felt compelled to operate at a musical level set by the Specials and expected by the press and media alike, while also facing his commitment to give up drinking. "The whole world was waiting but I was completely exhausted. There was so much pressure on me from everyone; I had lost the plot of what was really going on."

To the eye of an impartial observer, drug dependency littered the studio floor; where John Bradbury withdrew into himself and Gary McManus battled with heroin addiction, John Shipley says he succumbed to "a sort of breakdown. Somebody gave me a line of speed or something and it fucked me up for months. I wouldn't get on the train [to London] half the time. It was horrible. The repetition in the studio drove everyone nuts. It was like a form of Japanese torture: 'Do it again. Do it again.' There were three singers—Rhoda, Egidio [Newton] and Stan [Campbell]—and their voices didn't mix that well. I remember sitting in the studio listening to 'Break Down the Door' over and over for a month. Rhoda was in tears. Stan couldn't stand to look at Jerry. He closed the curtains between the live room and the studio. It was a nightmare. I should have gone when Horace left but I wanted to stay loyal."

Jerry Dammers, London, March 1984.

Former lead singer in Coventry group Channel A, Stan Campbell had always dreamed of pop stardom. "I thought it would be great: get on the road, have fun, go to parties, making lots of money. You don't think about any problems you have in the studio and things like that. I thought it was going to be America, Europe and having hit songs because I was working with this guy who wrote 'Ghost Town' and 'Too Much Too Young.' This guy who had started 2 Tone. It looked like a good move." More of a loner than a natural team player, the new lead singer challenged Jerry to write for a different voice. "With Terry there was a deadpan style of delivery which was more in tune with the way I felt," says Jerry. "I found it difficult to change and find lyrics that would suit Stan."

Distracted and restless, Campbell started an affair with the manager of Wessex Studios. "We were there that long he formed a long-term relationship with this older woman," laughs John Shipley. "We weren't supposed to know. But he turned up one day wearing her tartan trousers—'The game's up, Stan!'"

Allegedly accumulating £500,000 in costs, Chrysalis called time on the recording. "I never know when to stop," admitted Jerry. "I heard that when Francis Bacon does a painting, he keeps on putting more and more layers on so that it changes all the time. He has to employ someone to come in and grab it off him."[152] Whereas the first Specials album had taken two weeks to record and the second six months, the third—given the working title *Square One* and then *Obscurity Beckons*—pushed toward its third year in the making. Nevertheless, Jerry balanced the time spent on the record against the money Chrysalis had made from 2 Tone. "Maybe £2 million," he estimated. "So if they have to plough some of that back in when the going gets bad, when they didn't exactly do anything to dissuade the Fun Boy Three from leaving in the first place, then so be it. At the same time, it's not right that it costs that much. It must make people angry. I know it makes *me* angry."[153]

To plug the financial shortfall, Chrysalis released *This Are 2 Tone*, a compilation of sixteen A and B sides from the 2 Tone catalog. Presented in both pink and blue sleeves, the record—initially titled *2 Tone Chartbusters Vol. 1*—spent a healthy nine weeks on the UK album chart but peaked no higher than fifty-one. Greater hope rested on the Special AKA. When *In the Studio* was finally released on June 23, 1984, the timing of the wryly titled album could not have been worse. Not only was the country embroiled in a political standoff between the government and the National Union of Mineworkers, culminating in the infamous Battle of Orgreave which saw striking miners in a pitched battle against mounted police, there was also a nationwide industrial press dispute. Many, it transpired, were unaware that a new Specials record existed.

It was presented in a dense, blue-tinted sleeve reflecting the musical mood of the album and the familiar hallmarks of a Blue Note Records jazz sleeve. John Shipley says, "Originally we were going to call it *The Specials So Far*, with a picture of a sofa on the front cover." Instead, pieces of old recording equipment and instruments lined up in an empty recording studio. "No people. That sums it up," says Jerry. "Realistically, the Special AKA *aren't* as good as the old Specials. I was so sick of it by the time it came out . . . The thing is, people think two years in the studio, they think you're in there seven days a week for two years. Well, we *were*. Well, not quite, but everything that could possibly go wrong with it went wrong."

In the Studio was a peculiarly disparate album: a claustrophobic combination of African and Brazilian music mixed up with reggae, funk and Latin-influenced jazz grooves. Discussing the record's predominant melancholia, Jerry informed *Jamming!*: "There's two sides to it really. Some of it's political and some of it's more personal. I was really upset over the Specials splitting up and everything, so there's a lot of quite miserable songs on it. We had to wait till we got something a bit more positive like '[Free] Nelson Mandela' to finish it off with, otherwise it would have been all miserable! A lot of the tracks are great in the context of the LP, but they're not great singles; maybe we're more of an LP band."[154]

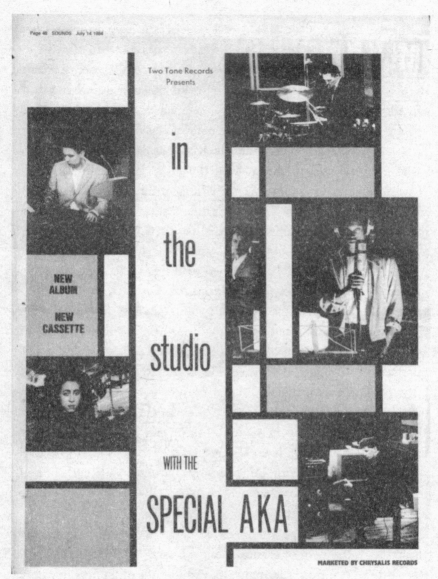

Ad for *In the Studio*, July 1984. Courtesy of Chrysalis Records.

In fact, prior to its release, five of the ten tracks on the album were issued as singles, and a sixth thereafter. Most dealt with their subject matter in uncompromising terms, and Jerry's decision to use songwriting as a means to address global political issues stretched the patience of more fainthearted fans. "War Crimes (the Crime Remains the Same)" protested against Israel's attack on a refugee camp in Lebanon on September 16, 1982. "The bombing of civilian targets in Beirut [Sabra and Shatila] was way over the top," Jerry told the *Daily Mirror* on December 21. "[The Israelis] are stooping to the same level as the Nazis."

The incendiary comment understandably drew much criticism, predominantly from Zionist and Jewish quarters. "There was no way I was comparing it to the scale of the Holocaust," cautioned Jerry. "I was saying that cruelty and the killing of innocent civilians is the same crime: wherever it is, whoever it is, whatever it is. The point being, can you tot things up in numbers like that? No innocent children should be killed under *any* circumstances."

A year earlier, Jerry had traveled to the Middle East to visit his brother, who worked for Oxfam in Beirut. On a trip to Cairo, Jerry was enamored by the spectacle of people dancing to a 5/4 rhythm. Captivated by the unusual time signature, more commonly associated with jazz, and the non-Western instrumentation on display, Jerry purchased a five-foot-wide cowhide drum. Returning to Coventry, he wrote a piece of music integrating a 5/4 rhythm with a reggae offbeat. "We'd been playing reggae for so long, I thought of trying to add something to it of my own, to use reggae with five beats to the bar instead of four. I've been taking piano lessons to learn the Latin American style of playing but I seem to naturally put seven beats in the bar instead of eight. Maybe," he joked, "it's because I've got one leg longer than the other."*[155]

In a scene worthy of a black comedy, "War Crimes"† was recorded with the help of session violin player Nick Parker, the son of a Jewish refugee from Germany. In a sudden fit of panic, Jerry beckoned Rhoda Dakar into the control room and blurted out, "I think he might be Jewish." Cautiously approaching the matter, Jerry asked

---

* Previous records to chart with a song in 5/4 timing included Dave Brubeck's "Take Five" (1959)—Rico performed the track live in 4/4, backed by members of the Specials—and Jethro Tull's "Living in the Past" (1969).

† Its working title, "Alphabet Lodge," came from the name of a house on the border of Coventry and Ansty.

Parker whether he was sure about playing on the track. Appalled by the recent bombings in Lebanon, Parker expressed his appreciation. "I'd had all those arguments about the difference between Zionism and Judaism and agreed with the sentiment of the lyrics." The public did not, however, and the record flopped. "Here's Christmas in the Special AKA," scoffs John Shipley of the winter release. "It wasn't exactly 'Jingle Bells.' It was commercial suicide."

Next up was "Racist Friend," demanding a severing of links with known racists: be it your sister, brother, cousin, uncle, best friend, husband, father, mother or lover. Based on personal experience, Jerry says, "I had a very good friend and he just persisted with these racist views. Eventually there came a point where I had to say, 'Enough is enough.'" Opening his address book, Jerry scribbled out the names of people whose prejudiced views he thought were unlikely to ever change. "You can't be a friend with somebody who is a racist, because you're supporting racism."

Provocative and disturbing, "Racist Friend" was designed to be an uncomfortable listening experience. Nevertheless, predictably, the uncompromising lyrical stance attracted no airplay and the single fell short of the Top 40. "People seem to think that if you ignore racism it will go away," commented Jerry, "but in fact they just ignored the record and the record went away." Maintaining that pop is "giving people what they want to hear," Jerry determined to give people "what they *don't* want to hear." After the Specials, he continued, "I went through a period where I wanted to say there's more to music than commerciality. You have to establish that you're also trying to create interesting music. But at that point, I didn't quite understand the implications of not having commercial success. I do now."[156]

Taking a swipe at pop's obsession with the cult of youth, Jerry asserted that it was a white American invention divorced from anything important. With George Michael and Andrew Ridgely in his sights, "Bright Lights" (issued with "Racist Friend") hollered, *Everyone goes WHAM! and has fun on the dole.* Angered by the rise of

Britain's latest carefree chart sensation, Wham!, Jerry blasted: "'Have fun. Don't worry about anything. Don't worry about not having a job. Don't worry about the future. Just stand up for yourself.' To me that's rubbish."[157] Written for lead singer Stan Campbell, "Bright Lights" read like a modern-day fable, describing the dream combination of moving to London and achieving pop stardom. In the second verse, fantasy gives way to the reality of work and rising anger on the streets—in this instance, Jerry's experience of coming face-to-face with a demonstration demanding an inquiry into the death of twenty-one-year-old Black man Colin Roach from a gunshot wound while in custody in the Stoke Newington police station in 1983.

To package the collection of songs presented on *In the Studio*, Chrysalis collated a commissioned set of nine promotional videos for VHS home release and the ill-fated LaserDisc format. "Chrysalis was at the forefront of promoting their artists and selling them as entertainment," explains film producer Danny Nissim. "Videos were good advertising, particularly if you could get them on *Top of the Pops*. And the television stations were getting high-value product for free." Brought in by Nissim as a cameraman, Jeff Baynes had previously worked on "Video Killed the Radio Star," "Turning Japanese" and a clutch of Madness videos, including "Baggy Trousers" and "Cardiac Arrest," for Stiff Records. "I was seen as a guy who was practical and could get on with musicians, so it was suggested I work with Jerry because I had a Midlands accent." With no overall budget, the record company paid for each video on a track-by-track basis. By eighties standards, the Special AKA investment was low. Where "What I Like Most About You Is Your Girlfriend" cost £10,500 and "[Free] Nelson Mandela" £12,500, "Pirates on the Airways" by Sunday Best featuring Pauline Black and Neville Staple totalled £18,500. Higher still, Debbie Harry's "Rush, Rush" commanded £20,000, Ultravox's "Dancing with Tears in My Eyes" £22,970, Spandau Ballet's "I'll Fly for You" £82,000, and "Wild Boys" by Duran Duran a staggering £250,000.

Storyboard for the Special AKA's "Girlfriend" video, 1984.

Viewing videos as an ideal platform for music promotion, Jerry meticulously drew each storyboard and turned to Baynes to interpret his ideas. "They worked very closely together," says Nissim. "They were on the same wavelength and shared the same sense of humor." "Alcohol" derived from the 1965 musical comedy *The Girl Can't Help It* starring Jayne Mansfield and Tom Ewell as an alcoholic who starts hallucinating. Cast as the femme fatale, Rhoda Dakar lay on top of Jerry's piano and crooned the lead vocal, *Heroin, why do you do it?* as brass instruments floated in and out of the picture. "Lonely Crowd" was filmed in the Wag Club and satirized London's posturing in-crowd. "It's sort of my version of 'Ain't No Love in the Heart of the City,'" says Jerry. "The other side of nightlife." Rumored to be about Terry Hall, "Housebound" was described by Jerry as a song "about an old friend who stays indoors all the time 'cos of the pressures of being a pop star." It was shot in the claustrophobic confines of John Shipley's flat, above a motorbike shop in Tottenham, and the closing frame zooms in on Buckingham Palace with its inherent connotation of wealth and isolation.

To support *In the Studio,* Chrysalis invested an estimated promotional spend of £9,000. "Considering all the time that had been spent on it, it was just ridiculous," Jerry lambasted. "The record company asks the computer, 'How much money will Jerry Dammers make?' And the computer says, 'Nothing.'" When the album spent a mere six weeks on the chart and reached no higher than thirty-four, its artistic merits did little to alleviate the financial disaster. When Chrysalis discovered there were to be no live dates to support the release, the frustration was palpable. "It wasn't a deliberate policy," said Jerry. "It just never really came together. There were a lot of problems, like the guitarist won't go on an airplane. And if we were gonna play live, we'd have probably played abroad first because there would have been too much pressure in England."

To breathe life into the album—notwithstanding the March top ten "(Free) Nelson Mandela," which provided the group with their only commercial chart hit—the Special AKA gave a late summer release to "What I Like Most About You Is Your Girlfriend." Cruel but gently comical, the song was written about a former rude boy on the Coventry scene and a girl named Nicolette who Jerry had a crush on. "She was going out with a guy called Francis who was a bit of a pain," reveals Lizzie Soden, "but Jerry used to talk to him so that he could get to know her." Francis was prone to boasting about his friendship with a pop star, and Soden says, "People would laugh at [him] behind his back."

Playing up to its comedic appeal, the song's accompanying video begins with a spaceship landing outside a nightclub. Intentionally lo-fi with a cheap, 1950s, B-movie, science-fiction quality, the lunar module was constructed from a three-legged stool with sparklers attached to the end and lowered to earth on a piece of fishing wire. Descending from an aluminum stepladder—to sound effects sourced from Delia Derbyshire and the BBC Radiophonic Workshop—a green-faced alien (Jerry), robed in a silver space suit, emerges. Inappropriately dressed, the extraterrestrial changes into black trousers, polo neck and shades—"de rigueur outfit for jazzbos of the period," says Jeff Baynes—and upon entering the club spends the evening chatting to a handsome sailor type in an attempt to reach his pouting blond girlfriend.

"It was hilarious," chuckles John Shipley. "Stan Campbell couldn't sing it as a ballad, so Jerry sang it trying to sound like Gregory Isaacs." Aware of his perceived miserable persona, Jerry commented, "It's difficult because it's not as if I can just sit down and write a silly sort of pop song. I've tried to do that and they're just terrible! If I try to write happy songs, they're just not convincing. I can only really write about things that make me personally angry, or that I feel strongly about."[158]

After making a rare live appearance on Channel 4's *Switch*, the Special AKA then popped up on the children's television program *Crackerjack*. It would be their last public performance. Presented by the ventriloquist Keith Harris, the group hatches an unsuccessful plan to kidnap Orville the Duck before performing a mimed version of "What I Like Most About You Is Your Girlfriend" to an audience of scouts and guides. "What a send-off!" laughs John Shipley. "They had an acrobatic troupe on from Morocco. I thought, *Right! I'll join in and do a cartwheel,* and ended up collapsed in a heap. After the program, we all got into separate cars. There was no communication."

The surprising commercial failure of "What I Like Most About You Is Your Girlfriend," which stalled outside the top fifty, cemented the ruin of the band. "Whatever music I do in the future has got to be a bit easier than this," lamented Jerry in August 1984, "because this has been a real grind and it should be a lot more enjoyable to actually play music. It may be too late, but I still feel proud of it. I think it's the lowest depths you can sink to because I was depressed about all sorts of things at that time. But in the future, I want whatever music I do to be a bit more upful."

CHAPTER 37

TWENTY-EIGHT DAYS OF MADNESS

THE FRIDAY CLUB. J.B.'S ALLSTARS.

In 1984, Jerry Dammers commented that 2 Tone had been "the kiss of death" for its most recent signings. "The days have long gone when having a record on the label would sell it," he said in an interview with the *Face*. "There isn't a 2 Tone sound anymore." But just as the label prepared to pull down the curtain on five fascinating years, Jerry signed the Friday Club. It was to be the final act in a thrilling drama. As the fat lady prepared to sing, the last company of 2 Tone players would exit in a gripping finale of tragicomedy, leaving in their wake a bewildering tale of misfortune and old-fashioned skulduggery.

The Friday Club belonged to Scarborough, described by founding member Michael Hodges as a "moribund mix of unemployment, grim nightclubs and street violence." Tribal division between punks, mods, rockers and Northern Soul factions was fierce. But when 2 Tone impacted, the cultural antagonism abruptly stopped. "It had a big effect on our audience," says Hodges. "2 Tone ended the civil war between middle class and working class. It changed everything." Together with guitarist and songwriter Andy Brooks, Hodges had been in bands since the age of fourteen and saw music as a way out. After several name changes and fluctuating lineups—"We used to do a cover of 'Nite Klub,'" informs bass player Graham Whitby—the Friday Club were formed in 1983, taking their name from a group of friends who got together on the fifth day of the week. "There was a sense that you could create your own micro-culture," says Hodges. "You didn't just have a band. You started clubs and played the records that mattered to you."

The Friday Club became one of the biggest bands on the scene and were soon securing bookings in nearby Leeds and Hull. Then, after recording an independent single, "What Is Soul?," they made a break for London.

Diagnosed with multiple sclerosis in later years, Adele Winter may have lost her ability to play piano but she still speaks with passion about her time in the Friday Club. The first to move to the capital, Winter encouraged the band to follow suit after a chance meeting with cofounder of the fashion shop Demob, Harry Cook. "Adele was going, 'Harry knows lots of people. We can do gigs and he could be our manager,'" remembers keyboard player Eddie Eave. With a checkered history running illegal warehouse parties, Cook promised that he could bag the band a record deal. The relationship with Cook would prove to be inflammatory and, over time, the harbinger of the Friday Club's downfall. "There are a lot of stories," teases Eave in a foreboding tone.

Playing clubs and picking up ad hoc support dates, the Friday Club attracted record label interest. On July 16, 1985, the group played a prestigious slot at the Alternative Top of the Pops held at the Camden Palais. The bill offered a tantalizing glimpse of tomorrow's stars, including Hipsway, Curiosity Killed the Cat and Swing Out Sister. Reviewing it in the *Observer*, John Peel was "very sniffy about us," says Michael Hodges, "but pretty much everybody else on the bill went on to be megastars." Laughing at the memory, vocalist Terry Bateman says, "As soon as the Pet Shop Boys came on with 'West End Girls,' you were like, 'Bloody Nora! We're not going to do any good here.'" In fact, Bateman was herself the subject of an advance from London Records wishing to sign her as a solo artist. Closing ranks, the group took affirmative action and, as Adele Winter recalls, "We told them to fuck off."

Nevertheless, record companies circled on sniffer alert. At one gig in Clapham, as many as five major record companies made their presence known. "It was looking fucking great," says Andy Brooks. "Dave Robinson at Stiff Records offered us a five-album deal. Then it went tits-up." When the label proposed including the group on a mod-influenced compilation album and a tour supporting the American ska-influenced band the Untouchables,* Brooks flatly refused. "It was everything we were trying not to be. Robinson went fucking ballistic and the feedback we got was the deal was off. Everyone was looking at me going, 'Great idea to say no, Andy!' I was thinking, *Fuck!*"

In danger of becoming record industry pariahs, the Friday Club discovered that Jerry Dammers was living two streets away near the Clapham North tube station "in this wonderful tenement block with fake Tudor beams on the outside." Bombarding his mailbox with demo tapes and gig flyers, Michael Hodges jokes, "Today it might qualify as stalking!" Curious, if not flattered, Jerry went to see the band play at the Railway Hotel in Brixton. Unaware of his presence, the Friday Club were having an off day. "We weren't far from giving up," acknowledges Hodges. "There were nine of us onstage playing to a barman. It wasn't one of those Broadway legends when someone comes in the dressing room and says, 'You won't believe who's here!' The gig was sparsely attended, so if anybody walked in you noticed them." After the gig, Jerry introduced himself and told them that he had never heard a band so woeful in all his life. "You're not only out of tune with each other, you're out of tune individually," he jested in his inimitable manner, "but I like the songs." With the band not knowing whether to be excited or despondent after playing such a wretched gig, a phone call the following morning offering them a record deal was as unexpected as it was joyous.

"It was a dream come true," beams Adele. "To get a deal with 2 Tone was everything you could want." "Absolutely unbelievable," agrees Terry, who since buying "On My Radio" and playing it over

---

* In 1985, Jerry Dammers produced the Untouchable's only UK hit single, "I Spy for the FBI."

and over in his sixth-form common room had been a massive 2 Tone fan. "I think everyone was sick of me. I just played it constantly. It blew your mind."

Choosing to record "Window Shopping," the Friday Club spent four days rehearsing with Jerry, arranging the song in a small studio in Clapham. In part, "Window Shopping" was a commentary on the dual effects of Thatcherism and consumerism. "When we emerged the full implications of the Tory agenda was clear," asserts lyricist Michael Hodges. "We came out of school and there was nothing. No jobs. Everyone was on the dole. Very few people escaped or went to university. We couldn't afford to go shopping." The idea for the song came from Andy Brooks, who shared a rented house with Hodges. Late one night, Brooks called upstairs and woke his sleeping flat-mate. Thinking it was the morning and he was therefore late for work, Hodges ran downstairs and started putting on his donkey jacket and work boots. "I've got a new song I want to play you," Brooks blurted out, clutching his acoustic guitar. "What time is it?" replied Hodges, half asleep. "Almost midnight," said Brooks. "Fuck off!" snarled Hodges and went back to bed.

Sessions began at Power Plant Studios, Willesden, home to recordings by Sade, Everything but the Girl, Working Week and Fine Young Cannibals.* "Half in fear and half in wonder," Hodges says of their producer, "for a man who appeared distracted and slightly daft away from the studio, once installed behind the mixing console, he became animated and utterly taken by the project, smoking unending cannabis roll-ups." Likewise smitten, Brooks says of Jerry Dammers: "The more time I spent with him the more his genius became apparent."

But when attempts to record a suitable drum take repeatedly fell short of the mark, Jerry's patience was soon tested. "After two days it was like, 'Forget it,'" says Brooks, thankful for Jerry's face-saving sug-

---

* Fine Young Cannibals were formed after the Beat split in July 1983 by David Steele and Andy Cox. Vocalist Roland Gift had once been a member of Hull ska band Akrylykz, which had supported the Specials, Madness and the Beat. Pauline Black remembers there was talk of signing Akrylykz and people wondering, "Might they be a good band on 2 Tone?"

gestion to program the rhythm track using a Roland drum machine. Subsequently, forced to record each instrument separately, Jerry opted to take a live feed of the bass from the studio's stairwell. To create a wah-wah sound, Jerry operated the foot pedal as Brooks strummed his guitar and marveled at the producer's "hands-on" approach. Next up, Adele added vibraphone. "They were from the forties," she laughs. "They were enormous. I played them with wooden beaters. Poor Jerry. I was playing it through, and he said, 'I think we might have to get something a bit more modern!'"

Having now spent ten days on the lead track and with studio costs rising, a decision to prepare an instrumental version of "Window Shopping" found favor over recording the proposed B-side, "The Easy Life." With the song augmented by a rudimentary "one note at a time" piano part, played as a guide for the lead vocal, Eddie Eave was aghast to hear it featured as the key melody line. Stunned by how long one track had taken to record, including a third week to mix, Andy Brooks says, "Sade was in the studio at the same time as us and recorded her second album in pretty much the same time we did 'Window Shopping.'" Adding to his despair, he says the finished track "was embarrassing. We were on the coolest label in the world and that was our contribution."

Exonerating Jerry—"He took the gamble because he liked the song"—Brooks says the general feeling was that a previous demo version recorded in Hull had captured the spirit of the band more effectively. "It was looser and more flowing," agrees Eddie Eave. "It was like, 'It's better when we play it live—why's it not like that?' I remember somebody at the studio said, 'It kind of goes like this,' and spread their hand across an imaginary flat line. It had no highs and lows." For the front cover of the record, each member of the band took off their right shoe to create a clock face of brogues and loafers.* But there was further disappointment when the inner label on the

* Michael Hodges: one o'clock; Graham Whitby: two o'clock; Terry Bateman: three o'clock; Andy Brooks: five o'clock; Adele Winter: eleven o'clock. Missing from the lineup, Eddie Eave says, "I had a pair of oxblood loafers on and everybody else's shoes were black."

twelve-inch of "Window Shopping" misspelled "Brookes" with an "e." "Andy was pissed off about that," says his writing partner. "You finally get your name on a vinyl and they spell it wrong."

The Friday Club's "Window Shopping" front and back sleeve bag, October 1985. Courtesy of Chrysalis Records/Jerry Dammers.

Originally scheduled for the new year, the release date of the single was brought forward to coincide with a tour supporting Madness. "Everyone was saying, 'It's suicide to release a new band in late October,'" rages Andy Brooks. "Chrysalis couldn't give a flying fuck about us. They were reducing their roster. We should have done 'Christmas Shopping' not 'Window Shopping.'" Eddie Eave recalls a meeting with Chrysalis. "They were bitter about Jerry not making any money," he speculates, "and then when he did '(Free) Nelson Mandela' he donated it all to the ANC. Chrysalis decided that having too many artists was competing against yourself. Everything was getting bumped in favor of Huey Lewis & the News."

"Window Shopping" garnered little press attention and less airplay. Then, as the band traveled to Manchester after a gig at UEA the night before, the single unexpectedly came on the radio. "We were somewhere in a wheat field in Norfolk," recalls Michael Hodges, "and it was suddenly, 'Shhh . . . shut up,' and we came on Radio 1. That's when you think, *It's really going to happen.* Simon Bates played us two or three times but then he went on holiday."

Vocalist Terry Bateman says it was crushing when "Window Shopping" didn't chart. "It just fizzled out," she says glumly. Evaluating their prospects, Michael Hodges reasoned that it was only their first single. "We had a sense that it didn't mean the end," he says. "But one of the problems facing 2 Tone was how it would survive its initial success. The great example of that is Tamla Motown . . . but they had Stevie Wonder and Diana Ross, not me and Charlie Higson."

On signing to 2 Tone, rather than a standard one-page agreement, the Friday Club were surprised to receive a thirty-page contract from Chrysalis. Detailed in the agreement was an offer to make a promotional video to support the release of "Window Shopping" or alternatively support Madness on a twenty-eight-day tour. Further agreeing to pay the industry standard buy-on fee of £3,500—turned down by an up-and-coming quartet from Hull called the Housemartins—Chrysalis would also cover losses up to £2,740. Weighing up the two choices, the Friday Club wisely chose the latter and readied to embark on what could loosely be called "the last 2 Tone Tour."

Viewing this as a favor to Jerry Dammers, Madness ventured down to the Marquee Club to get the measure of 2 Tone's new signing. "Yeah, you can come on tour with us," they told the group backstage. Terry was ecstatic. "We were just small town coming to London playing some big warehouse venues and then all of a sudden we were asked to support one of my favorite bands. It was like, 'Wow, unbelievable!' I remember seeing Madness every night and them just lighting up the place. That was incredible. I never got bored of watching them. They'd get the whole place rocking."

While the Friday Club played in theaters to audiences averaging 3,000 a night, weaknesses in their musical capabilities soon showed. "Mark Bedford came up to me and said, 'Where's your bass player? Is he back at the hotel practicing his scales?'" says Brooks, shuddering at the implied amateurism.

Resorting to impromptu rehearsals backstage to bring the rhythm section up to speed, the group recorded every gig to unpick the following day in the van. Struggling to project her naturally soft voice, Terry attracted the weight of criticism. "There would be something that was out and someone would get told off about it. I had a quiet voice. I could never hear myself in the monitors. Being criticized was not the best way if you want people to develop . . . They should have had my vocals up so I could hear what I was singing. It was not easy for me."

When not singing, Terry was playing saxophone. But hampered by incessant feedback, the front-of-house sound engineer simply turned her sound off. "It was making the horn section sound cheap," says Brooks dismissively. Claiming the criticism was unfair, Adele adds, "Brooksy got himself worked up. He wanted it perfect and said we were keeping him back. People were saying to us, 'Don't you know how lucky you are to be signed to 2 Tone? And you're falling out.'"

Dealing with news that his father was dying, Michael Hodges was struggling to cope with the outside world. "I did what countless humans had done before me and drank more and kept going. The fact that City Hall in Newcastle was a good gig and my father saw it in the place where he'd taken my mother on a date when they first met was a big thing for me. That was the gig that mattered."

The tour kicked off with six dates in Ireland, and the tenor was set in a private bar in Dublin called Pink Elephant, owned by U2. As the Friday Club played pool and mixed with various members of Spandau Ballet, Chas Smash unexpectedly approached the band and ambiguously announced, "This has got nothing to do with you guys, but I'm going to fucking kill your manager." Pointing at Harry Cook, he suddenly launched at him. "It was like a proper cowboy saloon fight," fizzes Brooks. "They rolled all the way along the bar until Suggs jumped in to pull them apart. Then it carried on down the stairs with punches flying in all directions and Suggs stuck in the middle." Eventually, Harry climbed back up the stairs with a bloody nose and a bruised face, and said to the band, "That's the last time I take a beating for you lot."

Six months earlier, it transpired, there had been an incident in a pub in Soho. "We were out one night and Harry fell down some steps onto Chas's girlfriend," says Adele Winter, piecing together the story. "Maybe he made fun of her or something and it caused a fight. I thought, *I'm off*, and left Harry and Chas to it." Allegedly, Harry stepped over the girl and carried on to the bathroom where Chas followed him and punched him in the face. Others say Harry then regained his composure, went back upstairs, found Madness's singer sitting at a table, and put his fist straight through his face, breaking his nose.

No stranger to trouble, Harry Cook operated under a number of pseudonyms to evade the attention of different police forces. "He was a mercurial figure," confides Hodges, "stuff happened around him. He was a fantasist who was occasionally right. You'd be drinking in the bar and suddenly he wouldn't be there. He called himself Harry Lime. That's your clue." Though Harry was a shady character in most people's descriptions, bass player Graham Whitby nevertheless maintains that he was "fantastic and got things done. Nothing stood in his way. We wouldn't have got anywhere near 2 Tone or Jerry Dammers if it wasn't for him. He went to record companies and made sure we got paid. Got us gigs. Nobody messed with him."

But as Eddie Eave observes, Chas was not the most easygoing person either. "He definitely had attitude. He didn't like being called Chas and got really offended if anyone called him that. Of course, it was the first thing everyone did: 'Alright, Chas!' 'It's not Chas, it's Carl.'"

As the English leg of the tour opened at the Birmingham Odeon, "Window Shopping" received its first review. Brooks was less than impressed. "*NME* more or less said, 'What does Jerry Dammers think he's doing? This band needs to think more about music and less about shoes.'" Brooks's response: "Fuck you! I'm on tour with Madness. I don't care!"

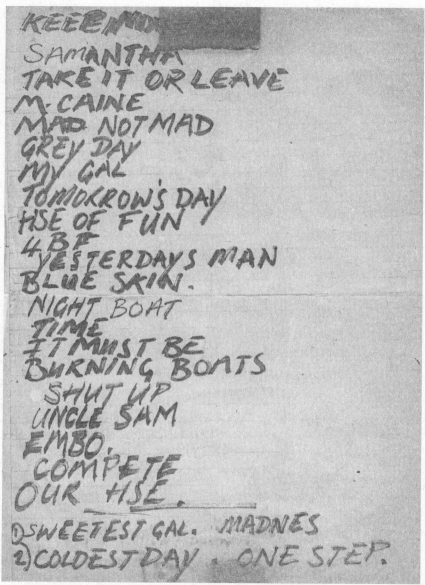

Set list for Madness at the Birmingham Odeon, October 30, 1985.

Indeed. After all, the party was in full swing. A piss-up in Bristol. Weed quickly thrown out the window in Aberdeen. Graham knocking over the drum kit in Leeds while dancing a Northern Soul stomp.

A case of dysentery sweeping through the band, driving Brooks to crawl down the road to "honk up" bent double in a ditch somewhere near Manchester; then Hodges sticking his head out of the window, gleefully announcing, "Brooksy, you were good but we'll find better," and the van pulling off. Illness spread into Madness's camp, too, with Chas forced to leave the stage on several occasions in Liverpool. And there was Suggs advising the Friday Club "to do something" to get the audience on their feet. Returning from a quick one down at the local pub, Suggs and Chas waltzed through the auditorium waving their arms until the whole audience erupted in laughter. "What did you think of us?" Brooks asked his dad backstage. "'It was really good,' he replied, 'apart from those two thugs walking through the audience who destroyed the whole thing.' He didn't realize who they were!"

In St. Austell, there was trouble between Hells Angels and skinheads. Madness stopped playing while their roadie Toks "kept flying out to sort trouble out in the audience," recalls trumpeter Tony Miller; while in Leeds, National Front hostility included shouting, heckling and saluting. "It was a disastrous gig," sighs Miller. In Canterbury, Jerry walked in during Madness's soundcheck and the reaction, says Brooks, "was beautiful. You could feel the warmth they felt toward him. It was truly touching to witness. They hadn't forgotten what he'd done for them." Stealing a quick word, Jerry forewarned Brooks of a touring tradition and to watch out on the last night. "We were thinking, 'Oh fuck, what's coming?' Sure enough, we started the first song at the Hammersmith Odeon and suddenly there was this voice coming through the monitors: 'Terry, you've got a lovely arse,' then, 'Oi! Keyboard player!' We were all looking at each other like, *What the fuck is that! Where's it coming from?* We found out after that Lee Thompson had laid down underneath the front-of-house desk and plugged a microphone into the monitor speakers. He harangued us all night."

"Lee told us all that he loved Terry," laughs Adele, "but nothing happened. They loved their wives. Terry had all the boys after her. But she was going out with Graham and I was going out with Harry. Suggsy—top, top man!—said to me, 'You look like my wife.' He used to go onstage and wave at me." On the last night, Suggs invited the band for drinks at Madness's hotel. As alcohol consumption increased, so did the antics. "Lee had a video camera and decided I was going to be his subject," confesses Brooks. "I ended up in his shower fully clothed reading out fire instructions soaked through to the skin. Then we found a wheelchair and he was pushing me up and down the corridor. I ended up pretending to be a dog on all fours, barking."

Although invited, no record companies showed at the Hammersmith Odeon. Out of contract and collapsing into arguments and fights, the Friday Club called time. "We killed 2 Tone," says Michael Hodges. Brooks disagrees: "Chrysalis were putting out fucking Wet Wet Wet, Climie Fisher and Sinéad O'Connor. Where does Jerry Dammers fit in the middle of all of that? Simon Cowell and Simon Fuller were junior A&R at that time. It was a whole new world of people who were just a bunch of wankers. They never would have got what Jerry was about in a million years. Can you imagine Jerry dealing with Simon Cowell? *In the Studio* was a killer album but it wasn't shifting units, which is what major record companies are about. That's what genius is. It's Miles Davies. Marvin Gaye. It's Jerry Dammers. They're one-offs. Geniuses like that don't fit well in the pop industry."

Although they were the last band to record on 2 Tone, the Friday Club were not the last release. Fittingly, the swansong belonged to the man who had appeared on both sides of 2 Tone's inaugural single.

John Bradbury was an advocate of free education for all. He had been raised with a political conscience; his mother was a nurse at Walsgrave Hospital in Coventry and involved with trade union and antiracist activity. Bradbury attended teacher training college in 1975 and, after qualifying, taught English as a second language in a community education center. Bradbury's time as the drummer of the Specials and its subsequent iteration as the Special AKA coincided with an education system increasingly undervalued by the incumbent government. A series of strikes and demands for fairer wages were routinely ignored. In solidarity with an undermined and undervalued profession, Bradbury wrote

"The Alphabet Army." The title belonged to a hugely successful campaign led by workers in Cuba who traveled from towns to the countryside to promote literacy after Fidel Castro became leader in 1959.

As band leader of J.B.'s Allstars, Bradbury had already recorded four singles—including "One Minute Every Hour" and "Backfield in Motion," a revival of the 1969 US million-seller, written and performed by Mel & Tim—and was the first artist to appear on the RCA Victor imprint since Elvis Presley. Offering distinctive Northern Soul rhythms, the records failed to make a notable impact. In response, Bradbury decided to change direction and recruit a new singer.

Born of Jamaican parents and raised in Stoke Newington, Dee Sharp (born Derek Trough) grew up listening to a heady mix of the Beatles, Motown and Dusty Springfield. Serving as an elite infantry soldier before becoming a musician, Sharp gave his first performance at age fifteen at a nightclub for a local talent contest. Signed as a solo artist to RCA Records, Sharp released a brace of singles, but it was performing as a backing vocalist for Nick Heyward, formerly of Haircut 100, that first landed the wannabe star on *Top of the Pops*.

Then one day, John Bradbury made contact. "We spoke on the phone and Brad said, 'I'm a great admirer of what you do. I think we could do some good work together. He told me that as part of 2 Tone he could do his own thing and he was looking for a new direction.'" Agreeing to work as coproducers, Sharp and Bradbury laid down a basic rhythm track at the Camden Sound Suite, later owned by Paul Hardcastle of "19" fame. Utilizing a range of available musicians, including session guitar player Robert Ahwai, bass player George Webley and pianist Steve Nieve, better known as one of Elvis Costello & the Attractions, "The Alphabet Army" was then mixed by Jerry Dammers between stints with the Friday Club. "Jerry kept making Brad go back and do different versions," recalls Andy Brooks. "He had Brad in tears one day because he was rejecting yet another version." Certain that he never met Jerry, Dee Sharp says he was nonetheless aware of a love/hate relationship. "Whenever Brad mentioned Jerry, it was like he was picking away an old sore."

John Bradbury (L) and Dee Sharp, 1985.

Released on January 2, 1986, "The Alphabet Army" flopped. The Allstars made a solitary appearance on *The Tube*—Sharp dressed in a tailor-made black-and-white checkered outfit and wraparound shades; "absolutely a nod to 2 Tone's past"—but never performed as a group live. "I thought it would be a hit," bemoans Sharp. "It got airplay and the reviews in the press were outstanding. I thought, *What the hell is going on here!* It blew all the other records in the chart out the water. You do your work, you give it your best and you move on."

Unfortunately, there was nowhere to move on to. 2 Tone was all but finished. And any hopes of the label maintaining an identity, independent of Chrysalis, had been dashed. All that remained was a tangle of contracts and debt between the Specials and Chrysalis, and an outstanding five-album deal. As the sole remaining signatory, Jerry Dammers was responsible for all unsettled debts. "I was what they call 'imprisoned' to the record company. After the *In the Studio* album came out, everyone drifted off. There was no point in trying to carry on. I needed to do something else, constructive." Then with characteristic self-effacing humor, Jerry speculates, "I could always do a contractual obligation of *Jerry Dammers Plays 2 Tone's Greatest Hits on the Hammond Organ!*"

In the public eye, 2 Tone represented a certain style of music and had long since progressed beyond the days of rude boys and porkpie hats. "So when we decided to move on," Jerry told *Jamming!*, "people thought, *This isn't really 2 Tone anymore.* I always thought of it as just a record label. I never put that much importance on it—obviously the public did."

After "Ghost Town," one can imagine a lone caretaker shuffling around the 2 Tone office, sweeping up the rubbish, shutting down the lights and gently closing a squeaking door. No fanfare. Just a brief reflective glance back at a time that had lit up an era and as quickly dimmed into a distant past. Yet, in danger of fading into obscurity, Jerry played his trump card. Capitalizing on an upswell in public condemnation of South Africa's apartheid regime, "(Free) Nelson Mandela" would prove to be one of the greatest political songs ever written. Pop music was about to change the world.

CHAPTER 38

PLEAD I CAUSE

FREE NELSON MANDELA

Having grown up with the Beatles, Jerry Dammers believed that an album was an opportunity to experiment. Then to bring it all together at the end, "one big killer single." After *More Specials*, it was "Ghost Town." And after *In the Studio*, it was "(Free) Nelson Mandela."

On Sunday, July 17, 1983, Jerry attended the Festival of African Sounds held at Alexandra Palace, north London, to celebrate Nelson Mandela's sixty-fifth birthday. Organized by the Anti-Apartheid Movement and exiled South African musician Julian Bahula, the all-star lineup included Hugh Masekela, Jazz Afrika, Dudu Pukwana and the Ipi Tombi dancers. "I bumped into an old school friend and he told me about this concert," says Jerry. "I'd never heard of Nelson Mandela, and Julian Bahula sang a song about him."

Leaving the concert hall armed with a selection of educational leaflets, Jerry learned that Mandela was serving life imprisonment for conspiring to overthrow South Africa's apartheid regime. As a fifteen-year-old, Jerry had campaigned against the Springboks's (South Africa's whites-only rugby team) tour of the United Kingdom. "I put anti-apartheid stickers all around school and tried to persuade people to demonstrate against them. It was probably the first demonstration I ever went on." Organized by Peter Hain, a white South African, the Stop the Seventy Tour campaign galvanized support to increase sanctions on South Africa and to highlight the injustices of racial segregation. Like his father before him, who canvassed alongside Bishop Trevor Huddleston and promoted anti-apartheid vigils, Jerry found racism abhorrent. "I remember when I was a little kid and my parents had this Chinese man come to stay with us, and we were walking down the street and these kids started abusing him and calling him a 'chink.' I was disgusted."

That summer of 1983, Jerry was developing an instrumental track with a Latin-African feel. "I hadn't worked out what it was," he says, "but it was very simple." Mulling over the anti-apartheid literature he had gathered from Alexandra Palace, Jerry honed in on a detail disclosing that the shoes Mandela wore in jail were too small for his feet. Realizing it would be easier for people to relate apartheid to one person's story, Jerry began to describe Mandela's condition—*Twenty-one years in captivity, shoes too small to fit his feet, his body abused but his mind is still free*, accompanied by an upbeat melody. "Writing the tune [on the piano] before the lyrics was key," says Jerry. "Otherwise I would have probably come up with some earnest thing on a strummed acoustic guitar and miserable lyrics. But this was very positive: taking some of the spirit of the music and looking to a positive outcome."

In November, Channel 4 filmed the Special AKA rehearsing "(Free) Nelson Mandela" for the documentary series *Play at Home*. Talking directly to the camera, Jerry informs viewers, "I've just written this song more or less for this program," before adding with a nervous smile, "It's only a rehearsal." Tentatively exploring the structure of the song, the group confidently deliver two verses before spontaneously jamming an extended coda imploring an unspecified party to free the imprisoned Mandela. "We were trying to finalize lyrics out in the hall before it was filmed," says vocalist Rhoda Dakar, who in the intervening years has claimed to have written elements of the song's second verse. Contacting the Anti-Apartheid Movement, Rhoda collected leaflets to share at rehearsals. *His body abused but his mind is still free* was "probably my line," she says, and *pleaded the cause of the ANC* (African National Congress) "definitely. I remember thinking *plead I cause*. It was from a reggae dub song: *pleading a cause*. It's like a case in Latin. By the time we got into the studio, Jerry thought he'd written or rewritten the song," she contends, "but my lines were still in there."

Outraged by the suggestion, Jerry wants it to be known, once and for all, that he was the sole author of "(Free) Nelson Mandela." "I was trying to work in 'ANC' and it may be that my line reminded Rhoda of the reggae track 'Plead I Cause.'" Striking a conciliatory tone, he concedes he was then stuck for a rhyme, to which Rhoda added *only one man in a large army*. "I thought it was a terrible rhyme," he says, "but it got the message across. I didn't particularly like the military aspect, but I knew the reality of the situation, so it was fine." Thereafter, the parties agreed that Rhoda would get "what they were calling an 'acknowledgment' for her one line."

But when Rhoda saw the pressed record, credited to "Dammers," she was furious. Phoning the head of Chrysalis, she insisted on an amendment. Moved by magnanimity, or perhaps to avoid a protracted legal case, the record company acceded to a second pressing bearing the writing credit "Dammers/Dakar." The small victory left a bitter aftertaste. Four decades on, neither entity is satisfied, while relations between the two former band members are decidedly frosty. "If you put the writing credit 'Dammers/Dakar,' it looks like it was a cowritten song," snarls Jerry. "It's misleading."

Stepping back, "(Free) Nelson Mandela" needed recording. The trouble was that the Special AKA were a band on the brink of collapse. The remedy came via on old friend, one who had not only produced the first Specials album but had also unofficially released a single on 2 Tone. When Elvis Costello stated in an interview that he thought "Racist Friend" had been an "important record," Jerry seized the opportunity and invited him to produce the new song, further reasoning that having an "outsider" involved would lend "a fresh pair of ears" and "bring everyone together."

The night before the session—December 16, 1983—John Shipley was hustling at a snooker club in Tottenham. By morning, with losses mounting, his opponent called in the debt. Light on cash, Shipley suggested withdrawing money from an ATM, only to discover his account was in the red. Thinking on his feet, Shipley proposed a detour. "I said, 'If you come to the studio, I'll give you the money.' I wasn't expecting him to say yes." Flanked by two burly men carrying snooker cues, Shipley took a tube to Oxford Circus. As they exited the station at exactly 1:21 p.m., there was a loud explosion, later attributed to an IRA bomb detonated outside Harrods department store, almost two miles away, killing six people, including three police officers, and leaving ninety more injured. Safely inside Air Studios, Shipley found Jerry and asked him to settle the outstanding debt. "He did," says the guitar player, "and then the two blokes stayed for the whole session."

Guests were to be the order of the day. Taking inspiration from "Let's Clean Up the Ghetto"—recorded in 1977 by the Philadelphia International All Stars to promote a cleaner environment—Jerry invited an ensemble of friends to sing on "(Free) Nelson Mandela." They included the Specials's guitarist Lynval Golding—"as an act of forgiveness"—and Dave Wakeling and Ranking Roger, who, having walked out on the Beat in July, were recording their debut record as General Public in an adjacent studio. To complement Stan Campbell's lead vocals, described by Elvis Costello as the Special AKA's secret weapon—"he had a voice that the microphone loved and he looked like he'd walked off a magazine cover"[159]—John Bradbury brought in backing vocalists and sisters Molly and Polly Jackson, who he had met in a bar in Camden. The sisters are heard at the beginning of the record singing a cappella, and Jerry suggests, "They might even be slightly out of tune with the rest of the song since it was added afterward, but it gives it a weird kind of lift when the main melody comes in." Supplemented by session vocalist Caron Wheeler—later heard on Soul II Soul's anthemic "Keep on Moving" and "Back to Life"—the Jackson sisters "passed a few spliffs of sensimilla around and the whole scene just went," laughs John Shipley. "Nobody could move."

* * *

Track completed, posters appeared in the surrounding area of Kentish Town inviting people to take part in a video shoot. Directed to Blackfriars Hall, St. Dominic's Priory Church, the request promised "an opportunity to be seen on television" and "a tenner on the day" for expenses. Inside the church hall, Nic Knowles, lighting director of the award-winning documentary *The Rhythm of Resistance*, filmed in South Africa four years earlier,* recreated the atmosphere of a South African township. On the day of the shoot—Wednesday, February 29, 1984—Stan Campbell arrived late with two peroxide-blond young women dressed in tinsel dresses hanging off each of his arms. "He'd lost the plot completely," says Shipley. "It was comical. He demanded £1,000 to appear in the video." Following a stand-up row with Jerry, Campbell reluctantly did the required filming and then, once paid off by manager Pete Hadfield, left.

To a selection of records played courtesy of one of London's hottest DJs—Baden Powell—Jeff Baynes's crew filmed images of breakdancers showing off the burgeoning body-spinning craze crossing over the Atlantic. Further shots of the four female vocalists in profile and three-quarter backlight added a haunting quality to the final cut. Yet, this was not the version viewed by the record company. Faced with a request to screen "(Free) Nelson Mandela" for representatives from Chrysalis International, at a point when the video was as yet unedited, Danny Nissim opted to show a compilation of outtakes of the Specials driving around in a car from "Ghost Town" over the soundtrack of "(Free) Nelson Mandela." "I'm not sure what Jerry Dammers might think about this," says Nissim, "but he'll never know." He does now.

Oddly, in the final edit, the only image of Nelson Mandela visible to the viewer is a poster pinned innocuously on the back of a black PA speaker. By contrast, the record sleeve artwork could not have been more radical. Seizing the opportunity to speak directly to every buying customer, the front cover featured a headshot of Mandela backed

---

* Directed by Jeremy Marre, the film was a critical influence on Paul Simon's *Graceland* album.

by a written history of South Africa's imposed apartheid regime. Reading more like a political pamphlet than the usual pop product copy, the didactic material urged readers to support the Anti-Apartheid Movement and quoted Mandela's famous statement made from the dock on April 20, 1964:

> *During my lifetime I have dedicated myself to this struggle of the African people. I have fought against white domination, and I have fought against Black domination. I have cherished the ideal of a democratic and free society in which all persons live together in harmony and with equal opportunities. It is an ideal which I hope to live for and to achieve. But if needs be, it is an ideal for which I am prepared to die.*

The "Nelson Mandela" sleeve bag, March 1984. Courtesy of Chrysalis Records.

Stan Campbell seemed oblivious to the importance of the record, and his increasingly irrational behavior was again on show when the Special AKA were booked to appear on *The Tube*. Campbell did not show. "He was too much of a superstar," snipes John Shipley, who chose to wear off-pink sharkskin trousers bought from a charity shop in Newcastle, prompting Jerry to liken him to "a Neapolitan ice cream."

Invited by the BBC to perform on *Top of the Pops*, Campbell demanded his own dressing room and £4,000 for his appearance. "His ego had got too much for him," says Tim Strickland, who chaperoned the disintegrating Special AKA to Television Centre. "It was the classic story: local lad, amazing looking, amazing voice, a great performer, gets picked up by a really big group and it's just ego. By that time, they didn't get on with each other. Stan was hardly speaking to Jerry. So the main thing was trying to keep the band amused; taking them to the bar but trying not to get them too drunk."

On the day of filming, a public transport strike rendered London gridlocked. Picked up from his favored snooker haunt in Tottenham, Shipley recalls arriving at the BBC "half asleep" and miming to the track without any makeup on. Recently forced to claim unemployment benefits when Chrysalis withdrew the group's wages, Shipley urged the "the guy on the dry ice machine" to create a cloud of mist so he wouldn't be spotted by dole officials.

Camouflaging his own exit, Campbell negotiated a solo record deal and promptly quit. Angry but mystified, Jerry says, "That was the trouble, it never came down to proper arguments. It was just all 'I'm leaving.' There was no real reasoning. Leaving like he did was unnecessary. He could have waited until the LP came out and promoted it properly. What he did was obviously intended to fuck everything up, which to me is pointless. If he wanted to pursue his own solo career, he should have used the band as a stepping stone. It's what Terry [Hall] and everybody else tried to do and I'm quite happy with that. It's a bit more like the jazz idea where people come and serve their time and go on to their solo career."[160]

Some years later, albeit long after he had had any contact with 2 Tone, Campbell was arrested following numerous complaints from women claiming to be harassed or verbally abused by the former singer. In 2000, a jury at Warwick Crown Court found Campbell guilty of kidnapping and indecently assaulting a fifteen-year-old girl and assaulting another woman in an unrelated incident. Fined and issued with a restraining order in a separate incident of harassment, Campbell was later committed to a psychiatric hospital. Addressing the court, Detective Constable Nicky Linn concluded that Campbell had a hatred for women, which made him potentially dangerous. "It was the way he spoke to me. There is no doubt in my mind that if the girls had not been able to get away when they did, they would have been subjected to very serious sexual assaults indeed," adding: "He kept going on about the Specials. He used to tell us he was a professional musician and had been in the charts. It was obviously something Campbell used to tell a lot of people."

Where the previous three Special AKA singles—"The Boiler," "War Crimes" and "Racist Friend"—had barely made a notable impact on the charts, lost to a paucity of media attention and wider public disinterest, "(Free) Nelson Mandela" found favor with two influential record pluggers. Huge fans of the Specials, Ferret 'n' Spanner pushed the track at Radio 1. The campaign took the record onto daytime pop radio. Simon Bates made it Record of the Week. Not only a smash hit in the UK, "(Free) Nelson Mandela" charted highly in a handful of other countries as well—Australia, Belgium, Ireland and the Netherlands—including the number one spot in New Zealand. "There was a lot of pain around the Special AKA," says Chrysalis press officer Julia Marcus. "Everything was a struggle and then suddenly '(Free) Nelson Mandela' came along. It was an aberration. But there was huge relief from this incredible song."

"A seamless marriage of heartfelt protest and surging hi-life exuberance," enthused Gavin Martin in *NME*. Enjoying a night out at the Fridge in Brixton, Andy Brooks recalls the DJ playing "Soul

Limbo" by Booker T. & the M.G.'s, when Jerry "turned and started singing, *Free Nelson Mandela*, over it to me." The overt influence of the sixties soul classic may have been part of the reason that the compelling and musically irresistible record rocketed to number one in New Zealand. The joyous celebration lasted until Chrysalis (South Africa) forwarded a telegram to London indicating that possession of the record was an imprisonable offense. Nevertheless, when a stadium full of Black people started singing the song's refrain, *Free Nelson Mandela*, at a United Democratic Front rally—broadcast on a BBC news item—Jerry watched on, stunned. "We didn't get him out of prison, but we did get a letter of congratulation from the United Nations, which was quite nice. And a letter from the ANC."

In another surreal turn of events, a communication arrived from Erich Honecker, chairman of the state council of East Germany, inviting the Special AKA to Berlin. "We were meant to be an example to young people of what pop music should be," says Jerry with a hearty chuckle, "which was incredible, but we didn't go."

If "(Free) Nelson Mandela" was the perfect example of how pop music can achieve an extraordinary effect, Clapham Common filled with half a million people rallying against the apartheid regime in South Africa provided the crowning glory. Organized by Jerry Dammers, the Festival for Freedom on Saturday, June 28, 1986, featured a sterling lineup including the Style Council, Elvis Costello and Gil Scott-Heron. The rallying cry was to free Nelson Mandela. Taking to the stage after a solo performance of "Don't Let Me Be Misunderstood" by Elvis Costello, Jerry led the jubilant crowd through a triumphant version of "(Free) Nelson Mandela" featuring a packed stage full of international musicians.

This was Jerry Dammers's moment of vindication, encapsulating all that he, and indeed the Specials, represented. Not only did "(Free) Nelson Mandela" galvanize momentum against apartheid but it achieved it with a glorious duality of educational lyrics and an intoxicating musical backing. Furthermore, if the song, or indeed 2 Tone, can lay claim to influencing a generation, one need only look to two spectacular concerts later held at Wembley Stadium: the first, in 1988, to celebrate Mandela's seventieth birthday in front of a televised global audience of 600 million—"one of the proudest moments of my life," grins Jerry, who initiated the spectacle—and the second, two years later, to honor the release of Mandela, twenty-seven years after his imprisonment, and to welcome him to London as a free man.

In the twenty years between his incarceration and the concert at Alexandra Palace in 1983, Nelson Mandela's name was spoken barely a dozen times in the debating chamber of the House of Commons, and only once by a serving prime minister—James Callaghan. On June 5, 1984, Margaret Thatcher, then in her second term as prime minister, spoke of her concern at the continued "detention" of Mr. Mandela, informing the members of Parliament that she had raised the issue with President Botha, including her concerns regarding South Africa's "recent constitutional measures."

"Margaret Thatcher had described the ANC as a terrorist organization and said Mandela provided the oxygen for terrorism," rails Jerry, anger rising with every word. "Then she got credit for telling Botha to release him. The hypocrisy of them all clambering on the bandwagon after the event was incredible. He was just left to rot as far as Parliament was concerned." Taking stock of his own contribution as a musician and a songwriter, Jerry adds, "I like to think my song might even have helped keep the pressure on her to take action. Thatcher knew something had to give and the sanctions campaign tipped the balance."

When Mandela stepped onto the stage at Wembley Stadium on April 14, 1990, at the International Tribute for a Free South Africa,* Jerry stood transfixed among the audience. "He got the most amazing standing ovation. It lasted about fifteen minutes. It was so powerful." At the end of the evening, Jerry joined a small coterie of guests introduced to Mandela. Perhaps not fully aware of his effort in organizing the concerts, not least the impact of the song itself, Mandela came face-to-face with its composer. "Ah yes," Mandela said, looking Jerry in the eye, "very good."

---

* Apartheid officially ended on April 27, 1994.

CHAPTER 39

THIS ARE 2 TONE

▰▰▰▰▰▰▰

People say that 2 Tone was an experiment waiting to happen. A phenomenon born of Coventry. But rather than a fully conceived idea, sold and executed for greater purpose, 2 Tone defined itself by its day-by-day existence. It was successful because it reflected and grew with its audience. It spoke to a disempowered generation and gave them hope; a reason to promote change. "All the bands believed in that," says the Selecter's manager Juliet de Vie. "It was such a fantastic ideal to aspire to."

2 Tone saw musicians of different classes, cultures and ethnicities behaving in extraordinary ways. Black and white people onstage, being creative together, making music and blending the rhythms of the Caribbean with the diverse influences of punk and rock and soul. "It changed culture and changed England," says the Beat's David Steele. "A lot of people like me came from a little town and it was the first time they'd seen bands like this. It opened their eyes to other things." Against a backdrop of division and despair, disaffected youth united and asked questions, challenging the status quo. "We weren't politicians," says singer Pauline Black. "We couldn't change things in the way that a policy or law can change society. But we changed attitudes. People talked about Blacks and whites together, but they didn't have a language that actually encompassed that."

"Before 2 Tone there was Black music and there was white music," says the Selecter's Compton Amanor, "and never the two shall mix. We didn't live in a segregated society but there were always those tensions. But for the first time my generation was saying, 'We're Black and we're British and we're here to stay,' not, 'We're Black and we want to go back to Africa or the West Indies.' 2 Tone helped to break away those edges and said you could be both." Juliet de Vie regards it as the transition generation: "It's why I think 2 Tone could happen. You had Black British youth rejecting the conservative parental Caribbean values of their elders and identifying with politically assertive reggae. For the first time Black and white youth found a common language in this unique hybrid of ska, fired up with the reality of growing up in seventies Britain. To see these musicians onstage together was a microcosm of what was starting to happen in broader society. It was a shared love of music."

Today, Suggs sees a young generation mixing their music "like it's nothing," he says. "But back then it was very delineated: Black people did this and white people did that. 2 Tone had a huge impact on changing that perspective." The word was unity. 2 Tone attempted to break through deeply rooted cultural bigotry and empower a young generation to believe in a brighter, multicultural future. It offered rhythm, three-minute bursts of finely crafted melody, fine threads and iconic artwork. "2 Tone was trying to reach everybody: Black or white," says the Specials's manager Rick Rogers. "It was trying to appeal to the better parts of people's human nature and celebrate them."

2 Tone propagated a strong message of racial unity and challenged right-wing thinking. "I think we did help to defuse the situation," argues its founder Jerry Dammers. Certainly, letters sent to the 2 Tone Fan Club suggest that hearts and minds were changed. In one instance, Jerry remembers a conversation with a teenage fan from the East End who would "definitely have gone into the National Front if it hadn't been for 2 Tone. We got so many letters from people who said similar things." After a Specials show in Portsmouth, guitarist Lynval Golding sat in a bar, talking to a skinhead with a British Movement emblem shaved into the back of his head. "That would be the photo," says his bandmate Horace Panter, "conquering England one fan at a time."

Decades on and Ranking Roger was still meeting former skinheads who used to spit and throw coins at him. "They thank me for the Beat changing their lives," he says. "One time, a big skinhead came up to me after a gig and said, 'I used to be a member of the British Movement but tonight I've seen unity, so fuck 'em!' Dave [Wakeling] and I were just smiling because we'd achieved something."

Yet 2 Tone also became a magnet for right-wing factions intent on disrupting concerts and luring away impressionable teenage audiences. Such was the magnitude of the problem, in December 1979, Madness threatened to split, while in 1981 Jerry Dammers spoke of his despair in "Ghost Town": *Bands won't play no more, too much fighting on the dance floor*. The minority voice attracted a national media platform and in the 1979 general election, the National Front contested seats in almost half the constituencies in Britain. They may have lost deposits in every instance, but they still polled near 200,000 votes. Nevertheless, throughout the eighties, support for the National Front incrementally waned. Is it conceivable that first-time voters, raised and inspired by antiracist movements such as 2 Tone and Rock Against Racism, rejected neo-fascism in favor of tolerance, compassion and the rewards of a multicultural society?

The very notion that 2 Tone might not have been a positive catalyst for change is met with indignation by Madness's Chas Smash. "2 Tone was absolutely successful," he proclaims. "It changed people: to dance for joy, for social awareness. 2 Tone at its very core was multiracial. It was a cultural movement. White boys danced, for fuck's sake!"

Attempting to quantify 2 Tone's achievement, Jerry aligns it with other campaigns like Rock Against Racism, asserting, "It helped make everyday racism unacceptable. In the sixties and early seventies, it was common to use language like 'nigger' and 'wog'; 2 Tone contributed to making that situation better. But racism didn't go away. It was part of an ongoing struggle. The Specials took the message into the lion's den, so to speak. I was always aware that strategy had risks and dangers and it was unlikely to work 100 percent."

Acknowledging the inevitable fallouts, contradictions and misunderstandings as "the price to pay for the incredible tornado that tore through British youth culture," Juliet de Vie argues that "record sales and the overall impact of 2 Tone suggests that the message was reaching a whole generation of young Black, white and Asian youths in their bedrooms up and down the country. I have nothing but respect for Jerry Dammers and the artists involved coming together and trying to find a better way forward for a multicultural society."

Likening it to letting the genie out of the bottle and taking on a life of its own, Pauline Black says that, as a movement, it enabled people "to have a way of looking at their racist attitudes, questioning them and hopefully coming out with a better viewpoint. If we did nothing more than that, then history owes us an incredible debt. People didn't use words like 'multiculturalism' or 'racism,' they said 'racialism,' and they'd get very embarrassed about even saying the word. There was still this Black world and this white world. In a way, we brought them together for that brief period. That was quite extraordinary given the time. There is a long thread that you can tug on and feel secure that whatever problems we had internally, within our bands, there was something deeper going on that maybe we weren't aware of that made it a cohesive whole."

In 1984, Terry Hall dared to suggest that there was no racism in Coventry before the Specials started talking about it. That he had participated in "Paki-bashing" and gang warfare against people of color in Coventry, including fighting his future bandmates Lynval Golding and Neville Staple. "Stupid!" explodes Jerry. "You expect some of the audience not to get the point of what you're doing, but when the lead singer of the group doesn't get the point . . . It wasn't true at all."[161] Such is his dismay at discovering this statement; Jerry says that had he known about Terry's racist attitude beforehand he would not have had him in the Specials.

Battling with the contradiction of a movement that on one hand achieved incredible levels of success, both commercially and culturally, lead guitarist Roddy Byers points to the level of antagonism and misunderstanding within its ranks. "I still find it disturbing to talk about certain periods of the Specials's history," he says despondently. "There were some very big egos in that band. People remember according to their own agenda and twist things to suit themselves." Horace Panter nods in agreement. "If you ask the seven people in the Specials the same question, you will invariably get seven different answers. History is written by the people who write the books."

Conjuring images of a war zone, Juliet de Vie suggests, "There was a lot of walking wounded at the end of 2 Tone." On the upside, "There were no Bill Wymans," laughs the Beat's David Steele, comparing the static presence of the Rolling Stones's bass player and the mayhem of a 2 Tone concert. "It's probably why we all fell apart. You've got six or seven really strong characters. It's like sticking all your favorite things in a suitcase and sitting on it: you know it's going to burst open. The energy and the mixture was amazing but we probably all could have done with a couple of nonentities."

While acknowledging the infighting and fractiousness within all the bands, the Bodysnatchers's saxophonist Miranda Joyce's abiding memory is of an exciting movement and all the bands hanging out together. "The egos felt very small somehow. We were all partying, going to the pub, going out for Sunday lunch. Everyone was friends, shagging each other, going to gigs together. It was amazing. There was no hierarchy. That was Jerry. He'd go, 'You can headline if you want.' He wasn't into the big band ego thing. There was a real melting pot of ideas and support for each other. It was a great feeling, like a family."

At its peak, 2 Tone lasted little more than eighteen months, from late 1979 to the summer of 1981. "A force of nature which came out of nowhere," describes Juliet de Vie, "burned unbelievably bright, and burned itself out just as quickly. You thought, *What happened!* It didn't make much sense to me. To have gone from that groundswell of that generation: how could their views and their beliefs change so fast? To go from actively supporting overtly radical influences and music to superficial clothes and hairstyles and politics becoming unfashion-able immediately."

2 Tone may have been a transient fashion. Where clothing man-ufacturers had once sold black-and-white checkered suits in abun-dance, the new demand was for bandannas, frilly shirts and pixie boots. "What was 2 Tone?" asks Pauline Black. "It was a two-year blip between the end of punk and New Romantics." "What I do know," says de Vie, picking up the thread, "is that musically and culturally we would be a lot poorer if it hadn't happened. It changed attitudes and it started something."

The movement's enduring legacy is perhaps best illustrated by the hundreds of comments posted on the fan wall of the 2 Tone Lives & Legacies exhibition hosted at the Herbert Museum, Coventry, in 2021. Scrawled notes on blank postcards tell of not "being alone" and having "a voice." Of the impact 2 Tone had on people's youth, "It shaped my soul," says one, "my musical and fashion explorations that followed are all inextricably linked to the seeds that were sown then." Another says, "2 Tone is in my blood. It was my introduction to the idea that black and white people could live and work together in harmony." Son of an immigrant from the Punjab, Coventry-born Sukhminder Singh says, "For people like me who were struggling with identity and a sense of belonging, we suddenly found something that stood up for us." While South Africa–born Shamala Naidro says, "We knew that many were supporting us—how wonderful to finally see how that support was routed in other struggles in the UK."

In 2014, Jerry Dammers received the Order of the Companions of O.R. Tambo from the president of South Africa, Jacob Zuma (Af-rican National Congress), which "recognizes eminent foreign nation-als for friendship shown to South Africa." Accepting the honor on the twentieth anniversary of the country's first democratic election, in which Nelson Mandela was elected president, Jerry said, "I never expected anything like this when I wrote '(Free) Nelson Mandela.' It's a fantastic honor and it's amazing that it's remembered in South Africa. But it's important to remember that I did what any decent person would do in my position. And it's nothing compared to the sacrifices the people in South Africa made to fight apartheid."

2 Tone was triumphant. It changed a generation. It had number ones and sold records in the hundreds of thousands. It launched the Specials, the Selecter, Madness, the Bodysnatchers, the Beat, the Swinging Cats. Every gig was an event and lured fans onto dance floors and onto the stage. It inspired a fashion that swept the country. It stood for antiracism, challenged sexism and encouraged people of all persuasions to embrace multiculturalism. Its impact will continue to inform voluminous sociological and political debates, be they in books or simply down at the pub. They are all-important and help to make sense of one of the greatest youth cults in British history. But for its originator, it distills down to one very simple and charming occurrence: "2 Tone happened," says Jerry Dammers, with a mischevious note in his voice, "because it came out of my head!"

Acknowledgments

First and foremost, I would like to thank Jerry Dammers, founder of the Specials and 2 Tone Records. 2 Tone begins and ends with Jerry and, although this account is not authorized nor fully confirmed, it was a privilege to have his commitment from the beginning. I have a lifetime of listening pleasure to thank you for and this book is greatly enhanced by your contribution.

An enormous thank you to everyone who generously gave their time to talk to me: Robert Ahwai, David Compton Amanor, Stella Barker, John Barrow, Mike Barson, Terry Bateman, Jane Bayley, Leigh Bayley, Jeff Baynes, Charles "Aitch" Bembridge, Gaz Birtles, Pauline Black, Andy Brooks, Tom Brown, Roddy Byers, Simon Charterton, Tony Cheetham, Doug D'Arcy, Chalkie Davies, Neol Davies, Joe Dunton, Eddie Eave, Roy Eldridge, Al Elias, Felicity Fairhurst, Chris Foreman, Lynval Golding, Paul Harris, Arthur "Gaps" Hendrickson, Paul Heskett, Charlie Higson, Michael Hodges, James Hunt, John Kehoe, Clive Langer, Stephen Leonard-Williams, Roger Lomas, Gavrik Losey, Julia Marcus, Jason Massot, Stuart McGeachin, Peter Millen, Tony Miller, Everett Morton, John Mostyn, Frank Murray, Danny Nissim, Sarah-Jane Owen, Horace Panter, Judy Parsons, Jeff Perks, Chris Poole, Ranking Roger, Joe Reynolds, Rick Rogers, Errol Ross, Bob Sargeant, Richard Scott, Dee Sharp, John Shipley, John Sims, Cathal Smyth, Lizzie Soden, Neville Staple, David Steele, Tim Strickland, Suggs, Nicky Summers, Kraig Thornber, Geoff Travis, Holly Beth Vincent, Juliet de Valero Wills, Dave Wakeling, Graham Whitby, Sarah Wills, Alan Winstanley, Adele Winter, Laurence Wood, and Steve Wynne.

Sadly, while I was writing this book, Terry Hall, Frank Murray, Everett Morton, Ranking Roger and Bob Sargeant passed away. Their words and music will never be forgotten.

A special thank you to Terry Edwards, Penny Leyton and Miranda Joyce for access to their private archives. And to Ronan O'Donnell (Mr. Wheeze) for incredible support, offering to fact-check the text, and sharing the most comprehensive and impressive 2 Tone collection I have seen.

Thank you to Welly Art, Billy Bragg, Rhoda Dakar, Dermot James, Blake Lewis, Marcia Morrison and John South, Nick Mirsky, Jason Weir, Richard Boon, Nick Grant, Stephen Shafer, Lloyd Bradley, Kevin Pocklington and Dave Simpson, Chris Wells, Katy Ellis, and Mark Harrison and Pete Chambers at the Coventry Music Museum/2 Tone Village, Coventry, for all your help and support.

Thank you to all the photographers who kindly shared their images in the spirit of the endeavor.

To the National Health Service, the staff, nurses and doctors at Barnet and Westmoreland hospitals.

To my literary agent, Carrie Kania, for rock-solid support, friendship and invaluable advice, edited manuscript notes, and everyday faith and commitment to my writing.

To Lee Brackstone for backing the book in unprecedented circumstances and having the faith and commitment to see it through. Also to your team at White Rabbit: Georgia Goodall (project editor), Susie Bertinshaw (project editor), Paul Baillie-Lane (copy editor), Seán Costello (proofreader) and Natalie Dawkins (picture editor).

In the US, an enormous thank you to Johnny Temple for your belief and enthusiasm, and to your team at Akashic Books: Johanna Ingalls (managing editor), Aaron Petrovich (production manager), Alexis Fleisig (designer), and Holly Watson (PR); and to Tara Hiatt (Hachette UK rights director).

And top of the heap, Susie McDonald for everything. You—and Lily, Eleanor and Lottie—are my world, xxxx.

DISCOGRAPHY 1979-1986

SINGLES

Title	Artist	Cat. No	Release Date
Gangsters/The Selecter	The Special AKA VS The Selecter	TT1/TT2	6/79
The Prince/Madness	Madness	CHS TT3	8/79
On My Radio/ Too Much Pressure	The Selecter	CHS TT4	9/79
A Message to You Rudy/ Nite Klub	The Selecter	CHS TT5	10/79
Tears of a Clown/ Ranking Full Stop	The Beat	CHS TT6	11/79
I Can't Stand Up for Falling Down/Girls Talk	Elvis Costello & The Attractions	CHS TT7	1/80
Too Much Too Young/ Guns of Navarone/ Longshot Kick de Bucket/Liquidator/ Skinhead Moonstomp	The Special AKA	CHS TT7	1/80
Three Minute Hero/ James Bond	The Selecter	CHS TT8	1/80
Let's Do Rock Steady/ Ruder Than You	The Bodysnatchers	CHS TT9	3/80

Missing Words/Carry Go Bring Come (Live)	The Selecter	CHS TT10	3/80
Rat Race/Rude Boys Outa Jail	The Specials	CHS TT11	5/80
Easy Life/ Too Experienced	The Bodysnatchers	CHS TT12	7/80
Stereotype/ International Jet Set	The Specials	CHS TT13	9/80
Mantovani/Away	The Swinging Cats	CHS TT14	9/80
Sea Cruise/Carolina	Rico	CHS TT15	10/80
Do Nothing/Maggie's Farm	The Specials	CHS TT16	12/80
Ghost Town/Why?/ Friday Night, Saturday Morning	The Specials	CHS TT17	6/81
The Boiler/ Theme from the Boiler	Rhoda & The Special AKA	CHS TT18	1/82
Jungle Music/ Rasta Call You	Rico & The Special AKA	CHS TT19	2/82
The Feeling's Gone/ The Feeling's Back	The Apollinaires	CHS TT20	10/82
Tear the Whole Thing Down/Ylang Ylang	The Higsons	CHS TT21	10/82
Envy the Love/Give It Up	The Apollinaires	CHS TT22	10/82
War Crimes/Version	The Special AKA	CHS TT23	1/83
Run Me Down/Put the Punk Back into Funk	The Higsons	CHS TT24	7/83
Racist Friend/Bright Lights	The Special AKA	CHS TT25	8/83
Nelson Mandela/ Break Down the Door!	The Special AKA	CHS TT26	3/84

What I Like Most About You Is Your Girlfriend/ Can't Get a Break	The Special AKA	CHS TT27	8/84
Window Shopping/ Instrumental	The Friday Club	CHS TT28	10/85
The Alphabet Army/ Al.Arm	J.B.'s Allstars	CHS TT29	1/86

ALBUMS

Specials	The Specials	CHR TT 5001	10/79
Too Much Pressure	The Selecter	CHR TT 5002	2/80
More Specials	The Specials	CHR TT 5003	9/80
Dance Craze	Various Artists	CHR TT 5004	2/81
That Man Is Forward	Rico	CHR TT 5005	3/81
Jama	Rico	CHR TT 5006	5/82
This Are 2 Tone	Various Artists	CHR TT 5007	11/83
In the Studio	The Special AKA	CHR TT 5008	6/84

2 Tone single and album front covers, 1979–1984. Courtesy of Chrysalis Records/Jerry Dammers.

LIST OF ILLUSTRATIONS

PART I

PART II

PART III

PHOTO INSERT

The Specials: (L–R) Roddy Byers, Neville Staple, Terry Hall, Horace Panter, Lynval Golding, John Bradbury, Jerry Dammers. Performing "Gangsters" on *Top of the Pops*, August 30, 1979. © Chalkie Davies

The Specials performing at the Hammersmith Palais, August 21, 1979. © Phil Grey/Bridgeman

Madness: (L–R) Mark Bedford, Suggs, Chas Smash, Chris Foreman, Mike Barson, at the Lyceum, London, August 26, 1979. © Justin Thomas

The Selecter, 1980. © Toni Tye

The Selecter: (L–R) Neol Davies, Pauline Black, Charley Anderson, Gaps Hendrickson, Compton Amanor, Aitch, Desmond Brown. On set filming the video for "Missing Words," November 1979. © Juliet de Valero Wills

Ranking Roger performing with the Beat, circa 1980. © Syd Shelton

The Beat: (L–R) Ranking Roger, Andy Cox, David Steele, circa 1980. © Syd Shelton

(L–R) Pauline Black, Suggs, Neville Staple, in front of the 2 Tone Tour bus, October 1979. © Chalkie Davies

Members of the Specials, Selecter and Madness, Blue Boar service station, Northamptonshire, October 1979.

Members of the Selecter, the Bodysnatchers and Holly & the Italians, February 16, 1980. © Getty/Virginia Turbett

Rico Rodriguez backstage with the Specials, Spa Centre, Leamington, April 15, 1981. © Steve Rapport

Rhoda Dakar dancing, Barrow-in-Furness, June 9, 1980. © Getty/Virginia Turbett

Sarah-Jane Owen and Miranda Joyce dancing, Barrow-in-Furness, June 9, 1980. © Getty/Virginia Turbett

The Bodysnatchers: (L–R) Stella Barker, Nicky Summers, Rhoda Dakar, Miranda Joyce, Sarah-Jane Owen, Penny Leyton, at the 101 Club, Clapham, London, December 13, 1979. © Getty/Virginia Turbett

Fans onstage with the Specials, Hammersmith Palais, August 21, 1979. © Ray Stevenson

Fans of the Specials dancing at "A Peaceful Protest Against Racism," Butts Stadium Coventry, June 20, 1981. © Mark Osborne

Fans watching the Specials at Northern Carnival Against Racism, Potternewton Park, Leeds, July 4, 1981. © Syd Shelton

Pauline Black on tour in the US, April 1980. © Juliet de Valero Wills

Gaps Hendrickson onstage with the Selecter, circa April 1980. © Juliet de Valero Wills

The Selecter playing live on *The Old Grey Whistle Test*, February 19, 1980. © Juliet de Valero Wills

Members of the Bodysnatchers, Go-Go's and Specials on the Seaside Tour, June 1980. © Penny Leyton

Sean Carasov and Miranda Joyce on the Seaside Tour, June 1980. © Penny Leyton

Nicky Summers and Sarah-Jane Owen with Gaz Mayall (top right) and Sarah Jane's boyfriend at her flat, London, 1980. © Penny Leyton

(L–R) Sean Carasov, Lynval Golding, Miranda Joyce, Jane Summers, Rhoda Dakar, on the Seaside Tour, June 1980. © Penny Leyton

Jerry Dammers on the Seaside Tour coach, June 1980. © Penny Leyton

Rhoda Dakar on the Seaside Tour coach, June 1980. © Penny Leyton

The Specials at the Rainbow Theatre, London, May 1, 1981. © Justin Thomas

The Specials at the Top Rank, Brighton, October 10, 1980. © Adrian Boot

Page from the diary of Miranda Joyce, October 1980. © Miranda Joyce

A Specials album shoot, Regent Hotel, Leamington Spa, 1980. © Chalkie Davies

The Selecter on tour in the US, 1980. © Juliet de Valero Wills

Northern Carnival Against Racism poster, July 4, 1981.

Storyboard for the Special AKA's "The Boiler" video, January 1982. © Lizzie Soden

Storyboard for Rico Rodriguez's "Jungle Music" video, February 1982. © Lizzie Soden

The Specials on location for the "Ghost Town" video, London, 1981. © Chalkie Davies

The Specials on location for the "Ghost Town" video, Tower Bridge, London, 1981. © Chalkie Davies

END PAGES

Members of the Specials, Selecter and Madness, Hove beach, October 19, 1979. © Chalkie Davies

Members of the Specials, Selecter and Madness, Hove beach, October, 19, 1979. © Chalkie Davies

ENDNOTES

Chapter 2: Son of a Preacher Man

1   Williams, Paul, *You're Wondering Now: from Conception to Reunion*, Cherry Red, p.14
2   Chambers, Pete, *The 2-Tone Trail: Dispatches from the 2-Tone City—30 Years On*, Tencton Planet
3   "2 Tone Lives & Legacies" pamphlet, Herbert Museum, 2021
4   "Celebrating Prince Buster," *Mojo*, 2008

Chapter 3: Bluebeat Attack

5   Hepworth, David, "Today Coventry, Tomorrow . . . Coventry," *Smash Hits*, May 29, 1980
6   *The 2 Tone Story*, BBC CWR, 2019
7   Frith, Simon, "Rude Boys Spread Manure in Yank Bed of Roses," *Creem*, April 1980
8   "Don't Get Angry, Get Even," Roddy Radiation online autobiography (available at: www.roddyradiation.com/history/history.htm)
9   Staples, Neville, with McMahon, Tony, *Original Rude Boy: From Borstal to the Specials*, Aurum Press, p.114
10 *Rock Legends: 2 Tone*, Carlton Television, 2002
11 Thompson, Dave, *Wheels Out of Gear: 2 Tone, the Specials and a World in Flame*, Helter Skelter, p.28
12 Petridis, Alexis, "Please Look After This Band," *Mojo*, 2002, p.75
13 Bushell, Garry, "The Clash/The Specials: Friar's, Aylesbury," *Sounds*, July 8, 1978

Chapter 4: Threatened by Gangsters

14 "The Colourfield," *Jamming!*, March 26, 1985, p.20
15 Williams, p.15
16 Williams, p.25
17 Williams, p.26
18 Panter, Horace, *Ska'd for Life: A Personal Journey with the Specials*, Sidgwick & Jackson, p.48
19 *Too Much, Too Young: The Story of 2 Tone*, BBC Radio 2, 2008
20 Marshall, George, *The Two Tone Story*, STP, p.18

Chapter 5: Ska Is Dead, Long Live Ska

21 Thrills, Adrian, "The Kids Who're Ska'd for Life," *New Musical Express*, May 26, 1979

22 Hepworth, David, "Don't Call Me Ska-Face!," *Smash Hits*, September 6, 1979

Chapter 6: Don't Call Me Ska Face

23 Thrills, Adrian, "Two-Tones Over Teuton!," *New Musical Express*, August 25, 1979

24 *The 2 Tone Story*, BBC CWR, 2019

25 Panter, p.66

Chapter 7: Rude Boys in the Jungle

26 *Sounds*, March 24, 1979

27 Wilson, Lois, "Original Gangsters," *Mojo*, May 2008, p.86

28 Snowden, Don, "Ska Jump: England to America," *Los Angeles Times*, March 16, 1980

29 "Walt Up Against the Wall," *Record Collector* Issue 395, October 26, 2011 (available at: www.recordcollectormag.com/articles/walt-up-against-the-wall)

30 *Too Much, Too Young: The Story of 2 Tone*, BBC Radio 2, 2008

Chapter 8: An Earthquake Is Erupting

31 Seven Ragged Men (available at: www.sevenraggedmen.com/years/)

32 Suggs, *That Close*, Quercus, p.133

33 Hepworth, David, "Madness: They Call It Madness," *Smash Hits*, November 29, 1979

34 *Smash Hits*, September 16, 1979

35 Madness with Doyle, Tom, *Before We Was We*, Virgin, p.200

36 Williams, p.40

37 Seven Ragged Men

38 Madness, p.170

39 *SMASH! The Madness Story*, dir. Leo Burley, 2002

40 Madness, p.216

41 Madness, p.22

42 Seven Ragged Men

Chapter 9: Going to a Go-Go

43 "Exclusive: Interview with Charley Anderson of the Selecter," Marco on the Bass blog, July 14, 2009 (available at: www.marcoonthebass.blogspot.com/2009/07/exclusive-interview-with-charley.html)

44 Goldman, Vivien, "The Selecter: Survival inna Suburbia," *Melody Maker*, February 23, 1980

45 Black, Pauline, *Black by Design: A 2-Tone Memoir*, Serpent's Tail, p.125

Chapter 10: Rude Boys

46 *Too Much, Too Young: The Story of 2 Tone*, BBC Radio 2, 2008
47 Simpson, Dave, "'A blur of legs, arms and adrenaline': the astonishing history of two-tone," *Guardian*, April 30, 2021 (available at www.theguardian.com/music/2021/apr/30/a-blur-of-legs-arms-and-adrenaline-the-astonishing-history-of-two-tone)
48 Pearson, Deanne, "A/K/A The Specials," *New York Rocker*, October 1979
49 "The 2-Toning of America," *New Musical Express*, February 9, 1980
50 Williams, p.49
51 "The 2-Toning of America," *New Musical Express*, February 9, 1980
52 Simpson, Dave, "'A blur of legs, arms and adrenaline': the astonishing history of two-tone," *Guardian*, April 30, 2021

Chapter 11: Battle of the Gap

53 *This Are Two Tone*, BBC Radio 4, 2008
54 Madness, p.250
55 *Melody Maker*, October 27, 1979
56 Madness, p.250
57 Pearson, Deanne, "Nice Band, Shame about the Fans," *New Musical Express*, November 24, 1979
58 Staples, p.147
59 Rambali, Paul, "The Specials, The Selecter: Lyceum, London," *New Musical Express*, December 15, 1979
60 Williams, p.61

Chapter 12: Nice Band, Shame about the Fans

61 *Too Much, Too Young: The Story of 2 Tone*, BBC Radio 2, 2008

Chapter 13: Man from Wareika

62 Eddington, Richard, *Sent from Coventry: The Checkered Past of Two Tone*, IMP, p.86
63 *Too Much, Too Young: The Story of 2 Tone*, BBC Radio 2, 2008
64 Thrills, Adrian, "Two-Tones Over Teuton!," *New Musical Express*, August 25, 1979
65 Albaum, Lars, "Rico Rodriguez Volles Horn var ausi Spex 3/1995," p.15, translated from German by Braunov
66 de Koningh, Michael & Griffith, Marc, *Tighten Up! The History of Reggae in the UK*, London: Sanctuary, 2003, p.14

Chapter 14: If It Ain't Stiff, It Ain't Worth a Fuck

67 Madness, p.228
68 *Too Much, Too Young: The Story of 2 Tone*, BBC Radio 2, 2008
69 *5 Years of Madness*, BBC Radio 1 documentary

Chapter 15: A Show of Gladness

70   "Bedders Digs The Beat," *Record Mirror*, September 27, 1980
71   *Smash Hits*, January 24, 1980
72   *Mojo*, p.84
73   *Record Collector*, August 2004, p.83
74   "A Career in Ranking," *Smash Hits*, September 3, 1980
75   Pearson, Deanne, "Don't Call Me Ska Face," *New Musical Express*, December 8, 1979
76   "Bedders Digs The Beat," *Record Mirror*, September 27, 1980
77   Pearson, Deanne, "Don't Call Me Ska Face," *New Musical Express*, December 8, 1979

Chapter 16: Calling Rude Girls

78   *Smash Hits*, May 1, 1980

Chapter 17: An Autumn of Misunderstanding

79   Panter, p.141
80   *Record Collector*, August 2004
81   "Walt Up Against the Wall," *Record Collector* Issue 395, October 26, 2011 (available at: www.recordcollectormag.com/articles/walt-up-against-the-wall)

Chapter 18: Rudies Come Back

82   *Uncut*, November 2016
83   Stand, Mike, "The Importance of Being Nutty," *Smash Hits*, April 17, 1980
84   *New York Rocker*, March 1980
85   *Too Much, Too Young: The Story of 2 Tone*, BBC Radio 2, 2008
86   Bushell, Garry, "Rude Boys Can't Fail," *Sounds*, March 15, 1980

Chapter 19: Backlash

87   *Record Collector*, August 2004, p.83
88   Williams, Mark, "Rankin' to Riches," *Melody Maker*, January 19, 1980
89   Bushell, Garry, "Live Injection," *Sounds*, March 1, 1980
90   *Sounds*, March 15, 1980
91   *New Musical Express*, September 27, 1980
92   *Black Music*, February 1980
93   Marshall, George, *The Two Tone Story*, STP, p.33
94   *New Musical Express*, September 27, 1980
95   Gardner, Mike, "The Black & White Minstrel Show," *Record Mirror*, May 17, 1980
96   *New Musical Express*, March 23, 1980
97   Pearson, Deanne, "A/K/A The Specials," *New York Rocker*, October 1979

Chapter 20: Go-Feet

98   *New Musical Express*, March 8, 1980
99   Williams, Mark, "Rankin' to Riches," *Melody Maker*, January 19, 1980
100 *Smash Hits*, May 1, 1980, p.13
101 Bushell, Garry, "Live Injection," *Sounds*, March 1, 1980

Chapter 21: Working at Your Leisure

102 *Too Much, Too Young: The Story of 2 Tone*, BBC Radio 2, 2008
103 *New Musical Express*, September 27, 1980

Chapter 22: Bravo Delta 80

104 Black, Pauline, "The Story So Far . . . Roddy 'Radiation' Byers (lead
     guitarist with the Specials)," the Blackroom, March 31, 1999 (available
     at: www.cwn.org.uk/blackroom/story-so-far/990331-roddy-byers.htm)
105 Hewitt, Paolo, "Too Much Too Young," *Melody Maker*, June 21, 1980
106 Williams, p.80.
107 Hewitt, Paolo, "Too Much Too Young," *Melody Maker*, June 21, 1980
108 Hewitt, Paolo, "Too Much Too Young," *Melody Maker*, June 21, 1980
109 "The 2-Toning of America," *New Musical Express*, February 9, 1980
110 *Record Collector*, August 2004, p.83

Chapter 23: Too Experienced

111 *Too Much, Too Young: The Story of 2 Tone*, BBC Radio 2, 2008

Chapter 24: Just a Whisper

112 *Two Tone Britain*, dir. Jason Collier, 2004

Chapter 25: Uno, Due, Tre, Quattro

113 *New Musical Express*, July 27, 1980
114 *Too Much, Too Young: The Story of 2 Tone*, BBC Radio 2, 2008

Chapter 26: International Jet Set

115 *New Musical Express*, September 27, 1980
116 Salewicz, Chris, "Stop the Tour, I Want to Get Off," *New Musical Express*, September 27, 1980
117 Eddington, p.167
118 Williams, p.81
119 Panter, p.243
120 *Too Much, Too Young: The Story of 2 Tone*, BBC Radio 2
121 Williams, p.56
122 Eddington, p.168
123 Williams, p.93
124 *Too Much, Too Young: The Story of 2 Tone*, BBC Radio 2

125 *Melody Maker*, December 15, 1979

126 *At the BBC: Madness*, BBC Radio 2, November 1, 2012

127 *Temporary Hoarding*, No. 12, 1980

128 *Rolling Stone*, 1980 Christmas message, quoted in *The Beat Twist & Crawl*, Halasa, Malu, Eel Pie Publishing, 1981, p.7

Chapter 27: Ghost of the Vox Continental

129 *Record Mirror*, November 8, 1980

Chapter 28: Blanket Coverage

130 Swift, Jon, "The Golding of 2 Tone," *Smash Hits*, January 21, 1981

131 Panter, p.196

132 Ludgate, Simon, "Stardust Memory"

Chapter 29: A Look at Life

133 *Q* Special, p.88

134 *Rock Legends*

135 Marshall, p.53

136 *London Trax*, No. 2, February 18–24, 1981

137 *London Trax*, No. 2, February 18–24, 1981

Chapter 30: Bands Won't Play No More

138 Petridis, Alexis, "Ska for the Madding Crowd," *Guardian*, March 8, 2002

139 *Uncut*, October 2007

Chapter 31: People Getting Angry

140 Williams, p.109

141 Perry, Andrew, "Rude Rules," *Q*, special edition

142 *Q* Special, p.98

Chapter 32: That Man Is Forward

143 www.olafkarnik.com/wp-content/uploads/2014/01/Konzert-Rico-11-81.pdf

144 Katz, David, "Remembering pioneering trombonist Rico Rodriguez," *Fact Magazine* (available at: www.factmag.com/2015/09/07/remembering-pioneering-trombonist-rico-rodriguez/)

145 *Record Mirror*, January 23, 1982

Chapter 33: The Feeling's Gone

146 Thrills, Adrian, "Black and White Unite," *New Musical Express*, December 11, 1982

Chapter 35: Put People First

147 Thrills, Adrian, "Black and White Unite," *New Musical Express*, December 11, 1982

Chapter 36: The Long Suicide

148 *Jamming!*, March 1984
149 Martin, Gavin, "26,732 Hours in the Studio with Jerry Dammers," *New Musical Express*, August 18, 1984
150 *Too Much, Too Young: The Story of 2 Tone*, BBC Radio 2, 2008
151 *New Musical Express*, August 18, 1984
152 Bell, Max, "Still Special (After All These Years)," the *Face*, June 1984
153 *New Musical Express*, August 18, 1984
154 *Jamming!*, March 1984
155 *New Musical Express*, August 18, 1984
156 *Melody Maker*, January 19, 1985
157 *New Musical Express*, August 18, 1984
158 *Jamming!*, March 1984

Chapter 38: Plead I Cause

159 Simpson, Dave, "'A blur of legs, arms and adrenaline': the astonishing history of two-tone," *Guardian*, April 30, 2021
160 *New Musical Express*, August 18, 1984

Chapter 39: This Are 2 Tone

161 *Jamming!*, March 1984

SONG CREDITS

Every effort has been made to trace the information for all copyright holders. The author and publishers would be pleased to rectify any errors or omissions at the earliest opportunity.

"Friday Night, Saturday Morning"/the Specials
Writer: Hall, Terry
Publisher: BMG Rights Management (UK) Ltd.

"Saturday Night Special"/Michael Dyke
Writer: Smith, Earl Stanley Chinna
Publisher: Jack Russell Music Ltd.

"Saturday Night Beneath the Plastic Palm Trees"/the Leyton Buzzards
Writers: Wilkerson, David; Rozelaar, Geoffrey
Publisher: B-A-M Music; Chappell Music Ltd.

"Gangsters"/the Specials
Writers: Bradbury, John Edward; Byers, Rod; Dammers, Jerry; Golding, Lynval; Hall, Terry; Panter, Stephen Graham; Staples, Neville Eugenton
Publisher: BMG Rights Management (UK) Ltd.

"It's Up to You"/the Specials
Writers: Bradbury, John Edward; Byers, Rod; Dammers, Jerry; Golding, Lynval; Hall, Terry; Panter, Stephen Graham; Staples, Neville Eugenton
Publisher: BMG Rights Management (UK) Ltd.

"Dreadlock Holiday"/10cc
Writers: Gouldman, Graham Keith; Stewart, Eric Michael
Publisher: EMI Music Publishing Ltd.

The Prince/Madness
Writers: Bedford, Mark William; Foreman, Christopher John; Smyth, Cathal Joseph; Woodgate, Daniel Mark; Barson, Michael; Thompson, Lee Jay; McPherson, Graham
Publisher: EMI Music Publishing Ltd.

"I'm the Leader of the Gang"/Gary Glitter
Writers: Leander, Mike; Glitter, Gary
Publisher: MCA Music Ltd.; Universal/MCA Music Ltd.

"On My Radio"/the Selecter
Writer: Davies, Neol
Publisher: Fairwood Music Ltd.

"Too Much Pressure"/the Selecter
Writers: Davies, Neol
Publisher: Fairwood Music Ltd.

"Judge Dread"/Prince Buster
Writer: Prince Buster
Publisher: Melodisc Music Ltd.

"007"/Desmond Dekker
Writers: Dacres, Desmond Adolphus; Kong, Leslie
Publisher: Beverley's Records Ltd.; Universal/Island Music Ltd.

"Dreader Than Dread"/Honey Boy Martin
Writers: Galnek, BMI Shares
Publisher: R-B-Music Ltd.; Sparta-Florida Music Group Ltd.; Chester Music

"Nite Klub"/the Specials
Writers: Bradbury, John Edward; Byers, Rod; Dammers, Jerry; Golding, Lynval; Hall, Terry; Panter, Stephen Graham; Staples, Neville Eugenton
Publisher: BMG Rights Management (UK) Ltd.

"Do the Dog"/the Specials
Writer: Thomas, Rufus
Publisher: Almo-Music Corporation; Universal Music Publishing International Ltd.

"Concrete Jungle"/the Specials
Writer: Byers, Roderick James
Publisher: BMG Rights Management (UK) Ltd.

"Burden of Shame"/UB40
Writers: Campbell, Ali; Brown, Jim; Campbell, Robin; Falconer, Earl; Travers, Brian; Hassan, Norman; Virtue, Michael
Publisher: Graduate Music Ltd.; Kassner Associated Publishers Ltd.; Universal SRG Music Publishing Ltd.

"King"/UB40
Writers: Campbell, Ali; Brown, Jim; Campbell, Robin; Falconer, Earl; Travers, Brian; Hassan, Norman; Virtue, Michael
Publisher: Graduate Music Ltd.; Kassner Associated Publishers Ltd.; Universal SRG Music Publishing Ltd.

"Ranking Full Stop"/the Beat
Writers: Wakeling, David Frederick; Charlery, Roger; Cox, Andrew; Morton, Everett; Steele, David
Publisher: Beat-Brothers-Ltd.; Songs of Mojo Two LLC; Mojo Universe Publishing

"Tears of a Clown"/the Beat
Writers: Robinson (Jun), William; Cosby, Henry; Wonder, Stevie
Publisher: Black-Bull-Music Inc; Jobete Music Co Inc; Sony/ATV Music Publishing Llc; EMI Music/ Jobete Music

"Danger"/the Selecter
Writers: Amanor, David Compton; Black, Pauline; Davies, Neol; Anderson, Charles Washington; Bembridge, Charles; Brown, Desmond Maximillian Mcgrath; Hendrickson, Anthony
Publisher: Fairwood Music Ltd.; Rak Publishing Ltd.

"Street Feeling"/the Selecter
Writer: Davies, Neol
Publisher: Fairwood Music Ltd.

"Time Hard"/the Selecter
Writers: Robinson, Loren Jackson; Crooks, Sydney Roy;
    Agard, George
Publisher: Music Like Dirt Sentric Music Ltd.; B and C
    Music Publishing Ltd.

"Too Much Too Young"/the Specials
Writer: Dammers, Jerry
Publisher: BMG Rights Management (UK) Ltd.

"Blank Expression"/the Specials
Writers: Bradbury, John Edward; Byers, Rod; Dammers, Jerry;
    Golding, Lynval; Hall, Terry; Panter, Stephen Graham;
    Staples, Neville Eugenton
Publisher: BMG Rights Management (UK) Ltd.

"Three Minute Hero"/the Selecter
Writer: Davies, Neol
Publisher: Fairwood Music Ltd.

"Ruder Than You"/the Bodysnatchers
Writers: Summers, Nicky; Joyce, Miranda Ann; Leyton, Penny
    Elizabeth; Owen, Sarah-Jane Mclaren; Barker, Stella;
    Mayall, Gary Vincent; Summers, Nicky; Dakar, Rhoda;
    Summers, Jane
Publisher: BMG Rights Management (UK) Ltd.

"Rat Race"/the Specials
Writers: Byers, Roderick James
Publisher: BMG Rights Management (UK) Ltd.

"Pearl's Café"/the Specials
Writer: Dammers, Jeremy David Hounsell Publisher: BMG
    Rights Management (UK) Ltd.

"Man at C&A"/the Specials
Writers: Dammers, Jerry; Hall, Terence Edward
Publisher: BMG Rights Management (UK) Ltd.

"Too Experienced"/the Bodysnatchers
Writer: Anderson, Keith Ainsley
Publisher: Andisongs; Jamrec Music; Third Side Music Inc;
    TSM UK Publishing

"Stereotype"/the Specials
Writer: Dammers, Jerry
Publisher: BMG Rights Management (UK) Ltd.

"International Jet Set"/the Specials
Writers: Dammers, Jeremy David Hounsell
Publisher: BMG Rights Management (UK) Ltd.

"Embarrassment"/Madness
Writers: Bedford, Mark William; Foreman, Christopher John;
    Smyth, Cathal Joseph; Woodgate, Daniel Mark; Barson,
    Michael; Thompson, Lee Jay; McPherson, Graham
Publisher: EMI Music Publishing Ltd.

"Do Nothing"/the Specials
Writer: Golding, Lynval
Publisher: BMG Rights Management (UK) Ltd.

"Why?"/the Specials
Writer: Golding, Lynval
Publisher: BMG Rights Management (UK) Ltd.

"Oh, What a Beautiful Morning"/*Oklahoma*
Writers: Hammerstein, Oscar II; Rodgers, Richard
Publisher: Williamson Music Company; Rodgers and
    Hammerstein Holdings Llc

"Ghost Town"/the Specials
Writers: Dammers, Jeremy David Hounsell
Publisher: BMG Rights Management (UK) Ltd.

"Jungle Music"/Rico Rodriguez
Writer: Rodriguez, Emmanuel
Publisher: BMG Rights Management (UK) Ltd.

"The Boiler"/Rhoda Dakar
Writers: Summers, Nicky; Joyce, Miranda Ann; Leyton, Penny
    Elizabeth; Owen, Sarah-Jane Mclaren; Barker, Stella
Publisher: BMG Rights Management (UK) Ltd.

"Tear the Whole Thing Down"/the Higsons
Writers: Charterton, Simon William Stelfox; Edwards, Terry
    David; Higson, Charles Murray; McGeachin, Stuart
    Francis; Williams, Colin
Publisher: Unknown

"Ylang Ylang"/the Higsons
Writers: Charterton, Simon William Stelfox; Edwards, Terry
    David; Higson, Charles Murray; McGeachin, Stuart
    Francis; Williams, Colin
Publisher: Unknown

"Envy the Love"/the Apollinaires
Writers: Kirk, Simon Andrew; Thornber, Kraig; Tickle, Paul
    Andrew; Hunt, James Robert; Brown, Francis Michael;
    Brown, Thomas Sidney
Publisher: BMG Rights Management (UK) Ltd.

"Put the Punk Back into Funk"/the Higsons
Writer: Charterton, Simon William Stelfox; Edwards, Terry
    David; Higson, Charles Murray; McGeachin, Stuart
    Francis; Williams, Colin
Publisher: Unknown

"Bright Lights"/the Special AKA
Writers: Bradbury, John Edward; Dammers, Jerry; Campbell,
    Stanley Hall; Cuthell, Dick
Publisher: BMG Rights Management (UK) Ltd.

"Alcohol"/the Special AKA
Writer: Dammers, Jeremy David Hounsell
Publisher: BMG Rights Management (UK) Ltd.

"(Free) Nelson Mandela"/the Special AKA
Writers: Dakar, Rhoda; Dammers, Jerry
Publisher: BMG Rights Management (UK) Ltd.